Developing Applications with Java™ and UML

Developing Applications with Java™ and UML

Paul R. Reed, Jr.

Addison-Wesley

Boston • San Francisco • New York • Toronto • Montreal
London • Munich • Paris • Madrid
Capetown • Sydney • Tokyo • Singapore • Mexico City

The publisher offers discounts on this book when ordered in quantity for special sales. For more information, please contact:

Pearson Education Corporate Sales Division
201 W. 103rd Street
Indianapolis, IN 46290
(800) 428-5331
corpsales@pearsoned.com

Visit AW on the Web: www.aw.com/cseng/

Library of Congress Cataloging-in-Publication Data

Reed, Paul R.
Developing applications with Java and UML / Paul R. Reed, Jr.
p. cm.
Includes bibliographical references and index.
ISBN 0-201-70252-5
1. Java (Computer program language) 2. Object-oriented methods (Computer science). 3. Computer software—Development. 4. UML (Computer science) I. Title.

QA76.73.J38 R44 2002
005.13'3—dc21 2001045883

ISBN 0-201-70252-5
Text printed on recycled paper
1 2 3 4 5 6 7 8 9 10—HT—0504030201
First printing, November 2001

To my parents, Paul and Jan, who showed me an honorable path

To my sister and brother, Elizabeth (Betsy) and Bill, with whose paths I share a common beginning

To my wife, Jeanette, who so graciously shares her path with mine

To my children, Micaela, Connor, and Natalie, for whose paths I hope to set a most admirable example

also

Thank you Grady Booch, Jim Rumbaugh, and Ivar Jacobson for giving us UML

Contents

Preface

This book focuses on the most powerful approach available today to modeling and building industrial-strength Java applications: the Unified Modeling Language (UML) adopted in 1997 by the Object Management Group (OMG). A project lifecycle and software process model are demonstrated (Rational's Unified Process) through a sample application from requirements gathering, using use-cases, through implementation via the creation Java code from class and sequence diagrams. This sample application uses the latest Java technology frameworks, such as JavaServer Pages (JSP), servlets, and most importantly, the Enterprise JavaBeans 2.0 (EJB) server-side enabling technology for implementation of the business rules. Products to implement these server-side solutions range from the Apache Tomcat server to commercial application servers such as BEA's WebLogic.

Reason for the Book

It took me many years to understand that writing a program is nothing more than a learned tactical skill. To program in a language like Java is to be a journeyman. But to capture someone's requirements in an intelligent fashion and organize the necessary resources and resulting software into a cohesive deliverable are the signs of a strategic craftsman.

To me, the majority of Java books never consider Java "in the large." They focus on the small view, covering single Java-enabled extensions such as JavaBeans, servlets, and JavaServer Pages. Although these views, too, are necessary, unfortunately no one seems to touch on project planning, software process, and the methodology for building enterprise-status Java applications. This is a difficult topic to explore and present because the whole subject of process spurs on many heartfelt debates and opinions. At the urging of many of my colleagues and supportive readers of my first book, *Developing Applications with Visual Basic and UML,* I have undertaken a similar project for Java.

Who Should Read This Book

This book is intended for anyone who wants to successfully build Java applications that can stand up over time. It provides an accurate road map for anyone to achieve the following goals:

- Review two processes: one commercially available through Rational Software called the Unified Process and one from my own experiences called Synergy. The greatest emphasis will be placed on the Unified Process.
- Establish a sound project plan (presented in depth in Appendix A).
- Estimate projects with confidence, rather than by using a rule-of-thumb approach.
- Understand and describe the requirements of the application using UML use-cases.
- Create a sound design based on UML class and sequence diagrams.
- Use a visual modeling tool such as Rose by Rational Software not only to create and track UML artifacts, but also to generate skeleton component code. Although I firmly believe that an automated code generation process is a big factor contributing to successful projects, it is certainly not mandatory.
- Use Java to build server-side Java functionality employing frameworks such as JavaServer Pages (JSP), servlets, and Enterprise JavaBeans 2.0 (EJB).

- Produce the code for the project using an evolutionary approach showing various technology options: (1) servlets, JSP, and Java Beans; (2) servlets, JSP, and bean-managed persistence (BMP); and (3) servlets, JSP, and container-managed persistence (CMP).
- Investigate the benefit of deploying Java applications on both open-source products like the Apache Tomcat server and commercial application server products such as BEA's WebLogic application server.

Anyone building Java applications today needs this book.

What You Need to Know to Use This Book

Maybe it's best to start out with what you don't need to know to benefit from this book. First, you don't need to know anything about UML. I present the essential aspects of UML and, more importantly, how they relate to Java deliverables. Although UML is expressed through nine separate diagrams, you will benefit the most from a core set.

Second, you don't need a formal background in object-oriented concepts (but it certainly doesn't hurt). I discuss standard object constructs in Chapter 2.

Third, you should have some conversational understanding of what Enterprise JavaBeans is. For a really thorough treatment of Enterprise JavaBeans (EJB), you should focus on one of the many texts that cover them in more detail. A favorite of mine is a book by Richard Monson-Haefel entitled *Enterprise JavaBeans*, published by O'Reilly. You will also benefit from some exposure to JavaServer Pages (JSP). One of my favorite sources on this topic is a book by Hans Bergsten entitled *Java Server Pages*, also published by O'Reilly.

This book assumes that you have a working knowledge of Java. Both the new Java programmer and the experienced Java programmer will benefit. I don't cover the basics of simple Java constructs, assuming that you already know these. I do briefly review the tenets of Java's support for object-oriented principles in Chapter 2, but only as a baseline for other topics related to UML. If you have had no exposure to Java, buy this book anyway and open it after you have had some initial training in that programming language.

This book emphasizes the most mainstream Java techniques and products that are used to build production applications. When I began this book, I planned to cover all kinds of Java technologies (i.e., applets, Java applications talking to servlets or JSPs). However, it quickly became apparent to me that the majority of my clients and my associates' clients were all pretty much cut from the same mold in terms of architecture. They consist of a light client browser on the front end (with minimal JavaScript for syntax editing), and a Web server intercepting those browser requests with either servlets and/or JavaServer Pages acting as a broker within a container product that houses the business rules. These business rules are implemented as either JavaBeans or Enterprise JavaBeans. The container products range from open-source solutions like Apache Tomcat to commercial products.

The two biggest of the commercial application server players I run across are BEA (with its WebLogic product) and IBM (with its WebSphere product). This doesn't mean there aren't other good commercial container products, but these two vendors have the lion's share of the market. This book will utilize a light client-side technology (no applets or Java applications), and a Web server running servlets and JavaServer Pages, which in turn send messages to either JavaBeans (Tomcat) or Enterprise JavaBeans (session and entity beans) residing in a commercial application server.

In the case of the latter, I have chosen to use BEA's WebLogic as my application server. Don't be discouraged if you are using another vendor's application server product because this book's coverage of EJB is based on the 2.0 specification. This release of EJB resolved many of the ambiguities that kept beans from being truly transportable across vendor implementations. So regardless of your EJB vendor, you will be able to use the code built in this book.

It would be unfair to say that you will know everything about EJBs after reading this book. If you already know about EJBs, this book will help you put them into a sound design architecture. The emphasis is on the notation (UML) and the process (Unified Process and Synergy) in beginning, developing, and implementing a software project using the Java language. The benefit of seeing an application from requirements gathering to implementation is the key goal of this book. This is where I shall place my emphasis.

Structure of the Book

The following sections summarize the contents of each chapter.

Chapter 1: The Project Dilemma

Chapter 1 reviews the current state of software development and my reasoning regarding why it's in the shape that it is today. It also reviews the concept of iterative and incremental software development and provides an overview of both Rational Software's Unified Process and my Synergy Process methodology. In addition, it touches on the primary components of UML that will be covered in more depth later in the book.

Chapter 2: Java, Object-Oriented Analysis and Design, and UML

Chapter 2 covers some of the benefits of adopting Java as a development environment, presented in the context of Java's implementation of encapsulation, inheritance, and polymorphism. It then maps UML to various Java deliverables. Highlights include mapping the UML diagrams to Java classes and Java interfaces; mapping use-case pathways to Java classes; and mapping component diagrams to Java classes and Java packages.

Chapter 3: Starting the Project

Chapter 3 explores the case study used in the book: Remulak Productions. This fictional company sells musical equipment and needs a new order entry system. The chapter introduces a project charter, along with a tool, called the event table, to help quickly solidify the application's features. Further, the chapter maps events to the first UML model, the use-case.

Chapter 4: Use-Cases

Chapter 4 reviews the use-case, one of the central UML diagrams. Included is a template to document the use-case. Actors and their roles in the use-cases are defined. The concept of use-case pathways, as well as the project's preliminary implementation architecture, is reviewed.

Also reviewed is an approach to estimating projects that are built with the use-case approach.

Chapter 5: Classes

Chapter 5 explores the class diagram, the king of UML diagrams. It offers tips on identifying good class selections and defines the various types of associations. It also covers business rule categorization and how these rules can be translated into both operations and attributes of the class. Finally, it discusses the utilization of a visual modeling tool as a means to better manage all UML artifacts.

Chapter 6: Building a User Interface Prototype

Chapter 6 reviews unique user interface requirements of each use-case. It develops an early user interface prototype flow and an eventual graphical prototype. Finally, it maps what was learned during the prototype to the UML artifacts.

Chapter 7: Dynamic Elements of the Application

Chapter 7 discusses the dynamic models supported by UML, exploring in depth the two key diagrams, often referred to as the interaction diagrams: sequence and collaboration. These are then directly tied back to the pathways found in the use-cases. Other dynamic diagrams discussed include the state and activity diagrams.

Chapter 8: The Technology Landscape

Chapter 8 covers the importance of separating logical services that are compliant with a model that separates services. It explores technology solutions specific to the Remulak Productions case study, including distributed solutions and the Internet using HTML forms, JSP, and servlets. Both JavaBeans and Enterprise JavaBeans as solutions for housing the business rules are also explored.

Chapter 9: Data Persistence: Storing the Objects

Chapter 9 explores the steps necessary to translate the class diagram into a relational design to be supported by both Microsoft SQL Server and Oracle databases. It offers rules of thumb regarding how to handle class inheritance and the resulting possible design alternatives for translation to an RDBMS. This book will deliver solutions that range from roll-your-own persistence using JavaBeans and JDBC, all the way to container-managed persistence (CMP) features of the EJB 2.0 specification. The latter removes all the requirements of the application to write SQL or control transactions. This chapter introduces the concept of value objects to reduce network traffic, as well as data access objects that encapsulate SQL calls.

Chapter 10: Infrastructure and Architecture Review

Chapter 10 finalizes the design necessary to implement the various layers of the application. It also presents the communication mechanism utilized between the layers and possible alternatives. Each class is delegated to one of three types: entity, boundary, or control. These types are used as the basis for the design implementation and as the solution to providing alternative deployment strategies.

Chapter 11: Constructing a Solution: Servlets, JSP, and JavaBeans

Chapter 11 builds the first architectural prototype for Remulak and does not rely on Enterprise JavaBeans. With the *Maintain Relationships* use-case as the base, the various components are constructed. The primary goal of the architectural prototype is to reduce risk early by eliminating any unknowns with the architecture. This chapter uses the Apache Tomcat server and introduces the concepts of user interface and use-case control classes.

Chapter 12: Constructing a Solution: Servlets, JSP, and Enterprise JavaBeans

Chapter 12 initially uses Rational Rose to generate EJB components. A primer on EJB is offered, along with a thorough discussion of the transaction management options in the EJB environment. Session beans are utilized as the use-case controller. Solutions that incorporate both container-managed persistence (CMP) and bean-managed persistence (BMP) are presented. Leveraging the data access objects created in Chapter 11 is crucial to the success of a BMP implementation.

Updates and Information

I have the good fortune to work with top companies and organizations not only in the United States, but also in Europe, Asia, and South America. In my many travels, I am always coming across inventive ideas for how to use and apply UML to build more-resilient applications that use not only Java, but also C++, C#, and Visual Basic. Please visit my Web site, at *www.jacksonreed.com,* for the latest on the training and consulting services that I offer, as well as all of the source code presented in this book. I welcome your input and encourage you to contact me at *prreed@jacksonreed.com.*

About the Author

Paul R. Reed, Jr., is president of Jackson-Reed, Inc., *www.jacksonreed.com,* and has consulted on the implementation of several object-oriented distributed systems. He is the author of the book *Developing Applications with Visual Basic and UML,* published by Addison-Wesley in 2000. He has published articles in *Database Programming & Design, DBMS,* and *Visual Basic Programmer's Journal,* and he has spoken at industry events such as DB/Expo, UML World, and VBITS. He is also the author of many high-technology seminars on such topics as object-oriented analysis and design using UML, use-case analysis, the Unified Process, Internet application development, and client/server technology. He has lectured and consulted extensively on implementing these technologies to companies and governments in the Middle East, South America, Europe, and the Pacific Rim.

Paul holds an MBA in finance from Seattle University. He also holds the Chartered Life Underwriter (CLU) and Chartered Financial Consultant (ChFC) designations from the American College and is a Fellow of the Life Management Institute (FLMI).

Acknowledgments

All of us today can trace our perceived success through the company we keep. I owe my good fortune to the many relationships, both professional and personal, that I have developed over the years.

I would like to thank Coby Sparks, Dale McElroy, Richard Dagit, Mike "mikey" Richardson, John "the japper" Peiffer, Kurt Herman, Steve "glacier man" Symonds, Jeff Kluth (a.k.a. Jeffery Homes of this book, backpacking buddy and the owner of the real Remulak, a DB2 consulting firm), Dave "daver" Remy, David Neustadt, John Girt, Robert Folie, Terry Lelievre, Daryl Kulak, Steve Jackson, Claudia Jackson, Bryan Foertsch, Debbie Foertsch, and Larry Deniston (the OO guru from Kalamazoo) and the other folks at Manatron (*www.manatron.com*). Thanks to Ellen Gottesdiener of EBG Consulting (*www.ebgconsulting.com* for her wonderful assistance on project charters, use-cases, and business rules. A big thank-you to Bill Kuffner, Nick Ouellet, Bill Reed, Betsy Reed, Rodney Yee (my wine mentor), and Brian and Susan Maecker (besides being one of the top realtors in the country, *www.maecker.com*, Brian shares my passion of the pursuit of the perfect glass of red wine).

Other individuals warrant commendation for shaping my thoughts about sound Java design and the use of its various technology offerings. In particular, I would like to thank Hans Bergsten for his excellent advice on the topic of JavaServer Pages, and Floyd Marinescu for the creation of his fantastic Web site (*www.theserverside.com*). Floyd's many articles on design patterns applicable to applications using Enterprise JavaBeans (EJB) were very helpful to me. I would like to thank Eric Stahl and Tyler Jewell, both of BEA Systems, for their assistance in using their marvelous products. I want to acknowledge Per Kroll from Rational Software for his assistance with using Rational's tools.

I have the benefit of working with some great clients in both the United States and abroad. I would like to explicitly thank Vicki Cerda at Florida Power Light; Sara Garrison at Visa USA; all my friends at the Federal Reserve Bank of San Francisco, including Mike Stan, Linda Jimerson, Matt Rodriguez, and Bill Matchette; and finally, my good friend and Asian partner Lawrence Lim at LK Solutions (Singapore, Malaysia, and United Arab Emirates, *www.lk-solutions.com*).

Finally, special thanks to Paul Becker of Addison-Wesley for putting up with my "whining" during this project. I would also like to thank Diane Freed of Diane Freed Publishing Services for helping organize the production of this book. I want to give a spweecial thanks to Stephanie Hiebert for her wonderful copyediting and for providing clarity to my most jumbled collection of prose.

The real heroes of this project are the reviewers who slugged their way through my early drafts and weren't shy at all to cast darts when necessary.

CHAPTER 1 The Project Dilemma

IN THIS CHAPTER

I have run across more projects after the fact that missed their initial goals than met them. One reason is that most of the project teams had no clue about what a development process was or how to customize one for a project's unique characteristics. In addition, most of the projects had little in the way of analysis and design artifacts to show how they got where they were. The whole endeavor lacked the ability to be tracked; that is, it lacked traceability.

This chapter lays the groundwork for the need of a software process. I will present two processes in this book: one that is commercially available from Rational Software called the Unified Process, the other based on my own experiences, which I call the Synergy Process. For reasons to be covered later, the Synergy Process will be presented in Appendix B. The primary process that will guide this book's efforts is the Unified Process, which is presented in greater depth in Appendix A.

This process, along with the Unified Modeling Language (UML), can ensure that your next Java projects have all of the muscle they need to succeed. More importantly, these projects will stand the test of time. They will be able to flex and bend with shifts in both the underlying businesses they support and the technology framework upon which they were built. They won't be declared legacy applications before they reach production status.

GOALS

- To review the dilemma that projects face.
- To explore the nature of an iterative, incremental, risk-based software development process.
- To become acquainted with the software process model used in this book, called the Unified Process.
- To examine how the project team can market the use of a process to project sponsors.
- To review the Unified Modeling Language and its artifacts, and how it serves as the primary modeling tool for a project's process.

The Sad Truth

The premise of my first book, *Developing Applications with Visual Basic and UML,* was that most software projects undertaken today don't come close to meeting their original goals or their estimated completion dates. My reasoning was that most project teams have a somewhat cavalier attitude toward project planning and software process. In addition, most projects have little in the way of analysis and design artifacts to show how they got where they are. That is, projects traditionally lack traceability. This holds true for applications built in any language—Java included.

My professional career with computers began after college in 1979, when I began working on large IBM mainframe applications using technologies such as IMS and later DB2, what many people today would call legacy applications. However, I prefer the terms *heritage* or *senior* to *legacy.*

Not only did I get to work with some really great tools and super sharp people, but I also learned the value of planning a project and establishing a clear architecture and design of the target application. I saw this approach pay back in a big way by establishing a clear line of communication for the project team. But more importantly, it set in place the stepping-stones for completing a successful project.

In 1990 I worked on a first-generation client/server application using SmallTalk on the OS/2 platform. This was the start of a new career path for me, and I was shocked by the "process" used to build "production" applications in the client/server environment. The planning was sketchy, as was the delivery of analysis and design artifacts (something that showed why we built what we built).

This pattern of "shooting from the hip" software development continued with my use of PowerBuilder, Visual Basic, and later Java. The applications delivered with these products worked, but they were fragile. Today many applications wear the *client/server* or *distributed* moniker when they are just as much a legacy as their mainframe counterparts, if not more so. Even worse, many of these become legacy applications a month or two after they go into production. The fault isn't with the tool or the language, but with the lack of a sound process model and methodology to ensure that what is built is what the users actually want and that what is designed doesn't fall apart the first time it is changed.

Most organizations today ship their staff off to a one-week Java class and expect miracles on the first application. Take this message to heart: The fact that you know Java doesn't mean you will necessarily build sound object-oriented applications. If you don't have a sound process in place and a very firm footing in sound object-oriented design concepts, your application will become a Neanderthal waiting in line for extinction.

Slowly I began to apply my own opinions about process and methodology to the applications built in these environments. This worked quite well. The applications were more resilient and accepted change more easily, and the users typically had smiles on their faces.

This book combines all of my experience building distributed applications with UML, which I feel is the best artifact repository for documenting the analysis and design of an application today. I would also like to think that my approach to this topic is exciting because I use a real example throughout the book utilizing various Java technologies and tools to demonstrate how you might approach solving some of your own problems.

The Project Dilemma

Few projects proceed totally as planned. Most start out with much enthusiasm but often end in a mad rush to get something out the door. The deliverable is often hobbled with inaccuracies, or worse, it invokes

FIGURE 1-1 *Time line of a typical project*

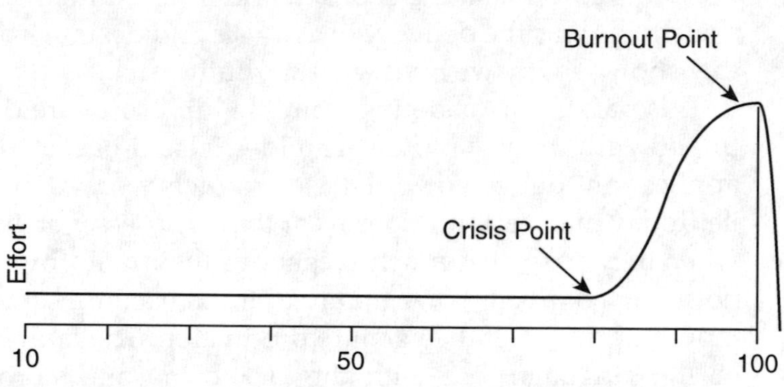

unrepeatable responses from the project sponsors. Figure 1-1 shows a time line/effort comparison of person-hour expenditures for most projects that don't meet their commitments.

You know the drill: The project plants a stake in the ground, with a big-bang deliverable two and half years away. And then you plod along, making adjustments and adding functionality until, toward the end, you realize, "We aren't going to make it." You are so far off the mark that you start adding more pounds of flesh to the effort. Before long, you begin to jettison functionality—for example, reporting, archiving, security, and auditing activities. You end up with a poor deliverable that adds to the black eye of the Information Technology (IT) department and further convinces the project sponsors that you can't develop software at all, let alone on time and within budget.

Unfortunately, like lemmings racing to the sea, companies repeat this saga again and again and again.

Iterative and Incremental Software Development

This dilemma of projects failing or not delivering promised functionality stems from the unwillingness of both the IT department and the project sponsors to take a learn-as-you-go approach to software development, more formally known as **iterative and incremental software development**.

In the context of a software project, many people confuse the terms *iterative* and *incremental.* The *American Heritage Dictionary,* Second College Edition, defines these terms as follows.

Iterative – 3. . . . procedure to produce a desired result by replication of a series of operations that successively better approximates the desired result.

Incremental – 1. An increase in number, size, or extent. 2. Something added or gained. . . . 4. One of a series of regular additions or contributions.

Let's give these academic definitions a bit of a software flavor:

Iterative: The application of tasks in a repetitive fashion that works toward bettering an interim or final product.

Incremental: The creation of interim deliverables such that each one adds significant value to the overall project, stands on its own or operates within a well-defined interface, or might take part as a subcomponent of a final product.

As an example, suppose you are constructing a wooden play set for children. You begin by simplifying the project by breaking it up into two incremental parts: (1) tower and attached slide chute and (2) swing and trapeze frame. You realize the project by iterating through the building of each increment. The iterations might be first to create a detailed drawing; then to buy, measure, and cut the wood; next to bolt together the pieces; and finally to stain the wood. Each iteration improves the chances of producing a product that stands on its own. This approach is powerful because many of the same iterative tasks (drawing, sawing, bolting, and staining) are to be applied to each increment (tower/slide and swing/trapeze).

The challenge, however, is to ensure that the first increment will bolt onto (interface with) subsequent increments. You must learn enough about all of the increments that you can approximate how they will work together as an integrated product. Figure 1-2 gives a sample time line for a project using an iterative, incremental approach.

After years of applying these concepts to many different types of projects, using many different tools and languages, I have no doubt that this is the only way that software can be successfully developed today and in the future.

FIGURE 1-2 *Time line of a project with iterative and incremental flow*

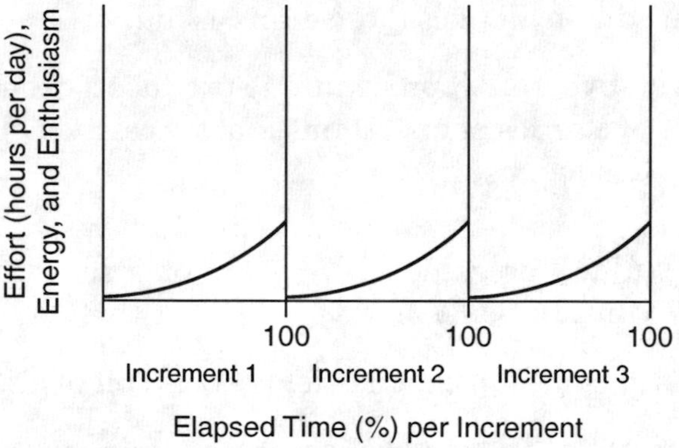

Risk-Based Software Development

Experience has taught me to always be a silent pessimist when I approach a new project. This idea stems from the repeated observation that something is always lurking nearby that will shift the project's course toward eventual disaster. Although this attitude might seem like a negative way to look at project development, it has saved many projects from disaster.

The project team must always be on the lookout for risks. Risks must be brought to the surface early and often. One way to do this is to extend the project development philosophy so that it is not only iterative and incremental, but also risk based. Appendix A presents project plan templates for the Unified Process. Figure 1-3 shows one possible visual representation of an iterative, incremental project framework founded on a risk-based approach.

One very positive side effect of this approach is the continual improvement of the end product. In addition, risks are addressed promptly because the project components that present the greatest risk are staged first.

The Iterative Software Process Model

It helps to visualize how combining the notions of iterative and incremental development might look graphically. Figure 1-4 shows an iterative and incremental process model. This framework is sometimes

FIGURE 1-3 *Iterative, incremental project framework with risk mitigation*

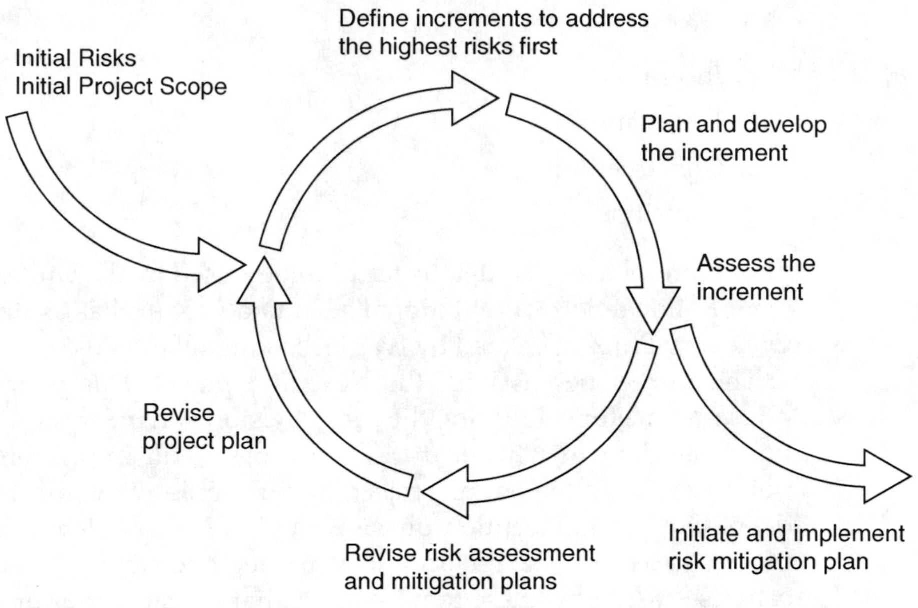

FIGURE 1-4 *Iterative and incremental process model: One-dimensional*

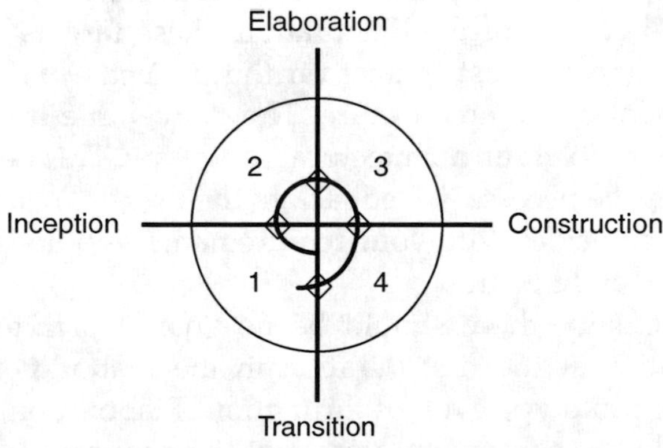

called the **spiral process model** and has been popularized by many practitioners. Each of the four quadrants shown in the figure is labeled as a phase:

1. Inception
2. Elaboration
3. Construction
4. Transition

These four phases parallel the terminology used by the Unified Process from Rational Software. Rational's Unified Process has as its roots the Objectory Process, created by Ivar Jacobson in the 1980s.

The project begins with the Inception phase. This is a discovery phase, a time for solidifying the project vision and incorporating a clear understanding of what features the project will implement. At this point we fly by the entire project, going a mile wide and five inches deep. Out of the Inception phase we will also have determined what the use-cases are. The project will also select the architecturally significant use-cases. It is these requirements that we target in our first iteration in the Elaboration phase. The milestone reached at the end of the Inception phase is called Lifecycle Objective.

In the Elaboration phase, early requirements identified in the Inception phase are solidified, and more rigor is added to the process. The first iteration of the Elaboration phase targets requirements that will have the greatest impact on the project's understanding and development of the architecture. The deliverable from the first iteration in Elaboration is an architectural prototype. This deliverable not only provides the necessary feedback to the user—"Yes, we can build software that coincides with your requirements"—but also it validates the proposed architecture.

Actually, there should be no "hard" architecture decisions to be made after the first iteration in the Elaboration phase. An architectural prototype evolves throughout Elaboration, as more use-cases are tackled in subsequent iterations. The milestone reached at the end of the Elaboration phase is called Lifecycle Architecture. In this book, our target is to make it through the first iteration in Elaboration and deliver an architectural prototype.

The Construction phase includes the mechanical aspects of implementing all the business rules and ensuring that subsystems integrate.

This phase is, for the most part, a software manufacturing process. Absolutely no architecture surprises should arise during Construction. It is in the Construction phase that alpha releases of the system are made available to the user. Packaging, rollout, support, and training issues are also dealt with in this phase. The milestone reached at the end of the Construction phase is called Initial Operational Capability.

In the Transition phase, components produced in the Construction phase are packaged into deployable units. At this time in the project the system is typically thought to be in beta status. Some parallel operations may also be taking place alongside existing heritage applications. This phase also details the support issues that surround the application and how the project will be maintained in a production environment. The milestone reached at the end of the Transition phase is called Product Release. In the Unified Process a product release is called an *evolution* or *generation.*

Within each phase, multiple iterations typically take place. The number of iterations within each phase might vary (Figure 1-5), depending

FIGURE 1-5 *Iterations within phases*

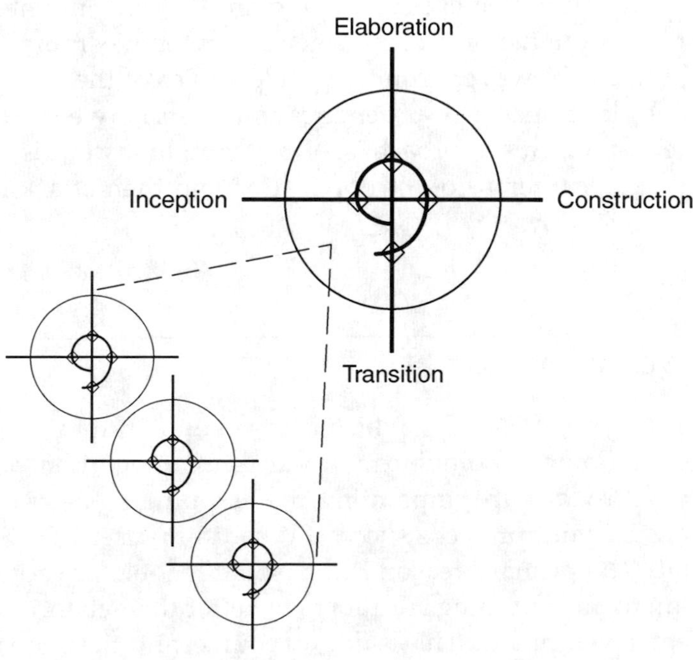

on the project's unique requirements. For projects with a higher risk factor or more unknown elements, more time will be spent learning and discovering. The resulting knowledge will have to be translated to other deliverables in a layered fashion.

To make the project even more interesting, the activities traditionally associated with any one phase may be performed in earlier or later phases. For example, if the project has a strong, unique visual component or is breaking new ground, you might need to simulate a prototype during Inception just to generate ideas and solidify the proof of concept going forward.

Combining Iterative with Incremental: Multidimensional View

Given that an iterative process is beneficial, next we envision the previous flow imposed on an incremental delivery schedule. Figure 1-6 illustrates the iterative nature of typical software development projects and shows that different increments will be in different stages of the lifecycle.

Notice that each increment (the three upper spirals) is in a different phase of its evolution. Each phase (e.g., Inception) might also be in its own iteration cycle. At first glance, all this might seem overly complex. From the project manager's perspective, more balls do need to be juggled. However, from the perspectives of the user, analyst, designer, and developer, a clear demarcation exists between each increment. The reason for this approach is, once again, to lessen risk by disassembling the logical seams of the application and then attacking each increment individually.

The Synergy Process

The Synergy Process, which is based on iterative, incremental software development, combines with an implementation project plan that is your road map pinpointing the stepping-stones you must follow to ensure your project's success. Why do I present the Synergy Process at all? The primary reason is that some readers are not interested in having to buy anything additional to better their chances of successful project development. This is fine, of course, and the Synergy Process will fit the bill.

FIGURE 1-6 *Iterative and incremental process model: Multidimensional*

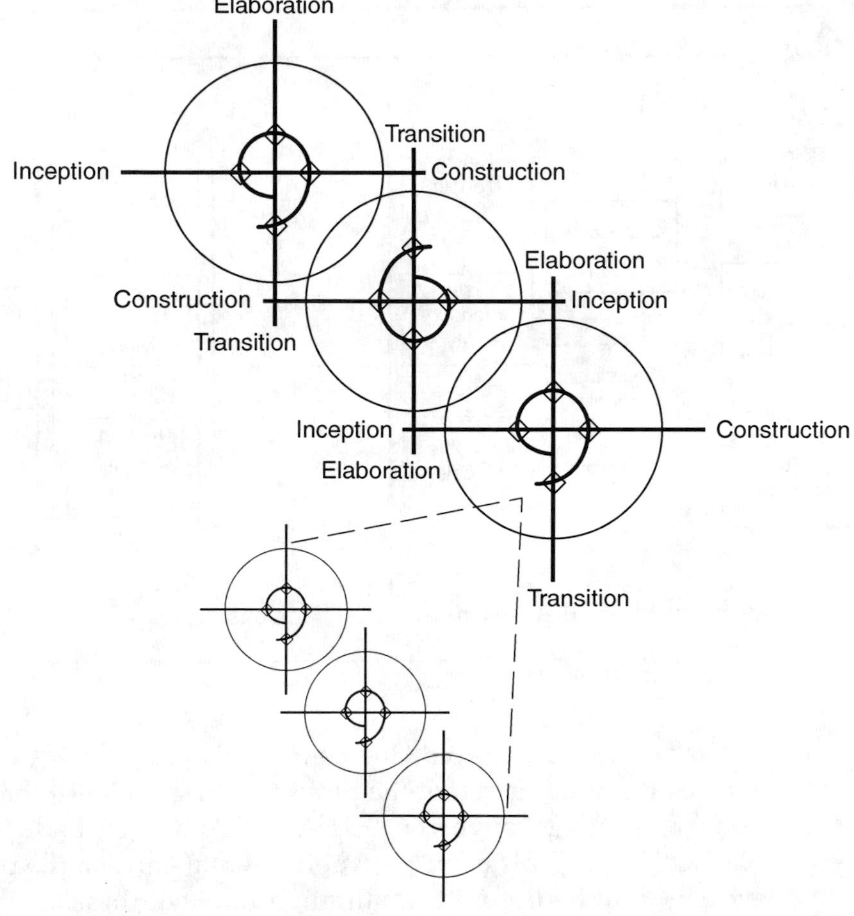

What Synergy lacks are the many guidelines and "how-tos" that the Unified Process has to offer. As a result, I will briefly present it here but cover it in more detail in Appendix B. In this book the Unified Process will be the process that guides our steps from project inception to coding.

Figure 1-7 previews the Synergy Process model. The boxes (e.g., "Release Cycle" and "Project Scope") represent categories of activities or processes. Although they are linked via a sample flow of order, recall that some tasks might be performed earlier or later, depending on a project's needs.

FIGURE 1-7 *Synergy Process model*

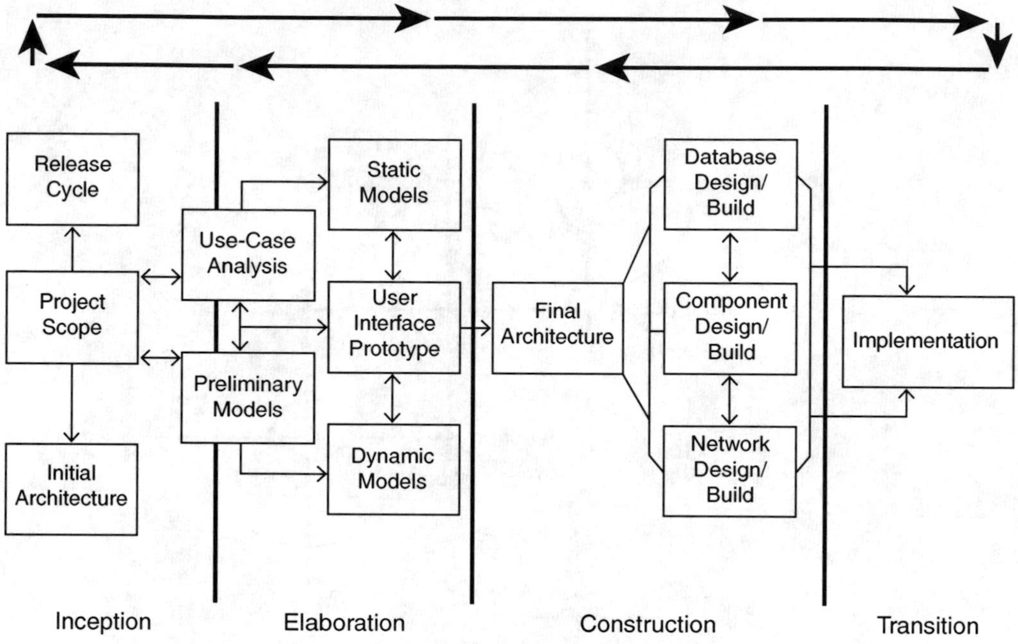

The vertical bars labeled "Inception," "Elaboration," "Construction," and "Transition" represent the project's phases. Notice that the Inception bar slices through the "Use-Case Analysis" and "Preliminary Models" boxes. This depicts graphically that early in the project's lifecycle we will fly by, or iterate through, some of these activities to estimate the duration and cost of our project.

The Unified Process

The Unified Process from Rational Software is a very complete and detailed software process. It can be quite overwhelming. Out of the box, the Unified Process contains 103 artifacts, 9 workflows, 8 project plan templates, 4 phases, 136 activities, 14 work guidelines, and 43 Word and HTML templates. However, having built my own training course on the Unified Process and having implemented it for a host of

FIGURE 1-8 *Rational Software's Unified Process*

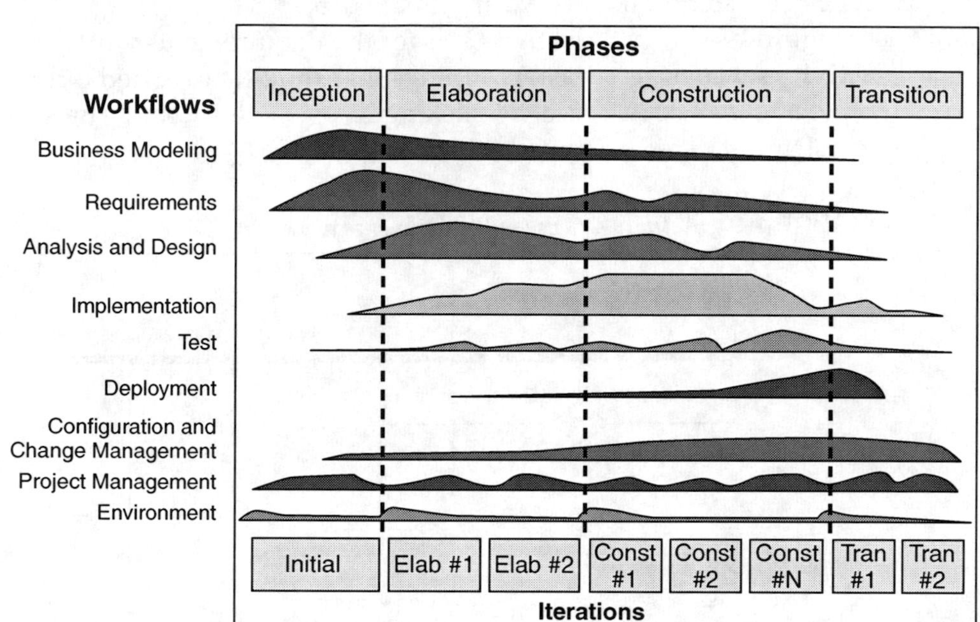

companies, I have found that most projects stick with ten "essential" artifacts. These will be presented in more detail in Appendix A.

The Unified Process takes the concept of **workflows**, which are horizontal, and **phases**, which are vertical, and presents a model that quite nicely implements the notion of iterative and incremental software development. In Figure 1-8 you can see the two concepts in action.

Notice that each iteration within a phase slices through all the workflows. This is a key point in the Unified Process. Looking horizontally across the Requirements workflow, for instance, you will notice that the emphasis on requirements is much heavier in the early phases (Inception and Elaboration). This should make sense because as we move further through the lifecycle toward the Construction phase, there should be less emphasis on requirements.

If you visit the Unified Process project plans in Appendix A, you will see a task in every iteration, even during Transition, that forces the project to address changes in requirements. Notice that the Implementation workflow shows up in the Inception phase, but without much emphasis.

This indicates that there may be some type of proof-of-concept prototype being undertaken very early in the project's lifecycle.

Figure 1-9 shows the activity sets for the Requirements workflow. An **activity set** consists of task groupings that should be carried out by the project team. For instance, by clicking on the activity set "Analyze the Problem," you are presented with Figure 1-10.

FIGURE 1-9 *Activity sets in the Requirements workflow*

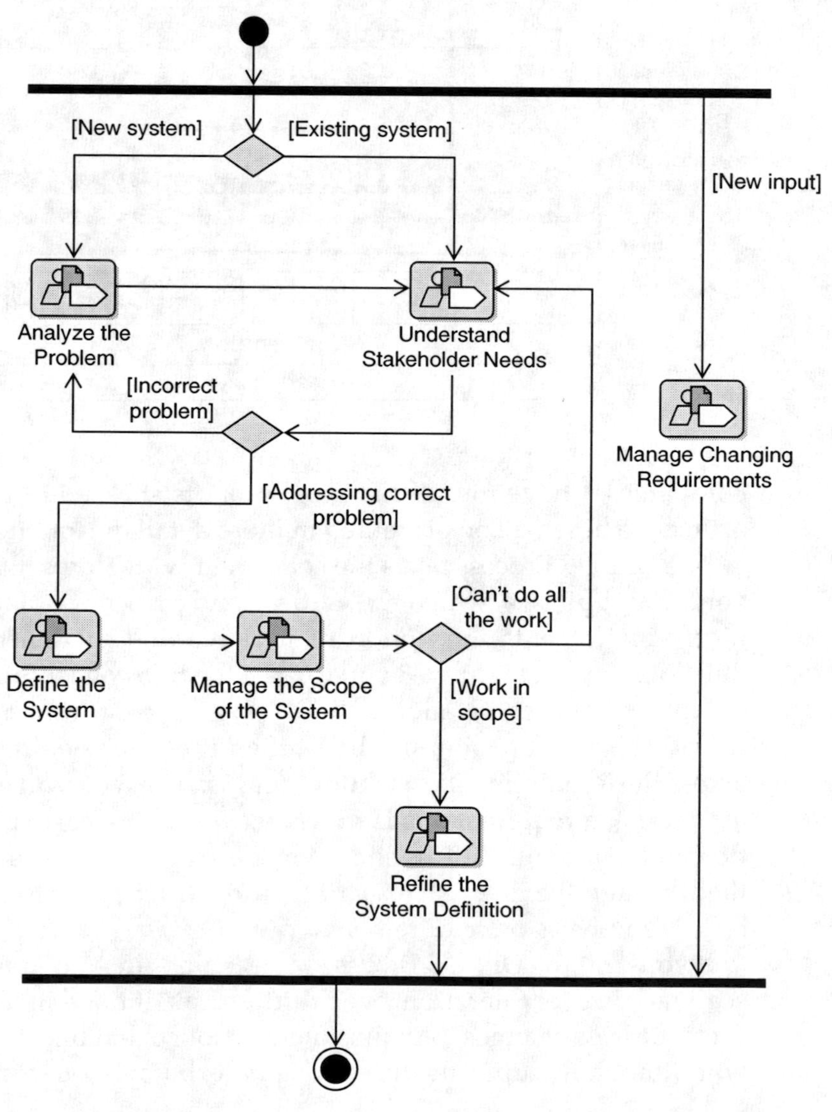

Figure 1-10 shows the tasks that make up the activity set "Analyze the Problem." When selecting, for instance, "Find Actors and Use-Cases," you are presented with several guidelines and templates to assist you in your efforts. This is just a cursory overview, but your next project should investigate what the Unified Process has to offer.

We will spend much more time with the Unified Process as we move through the book. As we cover each chapter, I will point out both the workflow and the activity sets that are being discussed. I encourage any project team to seriously consider the Unified Process for your project. At the time of this writing the product costs under $800 and runs on a Web server that can be referenced by everyone on the team. What you get for your money is well worth the investment. The fun part is separating the wheat from the chaff and working on only the artifacts that will provide the biggest bang for the buck. That's what this book intends to do.

FIGURE 1-10 *"Analyze the Problem" activity set within the Requirements workflow*

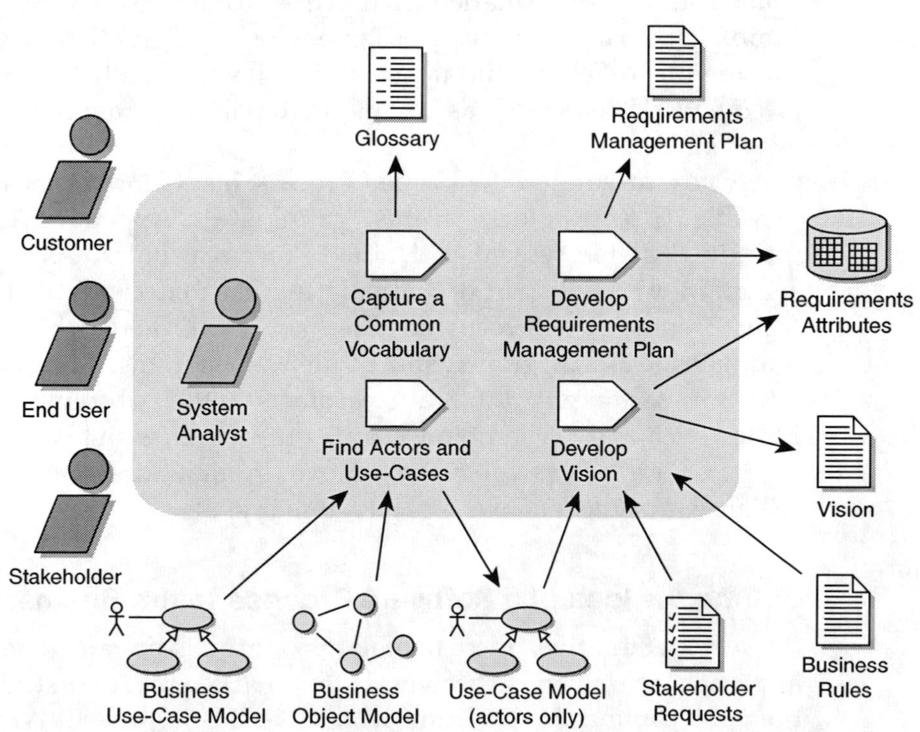

Other Processes: XP

A large groundswell in the market today is rallying around something called Extreme Programming, or XP for short. XP was pioneered by Kent Beck (a pioneer in the SmallTalk community as well). You can learn more about XP from its creators by checking out *eXtreme programming eXplained* by Kent Beck, published by Addison-Wesley. Without going into too much detail, I'll say that XP relies heavily on pair programming and full-time, 100 percent committed user input. Pair programming says that two sets of eyes see every line of code and that two individuals build the code collaboratively.

XP has immense promise as a software process, but even its creators admit that it isn't well suited for large projects. I have had the opportunity to be involved in a few projects using XP, and it absolutely demands strong resources. If the paired team is lopsided—one strong developer and one weak or inexperienced developer—the resources are wasted. XP is also very beneficial for the user interface aspects of the application, but I find it cumbersome with server-side rule-intensive applications. You still need well-defined and easy-to-understand requirements. I think I am in the same camp as James Gosling, Sun Microsystems Vice President and Fellow, and the creator of Java, when he was quoted in an *InfoWorld* interview as saying that pair programming sounded "kind of creepy."

My advice is to use the Unified Process; just tailor it to be as lean as possible. (I review some of this "pruning" in Appendix A, where I introduce my ten "essential" Unified Process artifacts.) As will be presented in this book, part of that tailoring has to do with the UML artifacts. This book will focus on three key UML deliverables: use-case templates, class diagrams, and sequence diagrams. Complementary efforts have attempted to reduce artifacts to their absolute minimum. Efforts such as that championed by Scott Ambler, with his agile modeling (*www.extreme-modeling.com*), move in that direction. The Agile Alliance (*www.agilealliance.org*) has similar goals.

Selling the Idea of a Software Process to the Business

To sell an iterative, incremental, risk-based software development approach, we all must become better marketers. At first glance the business community probably won't like this approach. Why? When project sponsors are told that their solution will be delivered in multiple increments, their usual reaction, from their past experience, is that phase 2 will never happen. Projects are canceled, resources are drawn away to other efforts, priorities shift. So as a rule, they will strive to put everything possible into the first increment. Thus the biggest challenge is selling the idea to project sponsors.

Here are some of the top benefits of a software process that must be worked into your marketing plan:

- The business gets useful increments in a staged fashion that continually build toward the final product.
- Each increment delivers value-added benefits, while increasing confidence that the project can be flexible enough to adjust to continually evolving business needs. The business doesn't stay static, so how can the software be expected to?
- Each increment is relatively short in duration, 3 to 9 months, so the possibility of the project's becoming a "runaway train" is lessened dramatically.
- Any problems with the design or the technology surface early, not 90 percent into the project time line.
- Users, analysts, designers, and developers stay very focused on each increment, so they can celebrate successes much sooner. The resulting team confidence is priceless.

This book stresses following a sound project plan, using a proven development process as the guide. To facilitate communication and extract both the requirements and design of the system, a common modeling language is applied: UML.

The Unified Modeling Language

The Object Management Group (OMG) adopted UML (version 1.0) in November 1997 (the most current release, version 1.4, was adopted in February 2001). This was a remarkable, unprecedented event because it marked the acceptance of a standard modeling language based on the best current practices for the analysis, design, and development of object-oriented software.

UML sprang from the combined efforts of the "three amigos": Grady Booch with his Booch method, James Rumbaugh with his Object Modeling Technique (OMT), and Ivar Jacobson with his Object-Oriented Software Engineering (OOSE) method. As mentioned earlier, some of the terminology and philosophy found in the Synergy Process is based on Jacobson's Objectory Process (later to be called Rational's Unified Process).

Beginning in 1994, under the auspices of Rational Software, UML began to take shape. Although UML clearly reflects the three amigos' combined approaches, it also includes the best practices of many others. Other contributions include insights from such organizations as Hewlett-Packard, IBM, and Microsoft, as well as other industry practitioners, such as Shlaer/Mellor, Coad/Yourdon, and Martin/Odell. UML was also submitted as a formal response to the OMG's Request for Proposal (RFP) for a standard object-oriented modeling notation.

The ramifications of the OMG's adoption of UML cannot be overestimated. Those of us who grew up in the Structured Analysis and Structured Design (SA/SD) world had numerous diagramming notations from which to choose and several software process models to apply. Wouldn't it have been wonderful if the likes of Ed Yourdon, James Martin, and Tom DeMarco, to name a few, had sat down one day in the late 1970s and agreed to put aside any and all egos and adopt one notation for the SA/SD approach to software development? Had there been only one way to express the application domain, many organizations would have benefited significantly. Not only would all of the organization's models have been similar, but also an individual moving from company to company or from application domain to application domain would have had a common notation as a baseline.

UML, then, is the first notation that has garnered consensus among most practitioners, software vendors, and academics as the de facto standard for expressing a business domain of the accompanying software solution.

The Place of UML in a Software Process

UML is not a software process model or a systems development methodology; it is a notation, a mechanism to "pen the problem" in such a way as to uncover the essence of an application domain. The combination of UML with a sound process model (Rational's Unified Process, Ernst and Young's Fusion, or the Synergy Process presented in this book) results in a powerful combination for building successful applications.

The goal of UML is twofold: One aim is to provide consistency in giving feedback to the project sponsor that the problem domain is well understood. The other is to provide a consistent model for proper software implementation. However, if you attempt to use UML without a sound process model and project plan (discussed throughout this book and fully presented in the appendices), your project will fail.

All of the artifacts that UML delivers are *traceable.* If developed in conjunction with a sound process, like the Unified Process, the UML models will build on one another. This element of traceability is key to the project. With UML, the project will not only produce less useless and "go-nowhere" deliverables, but it will serve as a checkpoint of the previous model's soundness. Because the UML models are interlocked in their creation, identifying when a component is missing or potentially incorrect is easier.

Some artifacts used in this book are not UML diagrams, nor are they covered in the Unified Process. As is explored later in the book, UML doesn't directly address some aspects of a project, including these:

- Graphical user interface (GUI)
- Process distribution
- Data distribution

In all cases, though, the information needed from these vital areas is based on knowledge gained from the UML diagrams. For example, one artifact useful in distributed systems is the object/location matrix. This matrix details geographically interested locations in the domain and assesses the kind of usage that they perceive for the objects in the system. Its input consists of the classes identified on the class diagram and the locations uncovered in the use-cases. Again, all artifacts must be traceable; otherwise, they aren't worth creating.

The Essence of Modeling

A key benefit of modeling is that it provides a communication pipeline for project team members. Without sound models, team members render their knowledge of the system from their own perspectives. A project can't tolerate individualized perspectives of, for example, requirements. If it did, the project would end up not meeting "perceived" requirements. And regardless of what the project charter says, the project team would be blamed for not meeting someone else's agenda.

Booch says that modeling should accomplish the following four goals:

1. Assist the project team in visualizing a system as it is or as it is intended to be.
2. Assist in specifying the system's structure or behavior.
3. Provide a template that guides in constructing the system.
4. Document the decisions that the project development team has made.

All of these goals echo the common theme of maintaining good communication. Without good communication, the project will fail. UML meets these goals, and more.

The UML Diagrams

UML consists of nine different, interlocking diagrams of a system:

1. Activity
2. Class
3. Collaboration
4. Component
5. Deployment
6. Object
7. Sequence
8. State
9. Use-case

The package diagram is also an important diagram in UML, but not one of the nine key diagrams. It was formerly called the subsystem diagram in other notations and can contain any and all of the diagrams listed here.

The diagrams are evolutionary in their construction. Nevertheless, they are merely different views of the domain. Because people have different backgrounds in modeling, categorizing the diagrams according to multiple perspectives can be helpful. (Figure 1-11 maps the nine diagrams to the five views of the software architecture, to be discussed shortly, for a given project.) The nine diagrams are divided into three categories: static, dynamic, and architectural.

A **static diagram** depicts the system's structure and responsibilities. Static diagrams are similar to the building contractor's "as-built" drawings, which depict multiple subsystems, all interacting within the framework of the physical structure. The static diagrams are

- Class
- Object
- Use-case

A **dynamic diagram** depicts the live interactions that the system supports. Dynamic diagrams detail the interaction among structural artifacts from the static diagrams (classes). These dynamic interactions are discovered in the use-cases as pathways performed in response to an external system stimulus. Dynamic diagrams also provide a much clearer picture of the intended, realized behavior of the system. The dynamic diagrams are

- Activity
- Collaboration
- Sequence
- State
- Use-case

An **architectural diagram** categorizes the system into running and executable components. Architectural diagrams also distinguish the physical location of execution and storage nodes and a framework within which they can interact. They often are produced very early in the project (e.g., during project scoping) to indicate the intended physical architecture. They are further detailed during the Construction and Transition phases to clarify early assumptions that will be physically implemented. The architectural diagrams are

- Component
- Deployment

UML and the 4+1 View of Architecture

An interesting perspective of a project's architecture and the UML modeling artifacts used to describe the system comes from the "4+1" view of software architecture. Developed by Philippe Kruchten and covered in his book *The Rational Unified Process: An Introduction* (published by Addison-Wesley), this view involves, in fact, five different views, as illustrated in Figure 1-11:

- Use-case
- Logical
- Implementation
- Process
- Deployment

The use-case view describes the functionality that the system should deliver as perceived by the external "actors" and the requirements of the system. Intended for users, analysts, designers, developers, and testers, the use-case view is central to all the other views because its contents drive the development of the other views. The use-case should be technology neutral, contain no object-speak, and focus on the *what* rather than the *how* of the system solution.

The logical view describes how the system functionality is provided. Intended mainly for designers and developers, it looks inside of the

FIGURE 1-11 *4+1 view of software architecture*

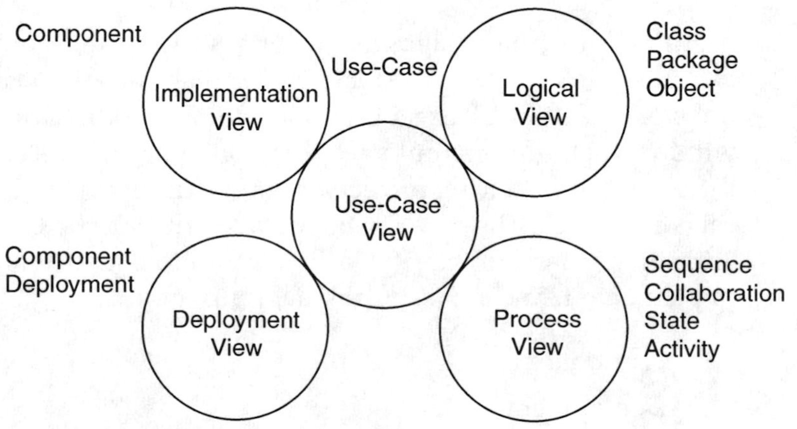

system, in contrast to the more macro use-case view. It describes both the static structure (classes, objects, and relationships) and the dynamic collaborations that occur when objects send messages in response to an external or internal event.

The implementation view describes the implementation modules and their dependencies. The modules can provide for cross-checks back to the other deliverables to ensure that all requirements are eventually actualized into code. It is mainly for developers and consists of the component diagram.

The process view (also called the concurrency view) describes the division of the system into processes and processors. This division allows for efficient resource usage, parallel execution, and the handling of asynchronous events. Intended for developers and integrators, it consists of the state, sequence, collaboration, and activity diagrams, as well as the component and deployment diagrams.

The deployment view describes the physical deployment of the system via the component and deployment diagrams. Developers, integrators, and testers utilize this view.

Using the UML Diagrams in Context

Although nine diagrams might seem a bit overwhelming, not every project will use all of them. For example, many projects might not require state or activity diagrams. A state diagram is used to model the lifecycle of instances of one class, and then only when that class exhibits complex or interesting dynamic behavior. Such classes are prevalent in embedded real-time applications but are not as common in business-oriented applications. Activity diagrams are useful for modeling complex steps within a use-case or an operation found in a class.

Other diagrams offer complementary views of the same thing, such as those found in the sequence and collaboration diagrams. Actually, many visual modeling tools allow you to create the collaboration diagram from the sequence diagram.

In practice, projects will always produce the following diagrams at a minimum:

- Class/collaboration
- Sequence
- Use-case

Projects would also be well served if they produced component and deployment diagrams. In my consulting work, I have encountered the recurring problem of the project team's not taking enough time to visualize and model the design's physical realization. The team assumes a cavalier attitude toward component assembly and, more importantly, the assignment of components to actual processors. Often the requirements are realized and the design is elegant, but response times are poor or ongoing issues of component distribution affect the application's supportability. Many of these issues can be resolved by the use of rich and expressive syntax of the component and deployment diagrams.

This book offers hints regarding when to apply which diagrams. It also stresses the importance of traceability between the diagrams. Early in my career, success as an analyst or designer depended on the weight and thickness of the requirements and design documents. I would like to think that after finishing this book, you will know better when to use which diagrams and will end up with project documentation that is as light as possible and yet complete.

Checkpoint

Where We've Been

- Successful software development requires that complex problems be broken down into smaller, more comprehensible and manageable tasks.
- By iteratively applying sound approaches to construct each increment, the project team manages risk while producing a quality deliverable.
- Successful projects require a sound software process model; the process model used in this book is called the Unified Process from Rational Software.
- The project team must effectively market the benefits of an iterative, incremental, risk-based approach to software development.
- The Unified Modeling Language consists of nine different, semantically rich, interlocked diagrams. These diagrams, when used in

conjunction with a sound software process, enable deliverables to be traced throughout the project's lifecycle.

- Not all of the UML diagrams need to be used in every project. At a minimum, all projects will produce class, sequence, and use-case diagrams.
- Some other artifacts aren't included in UML (e.g., graphical user interface, process and data distribution), but they add additional relevance to the picture of the application domain.
- A project that uses UML in a vacuum, without a sound software process and accompanying project plan, will fail.

Where We're Going Next

In the next chapter we:

- Explore why Java is one of today's most commonly used implementation languages.
- Discuss Java's capabilities for building sound, object-oriented applications.
- Cover why Java lends itself to utilizing a sound software process in conjunction with UML to improve a project's results.

CHAPTER 2

Java, Object-Oriented Analysis and Design, and UML

IN THIS CHAPTER

As mentioned in Chapter 1, to be successful in today's ever-changing business climate, software development must follow an approach that is different from the big-bang approach. The big-bang approach, or waterfall model, offers little risk aversion or support for modification of requirements during development. The waterfall model forces the project team to accept insurmountable risks and create software that usually doesn't approximate the original vision of the project sponsors.

This chapter looks at Java as an enterprise solution for constructing and implementing industrial-strength applications that will better approximate what the sponsors intended. Java is a language that not only supports object-oriented concepts, but also formally acknowledges many constructs not formally found in other object languages, such as the interface. This chapter explores Java's object strengths.

The UML is object-oriented, and its diagrams lend themselves to being implemented in software that is object-oriented. This chapter examines how UML, coupled with a sound software process model, such as the Unified Process, can produce applications that not only meet the project sponsor's goals, but also are adaptive to the ever-changing needs of the business.

GOALS

- To review Java's object capabilities.
- To explore Java and its relationship to UML.
- To review how UML diagrams are mapped to Java.

Java as an Industrial-Strength Development Language

Numerous tomes chronicle the emergence of Java onto the technology landscape. Suffice it to say, things have not been quite the same since James Gosling (the visionary behind Java's birth at Sun Microsystems) created Sun's first Java applet running in a Mosaic-clone Web browser.

Java has grown immensely since that time and gone through many upgrades and enhancements, including sizeable replacements of major components within Java (the Swing graphics library), along with the advent of enterprise-level Java commitment in the form of Enterprise JavaBeans (EJB). This book focuses on the most recent release of the Java Development Kit, JDK 1.3—more affectionately called Java 2.0. In addition, both JavaBeans and Enterprise JavaBeans will be used extensively to implement most of the Java components, and bean-managed and container-managed persistence using the EJB 2.0 specification will be used with commercial application servers.

Java as a career path has also turned out to be a smart decision. Studies have revealed that a majority of job postings in the U.S. market include Java experience as a requirement over other programming languages. In fact, a recent study by the Forrester research firm reported that 79 percent of all Fortune 1000 companies were deploying enterprise Java applications. Forrester also predicted that that figure will be 100 percent by the end of the year 2003.

Java and Object-Oriented Programming

Many seasoned Java developers will scoff at the fact that this section even exists in this book. It is here for two very important reasons. The first is that I continually run across Java applications built with a procedural mind-set. The fact that you know Java doesn't mean that you have the ability to transform that knowledge into well-designed object-oriented systems. As both an instructor and consultant, I see many data-processing shops send COBOL and/or Visual Basic developers to a three-day class on UML and a five-day class on Java and expect miracles. Case in point: I was recently asked to review a Java application to assess its design architecture and found that it had only two classes—`SystemController` and `ScreenController`—which contained over 70,000 lines of Java code.

The second reason for the emphasis on how the language maps to object-oriented principles is that people like language comparisons and how they stack up to their counterparts. To appease those that live and die by language comparisons, let's put Java under the scrutiny of what constitutes an object-oriented language.

No definitive definition of what makes a language object-oriented is globally accepted. However, a common set of criteria I personally find useful is that the language must support the following:

- Classes
- Complex types (Java reference types)
- Message passing
- Encapsulation
- Inheritance
- Polymorphism

These are discussed in the next subsections.

Java and Classes

Java allows classes to be defined. There are no stray functions floating around in Java. A **class** is a static template that contains the defined structure (attributes) and behavior (operations) of a real-world entity in the application domain. At runtime, the class is **instantiated**, or brought to life, as an object born in the image of that class. In my seminars, when several folks new to the object world are in attendance, I often use the analogy of a cookie cutter. The cookie cutter is merely the template used to stamp out what will become individually decorated and unique cookies. The cookie cutter is the class; the unique blue, green, and yellow gingerbread man is the object (which I trust supports a bite operation).

Java exposes the class to potential outside users through its public interface. A **public interface** consists of the signatures of the public operations supported by the class. A **signature** is the operation name and its input parameter types (the return type, if any, is not part of the operation's signature).

Good programming practice encourages developers to declare all attributes as private and allow access to them only via operations. As with most other languages, however, this is not enforced in Java. Figure 2-1 outlines the concept of a class and its interface.

The figure uses a common eggshell metaphor to describe the concept of the class's interface, as well as encapsulation. The internal details of the class are hidden from the outside via a well-defined interface. In this case, only four operations are exposed in the classes interface (`Operation_A`, `B`, `C`, and `D`). The other attributes and operations are protected from the outside world. Actually, to the outside world, it's as if they don't even exist.

FIGURE 2-1 *Public interface of a class*

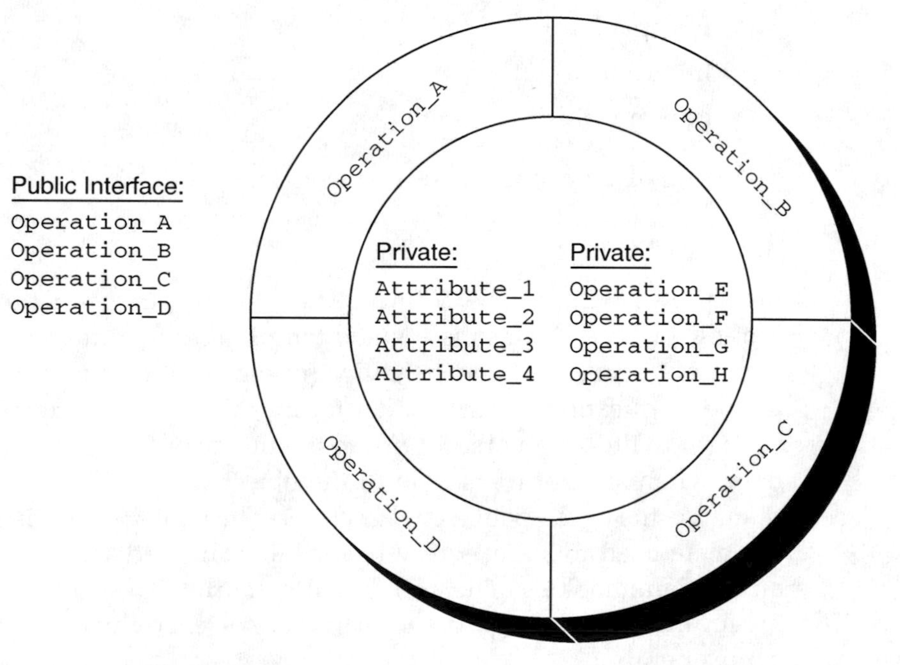

Suppose you want to create an `Order` class in Java that has three attributes—`orderNumber`, `orderDate`, and `orderTotal`—and two operations—`calcTotalValue()` and `getInfo()`. The class definition could look like this:

```
/**
 * Listing 1
 * This is the Order class for the Java/UML book
 */
package com.jacksonreed;
import java.util.*;

public class Order
{
  private Date orderDate;
  private long orderNumber;
  private long orderTotal;

  public Order()
  {
  }

  public boolean getInfo()
  {
    return true;
  }

  public long calcTotalValue()
  {
    return 0;
  }

  public Date getOrderDate()
  {
    return orderDate;
  }

  public void setOrderDate(Date aOrderDate)
  {
    orderDate = aOrderDate;
  }

  public long getOrderNumber()
  {
    return orderNumber;
  }
```

```
    public void setOrderNumber(long aOrderNumber)
    {
      orderNumber = aOrderNumber;
    }

    public long getOrderTotal()
    {
      return orderTotal;
    }

    public void setOrderTotal(long aOrderTotal)
    {
      orderTotal = aOrderTotal;
    }

    public static void main(String[] args)
    {
      Order order = new Order();
      System.out.println("instantiated Order");
      System.out.println(order.getClass().getName());
      System.out.println(order.calcTotalValue());

      try {
        Thread.currentThread().sleep(5*1000);
        } catch(InterruptedException e) {}
    }
}
```

A few things are notable about the first bit of Java code presented in this book. Notice that each of the three attributes has a get and a set operation to allow for the retrieval and setting of the `Order` object's properties. Although doing so is not required, it is common practice to provide these accessor-type operations for all attributes defined in a class. In addition, if the `Order` class ever wanted to be a JavaBean, it would have to have "getters and setters" defined in this way.

Some of the method code in the `main()` operation does a few things of note. Of interest is that a `try` block exists at the end of the operation that puts the current thread to sleep for a bit. This is to allow the console display to freeze so that you can see the results.

If you type in this class and then compile it and execute it in your favorite development tool or from the command prompt with

```
javac order.java //* to compile it
java order //* to run it
```

you should get results that look like this:

```
instantiated Order
com.jacksonreed.Order
0
```

Note: Going forward, I promise you will see no code samples with class, operation, or attribute names of `foo`, `bar`, or `foobar`.

More on Java and Classes

A class can also have what are called *class-level operations* and *attributes.* Java supports these with the `static` keyword. This keyword would go right after the visibility (public, private, protected) component of the operation or attribute. Static operations and attributes are needed to invoke either a service of the class before any real instances of that class are instantiated or a service that doesn't directly apply to any of the instances. The classic example of a static operation is the Java constructor. The constructor is what is called when an object is created with the `New` keyword. Perhaps a more business-focused example is an operation that retrieves a list of `Customer` instances based on particular search criteria.

A class-level attribute can be used to store information that all instances of that class may access. This attribute might be, for example, a count of the number of objects currently instantiated or a property about `Customer` that all instances might need to reference.

Java and Complex Types (Java Reference Types)

A **complex type**, which in Java is called a reference type, allows variables typed as something other than primitive types (e.g., `int` and `boolean`) to be declared. In Java, these are called reference types. In object-oriented systems, variables that are "of" a particular class, such as `Order`, `Customer`, or `Invoice`, must be defined. Taken a step further, `Order` could consist of other class instances, such as `OrderHeader` and `OrderLine`.

In Java, you can define different variables that are references to runtime objects of a particular class type:

```
Public Order myOrder;
Public Customer myCustomer;
Public Invoice myInvoice;
```

Such variables can then be used to store actual object instances and subsequently to serve as recipients of messages sent by other objects. In the previous code fragment, the variable `myOrder` is an instance of `Order`. After the `myOrder` object is created, a message can be sent to it and `myOrder` will respond, provided that the operation is supported by `myOrder`'s interface.

Java and Message Passing

Central to any object-oriented language is the ability to pass messages between objects. In later chapters you will see that work is done in a system only by objects that collaborate (by sending messages) to accomplish a goal (which is specified in a use-case) of the system.

Java doesn't allow stray functions floating around that are not attached to a class. In fact, Java demands this. Unfortunately, as my previous story suggested, just saying that a language requires everything to be packaged in classes doesn't mean that the class design will be robust, let alone correct.

Java supports message passing, which is central to the use of Java's object-oriented features. The format closely resembles the syntax of other languages, such as C++ and Visual Basic. In the following code fragment, assume that a variable called `myCustomer`, of type `Customer`, is defined and that an operation called `calcTotalValue()` is defined for `Customer`. Then the `calcTotalValue()` message being sent to the `myCustomer` object in Java would look like this:

```
myCustomer.calcTotalValue();
```

Many developers feel that, in any other structured language, this is just a fancy way of calling a procedure. Calling a procedure and sending a message are similar in that, once invoked, both a procedure and a message implement a set of well-defined steps. However, a message differs in two ways:

1. There is a designated receiver, the object. Procedures have no designated receiver.
2. The interpretation of the message—that is, the how-to code (called the *method*) used to respond to the message—can vary with different receivers. This point will become more important later in the chapter, when polymorphism is reviewed.

The concepts presented in this book rely heavily on classes and the messaging that takes place between their instances, or objects.

Java and Encapsulation

Recall that a class exposes itself to the outside world via its public interface and that this should be done through exposure to operations only, and not attributes. Java supports encapsulation via its ability to declare both attributes and operations as public, private, or protected. In UML this is called *visibility.*

Using the code from the previous `Order` example, suppose you want to set the value of the `orderDate` attribute. In this case, you should do so with an operation. An operation that gets or sets values is usually called a *getter* or a *setter,* respectively, and collectively such operations are called accessors. The local copy of the order date, `orderDate`, is declared private. (Actually, all attributes of a class should be declared private or protected, so that they are accessible only via operations exposed as public to the outside world.)

Encapsulation provides some powerful capabilities. To the outside world, the design can hide how it derives its attribute values. If the `orderTotal` attribute is stored in the `Order` object, the corresponding get operation defined previously looks like this:

```
public long getOrderTotal()
  {
    return orderTotal;
  }
```

This snippet of code would be invoked if the following code were executed by an interested client:

```
private long localTotal;
private Order localOrder;
localOrder = New Order();
localTotal = localOrder.getOrderTotal()
```

However, suppose the attribute `orderTotal` isn't kept as a local value of the `Order` class, but rather is derived via another mechanism (perhaps messaging to its `OrderLine` objects). If `Order` contains `OrderLine` objects (declared as a `Vector` or `ArrayList` of `OrderLine` objects called `myOrderLines`) and `OrderLine` knows how to obtain its line totals via the message `getOrderLineTotal()`, then the corresponding get operation for `orderTotal` within `Order` will look like this:

```
public long getOrderTotal()
   {
      long totalAmount=0;

      for (int i=0; i < myOrderLines.length; i++)
      {
         totalAmount = totalAmount +
                   myOrderLines[i].getOrderLineTotal();
      }
      return totalAmount;
   }
```

This code cycles through the `myOrderLines` collection, which contains all the `Orderline` objects related to the `Order` object, sending the `getOrderLineTotal()` message to each of `Order`'s `OrderLine` objects. The `getOrderTotal()` operation will be invoked if the following code is executed by an interested client:

```
long localTotal;
Order myOrder;
myOrder = new Order();
localTotal = localOrder.getOrderTotal()
```

Notice that the "client" code didn't change. To the outside world, the class still has an `orderTotal` attribute. However, you have hidden, or *encapsulated,* just how the value was obtained. This encapsulation allows the class's interface to remain the same (hey, I have an `orderTotal` that you can ask me about), while the class retains the flexibility to change its implementation in the future (sorry, how we do business has changed and now we must derive `orderTotal` like this). This kind of resiliency is one of the compelling business reasons to use an object-oriented programming language in general.

Java and Inheritance

The inclusion of inheritance is often the most cited reason for granting a language object-oriented status. There are two kinds of inheritance: *interface* and *implementation.* As we shall see, Java is one of the few languages that makes a clear distinction between the two.

Interface inheritance (Figure 2-2) declares that a class that is inheriting an interface will be responsible for implementing all of the method code of each operation defined in that interface. Only the signatures of the interface are inherited; there is no method or how-to code.

FIGURE 2-2 *Interface inheritance*

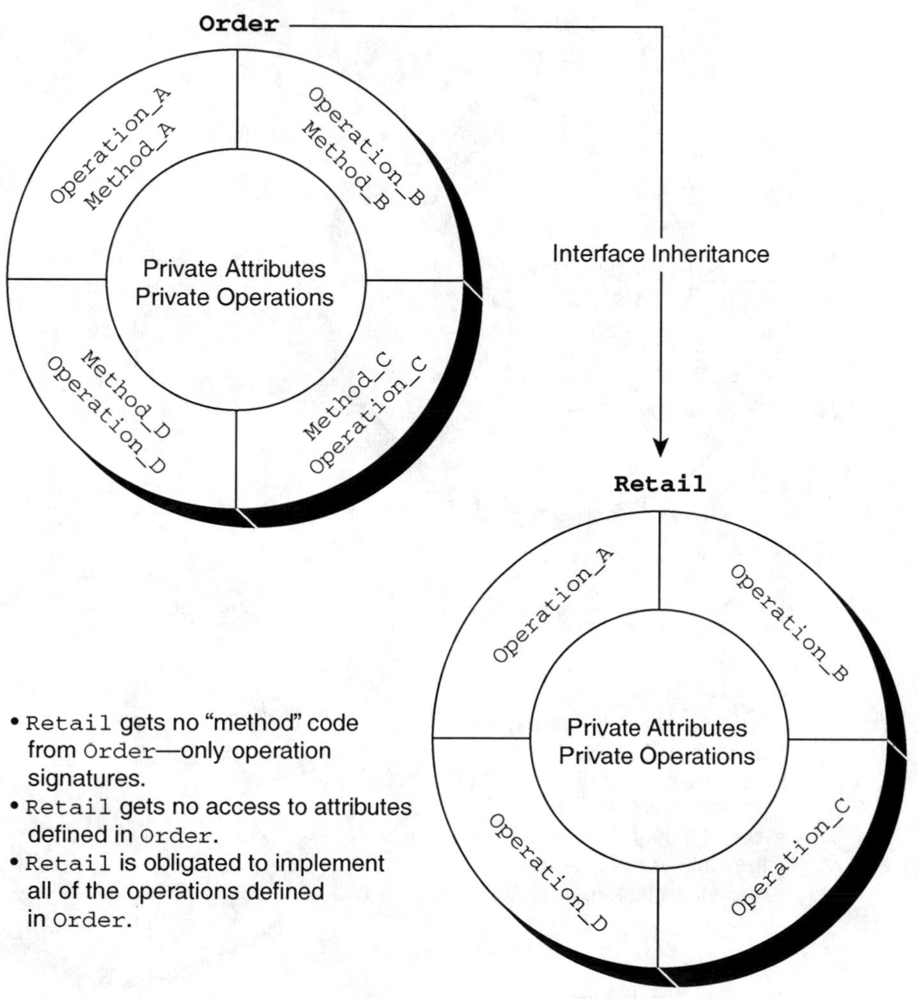

- `Retail` gets no "method" code from `Order`—only operation signatures.
- `Retail` gets no access to attributes defined in `Order`.
- `Retail` is obligated to implement all of the operations defined in `Order`.

Implementation inheritance (Figure 2-3) declares that a class that is inheriting an interface may, at its option, use the method code implementation already established for the interface. Alternatively, it may choose to implement its own version of the interface. In addition, the class inheriting the interface may extend that interface by adding its own operations and attributes.

FIGURE 2-3 *Implementation inheritance*

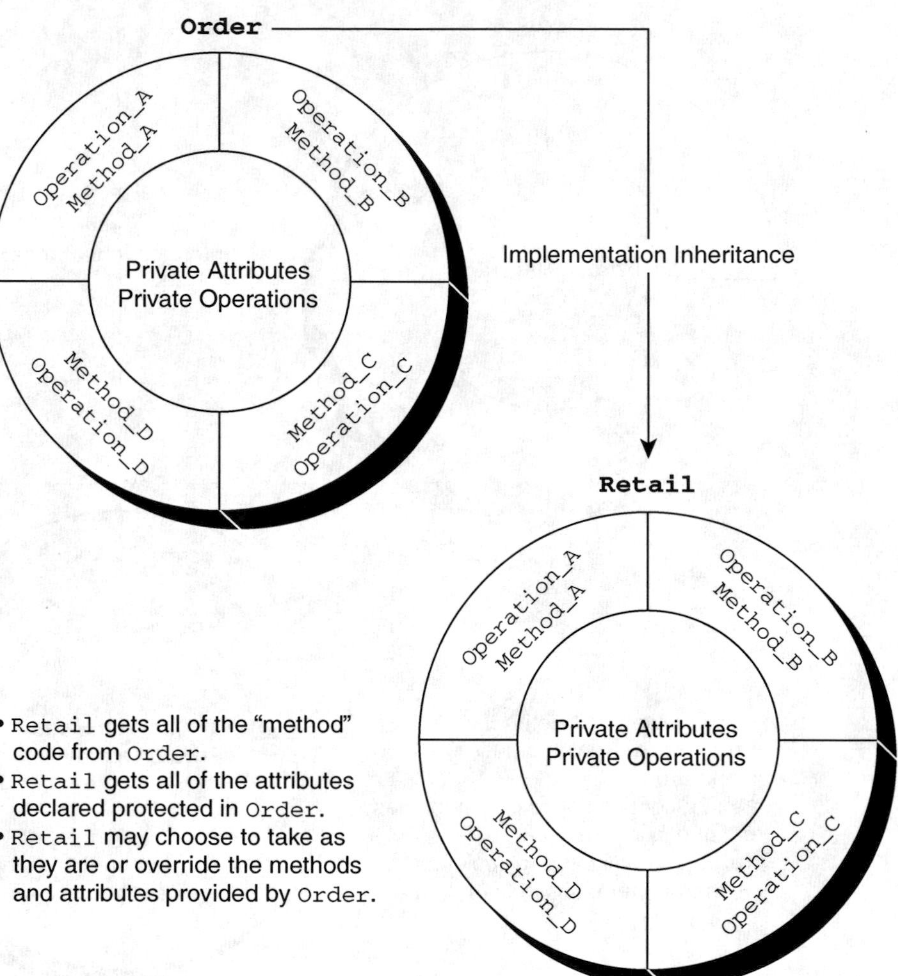

Each type of inheritance should be scrutinized and used in the appropriate setting. Interface inheritance is best used under the following conditions:

- The base class presents a generic facility, such as a table lookup, or a derivation of system-specific information, such as operating-system semantics or unique algorithms.

- The number of operations is small.
- The base class has few, if any, attributes.
- Classes realizing or implementing the interface are diverse, with little or no common code.

Implementation inheritance is best used under the following conditions:

- The class in question is a domain class that is of primary interest to the application (i.e., not a utility or controller class).
- The implementation is complex, with a large number of operations.
- Many attributes and operations are common across specialized implementations of the base class.

Some practitioners contend that implementation inheritance leads to a symptom called the *fragile base class* problem. Chiefly, this term refers to the fact that over time, what were once common code and attributes in the superclass may not stay common as the business evolves. The result is that many, if not all, of the subclasses, override the behavior of the superclass. Worse yet, the subclasses may find themselves overriding the superclass, doing their own work, and then invoking the same operation again on the superclass. These practitioners espouse the idea of using only interface inheritance. Particularly with the advent of Java and its raising of the interface to a first-class type, the concept and usage of interface-based programming have gained tremendous momentum.

As this book evolves, keeping in mind the pointers mentioned here when deciding between the two types of inheritance will be helpful. Examples of both constructs will be presented in the theme project that extends throughout this book.

Implementation Inheritance

Java supports implementation inheritance with the `extends` keyword. A class wanting to take advantage of implementation inheritance simply adds an `extendsClassName` statement to its class definition. To continue the previous example, suppose you have two different types of orders, both warranting their own subclasses: `Commercial` and `Retail`. You would still have an `Order` class (which isn't instantiated directly and which is called abstract). The previous fragment showed the code for the `Order` class. Following is the code for the `Commercial` class.

```
package com.jacksonreed;
public class Commercial extends Order
{
  public Commercial()
  {
  }

  /* Unique Commercial code goes here */
}
```

Implementation inheritance allows the `Commercial` class to utilize all attributes and operations defined in `Order`. This will be done automatically by the Java Virtual Machine (JVM) in conjunction with the language environment. In addition, implementation inheritance has the ability to override and/or extend any of `Order`'s behavior. `Commercial` may also add completely new behavior if it so chooses.

Interface Inheritance

Java supports interface inheritance with the `implements` keyword. A class wanting to realize a given interface (actually being responsible for the method code) simply adds an `implements InterfaceName` statement. However, unlike extension of one class by another class, implementation of an interface by a class requires that the interface be specifically defined as an interface beforehand.

Looking again at the previous example with `Order`, let's assume that this system will contain many classes—some built in this release, and some built in future releases—that need the ability to price themselves. Remember from earlier in this chapter that one of the indicators of using interface inheritance is the situation in which there is little or no common code but the functional intent of the classes is the same. This pricing functionality includes three services: the abilities to calculate tax, to calculate an extended price, and to calculate a total price. Let's call the operations for these services `calcExtendedPrice()`, `calcTax()`, and `calcTotalPrice()`, respectively, and assign them to a Java interface called `IPrice`. Sometimes interface names are prefixed with the letter *I* to distinguish them from other classes:

```
package com.jacksonreed;

interface IPrice
{
  long calcExtendedPrice();
  long calcTax();
  long calcTotalPrice();
}
```

Notice that the interface contains only operation signatures; it has no implementation code. It is up to other classes to implement the actual behavior of the operations. For the `Order` class to implement, or realize, the `IPrice` interface, it must include the `implements` keyword followed by the interface name:

```
public class Order implements IPrice
{
}
```

If you try to implement an interface without providing implementations for all of its operations, your class will not compile. Even if you don't want to implement any method code for some of the operations, you still must have the operations defined in your class.

One very powerful aspect of interface inheritance is that a class can implement many interfaces at the same time. For example, `Order` could implement the `IPrice` interface and perhaps a search interface called `ISearch`. However, a Java class may extend from only one other class.

Java and Polymorphism

Polymorphism is one of those $50 words that dazzles the uninformed and sounds really impressive. In fact, polymorphism is one of the most powerful features of any object-oriented language.

Roget's II: The New Thesaurus cross-references the term *polymorphism* to the main entry of *variety.* That will do for starters. Variety is the key to polymorphism. The Latin root for *polymorphism* means simply "many forms." Polymorphism applies to operations in the object-oriented context. So by combining these two thoughts, you could say that operations are *polymorphic* if they are identical (not just in name but also in signatures) but offer variety in their implementations.

Polymorphism is the ability of two different classes each to have an operation that has the same signature, while having two very different forms of method code for the operation. Note that to take advantage of polymorphism, either an interface inheritance or an implementation inheritance relationship must be involved.

In languages such as COBOL and FORTRAN, defining a routine to have the same name as another routine will cause a compile error. In object-oriented languages such as Java and C++, several classes might have an operation with the same signature. Such duplication is in fact encouraged because of the power and flexibility it brings to the design.

As mentioned previously, the `implements` and `extends` keywords let the application take advantage of polymorphism. As we shall see, the sample project presented later in this book is an order system for a company called Remulak Productions. Remulak sells musical equipment, as well as other types of products. There will be a `Product` class, as well as `Guitar`, `SheetMusic`, and `Supplies` classes.

Suppose, then, that differences exist in the fundamental algorithms used to determine the best time to reorder each type of product (called the economic order quantity, or EOQ). I don't want to let too much out of the bag at this point, but there will be an implementation inheritance relationship created with `Product` as the ancestor class (or superclass) and the other three classes as its descendants (or subclasses). The scenario that follows uses implementation inheritance with a polymorphic example. Note that interface inheritance would yield the same benefits and be implemented in the same fashion.

To facilitate extensibility and be able to add new products in the future in a sort of plug-and-play fashion, we can make `calcEOQ()` polymorphic. To do this in Java, `Product` would define `calcEOQ()` as abstract, thereby informing any inheriting subclass that it must provide the implementation. A key concept behind polymorphism is this: *A class implementing an interface or inheriting from an ancestor class can be treated as an instance of that ancestor class. In the case of a Java interface, the interface itself is a valid type.*

For example, assume that a collection of `Product` objects is defined as a property of the `Inventory` class. `Inventory` will support an operation, `getAverageEOQ()`, that needs to calculate the average economic order quantity for all products the company sells. To do this requires that we iterate over the collection of `Product` objects called `myProducts` to get each object's unique economic order quantity individually, with the goal of getting an average:

```
public long getAverageEOQ()
  {
    long totalAmount=0;

    for (int i=0; i < myProducts.length; i++)
    {
      totalAmount = totalAmount + myProducts[i].calcEOQ();
    }
    return totalAmount / myProducts.length;
  }
```

But wait! First of all, how can `Inventory` have a collection of `Product` objects when the `Product` class is abstract (no instances were ever created on their own)? Remember the maxim from earlier: Any class implementing an interface or extending from an ancestor class can be treated as an instance of that interface or extended class. A `Guitar` "is a" `Product`, `SheetMusic` "is a" `Product`, and `Supplies` "is a" `Product`. So anywhere you reference `Guitar`, `SheetMusic`, or `Supplies`, you can substitute `Product`.

Resident in the array `myProducts` within the `Inventory` class are individual concrete `Guitar`, `SheetMusic`, and `Supplies` objects. Java figures out dynamically which object should get its own unique `calcEOQ()` message. The beauty of this construct is that later, if you add a new type of `Product`—say, `Organ`—it will be totally transparent to the `Inventory` class. That class will still have a collection of `Product` types, but it will have four different ones instead of three, each of which will have its own unique implementation of the `calcEOQ()` operation.

This is polymorphism at its best. At runtime, the class related to the object in question will be identified and the correct "variety" of the operation will be invoked. Polymorphism provides powerful extensibility features to the application by letting future unknown classes implement a predictable and well-conceived interface without affecting how other classes deal with that interface.

Why UML and Java

When modeling elements, our goal is to sketch the application's framework with a keen eye toward using sound object-oriented principles. For this reason, UML, as an object-oriented notation, is a nice fit for any project using Java as its implementation language. Java was built from the ground up with the necessary "object plumbing" to benefit from the design elements of UML models. More importantly, when UML is combined with a sound software process such as the Unified Process, the chances for the project's success increase dramatically.

James Rumbaugh once said, "You can't expect a method to tell you everything to do. Writing software is a creative process, like painting, writing, or architectural design. There are principles of painting, for example, that give guidelines on composition, color selection, and perspective, but they won't make you a Picasso." You will see what he means when later in the book the UML elements are presented in a workable context during the development of an application using Java. At that time, artifacts will be chosen that add the most value to the problem. We will still need a sound process to be successful, however—and a little luck wouldn't hurt, either.

All of the UML artifacts used in this book will cumulatively lead to better-built Java applications. However, some of the UML deliverables will have a much closer counterpart to the actual Java code produced. For example, use-cases are technology neutral. Actually, use-cases would benefit any project, regardless of the software implementation technology employed, because they capture the application's essential requirements. All subsequent UML deliverables will derive from the foundations built in the use-cases.

For core business and commercial applications, three UML diagrams most heavily affect the Java deliverable: use-case, class, and sequence (or collaboration). Now, I run the risk already of having you think the other diagrams are never used; they are, depending on a project's characteristics and requirements. Yes, the project may also benefit, on the basis of its unique characteristics, from other diagrams, such as state and activity diagrams. In my experience, however, the previously mentioned three diagrams, along with their supporting documentation, are the pivotal models that will be most heavily used. Table 2-1 maps the UML diagrams to Java.

Class Diagram

The king of UML diagrams is the class diagram. This diagram is used to generate Java code with a visual modeling tool (in this book, Rational Software's Rose). In addition, everything learned from all of the

TABLE 2-1 *Mapping UML Diagrams to Java*

UML Diagram	Specific Element	Java Counterpart
Package	Instance of	Java packages
Use-case	Instance of	User interface artifacts (downplayed early on) in the form of pathways that will eventually become sequence diagrams
Class	Operations	Operations/methods
	Attributes	Member variables and related accessor operations
	Associations	Member variables and related accessor operations
Sequence	Instance of	Operation in a controller class to coordinate flow
	Message target	Operation in the target class
Collaboration	Instance of	Operation in a controller class to coordinate flow
	Message target	Operation in the target class
State	Actions/activities	Operations in the class being lifecycled
	Events	Operations in the class being lifecycled or in another collaborating class
	State variables	Attributes in the class being lifecycled
Activity	Action states	Method code to implement a complex operation or to coordinate the messaging of a use-case pathway
Component	Components	Typically one *.java* and/or one *.class* file
Deployment	Nodes	Physical, deployable install sets destined for client and/or server hosting

other diagrams will in one way or another influence this diagram. For example, the key class diagram components are represented in Java as follows:

- **Classes:** The classes identified will end up as automatically generated *.java* class files.
- **Attributes:** The attributes identified in the class will be generated as private (optionally public or protected) member variables in the class module. At the option of the designer, the generation process will also automatically generate the necessary accessor operations (i.e., get and set).

- **Interface:** Through the messaging patterns uncovered in the sequence diagrams, the interface of the class—that is, its public operations—will begin to take shape as operations are added to the class.
- **Operations:** Every operation defined for a class will end up as a public, private, or protected operation within the class. The operations initially will lack the complete signature specification (operation name only), but eventually they will contain fully specified signatures.
- **Associations:** The associations identified between classes will end up as attributes of the classes to enable messaging patterns as detailed by sequence diagrams.
- **Finalized classes:** Finalized classes can often be used to generate first-cut database schemas (assuming a relational database as the persistence store) in the form of Data Definition Language (DDL).

The UML class diagram and its Java counterpart, the class *.java* file, are the core of what drives the application's implementation.

Sequence Diagram

The tasks required to satisfy an application's goals are specified as *pathways* through a use-case. For a banking environment, one use-case might be Handle Deposits. A pathway through this use-case, one of many, might be deposits processed at the teller window. In most cases, each major pathway will have a sequence diagram created for it. Each, although logically stated in the use-case, will eventually end up as a dynamic collaboration between runtime objects, all sending messages to one another.

For example, when the `Customer` object wants each of its `Order` objects to perform the operation `calcTotalValue()`, it sends a message. Each message requires the receiver object (the `Order`) to have an operation defined to honor the request. Operations all end up in a class somewhere. These classes eventually are used to generate code in the Java environment.

The project team uses the sequence diagram to "walk through" the application. Once the project team has become comfortable with UML, and the accompanying Unified Process, it will no longer need to walk through code. Once the sequence diagram has passed inspection, the method-level coding can be implemented.

Eventually the sequence diagram walk-throughs will be the primary confirmation of whether a use-case pathway is correct. Most visual modeling tools, at present, do not generate Java code from the message patterns outlined in the sequence diagram (Together Control Center from TogetherSoft will reverse engineer sequence diagrams from Java code). However, I contend that this wouldn't be difficult for all visual modeling tools, and the next version of these products likely will support this ability. Having it would certainly differentiate competitors.

Component Diagram

The fully developed classes are assigned to components in the visual modeling tool's component diagrams. Many will fit a variety of possible physical manifestations:

- Graphical forms (applets and/or applications)
- Business-level rule components
- Transaction or persistence components

These component choices will be reflected in *.java* files.

Deployment Diagram

Components defined in the visual modeling tool are deployed on nodes specified in the deployment diagrams. These diagrams depict the physical machines that will house the components specified as components previously. These deployment strategies may be Web-based solutions, multitier solutions, or standalone Java applications.

Visual Modeling Tool Support

The UML and Java fit together well. The value that UML adds is enhanced by the use of a visual modeling tool that supports both forward and reverse engineering (creating code from models and creating models from code). The use of a visual modeling tool also aids traceability and cross-checking of the model components.

A project that combines an effective software process model and a robust modeling language such as UML nevertheless will be hindered if it lacks a visual modeling tool. Without such a tool, the project will produce paper models that won't be updated or, worse, that will be lost in the shuffle of day-to-day project activity. Many excellent products are available, and they continue to evolve. Pick a tool and make it part of your process. Personally, I wouldn't be caught dead without one.

Checkpoint

Where We've Been

- Once a set-top language destined to control the toasters of the world, Java has become the language darling in the software industry and is quickly eclipsing many other long-standing languages that have been around for years.
- Java has grown in acceptance for many reasons, including its support of a write-once, run-anywhere strategy. In addition, the vast middleware marketplace that affords multitier solutions has embraced Java as its prime source of enablement.
- Java cleanly implemented the notion of interface and implementation inheritance, allowing for a more natural and easy-to-understand use of the constructs.
- Java is greatly influenced by the work done in three UML diagrams: use-case, class, and sequence (or collaboration).

Where We're Going Next

In the next chapter we:

- Explore the project plan for the Unified Process model.
- Review the importance of creating a vision for a project, and look at deliverables from that effort.
- Get acquainted with the book's continuing project, Remulak Productions.
- Produce an event list as a precursor to use-case analysis.

CHAPTER 3 Starting the Project

IN THIS CHAPTER

This chapter lays the groundwork for how to start a project by creating a project vision. It shouldn't be surprising that this is where most projects take their first wrong turn. The project vision sets the stage for the project's Inception phase. As the first artifact to be produced, its importance should not be underestimated.

A project vision is driven by the following six key inputs:

- *The features that the system must support*
- *The stakeholders who will fund and/or oversee the system's use*
- *The actors who will interface with the system*
- *A framework to identify business rules*
- *The events that the system must be aware of and respond to*
- *The constraints and risks placed on the project*

The project vision also must put into place the administrative plumbing necessary for managing the project. This, too, is key to the project's success. Change control, risk assessment, and training are just as meaningful as requirements. These types of activities are taken care of in the Project Management workflow in the Unified Process. Many project teams take these housekeeping chores too lightly and end up the victims of scope creep, risky choices, and a staff with skills inadequate for performing their assigned tasks. The project vision identifies the stepping-stones for successful use of the Unified Process introduced in Chapter 1. Following its activities and observing its dependencies will move us closer to our goal of building quality, object-oriented Java applications.

GOALS

- To introduce Remulak Productions, the project specimen for the book.
- To introduce the process model activities pertinent to the Inception phase.
- To review the project vision template.
- To define and introduce the actors and their roles in the project.
- To explore the event table and its components, and how it forms the basis for identifying use-cases.

Establishing the Project Vision

Remulak Productions is the subject of the sample project that will unfold throughout the remaining chapters. A very small company located in Newport Hills, Washington, a suburb of Seattle, Remulak specializes in finding hard-to-locate musical instruments—in particular, guitars—ranging from traditional instruments to ancient varieties no longer produced. Remulak also sells rare and in-demand sheet music. Further, it is considering adding to its product line other products that are not as unique as its instruments, including recording and mixing technology, microphones, and recordable compact disk (CD) players. Remulak is a very ambitious company; it hopes to open a second order-processing location on the East Coast within a year.

Most of Remulak's orders are taken in-house by order entry clerks. However, some of its sales come from third-party commercial organizations. Remulak's founder, owner, and president, Jeffery Homes, realizes that he cannot effectively run his company with its current antiquated order entry and billing system. Our challenge is to design and implement a system that not only meets the company's immediate needs but also is flexible enough to support other types of products in the future.

The first step is to identify the features that the application needs and to scope the project. The vision will define the boundaries of the project and limit the possible features, as well as implement the housekeeping framework that will guide the project forward. Appendix A contains the project plan templates found in the Unified Process. Before beginning, however, let's reorient ourselves to the Unified Process.

The Process Model

Recall that the Unified Process is our guide to performing activities in a predictable order. Figure 3-1 shows the Unified Process model from Chapter 1, with the Inception phase highlighted.

The goal of the Inception phase is to "go a mile wide and five inches deep" through the entire system. Upon completion of the Inception phase the project team will have an idea of the following:

FIGURE 3-1 *Unified Process model: Inception phase*

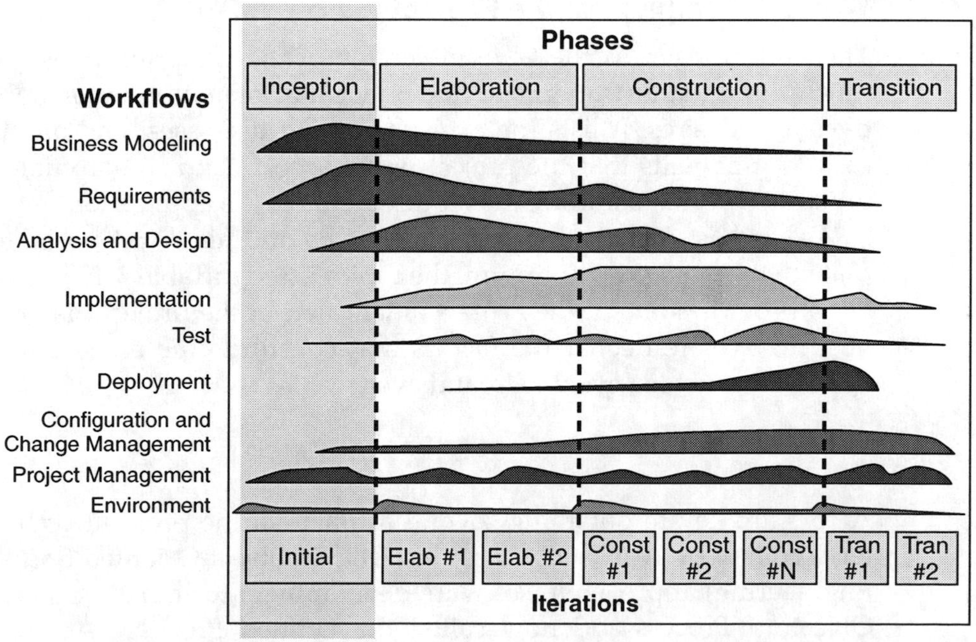

- The goals of the system from the perspective of the stakeholders
- The events the system must support
- The use-cases that make up the system under discussion
- The use-cases and/or use-case pathways that are architecturally significant
- A high-level phase plan for the four phases of the project (Inception, Elaboration, Construction, Transition) and a detailed iteration plan for the architecturally significant requirements identified in the previous step

In this chapter the following Unified Process workflows and activity sets are emphasized:

- Requirements: Understand Stakeholder Needs
- Requirements: Analyze the Problem
- Requirements: Define the System
- Requirements: Manage the Scope of the System

Working Template of the Project Vision

The project vision is the key deliverable of the Inception phase. It is much more than a superficial document that merely mentions objectives and desires. It lists the events, first-cut use-cases, and architectural components that the project will support. And it is a vital step toward our understanding the requirements of the application.

We can best describe the project vision by outlining a proposed template that covers, at a minimum, the topics listed in Table 3-1.

To provide some of the artifacts identified in the project vision, we need to explore deeper the factors that constitute the essence of the application: actors, event lists, and event tables.

Actors

Actors are key to obtaining several artifacts in the project. *Actor* is a term coined by Ivar Jacobson in his OOSE (Object-Oriented Software Engineering) approach to software development (originally called the Objectory Process and now called the Unified Process). Actors are essential in the project. Identifying them gives us better insight into the events that the system must support.

TABLE 3-1 *Proposed Project Vision Template*

Topic	Purpose
Business purpose	The business reason for undertaking this project.
Business objectives	The business objectives of the project. What bottom-line benefits will the project bring to the organization (e.g., the ability to remain competitive, profitable, leading edge, reactive)?
Desired features	The features that the project must support (e.g., order tracking and control, expedient billing, management of inventory, one-day turnaround on special orders).
Critical success factors	The key factors that will make the project a success (e.g., delivery of products on time and within budget, hiring of a talented project manager, reassignment of skilled analysts and developers from existing projects, acquisition of full-time user commitment).
Constraints	Constraints from time, cost, and functionality perspectives (e.g., the project must be completed by year's end, provide a payback within two years, implement a minimum of usable functionality before going into production).
Risks	The clear risks of the project (e.g., the project team has never used Java Basic, let alone object-oriented programming techniques and UML, the existing system will prove difficult to convert because of its antiquated design, the executive sponsor is giving only lip service to full-time user involvement).
Roles and responsibilities	The logical functions that will be performed and by whom (e.g., Executive Sponsor: Jeffery Homes, Lead Analyst: Rene Becnel, Lead User: Dan Fruge, Lead Designer: Todd Klock, Lead Architect: Jose Aponte).
Locations of interest	The geographic areas (if any) that will be expected to use the applications (e.g., New Orleans, Denver, Seattle).
Stakeholders/ actors	Entities that stimulate the system in one form or another. They are usually human beings, but they might also be other systems, timers or clocks, or hardware devices (e.g., order clerk, billing clerk, shipper, accounting system, bar-code reader).
Event list/ event table	Outline of the essential events that the system must be aware of and that will provoke a perceived system response. It might also be good to specify location, frequency of arrival, and arrival pattern (e.g., customer places order, customer inquires about order status, order is shipped, order is billed, order is back-ordered). The event list is delivered in the Software Requirements Specification (SRS) but is kicked off during work on the project vision.
Use-cases	The use-cases that represent the major goals of the application. These are delivered in the Software Requirements Specification (SRS), but they are kicked off during the work on the project vision. The use-cases will be reviewed in Chapter 4.

(continued)

TABLE 3-1 *(continued)*

Topic	Purpose
Preliminary execution architecture	The architecture that is initially envisioned for the construction and production maintenance of the application (e.g., Java over a TCP/IP wide-area network [WAN] using an multitier design approach). The database will initially be Microsoft SQL Server, but all data access will be made via Java Database Connectivity (JDBC) drivers to allow the application to migrate to a different relational database management system (RDBMS) in the future. Visual SourceSafe will be used for source control, and Microsoft's Systems Management Server (SMS) will be used to distribute software components to remote locations.
Project infrastructure	Details of how change control and risk assessments will be made (e.g., all changes will be tied back to the original event table, and any changes not defined within that event table will have to go through a change control procedure).
Project release strategy	Planned release strategy for the project, indicating the increments, duration of each, and anticipated implementation schedule (e.g., there will be three increments for the project: (1) order entry and maintenance, (2) billing, and (3) inventory management).

Actors are usually thought of as human beings, but they may also be other systems, timers and clocks, or hardware devices. Actors stimulate the system and are the initiators of events; they also can receive stimuli from the system and in this case are considered passive. They are discussed in more detail in Chapter 4. For now, they are represented as they are identified in UML, as stick figures, as shown in Figure 3-2. However, they may also be rendered graphically in other ways that more directly illustrate the specific domain of the application.

FIGURE 3-2 *Examples of the actors of a project*

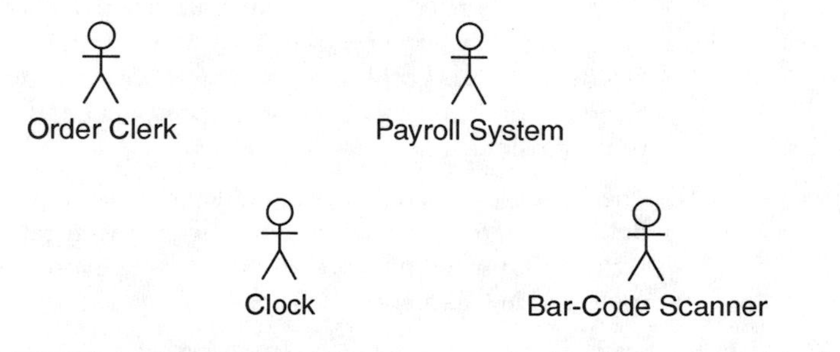

Too often, people attempt to understand a project by producing reams of paper describing what the system will support. This is a wasted exercise that we can remedy by first focusing on the actors—that is, the users—involved in the system. To find the actors, ask the following questions:

- Who/what will be interested in the system?
- Who/what will want to change the data in the system?
- Who/what will want to interface with the system?
- Who/what will want information from the system?

Be careful to focus specifically on the role that each actor will play. This is very important because a given person might play more than one role. As we uncover more information about how the actor interfaces with the system, lumping all of these roles together and treating them as the roles of one actor could be a mistake because that actor might not always play those multiple roles.

Logically, different roles might require different interface skills, knowledge of the system, and comprehension levels. We would err if we designed the interface on the basis of an assumption that the actor is superhuman and can cover lots of bases. Rather, we should analyze the role that each actor plays in the system. This approach will certainly make the system more pliable if the actor's responsibilities change.

Table 3-2 lists the proposed actors for Remulak.

TABLE 3-2 *Proposed Actors for Remulak's Application*

Actor	Definition
Customer	Places orders for products.
Supplier	Supplies products to the company for resale.
Accounting system	Gets accounting information from the system.
Billing clerk	Coordinates and tracks all sales from a financial perspective.
Shipping clerk	Coordinates the routing of fulfilled product orders.
Packaging clerk	Prepares the product for shipment.
Order clerk	Takes new orders and maintains existing orders.
Customer service clerk	Serves customers.
Manager	Requests reports on the status of the company's orders.

Now that we have identified the actors, we'll explore the events that they are responsible for generating.

Event List and Event Table

The event list is the catalyst that flushes out use-cases—something we will do in Chapter 4. Use-cases are not always intuitive. Events, on the other hand, are easy to identify and are very much on a project sponsor's mind. Once the events have been identified, the definition of use-cases is easier. You won't find an event list category in the vision template offered by the Unified Process, but I find it invaluable to the process.

The event list can be created separately from the event table, but one leads to the other. The system must be aware of many types of events. Typically, events fall into two categories: external and internal.

External events are the easiest to find. They are any stimuli to the system that originate from outside of the system's boundaries (e.g., the placement of an order by a customer). To identify external events, focus on the event and ask the question, Who or what is stimulating the event? Most events that we will identify are external.

Internal events are more diverse. One type, and the only one that we will identify now, is the clock or timer event. I view this type of internal event as "that big timer in the sky that goes off, causing the system to do something." Internal timer events are very common in most systems, across all types of domains. Examples of events that are stimulated by an internal timer are *Produce backorder reports nightly* and *Interface with the general ledger system every two days.* Again, focus on the event and ask the question, Who or what is stimulating the event?

Other types of internal events, which we won't discuss here, are those generated by the system. These events typically fall into the category of certain limits being reached or objects being created or deleted. For example, consider the following criterion: If a customer's credit is exceeded, we need a supervisor's approval to complete the sale. That the credit is exceeded is an event; however, this type of event will be specified as a *business rule* that is owned by a class in the domain.

Let's briefly examine the notion of business rules because they will come up quite a bit while your team is creating the event list.

Identifying and Categorizing Business Rules

The term *business rule* got quite a bit of attention in the 1990s. Entire seminars were devoted to the subject. Many practitioners—most notably Ronald Ross—did considerable work in this area.

At this point, some of you might be wondering why we're worrying about business rules. The reason is that they will come up quite often during the event-gathering process. It's a good idea to have a feel for what they are and how to categorize them. When I facilitate an event-gathering session, I usually have a separate easel on which I list the rules when they come up. Our goal is to categorize rules about the business that naturally arise during the Inception phase and that continue into the Elaboration phase.

Business rules can be categorized as follows:

- **Structural fact:** Requires certain facts or conditions to be true; for example, each order must have an order-taken date, each customer must have approved credit.
- **Action restricting:** Prohibits one or more actions on the basis of its condition; for example, add a new business customer only if that customer has a Dun & Bradstreet rating.
- **Action triggering:** Instigates one or more actions when its condition becomes true; for example, when an invoice is not paid by the due date, assess a one-percent penalty,
- **Inference:** States that if certain facts are true, a conclusion is inferred or new knowledge is known; for example, if a customer incorporates, the customer's status changes to business customer.
- **Derivation:** Performs computations and calculations; for example, the total value is the sum of all past orders plus the additional amount derived from the current order.

These categories are not hard-and-fast, but they do provide a method for gathering business rules. You can add additional categories to provide more granularity if you desire.

Event Capture Format

Sometimes project teams struggle with which external events to include in the project's scope. To help make this decision, ask if the system would be stable if you chose not to respond to the event. For example, the event *Customer Places Referral Order* might be a valid event; however, it is out of the scope of this project. An event that is critical to the integrity of a system, such as keeping creditworthy customers, isn't something that could be implemented optionally.

One last point on external events that might be out of scope: Don't exclude them during this initial brainstorming session. You might be surprised how many times you will revisit the list later, and you might resurrect some events that previously were deemed out of scope. It is a good exercise not to cloud the session with premature assumptions about boundaries. Here's a good maxim to follow: Ask for the sky, prioritize, and then simplify.

Now we can begin identifying the events. Think of an event as following this general form:

Subject + Verb + Object

where

- *Subject* is an actor defined earlier in the process—for example, customer or shipping clerk.
- *Verb* shows the action, such as places, sends, buys, or changes.
- *Object* is the focus of the action defined by *Verb.*

Here are some examples:

- *Customer + Places + Order*
- *Shipping Clerk + Sends + Order Items*
- *Customer + Buys + Warranty*
- *Order Clerk + Changes + Order*

It can be helpful to come up with events in one session and then, in another session, focus on adding information and placing the events in an event table. The goal is to get the events into the event table quickly because it is one of the first key artifacts produced as part of the project vision effort.

The event table identifies additional information that will provide important input to other areas of the organization (e.g., operations, network support). Table 3-3 shows a proposed format for the event table.

The importance of the arrival pattern might vary depending on the application domains. The following are typical values for it:

- **Periodic:** Events are defined by the period in which they arrive.
- **Episodic:** Events arrive unpredictably, showing no pattern.

Eventually we will want to be even more specific regarding the granularity of the arrival pattern (e.g., peak hour frequency) because this information will be vitally important to the network and operations staff. For example, 1,000 *Customer Places Order* events in a given day might not concern the network staff, but 900 such events between 8:00 A.M.

TABLE 3-3 *Proposed Format of an Event Table*

Subject	Verb	Object	Frequency	Arrival Pattern	Response
Customer	Places	Order	1,000/day	Episodic	Order is edited and saved in the system.
Shipping clerk	Sends	Order	700/day	Episodic	Order is packaged and shipped according to the shipping terms.
Customer	Buys	Warranty	60/day	Episodic	Order is validated as to terms and then recorded.
Customer	Changes	Order	5/day	Episodic	Order is edited to make the change and then recorded.
Supplier	Sends	Inventory	5–10/day	Episodic	New inventory is checked in.
Customer	Cancels	Order	1/week	Episodic	Order is removed from the system.
Time	Produces	Back-order report	3/week	Episodic	Report is produced.
Time	Produces	Accounting interface	1/week	Episodic	Interface is added to the system.
Customer service clerk	Changes	Address	5/week	Episodic	Address is changed.
Packaging clerk	Prepares	Order	100/day	Episodic	Package is readied for shipment.
Manager	Inquires about	Orders	5/day	Episodic	Request is honored.
Billing clerk	Inquires about	Past-due invoice	10/day	Episodic	Past-due report is produced.
Customer	Inquires about	Order	200/day	Episodic	Order information is provided.

and 9:00 A.M. definitely will. At this point in the project we might not know this level of detail; nevertheless, we must take a stab at predicting the arrival pattern. In addition, if the locations are known now, the frequency cells in the table should outline them and their unique frequencies.

The anticipated responses are at a relatively high level at this point. However, anticipated responses are an important component of the event table because they represent the expectations of the actors, many of whom are probably members of the project team. These responses will be realized as design components and actual code later in the project.

The Project Vision

In the first pass of the project vision, the project team must agree on the template's basic components (features, critical success factors, and so on), the actors, and the events to be supported. Although this effort can be accomplished in any of several different ways, a facilitated session works best, preferably supervised by a disinterested third party skilled in facilitating and in keeping things on track.

For very large projects, the project team should consider breaking up the sessions by logical subsystem—for example, accounting, billing, and order entry. Whether you do this depends on the size of the project. For example, I once worked with a large automobile company that was attempting to integrate state-of-the-art human interaction technology into the automobile. We broke up the project team into six separate teams along their functional boundaries (e.g., voice, cellular) and gave each team a week to come up with its part of the project vision.

In Chapter 4 we will assign events to use-cases. We will also add detail to some parts of the use-cases before attempting to estimate the project's release cycles (increments) and time frames; we need to know more about the project before we estimate the effort. Two new artifacts will begin to surface: the Software Requirements Specification and the Supplementary Specification. This is where the Unified Process differs from many other processes. (An approach to estimating use-cases is covered later in Chapter 4 and in Appendix C.) It is wise to remember that regardless of the caveats you put on an estimate, people later will recall only the estimate itself.

Checkpoint

Where We've Been

- Projects need boundaries and a way to express those boundaries coherently; the project vision provides this functionality.
- The actors and their roles need to be defined on the basis of information available about the application domain.
- The events are the embryo of what the system must support. They form the nucleus of the system's requirements and will be satisfied by use-cases defined in Chapter 4.
- Providing estimates too early damages credibility. Typically, more information is needed before workable release cycles (increments) and estimates can be provided.

Where We're Going Next

In the next chapter we:

- Review the concept of the use-case and its modeling components.
- Assign events to use-cases.
- Identify the primary, alternate, and exception pathways through the use-cases.
- Examine in detail some of the pathways through the use-cases.
- Prioritize and package the use-cases.
- Estimate release cycles (increments).
- Define preliminary software architecture.

CHAPTER 4 *Use-Cases*

IN THIS CHAPTER

Having defined the project vision, the actors, and the events of interest in the system, we next move to assigning the events to use-cases. The use-case is the one UML artifact that focuses on what *the system will be contracted to do, not* how *it will do it. Use-cases are the hub from which all requirements are derived.*

Every event identified in Chapter 3 as part of the Inception phase must be satisfied by a use-case. One use-case can satisfy many events. As a result, a use-case may have more than one pathway through it. A ***pathway*** *is the set of steps that must be carried out to satisfy the goal of the actor. This chapter examines how to identify these pathways, and it describes in detail the primary pathway through each use-case.*

The chapter also investigates a preliminary software architecture. This architecture is based on what is known about the application's execution domain and is represented by the UML component and deployment diagrams.

The Inception phase will also produce an estimate of both the number of iterations and increments in which the system will be realized and the time and costs incurred for deliverables. This grouping of functionality is visualized with the UML package diagram.

GOALS

- To add to our information about Remulak Productions, especially pertaining to preliminary technology needs and goals.
- To explore the concept of the use-case and the use-case diagram.
- To review a sample use-case template.
- To define the various pathways through use-cases: primary, alternate, and exception.
- To learn how to give a detailed description of the most common pathway through a use-case.
- To discuss a preliminary software and hardware architecture.
- To review the planned increments and implementation schedule.

The Sample Project

Recall from Chapter 3 that Remulak Productions, which specializes in locating hard-to-find musical instruments, primarily guitars, wants to replace its legacy order entry application. Company founder, owner, and president Jeffery Homes has contacted us to address his concern about his company's ability to keep up with technology.

Homes is not an IT expert, but he knows that success depends on the replacement system's extensibility into the future. His initial concern is the applicability of the Internet to his business. He wants to minimize cost outlays for the technology used while maintaining flexibility to change platforms later. He makes the following observations about the company:

- Many of its products are very expensive and require quite a bit of hand-holding and selling by the order clerk.
- Many, if not all, of its customers want to be able to get information on orders that have been placed and shipped without interacting with a company representative.
- Many of its customers want to order other products from Remulak that are not as unique as its instruments, including recording and mixing technology, microphones, and recordable CD players.

On the basis of these observations, Homes decides that an Internet-based inquiry capability could benefit Remulak. However, some cases still require customized, personal interaction, at least initially to enter the order in the system. So it appears that all but the most complicated orders could utilize an Internet-based order solution. These facts are crucial to consider as we devise our initial software architecture for Remulak.

The Process Model

Once again, the Unified Process model is spotlighted, again with emphasis on the Inception phase (Figure 4-1).

In this chapter, the following Unified Process workflows and activity sets are emphasized:

- Requirements: Analyze the Problem
- Requirements: Define the System

FIGURE 4-1 *Unified Process model: Inception phase*

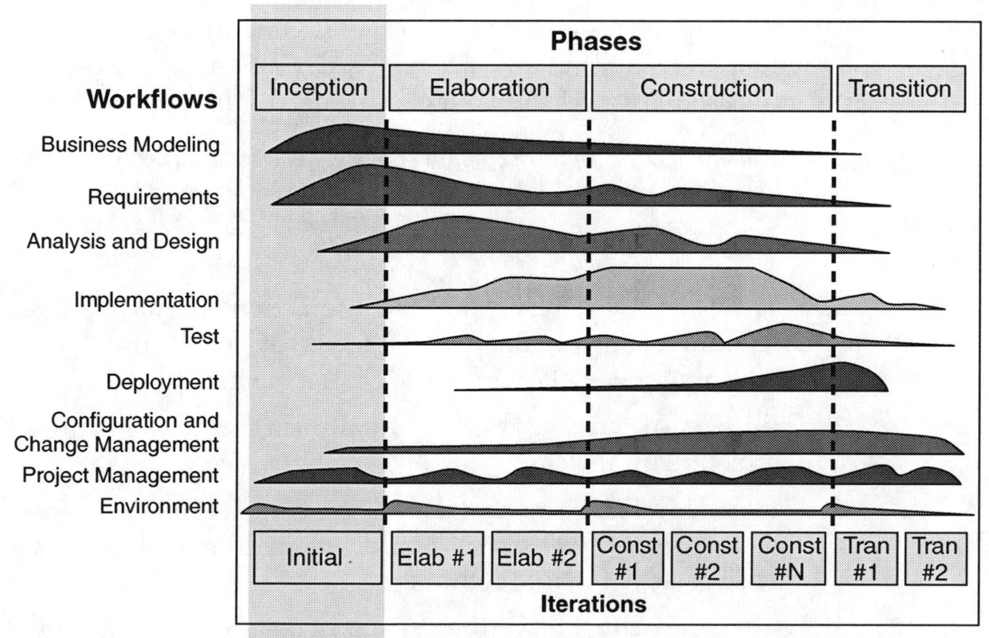

- Requirements: Manage the Scope of the System
- Test: Plan Test

Use-Cases

The project's success depends largely on defining requirements in a manner that is intuitive to both the IT staff and the project sponsors. The requirements documentation not only serves as a key artifact, but also must be a living artifact. Requirements cannot be expected to remain stable throughout the project effort, so they must be in a format that can be easily assimilated by the current project team, as well as by new team members. The key vehicle to capturing requirements is the **use-case**. Many people I work with ask, "But when do you do functional requirements?" Use-cases are the functional requirements of the application.

The concept of the use-case sprang from Ivar Jacobson's early work on large telecommunications switching systems at Ericsson. This was his primary contribution to UML. As mentioned in earlier chapters, Jacobson's Objectory Process was transformed into Rational Software's popular process model, the Unified Process.

Use-cases are goal-oriented and serve as containers of sorts for the interactions that they satisfy. Jacobson's definition of a use-case will serve as a baseline as we begin our exploration of this key UML artifact:

> *A behaviorally related sequence of interactions performed by an actor in a dialog with the system to provide some measurable value to the actor.*

Let's examine this definition in more detail.

1. *Behaviorally related* means that the interactions should, as a group, constitute a self-contained unit that is an end in itself, with no intervening time delays imposed by the business.
2. The use-case must be initiated by an actor and seen through to completion by an actor.
3. *Measurable value* means that the use-case must achieve a particular business goal. If we cannot find a business-related objective for the use-case, we should rethink it.
4. The use-case must leave the system in a stable state; it cannot be half done.

Use-cases are goal-oriented. Remembering this is key to using them effectively. They represent the *what* of the system, not the *how*. Use-cases are also technology neutral, so they can apply to any application architecture or process. Even if you were to throw out all that UML offers and use only use-cases, a project's requirements would be defined in a much clearer and more coherent fashion than if use-cases were not used. Figure 4-2 identifies the sequence that we follow to arrive at the use-cases.

The process of identifying use-cases is easier if the event table is grouped by actor, as in Table 4-1. Often a use-case will be associated with only one actor. However, some types of use-cases—for example, those that provide information such as reports—often have more than one actor.

Notice that certain events in the table tend to cluster together, such as those dealing with order entry. Also some events deal with maintaining an order, as well as inquiring about an existing order. We take these natural groupings and write a short descriptive phrase (one or two words) for each, asking these questions:

- What do these events have in common?
- Do these events have the same ultimate goal? If so, what is it?

FIGURE 4-2 *Getting to use-cases*

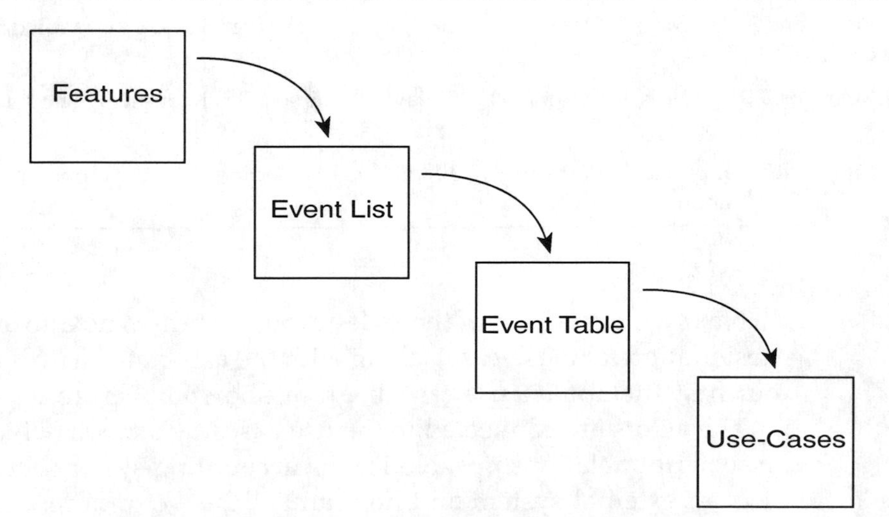

TABLE 4-1 *Event Table with Events Grouped by Actor*

Subject	Verb	Object	Frequency	Arrival Pattern	Response
Customer	Places	Order	1,000/day	Episodic	Order is edited and saved in the system.
Customer	Buys	Warranty	60/day	Episodic	Order is validated as to terms and then recorded.
Customer	Changes	Order	5/day	Episodic	Order is edited to make the change and then recorded.
Customer	Cancels	Order	1/week	Episodic	Order is removed from the system.
Customer	Inquires about	Order	200/day	Episodic	Order information is provided.
Customer service clerk	Changes	Address	5/week	Episodic	Address is changed.
Shipping clerk	Sends	Order	700/day	Episodic	Order is packaged and shipped according to the shipping terms.
Supplier	Sends	Inventory	5–10/day	Episodic	New inventory is checked in.
Time	Produces	Back-order report	3/week	Episodic	Report is produced.
Time	Produces	Accounting interface	1/week	Episodic	Interface is added to the system.
Packaging clerk	Prepares	Order	100/day	Episodic	Package is readied for shipment.
Manager	Inquires about	Orders	5/day	Episodic	Request is honored.
Billing clerk	Inquires about	Past-due invoice	10/day	Episodic	Past-due report is produced.

Next we place each of these descriptive phrases next to an oval (the designation for a use-case), along with the associated actors to produce our first attempt at a use-case diagram, shown in Figure 4-3.

The actors are connected to the use-cases by arrows, which indicate **association** relationships. Notice the accounting system actor. Because it is an external system and nonhuman, this actor is rendered by the *interface stereotype* and drawn as a box. Stereotypes are discussed in

FIGURE 4-3 *Remulak use-case diagram*

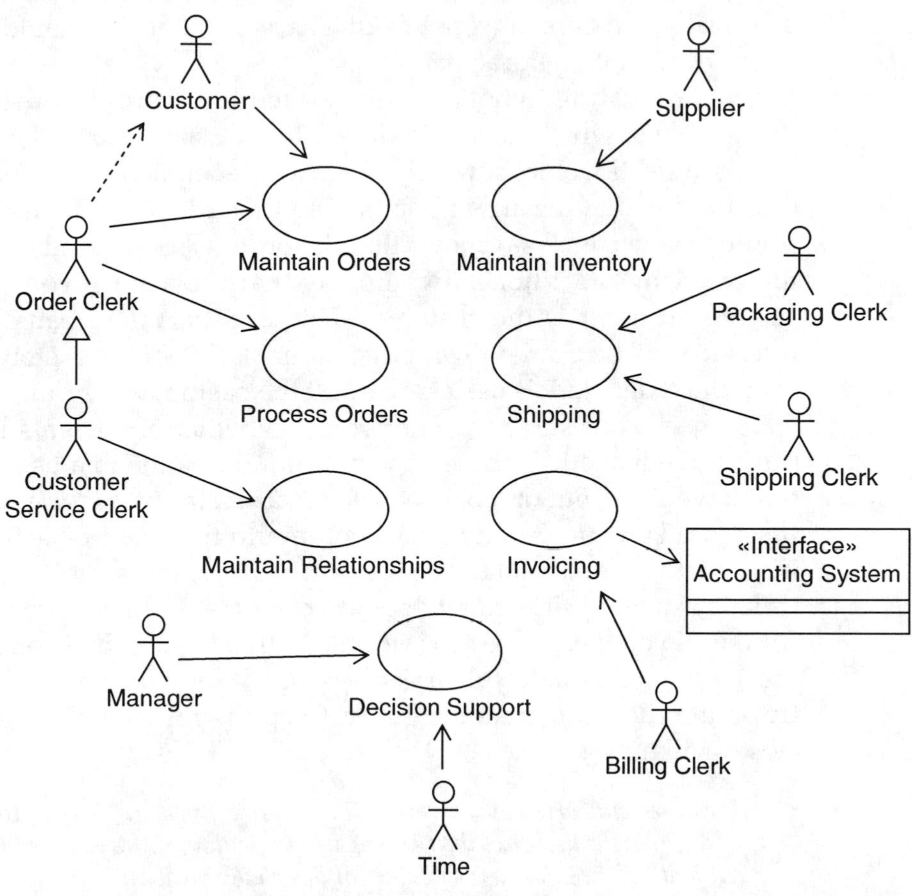

more detail later in the chapter. For now, think of a stereotype as a categorization or grouping mechanism. Using stereotypes is optional; there is nothing semantically incorrect about representing this actor as a stick figure. I consulted on a project whose management took a dim view of stick figures as part of the deliverables, so we went with the box notation. You can probably guess that this organization had quite a few other hurdles to clear before it became successful at using UML.

Notice also the line with the large triangle arrow connecting the customer service clerk and order clerk actors. This arrow means that a customer service clerk "is an" order clerk, thereby denoting a **generalization** relationship. That is, the two actors can be substituted for the same thing, and they perform the same logical function but happen to be physically one person (recall from Chapter 3 that we should focus on the role and not on the actor).

One last feature to notice is the dashed line from the order clerk to the customer, which denotes a **dependency association** relationship—that is, a relationship in which one actor depends on the other. In this case the fact that the arrow points from the order clerk to the customer (rather than vice versa) shows that the order clerk depends on the customer. Many practitioners would say that the actor involved in processing an order is the customer. This is debatable because the user interface will be geared toward the order clerk, not the customer. However, the order clerk is useless without the customer's input.

To check consistency, we determine whether any events identified during the Inception phase have not found a home in a use-case. Any that haven't are out of scope, worded incorrectly, or missing a use-case. It's a good practice to add a new column to the event table for recording which use-case satisfies each event.

This is a good time to talk about **scope creep**. Every project suffers from it. If you have experience with one that hasn't, then you have had the luxury of wonderful project sponsors, or you aren't telling the truth, in order to protect the guilty. Keep the following bit of wisdom close at all times:

> *All requirements originate as features in the project vision. These features lead to events that the use-cases then satisfy. If a particular feature isn't defined as an event and satisfied by a use-case, then it is a change request that requires some form of change control action.*

This doesn't mean that the project won't accept changes. Rather it says that to keep your schedule true to the increments to be implemented, changes must be tracked and assigned to a later-scheduled increment that will satisfy them. Do you need to update the event table and related use-case documentation? You bet. If the event table and use-cases are not kept up-to-date, you will lose all traceability.

We have now completed the first UML diagram: the use-case diagram (although it is subject to change). From the perspectives of the project sponsors, this is the most important diagram because it represents their domain; that is, it represents the boundaries of the project scope from a high-level perspective, and it is the basis for dividing the project into multiple increments.

Finding the Pathways through Use-Cases

Before we can complete the project vision, we need to do more work: We need to find the various pathways through each use-case. We will identify three levels of pathways—primary, alternate, and exception—as well as present a use-case template to be used across the entire project.

Unfortunately, the authors of UML provided us little, if any, input on what goes inside of a use-case. The official UML notation, as maintained by the Object Management Group, ventures no further than describing the diagrammatic components. This is little help to the practitioner. In defense of the UML authors, how we choose to capture the detail of the use-case is subjective to some degree. So it is crucial that a template be agreed upon for the project. The template presented here is what I consider to represent best practices after having been through many iterations of tweaking the process. The Unified Process also offers a use-case template, but it is a bit on the light side.

Other excellent use-case templates are available. A popular template is provided by Geri Schneider in her book *Applying Use Cases: A Practical Guide* (Addison-Wesley, 2001); another format is presented by Daryl Kulak and Eamonn Guiney in their excellent book *Use Cases: Requirements in Context* (Addison-Wesley, 2000).

We have assigned events to use-cases. Recall that use-cases are goal oriented and serve as containers for the interactions that they satisfy. Also recall from Ivar Jacobson that "the interactions should, as a group, be a self-contained unit that is an end in itself." To document the use-cases better, we employ a use-case template. The template is broken up into four sections that we apply to all use-cases.

Use-Case Template: Section 1

Section 1 of the template focuses on the high-level information gathered about the use-case. Most of what is contained here is informative and portrays the overall goal of the use-case. The "Trigger Event(s)" category is tied back to the event list produced in the previous section (see Table 4-1). It acts as a cross-check and balance to ensure that all the events are being assigned to a use-case. Trigger events are also important because if the team does not conduct an event generation exercise, at this point the events that kick the use-case into action should be identified.

Here's Section 1:

1. Use-Case Description Information

The following defines information that pertains to this particular use-case. Each piece of information is important in understanding the purpose behind the use-case.

1.1 Name

<Short, descriptive verb phrase naming the use-case.>

1.2 Goal

<A few sentences describing the ultimate goal of the use-case from the perspective of the user.>

1.3 Use-Case Team Leader/Members

<The person assigned the ultimate responsibility of completing the use-case, along with his/her team members.>

1.4 Precondition

<The state the system must be in before a use-case pathway can begin; may be specified further at the pathway level as well.>

1.5 Postcondition

<The state the system must be in after a use-case pathway has completed; may be specified further at the pathway level as well.>

1.6 Constraints/Issues/Risks

<Any items that may place a burden on the team that is describing the details of the use-case; may be specified further at the pathway level as well. It may be beneficial to assign each issue to a specific individual on the team.>

1.7 Trigger Event(s)

<The external event(s) or internal timer event(s) that stimulate a pathway through the use-case; may be defined at the individual pathway level as well.>

1.8 Primary Actor

<The key actor in the use-case. Typically this individual is the source of the event that stimulates the use-case pathway into action.>

1.9 Secondary Actor(s)

<Other actor(s) that play a part in the use-case.>

Use-Case Template: Section 2

Section 2 of the template focuses on the pathway names supported by the use-case. These are divided into three categories: primary, alternate, and exception. Note that these are only the names of the pathways, not the underlying tasks necessary to carry out the pathways. The details will be captured in the third section of the template.

Here's Section 2:

2. Use-Case Pathway Names

<The names of the pathways, serving only as a summary list to the subsequent detail of the pathways in Section 3.>

2.1 Primary Pathway (Happy Path)

<The most common pathway through the use-case. This path has no error conditions, with everything resulting in a positive outcome. More than one pathway may result in a positive outcome in the use-case; this one, however, occurs the most frequently.>

2.2 Alternate Pathway(s)

<Alternate pathway(s) through the use-case. Depending on the levels within the use-case, these may be just as detailed in content as the primary path.>

2.3 Exception Pathway(s)

<The primary exception(s) expected to occur in this use-case.>

Use-Case Template: Section 3

Section 3 of the template focuses on the detailed tasks, or steps, necessary to carry out a given use-case pathway. In many use-cases, completing this part of the template first for the primary (happy) pathway will satisfy a large majority of the effort in the use-case process. In addition, on the basis of the granularity of the project's use-cases, many of the alternate paths may be happy pathways as well—just not the most commonly occurring one.

Note that there will be a Section 3 of the template for each pathway. The "Business Rules" category of this section is a vital piece of information to the project at this point. Probably many business rules will have come up during the event generation exercise. If you recall, these rules are captured at that point, but here they are assigned ownership within a use-case.

Here's Section 3:

3. Use-Case Detail

<This section is completed for all pathways, regardless of the category of the pathway (i.e., primary, alternate, exception), which are usually documented in the three category groups. If the alternate and exception pathways are simple, they may refer back to a step within the main sequence of steps they are modifying or defining.>

3.1 Pathway Name

<The name of the pathway, as specified in Section 2.>

3.2 Trigger Event(s)

<Depending on the use-case granularity, events may be tied directly to a specific pathway.>

3.3 Main Sequence of Steps

<The detailed tasks, or steps, to be carried out in response to the event that started this pathway. The focus is on the what, *not the* how. *In addition, or in replacement, of the outline below, a UML activity diagram may be included. If a pathway step references a different use-case, the reference step is underscored. In addition, in the use-case diagram the included use-case is noted with the* <<includes>> *relationship.>*

Step	Description
<step #>	*<A one-sentence description of the step>*

optionally, for an <<*includes*>> relationship, underscore the step:

<step #>	*<A one-sentence description of the step>*

3.4 Variations (optional)

<Steps in an abbreviated alternate pathway that are documented as modifiers to one of the main-sequence steps. These may not be found for all pathways. If the alternative is not as simple as a variation to a previously defined main-sequence step, then provide a complete main sequence of steps for the alternative.>

Step	Description
<main sequence step #>	*<A one-sentence description of the step>*
<variation step #>	*<A one-sentence description of the step>*

3.5 Extensions (optional)

<Conditional steps that extend the use-case from a particular point. These may also be referred to as extension points. *They extend from a point within the main sequence of either the primary pathway or an alternate pathway within the use-case. The extension, if central to the overall understanding of the use-case, may be shown in the use-case diagram with an* <<extends>> *relationship to the extended use-case.>*

3.6 Business Rules (optional)

<Business rules that are pathway-specific. They may be global to the entire pathway, or they may be tied directly to a particular step within the pathway.>

3.7 Constraints/Issues/Risks (optional)

<Any items that may place a burden on the team that is describing the details of the use-case pathway. They may be global to the entire pathway, or they may be tied directly to a particular step within the pathway. It may be beneficial to assign each issue to a specific individual on the team.>

Use-Case Template: Section 4

Section 4 of the template focuses on more tactical elements of the use-case. Some practitioners label this section *Nonfunctional Requirements.* The Unified Process has a formal document to capture nonfunctional requirements, called the Supplementary Specification. Nevertheless, the items refer to many physical aspects of the use-case; some are even design focused. Some of you may be shuddering here because use-cases focus on the *what,* not the *how,* and are supposed to be technology neutral. However, I have found that to have a place to capture these aspects in the use-case process is very important for ensuring that the artifacts are not lost.

Here's Section 4:

4. Use-Case Tactical Information

<Information about the use-case that deals with scheduling, priorities, frequency, user interface, and performance topics. These items are usually not known early in the use-case Inception phase but are uncovered later, during Elaboration.>

4.1 Priority

<The priority of the use-case relative to others, indicating how this use-case will be packaged and delivered. It is possible to attach priorities to individual pathways.>

4.2 Performance Target(s)

<Specific performance expectations of the use-case. It is possible to attach these to individual pathways.>

4.3 Frequency

<The frequency at which the use-case pathways occur will eventually indicate potential transaction loadings in the system. This is usually stated in a base frequency such as x/day, x/hour, x/week. It is possible to attach this information to individual pathways.>

4.4 User Interface

<User interface issues or requirements for the use-case. This information will be described in detail later, during the Elaboration phase of the project.>

4.5 Location of Source

<If the application has a geographically dispersed nature, it is valuable to identify the relevant locations.>

Finding the Happy Path

We need to know more about the interactions stimulated by events and now assigned to use-cases. Specifically, we need more information about what happens when a use-case responds to an event. We obtain this information by identifying the steps within the pathway that a use-case must enforce in response to an event.

The use-case template is initially used to define the primary pathway, called the **happy path**, or more formally, the Basic Course of Events (BCOE). The happy path (or, as one of my seminar attendees called it, the "sunny-day path") is the most common pathway through the use-case. It usually depicts the perfect situation, in which nothing goes wrong. If a use-case has a lot of happy pathways, we arbitrarily pick one as *the* happy path. However, I contend that with a little work, we'll likely find that one of these potential happy paths either happens more often than the others or is more interesting to the project sponsor. In addition, the existence of more than one happy path for a use-case

TABLE 4-2 *Happy Paths for the Remulak Use-Cases*

Use-Case	Happy Path
Maintain Orders	A customer calls to inquire about an order's status.
Maintain Inventory	The products arrive at the warehouse with a copy of the purchase order attached.
Process Orders	A customer calls and orders a guitar and supplies, and pays with a credit card.
Shipping	An entire order is shipped from stock on hand to a customer.
Invoicing	An order is invoiced and sent to the customer, indicating that payment was satisfied via credit card billing.
Maintain Relationships	A customer calls to change his/her mailing address.
Decision Support	The manager requests a back-order status report.

may indicate that the use-case is too coarse-grained and may, in fact, be two use-cases.

We want to identify the happy path for every use-case we have at this point. Table 4-2 does this for Remulak Productions.

Finding the Alternate Pathways

Having identified the happy pathway for each use-case, we next tackle finding the alternate pathways. An **alternate pathway** is a pathway that is still considered a good pathway; it's just not the most heavily traveled one. Another term often used for this type of pathway is Alternate Course of Events (ACOE). Table 4-3 describes the alternate pathways for the Remulak Productions use-cases.

Finding the Exception Pathways

Things don't always go as planned. An **exception pathway** is intended to capture an "unhappy" pathway or, as one of my seminar attendees called it, the "crappy path." An **exception** is an error condition that is important enough to the application to capture. In some application domains (such as failure analysis), the error conditions are more important than the success-oriented happy path. Some use-cases, however, might not have exceptions that are interesting enough to capture; don't be concerned about those.

TABLE 4-3 *Alternate Pathways for the Remulak Use-Cases*

Use-Case	Alternate Pathways
Maintain Orders	A customer calls to change a product quantity for one order item on an order.
	A customer calls to cancel an order.
	A customer calls to add a new item to an order.
	A customer calls to delete an item from an order.
	A customer calls to change the shipping terms of an order.
	A customer buys an extended warranty on an item.
	A customer calls to change the billing method on an order.
Maintain Inventory	A product arrives at the warehouse with a purchase order that is attached but incomplete as to the products ordered.
	A product is ordered to replenish stock on hand.
	A product is ordered to fill a special order.
	A product is ordered to fill a back order.
	Products are accounted for through a physical inventory count.
Process Orders	A customer calls and orders a guitar and supplies, and uses a purchase order.
	A customer calls and orders a guitar and supplies, and uses the Remulak easy finance plan to pay.
	A customer calls and orders an organ, and pays with a credit card.
	A customer calls and orders an organ, and uses a purchase order.
Shipping	A partial order is shipped from stock on hand to a customer.
	An entire order is shipped to a customer sourced directly from a third-party supplier.
Invoicing	An overdue notice is sent to a customer for a past-due account.
	Subledger transactions are interfaced to the accounting system.
Maintain Relationships	A customer calls to change his/her default payment terms and payment method.
	A new customer is added to the system.
	A prospective customer is added to the system.
	A new supplier is added to the system.
	A supplier calls to change its billing address.
Decision Support	It is time to print the back-order report.

Table 4-4 lists the exceptions for Remulak Productions.

TABLE 4-4 *Exception Pathways for the Remulak Use-Cases*

Use-Case	Exception Pathways
Maintain Orders	A customer calls to cancel an order that can't be found in the system.
	A customer calls to add a warranty that is no longer valid for the time that the product has been owned.
	A customer calls to add to an order, and the product to be added can't be found in the system.
Maintain Inventory	A product arrives with no purchase order or bill of lading.
Process Orders	A customer calls to place an order using a credit card, and the card is invalid.
	A customer calls with a purchase order but has not been approved to use the purchase order method.
	A customer calls to place an order, and the desired items are not in stock.
Shipping	An order is ready to ship, and there is no shipping address.
Invoicing	None.
Maintain Relationships	None.
Decision Support	None.

Common Use-Case Pitfalls

If a use-case has only one pathway, the granularity of the use-case is much too fine. The effort has probably produced a functional decomposition of the domain. For example, while on a consulting assignment at an international banking organization, I was introduced to its use-case diagram. I was awestruck to learn that the firm had identified almost 300 use-cases. Closer examination revealed that simple pathways of a use-case had been elevated to the rank of use-case. After a little work, we ended up with 17 use-cases. Now that's more like it.

Having too many use-cases that lack what I call *functional entitlement* is a very common mistake that projects make. **Functional entitlement** means there is a clear mission defined for the use-case. After you decide on what you think the use-cases are, ask yourself the question,

Is this use-case an expression of a key goal of the application *in the eyes of the user?* Quite often I find projects that have defined use-cases with names like *Validate customer number.* Is this a key goal of the application? I don't think so. What is it then? It is merely a step within the detail of a pathway through a use-case.

All that aside, I'm afraid the granularity of use-case definition is very subjective. I must also be up-front and say that unless the use-case assignments have gone way overboard, the resulting software solutions will probably be the same. Where I find the key difference in getting the granularity right is the subsequent breakdown of the increments and how the resulting project is managed. A use-case that is too coarse-grained, such as *Process Transaction,* would be hard to break down into perhaps multiple increments of development. There isn't clear functional entitlement for this use-case. There are lots of transactions to process, but what is the goal? A little more work might find that there are transactions that deal with placing orders, paying invoices, and ordering supplies. These, I suspect, are the use-cases; they clearly have functional entitlement.

Shadow Use-Cases

Traditionally, use-cases have been viewed from the eyes of the business—that is, the user. In many application domains, however, some use-cases are never properly accounted for. These represent areas of functionality that meet all of the criteria of use-cases but that often have more meaning to the IT staff, which is their "user." The business sponsor might acknowledge them but often underestimates their impact on the application and the estimated time to completion. These use-cases often end up being budget busters.

I call these **shadow use-cases** because they are not given their due respect in most applications. Figure 4-4 shows the most common shadow use-cases found across all application domains: *Security, Audit, Parameter Maintenance, Archiving,* and *Architecture Infrastructure.*

Often both *Security* and *Audit* will show up in "includes" relationships to other use-cases (*Process Orders* "includes" *Security*). However, both are usually much more complicated than just logging onto a system (e.g., maintaining users and profiles, application functionality,

FIGURE 4-4 *Shadow use-cases*

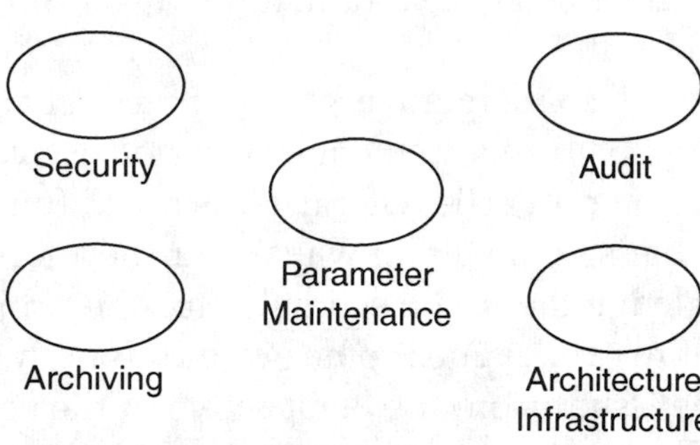

value-level security, and field-level security). Both should be represented on the business view of the use-case diagram. I worked on one project whose security package alone contained 15 distinct classes and consumed about 500 person-hours to build. All this grew from an innocuous statement found in a use-case pathway: "Clerk is validated by the system."

Parameter Maintenance is a use-case that tends to consume too many resource cycles in development and also leads to project cost overruns. Items satisfied by this use-case are setting up and maintaining things like code tables and system parameters. These items always end up being hacked together at the last minute. Worse yet, they are maintained by a database administrator through hand-edited SQL statements (nothing against database administrators; I married one so they can't be all that bad!). Tell me that isn't a disaster waiting to happen.

Archiving also belongs on the business view of the use-case diagram, but it typically is given little consideration. Archiving is not as easy as just backing something up and deleting objects. For example, for a project that is complicated by effective dating schemes, what and when to archive something isn't all that straightforward.

Architecture Infrastructure relates to the plumbing that must be in place to allow the layers of the application to communicate—for example, the components that allow a user interface to communicate to the business rules of the application (Remote Method Invocation, RMI; Common Object Request Broker Architecture, CORBA; Component Object Model, COM+). The same applies to communication from the business rules to the data management component (JDBC, Java

Database Connectivity). This use-case should not be on the business view of the use-case diagram; rather it should be a use-case specifically for the IT staff.

Although some might argue that these shadow use-cases are simply "nonfunctional requirements" and not use-cases, I contend that they have all the properties of a use-case (i.e., functional entitlement, goal-orientedness, many pathways). Furthermore, if the project doesn't acknowledge them, the estimates for the project will be very skewed. Some of my colleagues come around to my way of thinking after they view the issues from the perspective of the actor, which in many cases is the IT department. In practice, if these items are brought to the surface and treated as first-class use-cases, they will be given the attention they demand and deserve, along with a representative portion of the project budget.

Describing Details of the Happy Path

Now the use-cases have been defined, along with their primary, alternate, and exception pathways. For the Inception phase, we have one more task to do regarding use-cases: describe the details of the happy path. We do this for the happy path (or any other pathway) by outlining the necessary steps to implement the pathway's functionality. As with the previous caveat regarding use-cases, use-case pathways derive from a *what* perspective, not a *how* perspective.

A detailed description is necessary so that we can better understand the complexity that might be involved in realizing the use-cases. We need this level of understanding also to estimate both the incremental release strategy and the accompanying time and cost components. The detailed steps of the happy pathway for the *Process Orders* use-case (*A customer calls and orders a guitar and supplies, and pays with a credit card*) are identified as follows:

1. Customer supplies customer number.
2. Customer is acknowledged as current.
3. For each product the customer desires:
   3.1 Product ID or description is requested.
   3.2 Product description is resolved with its ID if necessary.

3.3 Quantity is requested.
3.4 Item price is calculated.

4. Extended order total is calculated.
5. Tax is applied.
6. Shipping charges are applied.
7. Extended price is quoted to the customer.
8. Customer supplies credit card number.
9. Customer's credit card is validated.
10. Inventory is reduced.
11. Sale is finalized.

The detailed steps for the pathway are meant to be at a relatively high level. Notice that there are no specific references to technology in the form of, for example, "button clicks" or "scanning." The details we describe for the pathway will be determined by both the features identified in the charter and any assumptions made about the use-case. Section 4 of the use-case template is a place to document some of the user-centric requirements, as well as throughput requirements. However, it is best to hold off on the user interface portion until the project is closer to producing more design-oriented artifacts. Appendix D contains a complete listing of the detailed steps for the happy path of each use-case.

Most projects seem to work well with the outline format of the use-case details. One reason for this, as cognitive psychologists have known for years, may be that people remember things as outlines in their brains. The processes of driving to the store or fixing your car, for example, are series of predetermined outlines stored away for recall. Another option for documenting Section 3 of the use-case template is the UML activity diagram. We will explore this diagram in Chapter 7; for now, suffice it to say that it is as close to a flowchart as you can get.

The Completed Process Orders *Use-Case Template*

Now that we have completed most of the framework for the use-cases, a sample of a completed template is in order. What follows is the use-case template for *Process Orders.*

1. Use-Case Description Information

1.1 Name

Process Orders.

1.2 Goal

This use-case satisfies all of the goals of setting up a new order. This applies for both new and existing customers. All aspects of the order entry process are covered, from initial entry to ultimate pricing.

1.3 Use-Case Team Leader/Members

Rene Becnel (team lead), Stan Young, Todd, Klock, Jose Aponte.

1.4 Precondition

Order clerk has logged onto the system.

1.5 Postcondition

Order is placed, inventory is reduced.

1.6 Constraints/Issues/Risks

The new system might not be ready in time for the summer product promotions.

1.7 Trigger Event(s)

All events dealing with new and existing customers calling and placing orders.

1.8 Primary Actor

Order clerk.

1.9 Secondary Actor(s)

Customer.

2. Use-Case Pathway Names

2.1 Primary Pathway (Happy Path)

Customer calls and orders a guitar and supplies, and pays with a credit card.

2.2 Alternate Pathway(s)

- *Customer calls and orders a guitar and supplies, and uses a purchase order.*

- *Customer calls and orders a guitar and supplies, and uses the Remulak easy finance plan.*
- *Customer calls and orders an organ, and pays with a credit card.*
- *Customer calls and orders an organ, and pays with a purchase order.*

2.3 Exception Pathway(s)

- *Customer calls to place an order using a credit card, and the card is invalid.*
- *Customer calls with a purchase order but has not been approved to use the purchase order method.*
- *Customer calls to place an order, and the desired items are not in stock.*

3. Use-Case Detail

A Section 3 will exist for all use-case pathways that are detailed enough to warrant their own unique set of steps. In this case only the happy path and the payment variation are shown.

3.1 Pathway Name

Customer calls and orders a guitar and supplies, and pays with a credit card.

3.2 Trigger Event(s)

All events dealing with new and existing customers calling and placing an order.

3.3 Main Sequence of Steps

Step	Description
1	*Customer supplies customer number.*
2	*Customer is acknowledged as current.*
3	*For each product the customer desires:*
3.1	*- Product ID or description is requested.*
3.2	*- Product description is resolved with its ID if necessary.*
3.3	*- Quantity is requested.*
3.4	*- Item price is calculated.*
4	*Extended order total is calculated.*
5	*Tax is applied.*
6	*Shipping charges are applied.*

7	*Extended price is quoted to the customer.*
8	*Customer supplies credit card number.*
9	*Customer's credit card is validated.*
10	*Inventory is reduced.*
11	*Sale is finalized.*

3.4 Variations

Step	**Description**
8.1	*Customer may pay with purchase order or easy-finance plan.*

3.5 Extensions (optional)
None.

3.6 Business Rules (optional)
- *Customers may not order more than ten products at one time.*
- *Any sale over $50,000 requires supervisor approval.*
- *Any sale over $20,000 receives a five-percent discount.*

3.7 Constraints/Issues/Risks (optional)
Timeliness of the product is key to the next sales promotion.

4. Use-Case Tactical Information

4.1 Priority
Highest (#1).

4.2 Performance Target(s)
None indicated.

4.3 Frequency
- *Customer calls and orders a guitar and supplies, and pays with a credit card (800/day).*
- *Customer calls and orders a guitar and supplies, and uses a purchase order (120/day).*
- *Customer calls and orders a guitar and supplies, and uses the Remulak easy finance plan (25/day).*
- *Customer calls and orders an organ, and pays with a credit card (40/day).*
- *Customer calls and orders an organ, and pays with a purchase order (15/day).*

4.4 User Interface

This portion of the application will not use the Web as a form of entry because of the need for clerk assistance.

4.5 Location of Source

- *Newport Hills, Washington.*
- *Portland, Maine (in the future).*

The detailed use-case pathways are then specified for all of the individual pathways in each category (primary, alternate, and exception). Each section can be documented at different times. Actually, each section can be done as a mini-iteration. I think one of the most important sections is Use-Case Pathway Names (Section 3) because it gives the analyst and user a succinct look at what the pathways are anticipated to be without documenting all details of each pathway up front. Doing this for all use-cases is crucial for producing an overall estimate for the project. Some practitioners collapse Sections 2 and 3 together; this approach is fine as long as you can first identify the pathway names, and then just fill in the body detail as the use-case evolves.

The use-case detail is reflected in the Unified Process via the Software Requirements Specification (SRS). The nonfunctional elements are captured in the Supplementary Specification. As I pointed out earlier, I prefer to put the nonfunctional elements that relate directly to the use-case in Section 4 of the use-case template. Nonfunctional elements such as the database that will be used I place in the Supplementary Specification.

Preparing the Preliminary Architecture

We now know a lot more about Remulak Productions' requirements, as well as some of its technology needs and desires. The last artifact we need to begin, but not finish, before completing the Inception phase is the framework of the preliminary architecture. The project vision template contains some high-level architecture placeholders, but the primary resting place of the project architecture is the Software Architecture Document (SAD) of the Unified Process. Officially, the SAD isn't produced until the Elaboration phase, but I choose to begin fleshing it out with elements that we already know about when we're in

TABLE 4-5 *Preliminary Architecture of the Remulak Order-Processing Application*

Component	Implementation
Hardware: Client	600MHz Pentium III–based clients with 128MB of RAM and an 8GB hard disk
Hardware: Server	Dual-CPU 700MHz Pentium III–based server with 1GB of RAM and RAID5 I/O subsystem supporting 60GB of storage
Software: Operating system (server)	Windows 2000 Server
Software: Operating system (client)	Windows 2000 Professional
Software: Application (client)	Any browser
Software: Database (server)	Microsoft SQL Server 2000 or Oracle 9i
Software: Transaction (server)	JavaBeans with JDBC transaction support, or Enterprise JavaBeans (where appropriate)
Software: Web (server)	Microsoft Internet Information Server, Apache Tomcat server, or commercial application server such as BEA WebLogic
Software: Web interface (server)	Servlets and JavaServer Pages
Software: Visual modeling	Rational Rose (Enterprise Edition), Together Control Center from TogetherSoft
Protocol: Network	TCP/IP
Protocol: Database	JDBC-ODBC Bridge

the Inception phase. Table 4-5 lists the technology components of the architecture.

To depict this architecture better, we use two different UML diagrams, which we combine to show both the software realization (component diagram) and hardware hosts (deployment diagram). Remember that this is a preliminary architecture. It is a snapshot based on what is known at this juncture of the project. Figure 4-5 shows the preliminary architecture model rendered in a hybrid UML component in the deployment diagram format.

For scalability, the architecture must allow various layers of the application to run on a processor other than the client's. In addition, we will want to take advantage of Enterprise JavaBeans to coordinate all of the various resources of the application. We will explore these and other technical considerations as the application evolves.

FIGURE 4-5 *Preliminary architecture with UML component and deployment diagrams*

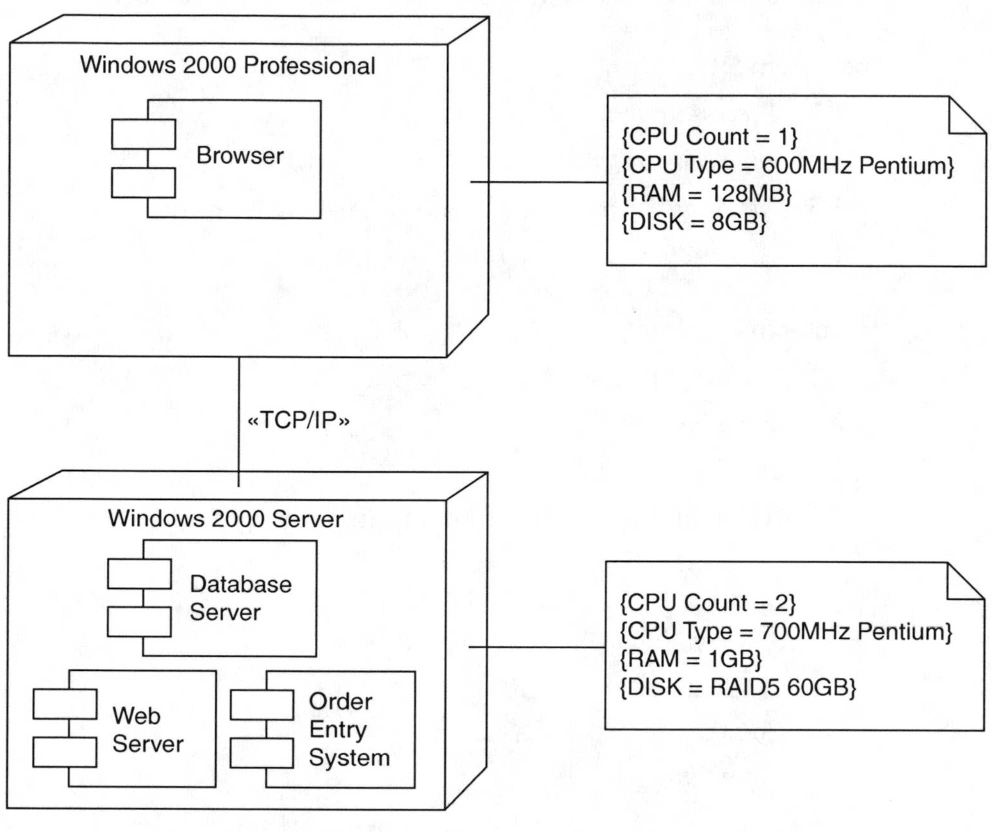

Project Charter: Increments and Estimates

Increments

So far, our mantra has been to approach any application development effort with an eye toward incremental releases. Recall from Chapter 1 that risk is reduced exponentially if we tackle the project in stages. To align our terminology with the Unified Process, we will produce each of these increments by conducting many different iterations through the four phases (Inception, Elaboration, Construction, Transition). This approach will allow the project to focus first on the riskiest requirements. Toward that end, we propose the following release cycles as the staged increments for Remulak Productions:

Increment 1:

1.1 *Process Orders*

1.2 *Maintain Orders*

1.3 *Maintain Relationships* (customer pathways only)

1.4 *Architecture Infrastructure*

Increment 2:

2.1 *Maintain Inventory*

2.2 *Shipping*

2.3 *Invoicing*

2.4 *Maintain Relationships* (remaining pathways)

Increment 3:

3.1 *Decision Support*

3.2 *Security*

3.3 *Audit*

3.4 *Archiving*

Estimates: The Issues

For years, analysts and designers have been told in classroom settings never to provide estimates until all of the requirements are known. With the Unified Process, and any other process that is iterative and incremental, we use the learn-as-you-go approach. Our bases are somewhat covered because we have done a flyby of all of the events, use-cases, and pathways and we have detailed the happy pathways. However, we still don't know all of the supporting detail behind the requirements. Yet the project sponsors need an estimate; without it, they can't decide whether or not to give the go-ahead.

Before I stray into the semantics of estimating using use-cases, let me say a few words about estimates and the project sponsor. When I am consulting or teaching seminars, one question that always comes up is, "Well, this is all fine and good, but what do you do when your sponsor wants all the functionality you've specified for the same price, but in half the time?" My initial answer is that I feel sorry for the project team. At the same time, I usually sketch a little diagram and discuss its merits and meaning (see Figure 4-6).

I contend that all projects must face the reality of the equilateral triangle creed. Once the information technology group has estimated the project and calculated a delivery schedule, the ratios generated form the basis of the equilateral triangle. The edict is: *All sides must remain in the same proportion as to the initial ratios.* Quality is *never* negotiable.

This creed implies that if a sponsor wants more functionality, the time and cost factors will increase in proportion to the increase in functionality. Typically, however, the request of the project sponsor yields a picture of these factors that looks like Figure 4-7.

FIGURE 4-6 *Realistic time, cost, functionality, and quality relationships*

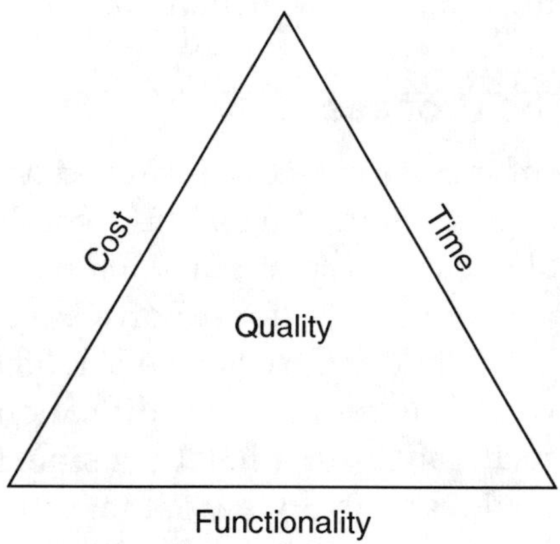

FIGURE 4-7 *Project sponsor's preferred time, cost, functionality, and quality relationships*

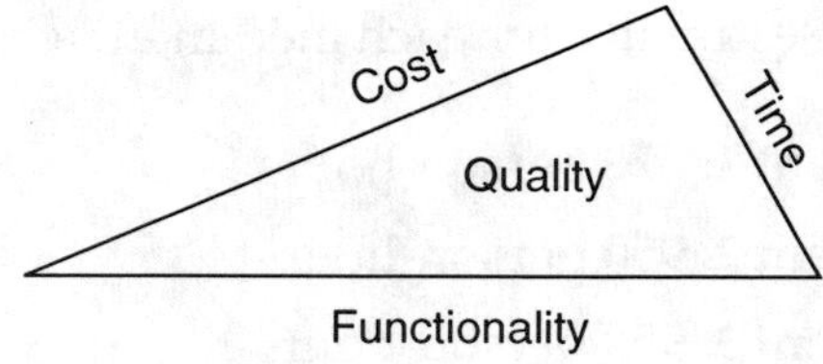

This situation is not feasible. The sponsors want the project done in half the time, but at the same cost and of course the same level of functionality. These types of no-win situations are worth walking away from. What ends up being sacrificed is quality. If the discussion about keeping time, cost, and functionality ratios equal doesn't help the project sponsor see the light, then I usually launch into a lecture pointing out that a building contractor would laugh in our face if we suggested such foolishness. And how about a plastic surgeon practicing his/her craft on an accident victim. What would the response be in that situation? Would we want either one of these professionals to sacrifice quality or to somehow rush the job while still attaining all the original goals?

The solution is to look at the problem and break it down into even more elemental pieces—that is, more increments. As mentioned in the preface and in Chapter 1, we must avoid risk if we are going to build software that meets the needs of a business but can stand the test of time. Working 100-hour workweeks is a perceived temporary solution that has absolutely no long-term benefit.

Estimates: The Process

Varying levels of success have been realized with structured approaches to project estimating. Estimating still is a combination of mystic art, the school of hard knocks, and plain luck. However, some very interesting research has been done at Rational Software by Gustav Karner (which he begain initially while at Objectory AB, which was later purchased by Rational Software). The result is a modification of work originally done by Allan Albrecht on estimating by using function point analysis. Appendix C provides an overview of that estimating technique, as well as how the estimates were reached for Remulak Productions.

Remulak Productions' deliverable will be realized by implementation of three different increments, staged as three different release cycles. This will enable Remulak to manage the risk of the project, as well as ease it into the new millennium without too much new-system shock. The estimates for each increment are as follows:

Increment 1: 670 person-hours

Increment 2: 950 person-hours

Increment 3: 950 person-hours

Figure 4-8 depicts the project with all of the increments in process. This figure does a good job of showing the iterative, incremental approach that we will take for the Remulak Productions application. The middle spiral is flipped to indicate that many increments or deliverables can be active at any one time, each in its own phase.

FIGURE 4-8 *Increments for the Remulak application*

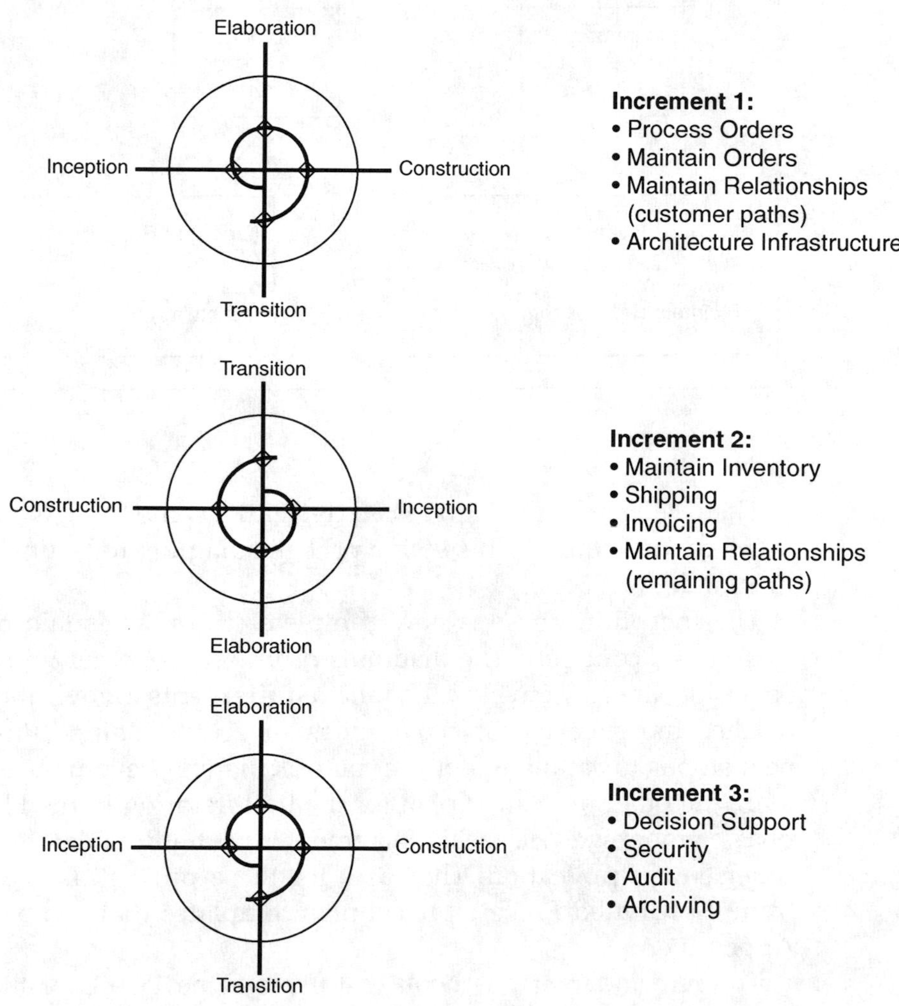

Increment 1:
- Process Orders
- Maintain Orders
- Maintain Relationships (customer paths)
- Architecture Infrastructure

Increment 2:
- Maintain Inventory
- Shipping
- Invoicing
- Maintain Relationships (remaining paths)

Increment 3:
- Decision Support
- Security
- Audit
- Archiving

FIGURE 4-9 *Remulak package diagram*

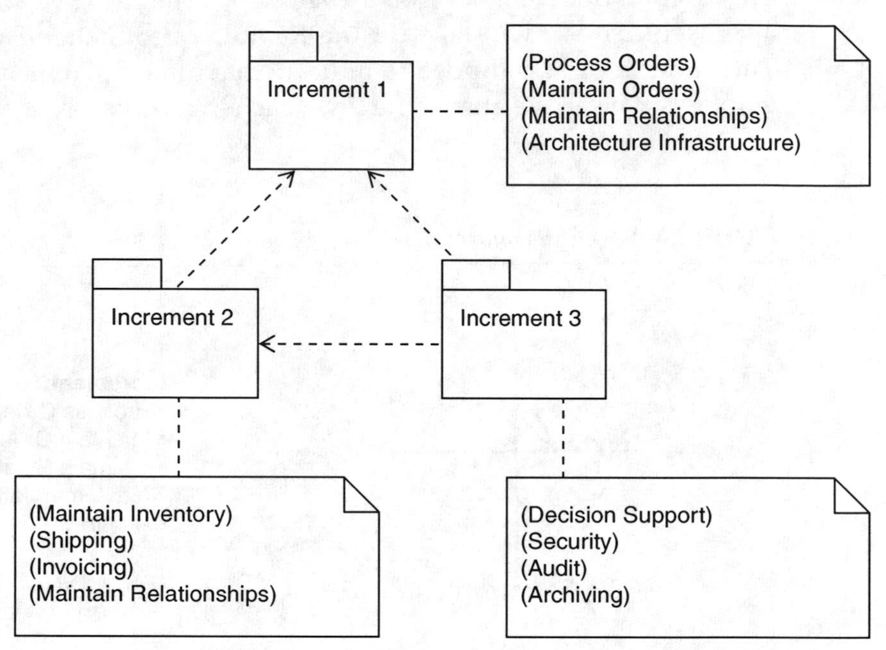

The UML package diagram can depict the same thing, while hiding much of the detail. Figure 4-9 is a package diagram reflecting the incremental deliverables.

The Inception phase is now complete. The road is laid out for us clearly and concisely. The diagrams produced, together with the project vision, are collectively called the **requirements model**, and we have reached the Lifecycle Objective milestone in the Unified Process. The next step is to create two project plans: One will be a high-level phase plan, the other a detailed plan for the first iteration in the Elaboration phase, where we will tackle Increment 1 of the Remulak Productions order entry application. The bases for these project plans are drawn from the Unified Process project plan templates that can be found in Appendix A.

The remainder of this book will explore the details of the first increment for Remulak Productions. The remaining two increments are not presented in this book, but they would be developed in the same fashion.

FIGURE 4-10 *Workflows and phases in the Unified Process*

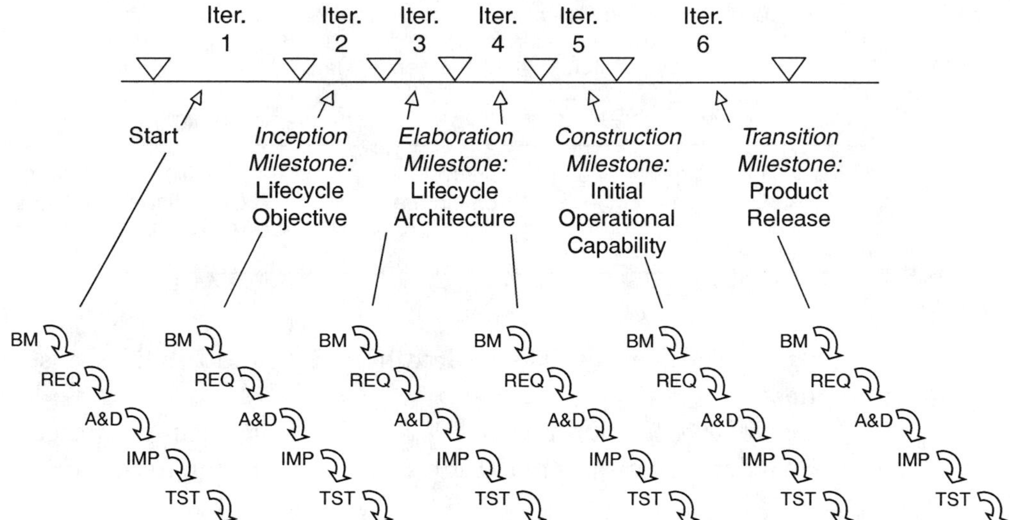

Let's now look at how the project-planning process is laid out in the Unified Process. Figure 4-10 shows how each iteration cuts vertically through all the workflows offered in the Unified Process (Business Modeling, Requirements, and so on). Just remember that as the project moves farther to the right in its lifecycle, the project plan tasks will shift more toward design and construction activities.

Here the timeline shows multiple iterations: one in Inception, two in Elaboration, two in Construction, and one in Transition. For Remulak, because there are three packages or increments of delivery, the proposition is to stretch both the Elaboration and Construction phases into three iterations each. This approach maps nicely to the packages and spreads out the risk. Figure 4-11 shows the phase timeline with the proper number of iterations. So the increment packages shown in Figure 4-9 will map to Iterations 2, 3, and 4 for the Elaboration phase of the

FIGURE 4-11 *Remulak iteration/package mappings*

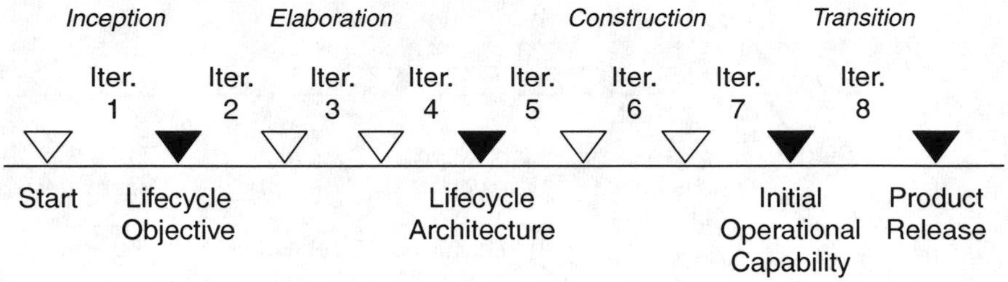

Inception *Elaboration* *Construction* *Transition*

Iter. 1 Iter. 2 Iter. 3 Iter. 4 Iter. 5 Iter. 6 Iter. 7 Iter. 8

Start Lifecycle Objective Lifecycle Architecture Initial Operational Capability Product Release

application. The same applies for Iterations 5, 6, and 7 in the Construction phase.

There we have the outline of our phase plan and the input necessary to create a detailed project plan for the first Elaboration iteration.

Checkpoint

Where We've Been

- Use-cases are technology neutral and applicable to any process or methodology used by a project team.
- Each use-case is a behaviorally related sequence of interactions performed by an actor in a dialog with the system to provide some measurable value to the actor. Use-cases are goal oriented and are significant to a business.
- The primary pathway, or Basic Course of Events, is considered the most common pathway through a use-case. It is also called the happy pathway.
- Alternate pathways are also good pathways, but they are not traveled as often.
- A detailed description of the pathway chronicles the steps that must be undertaken to satisfy the originating event. The steps should avoid, if possible, reference to *how* the event is being performed.

- All of the pieces of documentation produced up to this point, including the UML diagrams, are collectively called the requirements model.

Where We're Going Next

In the next chapter we:

- Identify more detail about the use-cases in the first iteration of the Elaboration phase.
- Explore how to derive classes from the use-cases.
- Explore how to derive associations.
- Review various UML diagramming constructs for various types of associations (generalization, composition, and aggregation) and how they relate to the Remulak Productions solution.
- Create a complete class diagram for Remulak Productions.
- Begin to identify attributes and operations for Remulak Productions' classes.

CHAPTER 5 Classes

IN THIS CHAPTER

The project is taking shape. Chapters 1 through 4 culminated in completion of the project's Inception phase. Some key deliverables were produced, including a requirements model consisting of two UML diagrams and the project vision. In the next phase, Elaboration, we expand the boundaries established by the requirements model.

Our flyby of the entire application during the Inception phase produced a list of in-scope use-cases and all of their individual pathways (primary, alternate, and exception), and described in detail their happy pathways. The idea was to gain enough knowledge about the project to be able to plan implementation increments and estimate required resources. The project also selected use-cases that were deemed architecturally significant. Remember that to reduce risk, we need to address areas of the project that will flesh out and challenge the candidate architecture.

Among the most important deliverables produced thus far, from the project sponsors' viewpoints, are the incremental delivery schedule and the supported functionality. The functionality was expressed in the form of use-cases and project estimates accompanying each of the three delivery increments.

From an IT viewpoint, a key deliverable was the list of use-cases, which provided a clear, easily understood format for sketching out the application's preliminary requirements. They were created in conjunction with the project sponsors and framed in their terminology.

This chapter covers the Elaboration phase of the project, which further fleshes out the application's requirements and proposes a design for the solution. It also explores the additional static and dynamic components through the use of more UML diagrams. It identifies, refines, and adopts a collection of interesting application entities called classes. Then it explores the associations that are explicitly and implicitly found in the use-cases.

We will use the class diagram to build the skeleton of the application's design and the sequence diagram to indicate the arteries of the application, representing the flow of messages between the skeletal components, or classes.

GOALS

- To describe in detail all of the alternate and exception pathways for the first iteration (and the first package within Remulak) of the Remulak Productions project.
- To examine the notion of classes and how to identify them.
- To explore ways to refine the class list by applying some common class-filtering rules.
- To define the concept of associations and how to identify them among the components of the use-cases.
- To explain how and when to use an object diagram, a runtime version of the class diagram.
- To review the class diagram for Remulak Productions.
- To begin to identify both attributes and operations for the classes identified for Remulak Productions.

The Elaboration Phase

Before completing the pathway detail for all the use-cases of the first package, let's review the Unified Process model. Figure 5-1 shows the model, with the first iteration of the Elaboration phase highlighted.

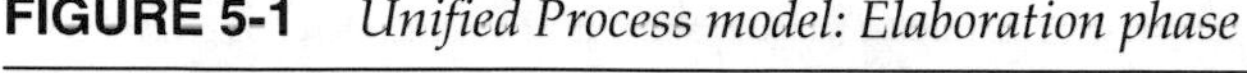

FIGURE 5-1 *Unified Process model: Elaboration phase*

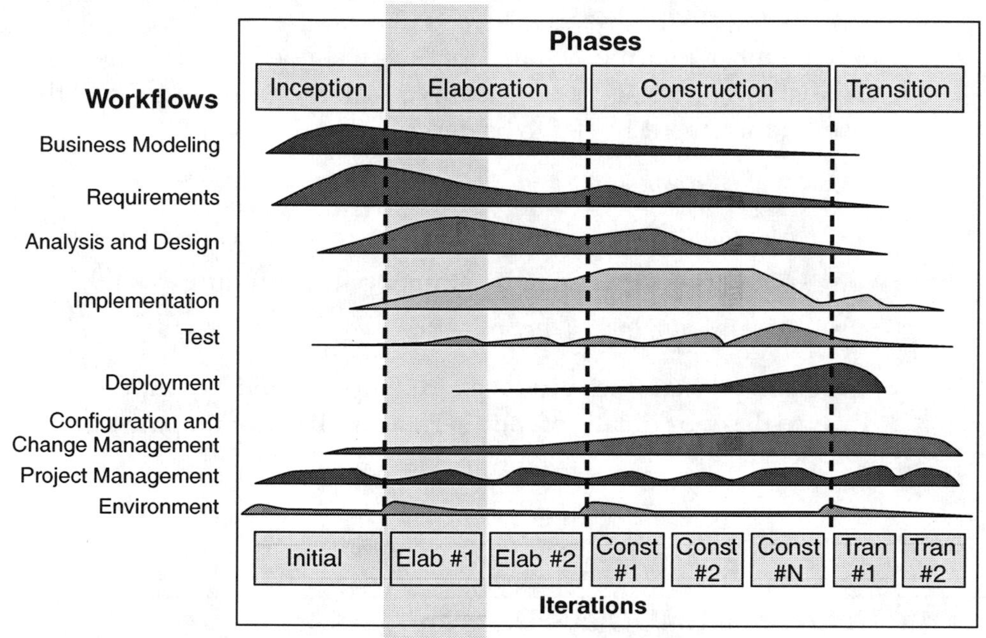

In this chapter the following Unified Process workflows and activity sets are emphasized:

- Requirements: Analyze the Problem
- Analysis and Design: Analyze Behavior
- Analysis and Design: Design Components

Describing Details of Pathways

The first goal of the project will be to further flesh out the detailed pathways for all the alternate and exception pathways in the use-cases. The use-cases referred to here are only those that will be implemented in the first increment. Remember from the previous chapter that pathway detail was already completed for each use-cases happy path (for all the increments). In that chapter, as an example we described in detail the happy path (*Customer calls and orders a guitar and supplies, and pays with a credit card*) for the use-case *Process Orders*.

Remember that the detailed pathway shows the tasks necessary to satisfy that course of the use-case. Now all the pathways for all the use-cases in Increment 1 need to be described in detail:

- *Process Orders*
- *Maintain Orders*
- *Maintain Relationships* (customer pathways only)
- *Architecture Infrastructure*

We use the examples produced in Chapter 4 and expanded in Appendix D to describe details of the alternate and exception pathways.

Identifying Classes

Role of the UML Class Diagram

The class diagram will eventually become the most important UML artifact we produce. By *eventually,* I mean that initially it will be somewhat sparse and lacking in anything of significant value. With each iteration, however, as we learn more about the static and dynamic features of the application, it will begin to evolve into the pivotal diagram from which all else going forward is derived. Even the UML component and deployment diagrams depict how classes will be packaged and ultimately delivered in runtime form.

Chapter 2 noted that the majority of visual modeling tools today generate their code structures directly from the class diagram. Tools that support reverse engineering derive their diagrammatic elements from the classes built by the specific language environment (e.g., header files in C++, *.java* files in Java, class modules in Visual Basic).

What Makes a Good Class?

Selecting classes requires skill; it can be difficult and tricky at times. The next several sections provide guidelines to help you learn how. With a little practice, you will see that there is a methodology to the madness of selecting classes.

The **class** is the key entity in the application domain. It represents an interesting abstraction of something that contains structure (**attributes**), as well as behavior (**operations**). Often a project team, depending on the level of its familiarity with an application domain, initially comes up with the classes just by using facilitated sessions to produce a list of entities.

Another, more methodical approach that has its roots in the relational modeling world is to review the source of the requirements produced thus far and simply extract the nouns. In the context of UML, the source for this noun extraction exercise consists of the completed use-cases. In a very quick and unstructured manner, you simply scan the use-cases and pull out all of the nouns. As you improve at the exercise, you should begin to apply some noun filtering to eliminate nouns that obviously will not make good classes. The most common nouns filtered out are those that represent domain attributes, which are characteristics of another class in the application. I find it is beneficial to put this initial list on Post-it notes. Then as you weed them out, those that become attributes of a class can be appended to the back of the owning Post-it note.

With Remulak Productions, for instance, detailed description of the use-cases produced the noun *credit card number.* Although this is undoubtedly a noun, ask yourself if it is something that will have both structure and behavior. Probably not. It is an attribute of another class (e.g., `Order`, `Customer`, or both) that might not have been identified yet. My rule of thumb, however, is not to filter out anything on the first iteration of the exercise. I just create a list.

A third mechanism for identifying classes is to hold a **CRC session**, where CRC stands for Classes, Responsibilities, Collaborations. CRC is a role-playing exercise used to identify classes and their individual roles in an application's life. See, for example, *The CRC Card Book* by Bellin and Simone (published by Addison-Wesley, 1997). On occasion, I use CRC sessions as an icebreaker for people new to object-oriented techniques. However, my only concern with CRC sessions is that they require a strong facilitator and the team must be agreeable to role-playing. For very complex interactions, CRC sessions can get really out of hand. In general, people seem to find CRC sessions just a bit too touchy-feely.

Applying Filter Rules

Once we have completed the initial list of nouns, we apply simple filtering rules to whittle it down. Seven different filters can be applied to the domain of nouns. We remove candidate classes that have any of the following characteristics:

1. **Redundancy:** Two nouns that represent the same thing are redundant. For example, *order* and *product order* are really the same thing. Settle on *order* because it is more succinct and represents what is actually being modeled.
2. **Irrelevance:** Nouns that have nothing to do with the problem domain are irrelevant. They might be valid classes, but not within the scope of the current project. For example, *employee performance rating* is a noun, but Remulak's system will not measure or track performance, so it is irrelevant for this project. Any temptation to include it might be an indication of scope creep. If anyone debates the exclusion of a class that appears to be out of scope, perhaps they need to reaffirm what was agreed upon in the prior deliverable.
3. **An attribute:** Nouns that really describe the structure of another class are attributes. This is the most common filter applied in most domains. Be careful not to completely remove these nouns, however, because they will end up as attributes in a class. Credit card number is a noun that describes something else in the system. However, it is not a class.

   Be careful with attribute recognition versus class recognition, especially in the context of the application domain. For example, a common noun, ZIP code, is usually thought of as an attribute of an address class. Depending on the domain, however, it might be a class. For example, to the postal service the noun ZIP code is a class because it contains both attributes (geographic location, census, rate structures, and shipping information) and behavior (routing and scheduling of deliveries).
4. **An operation:** A noun describing the responsibility of another class is not a class in its own right; it is an operation. Tax calculations is the responsibility of another class (perhaps an algorithm class), but it is not itself a class.
5. **A role:** A noun describing the state of a particular entity or its classification is likely not a class; it is a role. For example, preferred

customer is the state of a customer at a given time. `Customer` is actually the class, and the fact that a customer is preferred is probably indicated by an attribute within `Customer` (`status`).

A word of caution when dealing with roles: Often roles that are removed return later when the concept of class generalization and specialization (a.k.a. inheritance) is reviewed. If it is known upfront that the role has unique structural and behavioral elements that the domain is interested in tracking, don't be too hasty to remove the role. If removed, however, the role will be addressed later as the class diagram is iteratively refined.

6. **An event:** Nouns that describe a particular time frequency usually depict a dynamic element that the domain must support. Print invoices once a week is a timer-oriented event that the system must support. Week is not a candidate class.

   In some real-time, embedded applications, events are in fact classes. If an event has some interesting structural elements or behavior that is important to the domain, it might be a class.

7. **An implementation construct:** A noun that depicts a hardware element (e.g., printer) or an algorithm (e.g., compound interest) is best dealt with by being removed and assigned as an operation of another class.

   In many real-time, embedded applications, hardware components are classes (controller, servo). They have attributes (current position, head) and behavior (seek, set position) that meet all the criteria of a class. The act of creating a class out of an inanimate object and assigning structure and behavior to it is called **reification.**

When selecting the final name for a class, always use clear and concise terms. Favor the singular tense (`Customer`, `Order`) over the plural (`Customers`, `Orders`). Also note that class names are always capitalized when used on diagrams or in other documentation.

Types of Classes

Many people confuse classes with database entities. Database entities have the sole mission of recording only structural (persistent) elements of the application. Classes are very similar. In fact, they are a superset of what is provided by the database entity. However, classes also have behavioral characteristics that entities don't have. The project is very concerned about the data attributes, and that's where traditional entity data modeling ends—capturing the data structures.

Classes bring much more to the understanding of the application in the form of behavior (operations) that the class is responsible for implementing. The operations represent the services that the class is committed to carrying out when requested by other classes in the application domain. From a relational perspective, entities have been said not to have any *class* or to know how to *behave.*

In object systems, and through our modeling efforts, classes must be categorized into groups. Ivar Jacobson groups classes into three groups, or what UML refers to as **stereotypes**. Think of a stereotype as being a "flavor" of something:

1. **Entity:** Entity classes represent the core of the application domain (e.g., `Customer`, `Order`). They are meant to keep information about the persistent application entities over time, as well as to capture the services that drive the majority of interactions in the application. Don't confuse the term *entity* as used here with the more traditional use of the word when describing a relational entity. An entity class may not become a relational entity. Some practitioners use the term *domain class* to provide a better distinction (which I personally prefer). These classes will eventually end up as either JavaBeans or entity-type Enterprise JavaBeans (EJB).
2. **Boundary:** Boundary classes serve as a boundary between the external actors wishing to interact with the application and the entity classes. Typically, boundary classes are meant as a shield, or go-between of sorts, that segregates much of the interaction details of how to reach services offered by the application. Most boundary classes are user interface components, which take the shape of forms and screens used to interact with the application. Boundary classes can also be found in messaging to external application systems or as wrappers around existing legacy components.

   Note that not long ago, this category of classes was called *interface classes.* Now that the notion of interfaces has become much more popular and flexible, especially with Java, *boundary classes* is the name used in this text. For Remulak Productions, these classes will be JavaServer Pages, which are compiled into servlets at runtime. So, we could indirectly say that boundary classes will be Java classes implementing the servlet interface.

3. **Control:** Control classes are coordinators of activity in the application domain. Sometimes called *controllers,* they are repositories of both structure and behavior that aren't easily placed in either of the other two types of classes. These classes will eventually end up as JavaBeans or session-type Enterprise JavaBeans (EJB). Typically, a control class can play any of several roles:
   - As transaction-related behavior
   - As a control sequence that is specific to one or a few use-cases (or pathways through a use-case)
   - As a service that separates the entity objects from the boundary objects

Categorizing the classes into these three types makes the application less fragile to change. These changes may result from the business's evolution in a dynamic marketplace or because individuals want to view information in the application differently. Figure 5-2 shows the three types of classes in action, and the subsections that follow discuss each one in more detail.

FIGURE 5-2 *Entity, boundary, and control types of classes*

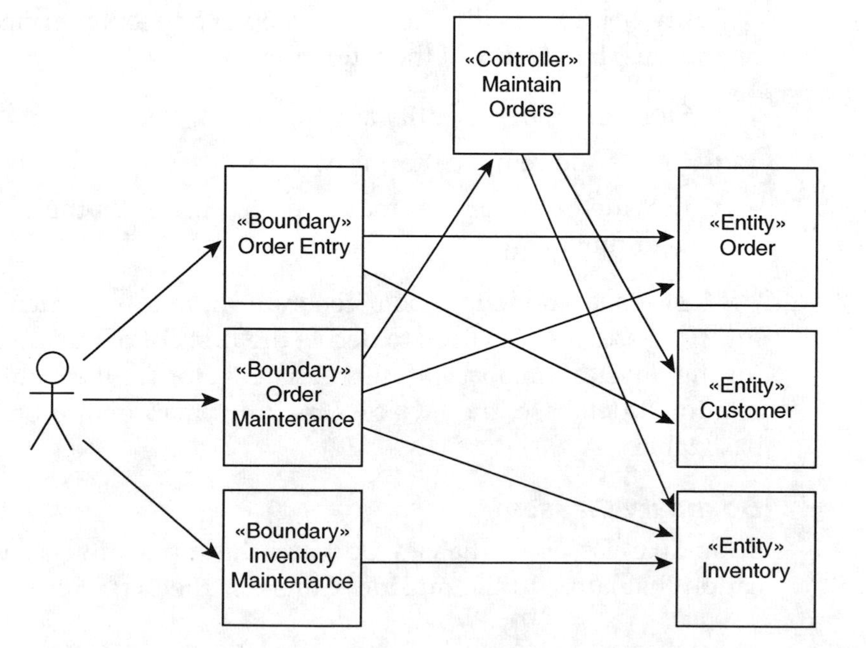

Entity Classes

For Remulak Productions, the following list identifies the potential entity classes (with filters applied) for the application. It covers all of the use-cases documented so far (all of the use-cases of Increment 1, and the happy pathways of the remaining use-cases):

- `Address`
- `Customer`
- `Order`
- `Invoice`
- `Product`
- `OrderLine`
- `OrderSummary`
- `Payment`
- `Shipment`
- `Guitar`
- `Supplies`
- `SheetMusic`

Entity objects usually provide some very specific services, typically operations that do any of the following:

- Store and retrieve entity attributes.
- Create and remove the entity.
- Provide behavior that may need to change as the entity changes over time.

Most visual modeling tools generate these class structures for you. Entity classes are also used to derive the first cut of the implementation for the physical database. If the persistent storage mechanism will be a relational database, these classes may not map one to one with database tables.

Boundary Classes

Boundary classes are the viewport into the application, as well as application insulators to the outside. Consider the `Order` class. It probably won't change much over time; it might undergo some behavioral changes (e.g., how pricing discounts are applied), but probably not many structural changes (attributes). Likely to change are the following:

- How people (actors) want to place orders (e.g., via telephone response systems, via the Internet)
- How other systems (actors) want to interface with the order application and how the order application will be expected to interface with other systems (actors)
- How people (actors) want to view information from a reporting and decision support perspective

To facilitate these trends better and to insulate the entity classes, you should place all behavior relating to interfacing with the application into boundary classes. Also place in boundary classes all functionality that is specified in the use-case descriptions pertaining to user interface and that depends directly on the system environment.

The easiest way to identify boundary classes is to focus on the actors in the system. Each actor will need its own interface into the system. The classes can be further refined from information found in the use-case description and the use-case pathway details. A boundary class will usually exist for each screen-oriented form and each report, as well as for each interface to an external system (e.g., accounting, billing, credit card authorization). The following list shows the potential boundary classes for Remulak Productions.

- `MaintainOrderPanel`
- `InquireOrderPanel`
- `ProcessOrderPanel`
- `MaintainRelationshipsPanel`
- `CreditCardInterface`
- `AccountingSystemInterface`

Control Classes

One excellent use of control classes is to act as the conductor of the work necessary to implement the pathways through the use-cases.

Control classes are usually transient (not persisted to external storage). Their lifecycle is only as long as it takes the interaction to complete or as long as a user session is active.

For example, where do we place the tasks necessary to orchestrate messaging for the happy pathway (*Customer calls and orders a guitar and supplies, and pays with a credit card*) for the use-case *Process Orders*? We'll place such "scripting" tasks in a control class. So we create one control class for each use-case. In addition, another pattern will emerge in that each happy and alternate path will have a corresponding operation in the control class that houses these scripting tasks.

The following list shows the potential control classes for Remulak's Increment 1:

- *Process Orders* controller
- *Maintain Orders* controller
- *Maintain Relationships* controller
- *Architecture Infrastructure* controller

Relationships

Relationships between classes are necessary because object-oriented systems are based on the collaboration of objects to accomplish a particular end goal (articulated in the use-cases). Like a network, relationships define the pathways between classes and serve as the *messaging media* across which objects can communicate. Relationships also define a context between classes prior to instantiation and as objects after instantiation. They then define how the classes of the application function as an integrated whole.

UML is quite rich in its ability to represent relationships between classes. It supports three types of relationships:

1. **Association:** The most common type of UML relationship, an association, defines how objects of one class are connected to objects of another class. Without these connections, or associations, no direct messages can pass between objects of these classes in the runtime environment (note that dependencies, discussed below,

also indicate a messaging relationship). A simple association for Remulak Productions would be the one defined between a customer and his/her order(s).

2. **Generalization:** A generalization defines a lattice of classes such that one class refines—that is, specializes details about—a more general class. The generalized class is often called the **superclass**, and the specialized class the **subclass**. All attributes (structure) and operations (behavior) of the generalized class that have public or protected visibility are available to (inherited by) the subclasses. Generalizations are such that any subclass "is a" valid example of the superclass.

   As was pointed out in Chapter 2, an example of a generalization/specialization relationship for Remulak Productions is the `Product` (superclass) and the subclasses `Guitar`, `SheetMusic`, and `Supplies`. Structure (attributes) and behavior (operations) will be defined for `Product` and will apply to all of its subclasses. Structure (attributes) and behavior (operations) also will be defined for `Guitar`, `SheetMusic`, and `Supplies`. These attributes and operations are unique to the subclasses and further specialize the definition of a particular instance of `Product`.

3. **Dependency:** A dependency is a relationship in which a change to one class may affect the behavior or state of another class. Typically, dependencies are used in the context of classes to show that one class uses another class as an argument in the signature of an operation.

   Dependencies are more commonly found in package diagrams than in class diagrams. A dependency relationship exists among the three increments for Remulak Productions.

We use association and generalization relationships in the Remulak Productions class diagram.

Establishing Associations

Where do we find associations in the application domain? Explicit associations can be found in the use-cases. However, an early indicator of associations can be found in the event table created during project scoping.

Recall that the use-cases describe the intended uses of the system from the actor's perspective. For an event such as *Customer Places Order* that is encountered in the dialog for the *Process Orders* use-case, an explicit association exists between the two classes `Customer` and `Order`. When the use-cases were initially created, we had no clear idea what the classes would be. Now that the class creation exercise has been completed, we need to revisit the use-cases in search of associations. Table 5-1 lists the associations for Remulak Productions.

Not all associations are explicitly stated in the use-cases. For example, the association *`Order` is paid by `Invoice`* isn't stated directly in the use-cases. However, it is an implicit association that is necessary to facilitate the messaging described in the pathways of the use-cases.

To construct the class diagram, we draw the classes as rectangles, connect rectangles with a solid line, and place the verb describing the association on the line. In UML, associations are read left to right, top to bottom. However, this isn't always possible, especially with complex diagrams. A small solid triangle can be placed next to the association name to indicate how to read the association. Finally, it isn't absolutely necessary to define an association name, especially if the association is obvious from the classes involved. Figure 5-3 shows an example of a simple association for Remulak Productions.

TABLE 5-1 *Remulak Class Associations*

Class	Association	Class
`Customer`	places	`Order`
`Address`	locates	`Customer`
`Order`	contains	`OrderLine`
`Order`	is paid by	`Invoice`
`Order`	is satisfied by	`Shipment`
`Product`	is specialized by	`Guitar`
`Product`	is specialized by	`SheetMusic`
`Product`	is specialized by	`Supplies`
`Product`	references	`OrderLine`

FIGURE 5-3 *Remulak association example*

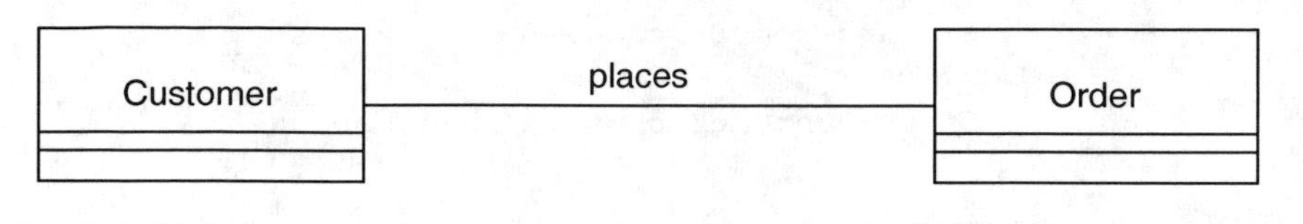

Notice that the top rectangle contains the class name. A class has three compartments, which define the following:

Compartment 1: Class name, displayed in proper case format

Compartment 2: Attributes (which define the structure of the class)

Compartment 3: Operations (which define the behavior supported by the class)

In many cases, depending on the stage of the project and the reviewing audience, not all of the compartments will be displayed. Attributes and operations are explored in more depth later in this chapter.

Establishing Roles

A **role** is a UML construct that better qualifies how a particular object will act in its relationship to another class. Roles are optional, but at times they can clarify a class diagram, thereby preventing misinterpretation of what the authors meant (and misinterpretation often happens).

On the association diagram the role is placed next to the class to which it is related. In the case of Remulak Productions, `Order` could play the role of *purchase,* while `Customer` could play the role of *purchaser.* The next section shows how to diagram this relationship, as well as how to correctly read the association.

A side note for those of you itching to get to the Java code: Roles have a direct impact on the code generation process when you're using a visual modeling tool. In most tools, if you were to generate code from the class diagram expressed in Figure 5-4, the attribute name of the related class would be the role name. In addition, most tools allow a prefix to be appended to the front of the name (e.g., *my, the*). So for the two classes `Customer` and `Order`, we might have the following:

```
public class Customer
{
  public Order myPurchase;

  // Other Customer class detail goes here
}

public class Order
{
  public Customer myPurchaser;

  // Other Order class detail goes here
}
```

If you don't supply a role name, don't worry; most tools will default the attribute name to that of the class name. In our Java example, then, if role names were not supplied on the class diagram, the class-referencing attribute names would be `myOrder` in the `Customer` class and `myCustomer` in the `Order` class. Again, usually you have some control over the prefix; some people prefer *the* or *an*. Some of you might think that the solution presented here is incorrect, for how can you have just one instance of `Order` in the `Customer` class? Enter UML's multiplicity.

Establishing Multiplicity

In the modeling of the application, it helps to define the number of possible objects involved in an association. This definition is expressed in the class diagram via the multiplicity property. **Multiplicity** can take several forms, from very specific (1) to infinite (*). In addition, these designations can be combined to form unique multiplicity statements for the applications; for example, *1..** means "1 or more."

Figure 5-4 is an example of the `Customer/Order` association using all of the adornments discussed thus far. The figure is read as follows:

`Customer` places zero or more `Order`(s), and `Order` is acting in the role of *purchase.*

`Order`(s) are placed by only one `Customer`, and `Customer` is acting in the role of *purchaser.*

Multiplicity has a direct impact on code generation as well. For the preceding example, with multiplicity the class definition for `Customer` would change. The reason is that there must be a receptacle to hold the

FIGURE 5-4 *Remulak fully adorned* `Customer/Order` *association*

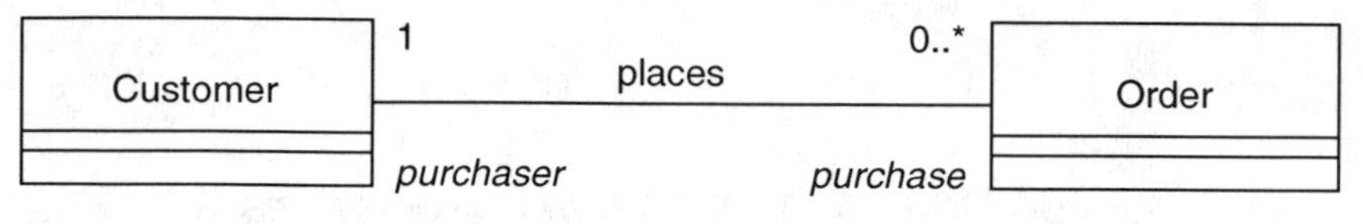

`Order` objects related to the `Customer`. It wouldn't do simply to have an attribute defined as type `Order` because then we could have only one `Order` related to an instance of `Customer`. In Chapter 2, with our brief glimpse of Java code, we used an array to handle this situation.

As many of you know, although arrays are very efficient and quite speedy in Java, they are very inflexible for managing relationships between classes. Probably the biggest drawback of an array is the requirement that we define ahead of time how many occurrences there will be. We will get the most flexibility with a Java `Collection` framework and its implementation of `ArrayList`. `ArrayList` is an instance of `Vector`; however, its methods are not synchronized, so performance is much better.

```
public class Customer
{
  public ArrayList myPurchase = new ArrayList();

  // Other Customer class detail goes here
}
```

We need `ArrayList` because the multiplicity is 0..*.

With roles, it really comes down to a matter of style. Role names can provide good customization for code generation. On the other hand, roles often provide extraneous information that does not add much value to the class diagram, as is the case with the `Customer/Order` example.

Advanced Associations

Many types of associations are possible—some more complex than others. To appreciate better what UML can offer regarding associations, we next explore more-advanced association types:

- Aggregation
- Composition

- Link
- Reflexive
- Qualification

Aggregation and Composition Associations

Aggregation and composition associations model *whole/part* contexts. In most application domains, a special relationship exists between a collection of classes in which one class clearly exhibits either control or ownership of the others. Simple examples found in the everyday world are an investment portfolio or a book. An investment portfolio is made up of assets (stocks, bonds, other securities); a book is made up of lots of parts (cover, table of contents, chapters, bibliography, index).

Distinguishing aggregation and composition associations from others is important because this distinction will later affect how the application treats the association from an implementation perspective (e.g., in implementing messaging patterns and persistence). Composition is essentially a strong form of aggregation.

Aggregation means that any of the parts may also be related to other wholes. A good example of aggregation is the investment portfolio. For example, Remulak Productions' stock can be part of several individual portfolios. **Composition** means that any of the parts have only one whole. A book is a good example of composition. The table of contents for this book is associated with this book and this book alone.

For Remulak Productions, composition associations exist between `Order` and `OrderLine`. Figure 5-5 shows an example of the `Order/OrderLine` composition association.

In UML, composition is shown as a solid diamond and aggregation as a hollow diamond. Aggregation and composition might yield two different solutions, from a program code perspective, depending on the language being used. In Java, the effect would be the same. In C++, an aggregation relationship (the whole) will define its component variables (the parts) by declaring them as "by reference" using a pointer. Composition, on the other hand, will be "by value" by declaring a variable of the class type. Put another way, with composition when the whole is destroyed the parts are destroyed with it. This is not the case with aggregation.

Remember that you do not always have to define an association name, especially when the name is obvious from the context. For ex-

FIGURE 5-5 *Remulak composition example*

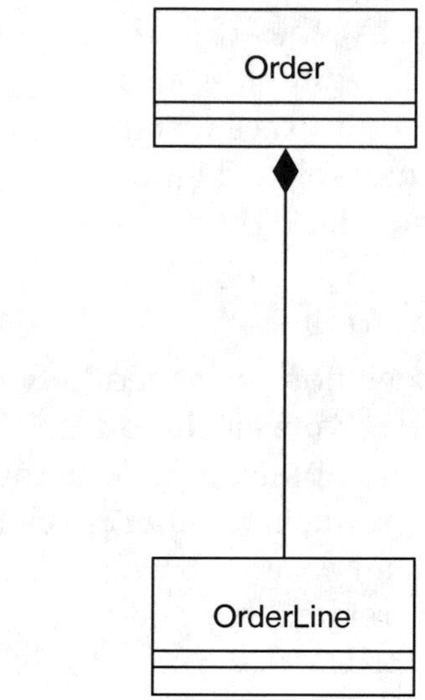

ample, placing the word *contain(s)* on each of the three composition associations would be redundant, so it is simply omitted.

Link Associations

Often there is no logical place to define certain information, usually attributes, about the association between two classes. You might need to define a class as a go-between for the actual link between two objects. A **link** is a runtime version of an association. Note that *links are to objects as associations are to classes.*

From experience, I know that if an application has an `Address` class related to another class (`Customer` in the Remulak case), another type of class likely is needed to hold unique information about that association. So if a `Customer` can have different shipping and billing addresses, where should the attribute that defines the type of `Address` exist?

Be careful! An instance of `Address` might contain a physical shipping address for customer Ryan Maecker, but it might also contain the billing address for customer Mike Richardson. Thus the `Address`-type attribute won't fit in either `Customer` or `Address`. This situation requires what UML calls a **link association**, or **association class**, a class that is related to the association of other classes. Perhaps in this class (`Role` for Remulak Productions), the attributes `addressType` and `dateAssigned` can be kept. Implicitly, the class also will contain the information necessary to determine the exact instances of `Customer` and `Address` to which these attributes relate. Figure 5-6 shows an example of an association class for Remulak Productions.

Reflexive Associations

Sometimes an association is needed between two objects of the same class. Called a **reflexive association**, this type of association is commonly used by many application domains. For Remulak Productions, we want to relate products to other products. This could be beneficial, for example, when an order entry clerk is selling a guitar and wants to recommend some related supplies. To provide this feature, and to model it according to UML, we need to set up a reflexive association on `Product`. Figure 5-7 shows an example of this association. Notice that the association leaves from and returns to the same class.

FIGURE 5-6 *A Remulak association class*

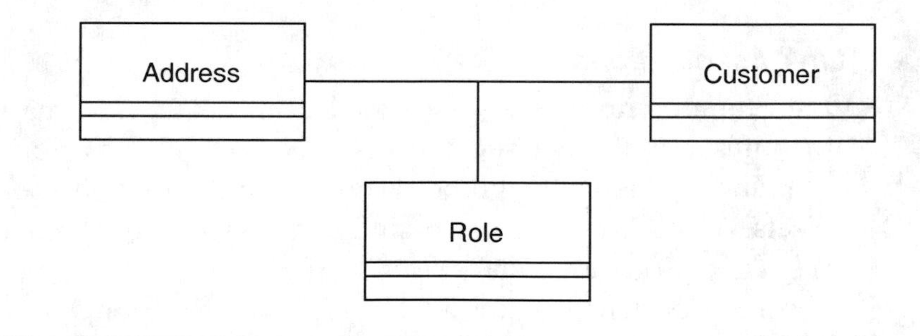

FIGURE 5-7 *A Remulak reflexive association*

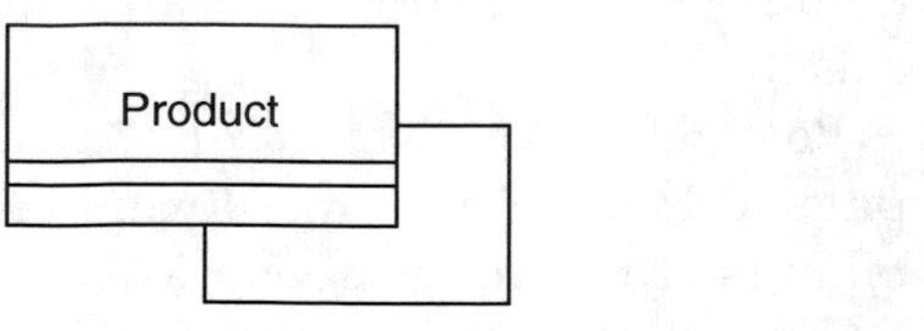

Qualification Associations

When the class diagram is created, no distinction is made regarding how the association is traversed. Rather, one class is viewed as simply having access to all of the possible associations (links in runtime between objects) to their related classes. In some cases it might be important enough in the domain to specify how the association will be traversed. Qualifiers provide this ability in UML. A **qualifier** allows a set of related objects to be returned on the basis of the qualification of some specific attribute(s).

For Remulak Productions, a qualifier could be placed, if needed, on the association between `Customer` and `Order`, as shown in Figure 5-8. The source object (`Customer`) and the qualifier's attributes (`orderId`) together yield a target set of object(s) (`Order`). In the case of Remulak Productions, either nothing or one `Order` object will be returned.

For the class diagram for Remulak Productions (outlined later in this chapter), we will diagram no qualified associations.

Generalization

Recall from earlier in the chapter that generalization is a way to depict a lattice of classes and to portray the fact that one class can be made to hold both structure (attributes) and behavior (operations) that apply to one or more specialized classes. These specialized classes can then add additional structure and behavior as necessary to portray their unique characteristics. Every instance of the specialized class also "is an" instance of the generalized class.

For Remulak Productions, a generalization/specialization relationship exists between `Product` and the classes `Guitar`, `SheetMusic`, and `Supplies`. `Product` is the generalized class, and the other three are specializations of `Product`. Common components will be defined in `Product` that will apply to all of the specialized classes. Figure 5-9 shows this generalization/specialization association.

FIGURE 5-8 *A Remulak qualified association*

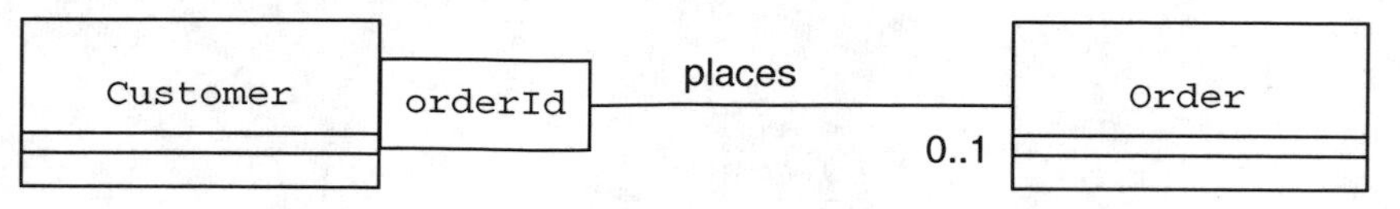

FIGURE 5-9 *A Remulak generalization/specialization class diagram*

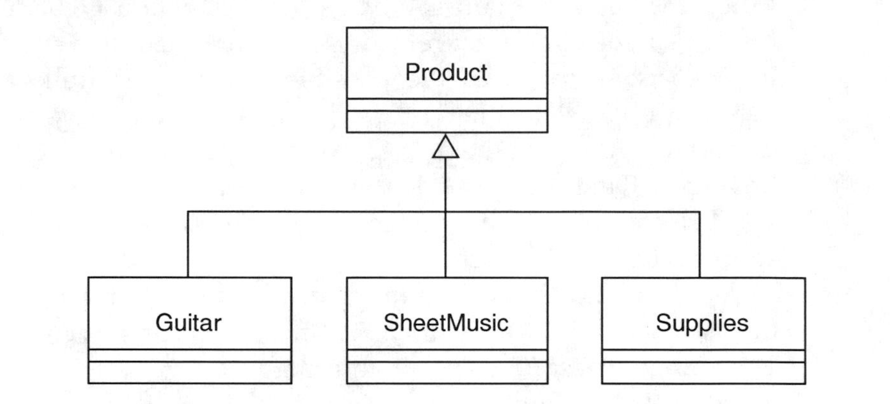

Creating the Class Diagram

A word of caution, and perhaps comfort, is in order. The preliminary list of classes and associations are just that—preliminary. We will add more classes as we progress through the Elaboration phase of the project. Some classes might be added to provide more detail about the project as it progresses. Some will be added to help resolve context-related issues about other, already defined associations.

Figure 5-10 is a first attempt at the class diagram for Remulak Productions. The diagram is rendered in the visual modeling tool (Rational Rose in this case). We do this to begin integrating our requirements and analysis work within a tool that will make it easier to produce other deliverables.

Figure 5-11 shows the user interface for Rational Rose and the class diagram for Remulak Productions. Notice the tree view pane on the left side of the window, which currently displays the logical view of Increment 1 entity classes.

FIGURE 5-10 *Remulak class diagram*

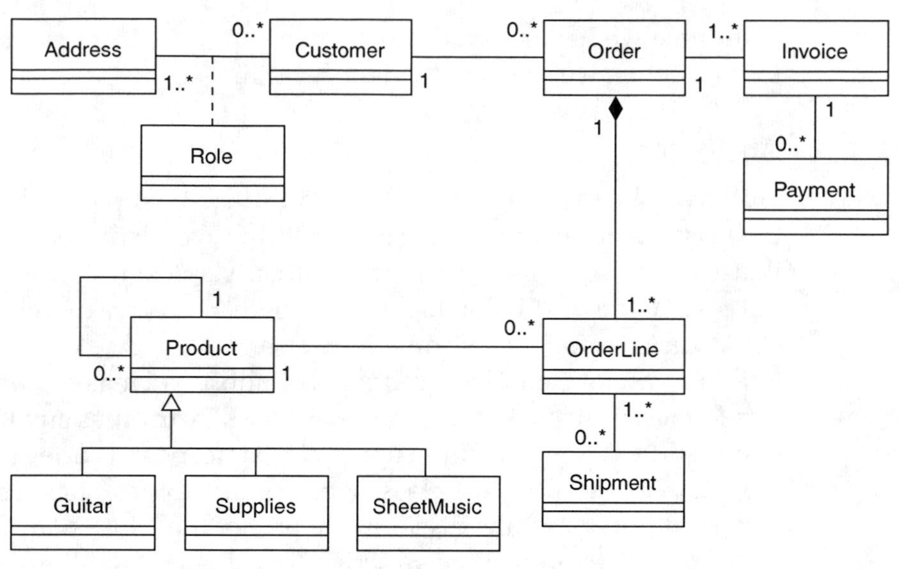

FIGURE 5-11 *Remulak class diagram in Rational Rose*

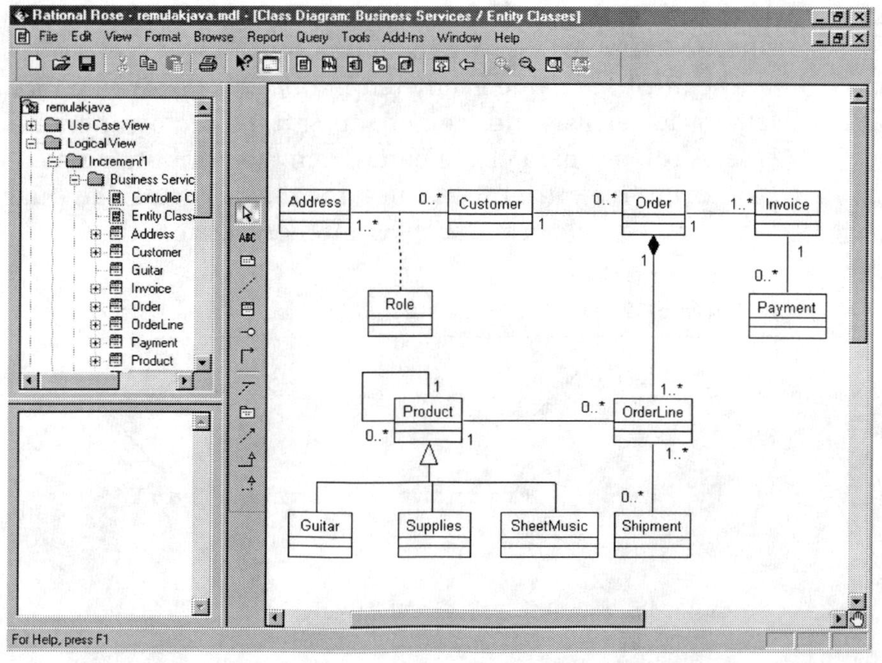

Identifying Attributes and Operations

Until now we haven't paid much attention to attributes or operations. In this section we see how to identify both.

Attributes

We have already encountered several attributes, particularly during the class identification exercise. Recall that we identified many nouns that were actually attributes (rather than classes) because they didn't have structure and behavior in their own right but merely served as structural components of something else.

In the case of Remulak Productions, nouns such as *first name, name,* and *last name* are part of the `Customer` class. Attributes such as address line 1, address line 2, address line 3, city, state, postal code, and country are part of the `Address` class, whereas attributes such as quantity, extended price, and line discount are part of the `OrderLine` class. Soon the attributes that form the structural backbone of the Remulak classes begin to take shape.

Recall that the previous UML class diagram showed three compartments for a class, containing the class name, attributes, and operations. The attributes go in the second compartment and have a defined structure; an example is shown in Figure 5-12.

The attribute name is entered in *camelback* notation; that is, the first letter is lowercase, and the remaining full word components are uppercase. A colon separates the name from the attribute type. The type may be a primitive attribute defined for the particular language environment or a complex type such as another class or structure. Any default

FIGURE 5-12 *UML attribute definition*

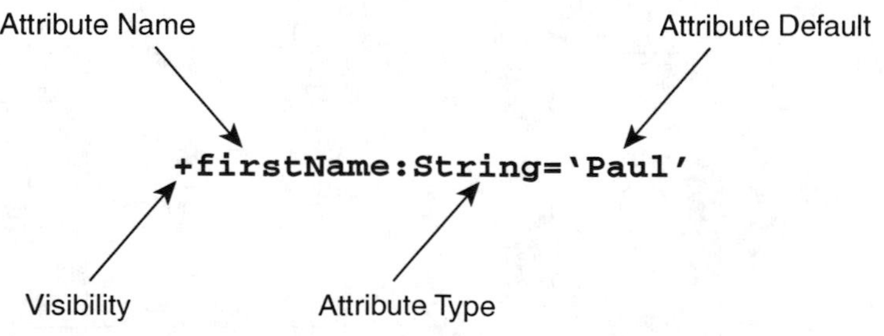

initial value for a particular attribute may also be specified as shown. Visibility specifies the attribute's accessibility to the outside consumer. In UML, there are three types of visibility: public (+), private (–), and protected (#).

We don't want to get hung up on completing the entire attribute definition. We might not know the type or default initial values, if any, at this time. Eventually, however, we will need all of this information before we can generate any program code and use it meaningfully.

Operations

Operations define the behavior supported by a given class. At this point we might not have a clear idea of the exact operations that each class will support; that will be driven by the work to be done as specified in the use-cases. The operations will take more shape as the project moves into the dynamic modeling stage, which is explored in Chapter 7. However, answering some basic questions will help us begin to identify the operations:

- What does the class know how to do?
- What is the class expected to do for others?
- What are the responsibilities of the class?

For example, the `Order` class should know how to calculate some type of total due, and it should know if anything is back-ordered.

The operation goes in the third compartment of the class and has a defined structure, as illustrated in Figure 5-13. Like the attribute name, the operation name is entered in camelback notation. After the

FIGURE 5-13 *UML operation specification*

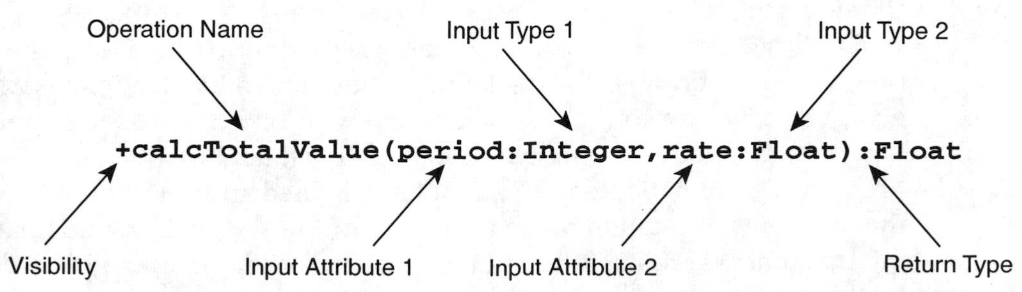

operation name, the parameters (arguments) that make up the input to the operation are defined (within parentheses). The argument specification conveniently takes the same form as the attribute specification outlined in the attribute section. Multiple input arguments are allowed and are separated by commas. Finally, the type of the output returned by the operation, if any, may be specified.

The entire set of arguments, with the exception of the return type, is called the **operation signature**. Operation signatures are important to polymorphism, as we will see when the nuances of polymorphism are explored during the Elaboration and Construction phases of the project.

As with attributes, we don't worry about completing the entire signature for each operation because we might not know them at this point. We will need to complete all of this information before we can generate any program code and use it meaningfully, but from experience I have found that the developers, not the designers, are the biggest contributors to the pool of private operations.

Interfaces

Chapter 2 briefly defined two types of inheritance: implementation and interface. Interface inheritance and how it is treated in Java is quite unique among object-oriented languages. This isn't to say that other languages don't support interfaces. C++ doesn't formally distinguish the construct, but an interface can be implemented by extension of a class in which nothing but pure virtual functions are defined. In Visual Basic, interface inheritance is accomplished through the `implements` keyword. Java has a little in common with Visual Basic in that regard because it, too, uses the keyword `implements`. However, this is where the similarity ends.

The designers of the Java language wisely granted interfaces their own unique definition. The declaration looks much like that of a class, except that the keyword `class` is replaced with `interface`. The important point about the interface in this chapter is that UML offers its own unique diagrammatic elements. Chapter 2 defined an interface, `IPrice`, that provided a common pricing contract for the `Order` class, anticipating that other classes (a future `Service` class, for example) might abide by this contract as well. UML offers two options to the modeler.

FIGURE 5-14 *UML notation for interface inheritance*

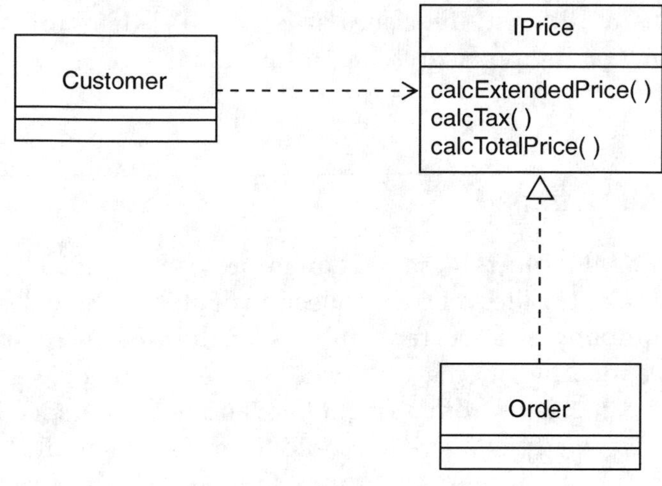

Figure 5-14 diagrams the `Order` class, which *realizes*—that is, provides the concrete implementation for—the interface `IPrice`. The realizes relationship is a combination of the inheritance notation (triangle with solid line) and the dependency relationship (dashed line with an arrowhead). Notice that the `Customer` class *depends* on the interface `IPrice`. The attractive features of this view of interface inheritance are that the operations of the interface are clear, and thus so is the responsibility of the `Order` class to abide by the interface.

Figure 5-15, on the other hand, denotes the alternative modeling convention for interface inheritance. This view may be more familiar to some of you, particularly if you have been exposed to the Microsoft technology architectures (of course there is more than one). Some people refer to this as the lollipop view of interface inheritance.

FIGURE 5-15 *UML and interface inheritance: Alternate form*

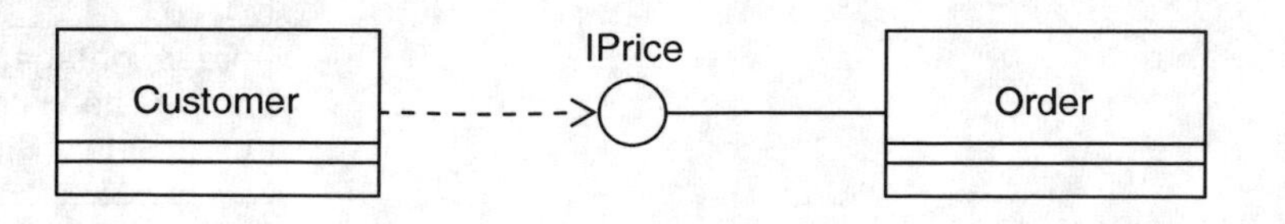

Although this view is cleaner and abbreviated, it lacks the operations that make up the interface. Because a class in Java may implement many different interfaces, it is possible, then, to have a class that has several lollipop icons extending from it.

Object Diagrams

A UML **object diagram** is an improvisation of a class diagram, a snapshot of the lifecycle of a collection of objects. Like the balance sheet for a company, it is current only as of the time it is printed or rendered. Depending on the audience, however, an object diagram can help depict classes from a "right here and now" perspective. It is most often used to depict a live example to management and to members of the organization who are not as familiar with the project as the project team is.

Figure 5-16 shows an example of an object diagram for customer Mike Richardson and his two orders with Remulak Productions. The object diagram is read as follows: *The R. Michael Richardson object of class*

FIGURE 5-16 *Remulak object diagram for* `Customer` *and* `Order`

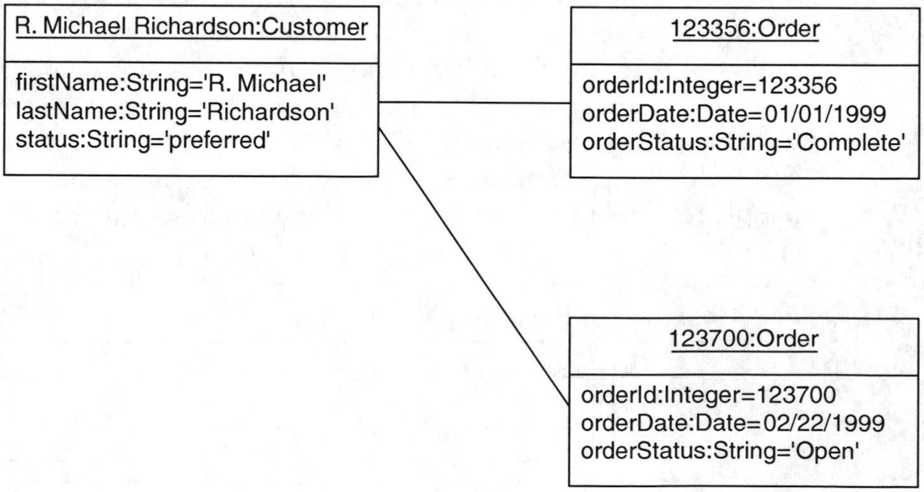

`Customer` is *linked* to both *the 123356 object of class* `Order` and *the 123700 object of class* `Order`. Notice that the attribute compartment shows the live object data for these instances. In addition, the operation compartment is dropped for object diagrams because operations are related to the class. If it is a member of the class, the object automatically has access to the operations.

In later UML diagrams (sequence and collaboration), the object view is used. Otherwise, the IT side of the project likely will seldom use object diagrams.

Figure 5-17 is a class diagram of the relationships of several concepts discussed so far. The figure indicates that the use-case is the embryo of all that we know about the project. Also shown are the primary, alternate, and exception pathways, which we will model with an interaction diagram in Chapter 7. Classes initially show up in the use-case and are used, as objects, in interaction diagrams. The other components of this class diagram will be clearer when we discuss the dynamic view of the project in Chapter 7.

FIGURE 5-17 *Class diagram of project concepts and UML deliverables*

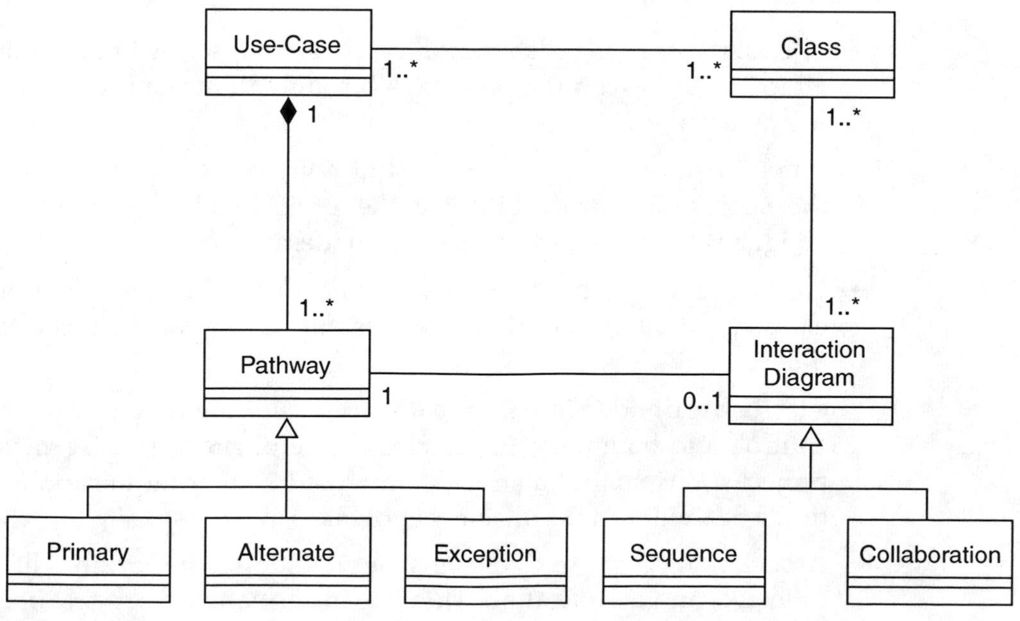

Finishing Up: The Analysis Model

With the completion of the use-cases, classes (entity, control, and boundary), class diagram, and related associations, we have completed the **analysis model**. The analysis model consists of everything completed so far. Recall that the requirements model consisted of the use-cases delivered at the completion of the Inception phase. The use-cases for Remulak Productions have been described in great detail, and from them we have derived additional diagrams and supporting artifacts (multiplicity, roles, and association names).

In the remaining chapters that deal with the Elaboration phase, we further flesh out the classes, adding more attributes and operations. In addition, the control and boundary classes, in their own contexts with the entity classes, begin to meld. The eventual result will be the design model for Remulak Productions.

Checkpoint

Where We've Been

- The first step in the Elaboration phase is to describe in detail the alternate and exception pathways through all of the use-cases in Increment 1.
- Categorization of business rules, but not UML artifacts, is key to the success and traceability of the project. Business rules are assigned to the use-cases that enforce them.
- We can develop a preliminary list of candidate classes by simply extracting nouns from the use-cases and applying various class filters.
- Classes are divided into three categories called stereotypes: entity, control, and boundary. Entity classes are of most interest to the project sponsors, but all classes are vital to ensuring the application's flexibility as the business evolves.
- Associations come in five forms: aggregation, composition, link, reflexive, and qualification. They are instantiated to provide links over which messages flow to carry out the functionality of the use-cases.

- A class has three compartments, containing the class's name, attributes, and operations. Not all of the detail for attributes and operations needs to be completely specified at this point in the project. However, this needs to be done before program code is generated.
- The analysis model for Remulak Productions is complete and includes the details of all use-case pathways, the results of the class identification process and association assignments, and the detailed description of multiplicity.

Where We're Going Next

In the next chapter we:

- Begin a high-level prototype effort for some of the use-case pathways.
- Create screen flow structure charts (storyboards) before creating the prototype.
- Identify ways to use the use-cases and actors to match navigational requirements with the prototype.
- Create screen dialogs to get users' perspectives on the anticipated goals of the user interface and what they expect it to do.
- Modify UML artifacts to reflect what is learned in the prototyping process.
- Examine the need for change control and the ability to maintain traceability throughout the project deliverables.

CHAPTER 6

Building a User Interface Prototype

IN THIS CHAPTER

*At this point in the project we need to create a concrete visualization, called a **user interface prototype**, of some of what we have learned so far. This visualization should focus on areas of the project that need further validation. It can also be an excellent way to discover more about the application requirements, which might involve not only new functionality but also usability needs.*

A prototype's goal is not only to mock up the visual interface but also to visually exercise many of the pathways through the use-cases. In the case of Remulak Productions, the prototype focuses on the happy path through the Process Orders *use-case. It also sets the stage for establishing some future standards for the project team, particularly as those standards relate to the user interface.*

GOALS

- To examine the use-cases, focusing on the gathering of user interface requirements.
- To create a user interface artifacts section for each use-case.
- To discuss the concept of use-case coupling.

- To create screen structure charts as a preliminary storyboard of the user interface flow.
- To construct the user interface prototype.
- To create screen dialogs to outline perceived interactions and desired outcomes.
- To evaluate the user interface prototype.
- To outline the changes to the use-case and class diagrams on the basis of additional information found during the prototyping effort.

Building an Early Prototype

Before we begin reviewing the use-cases, focusing on the user interface prototype, let's revisit the Unified Process model. Figure 6-1 shows the process model with the focus of the project on the Elaboration phase.

FIGURE 6-1 *Unified Process model: Elaboration phase*

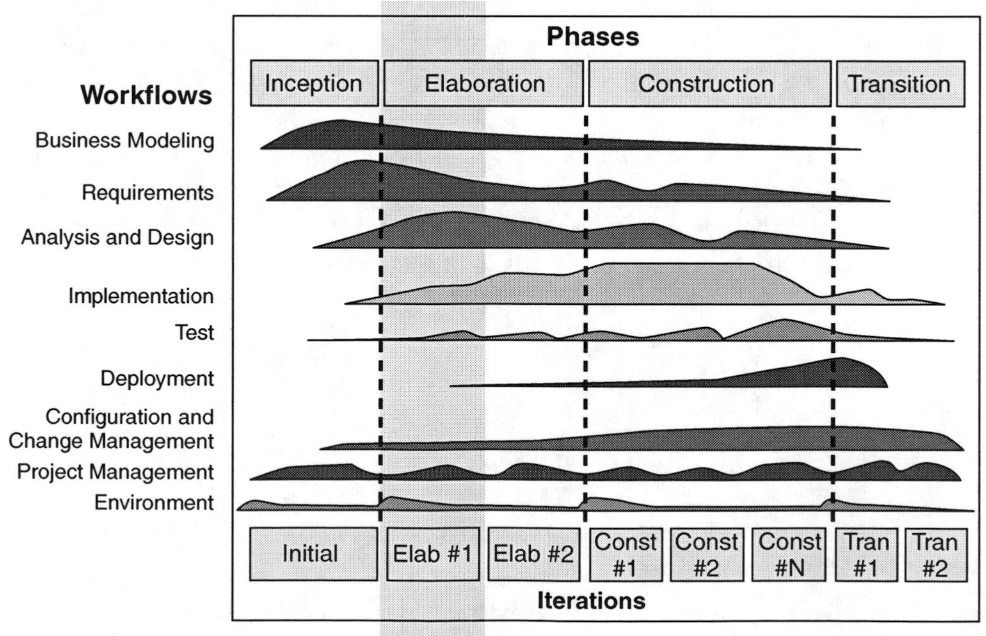

The Prototype

The user interface prototype serves many functions at this stage of the project:

- It further refines the actor and use-case boundaries, clarifies any misconceptions, and provides missing details that remain to be collected.
- It provides early feedback to the project sponsors of the many visual features that the application will provide.
- It expands the detailed description of the use-cases by adding an additional section, on user interface artifacts.

In this chapter the following Unified Process workflows and activity sets are emphasized:

- Requirements: Analyze the Problem
- Analysis and Design: Analyze Behavior
- Analysis and Design: Design Components

The prototype can also serve as an excellent eye-opener for many project participants. Many times in design sessions I have heard the statement, "I can't tell you what I want, but if I could show you a picture. . . ." The user interface prototype is our first picture into the future.

Gathering Requirements

User Interface Prototype

In this chapter we look at how we can use the UML deliverables created so far to leverage the prototyping effort. The prime input consists of the use-cases. Until now, however, we have purposely avoided adding to them any user interface specifications or usability requirements, instead keeping them technology neutral. There is a section in the use-case template for documenting user interface artifacts because they do come up early in the project. However, every attempt should be made to prevent the user from clouding the goal of gathering *what* in favor of *how*.

Before we begin the prototype discovery process, I want to offer a caution about using prototypes. Although the prototype succeeds in discovering and reconfirming existing requirements, it can foster unrealistic expectations by the project sponsors. Often I have heard from a project sponsor, "My, that took only two weeks, but you say the entire system will take a year and half. What gives?" It is very important that we educate the entire project team on the prototype's goal, and that we do this early and with the right focus. The best way to communicate this information is through the business members of the project team because the project sponsors consider them one of "theirs."

The goals of the prototype are as follows:

- To assess specific user interface requirements for the key pathways of the application.
- To provide feedback to the project sponsors in the form of visual clues so that the stated requirements found in the use-cases are understood and can be realized.
- To begin the early development of user interface standards for the project.
- To begin constructing the working on-screen templates to be used during the construction phase.

We must tell the project sponsors up front that what is behind the prototype is actually "smoke and mirrors"; most of the logic and data aspects of the prototype are hard-wired. The only thing representative of the production deliverable is the anticipated flow and look and feel. We need to communicate this message early and often. Again, the business team members on the project should communicate this to the project sponsors.

Actor and Use-Case Boundaries

To reinforce the notion that UML, combined with a sound process model such as the Unified Process, provides traceability, prototyping is driven by the use-cases created at the project's beginning. To be more precise, the initial focus of the user interface prototype is the point at which the actor crosses the boundary of the use-case.

Every point in the use-case at which the actor is involved warrants some type of user interface. The user interface doesn't have to be graphical. Recall from Chapter 3 that an actor can also be a hardware device, a timer, or a system. Thus it is also possible to prototype something that isn't visual. (This is certainly true for systems that have a very strong hardware element, which Remulak Productions' system does not.) For Remulak Productions, however, at least two system actors are needed: the *credit card switch* and the *accounting system*.

The key pathways that we will prototype deal with order entry. This prototype will exercise quite a bit of the flow of the application. Although the pathway details in the use-cases so far have been technology neutral, we still must provide a mapping between those essential steps and the realization of those steps into a physical user interface flow.

Figure 6-2 is a cutaway of the use-case diagram created in Chapter 4 (see Figure 4-3), showing *Process Orders* and its specific actor interface, the order clerk.

A good way to begin the prototyping process is to investigate the actor's interface expectations with the use-case by asking certain questions. Table 6-1 offers a set of questions about the *Process Orders* use-case that are geared toward human actors. The answers might lead the prototype into different directions based on the findings. In the table, the answers pertain to the order clerk actor.

In Appendix C, where the project estimation detail is presented, the order clerk is given a rating of "complex" because this actor will deal with a *graphical* user interface (GUI). Responses to the questionnaire indicate that the order clerk has intimate knowledge about the business but can benefit from a sophisticated and somewhat complex user interface.

FIGURE 6-2 Process Orders *use-case*

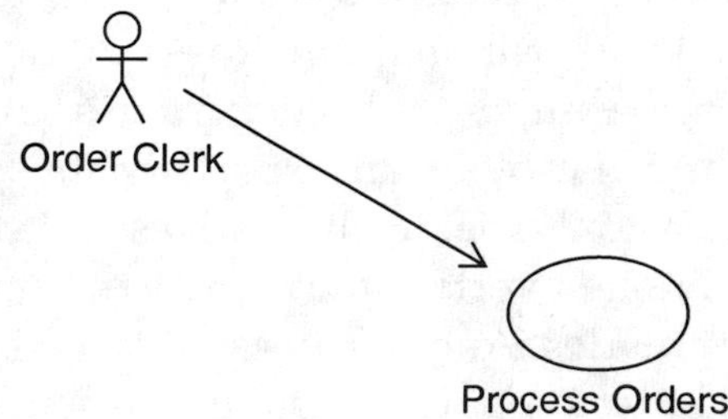

TABLE 6-1 *Sample Questions to Ask about a Human Actor at Remulak Productions*

Question	Answer
What level of skill, irrespective of any computer knowledge, does this actor need to have to perform his/her tasks?	The order clerk must be very knowledgeable about the order process. Often the order clerk will be required to answer somewhat technical questions about musical instruments and supplies.
Does the actor have experience in a windowing environment?	Yes, all order clerks at Remulak Productions have extensive experience in using Microsoft Windows.
Does the actor have experience with an automated business application?	Yes, all order clerks are currently using Remulak Productions' older systems.
Will the actor be required to leave the application and consult manual information such as catalogs during the work processes?	Yes, order entry specifically will require external catalog resources. This is the only area of Remulak Productions that will require consultation of manual information.
Will the actor require that the application have a save-and-resume capability?	Yes, all pathways through the *Process Orders* use-case will be dealing with an order that is new. An order is not saved until the order process is complete. If an order is partially completed but lacking something such as payment information, the order will be saved as an incomplete order.

User Interface Artifacts

Each use-case (or use-case pathway, depending on the level of separation in the individual use-case) will have a user interface artifacts section that will list key items geared toward the user interface for a particular actor/use-case pair. This was described in detail in Section 4 of the use-case template (see Chapter 4). In the case of *Process Orders,* there is only one primary actor.

What if a use-case has more than one actor/use-case pair? And what if the individual pairs require access to the same pathways but differ vastly in their abilities to deal with a user interface; for example, one is a novice and the other an expert? Many designs face this common dilemma. The only viable alternatives are to create either two different interfaces or one interface that has an option providing for both novice and expert modes. Another possibility is that the user interface could be designed to support the common denominator for both types of users, which is the easiest of the two interfaces. However, I have found that this quickly alienates the expert user. (I also believe that humans improve over time and those who start as novices will eventually become experts.) Because most users are familiar with a shopping cart from their personal lives, the Remulak order process will use the common shopping cart metaphor popularized today by the Internet.

Because there will probably always be new users, we have to deal with the dilemma. Often novices can interface with a script manager in the user interface that guides them through the steps of the use-case pathway. Scripts are much like the popular wizards in many Windows-based products.

Table 6-2 reviews the user interface artifacts section for each use-case in Increment 1.

All of these artifacts are used as input to the user interface storyboarding and subsequent physical screen creation steps. They are very "soft" in that they often describe concepts and generalizations and seldom specifics such as "use a spinner control."

TABLE 6-2 *Use-Case User Interface Artifacts Sections*

Use-Case	User Interface Artifacts
Maintain Orders	Requires as few screens as possible because the user will be on the phone with the client and needs a minimum of "window open" sequences. Users want an easy way to tell who last changed an order and on what date.
Process Orders	Requires as few screens as possible because the user will be on the phone with the client and needs a minimum of "window open" sequences.
Maintain Relationships (*customer* pathway only)	The customer search must be integrated onto the screen; the users want to avoid a separate screen if possible. Associating customers with addresses and specifying their associated roles should be very easy. Because many users work only certain states, default fields on the screens should be based on user preferences.
Architecture Infrastructure	This is a shadow use-case and will have user interface components that are geared toward the IT group.
Use-cases (general user interface comments)	All backgrounds will be white with black labels. All headings will have a blue background with white letters. As much faultless entry of information as possible should occur in the user interface. Date processing is important; manually entry of dates in a particular format should be avoided.

Use-Case Coupling

Often we want to know if a given use-case, from a workflow perspective, has a close association with other use-cases. This knowledge provides some degree of coupling information that can be quite beneficial for the user interface flow. Using a matrix of use-cases and describing their relationship can assess how closely use-cases are related. Figure 6-3 provides a first attempt at the matrix based on what we know about Remulak Productions.

Here's an example of how to read the matrix. Consider the *Maintain Orders* use-case from the *y*-axis and the *Maintain Relationships* use-case from the *x*-axis. From this you can see that 60 percent of the time, a person who is in the *Maintain Orders* use-case will subsequently navigate to the *Maintain Relationships* use-case. Notice that this value is not the same for the reverse relationship: While in the *Maintain Relationships* use-case, the person has a 0 percent chance of going to the *Maintain Orders* use-case.

You might want to use some other type of grading system instead of percentages (such as 0 for never, 1 for sometimes, and 2 for very often). Keep in mind that these occurrences are random and reflect the nature of the business at a given point in time. Note, too, that the relationships between use-cases are not "includes" or "extends" relationships but merely related to workflow and navigation.

The matrix in Figure 6-3 can help us determine how the user interface might be traversed, as well as demonstrate how easy it is to access other use-cases from an associated use-case pathway.

FIGURE 6-3 *Use-case coupling matrix*

	Maintain Orders	Maintain Inventory	Process Orders	Shipping	Invoicing	Maintain Relationships	Decision Support
Maintain Orders	X	0%	10%	40%	10%	60%	0%
Maintain Inventory	0%	X	0%	50%	0%	0%	0%
Process Orders	40%	0%	X	0%	0%	50%	0%
Shipping	30%	60%	0%	X	25%	5%	0%
Invoicing	20%	0%	0%	0%	X	0%	0%
Maintain Relationships	0%	0%	0%	0%	0%	X	0%
Decision Support	0%	0%	0%	0%	0%	0%	X

The First Pass

Screen Structure Charts

In my early days as a developer of client/server applications, I created physical screen layouts immediately during prototyping. All too often, I then found myself in discussions with my business sponsor tackling issues along the lines of, "Move the **OK** button over 4 pixels" and "Wouldn't a gray background be more appealing?" Discussions like these shouldn't dominate the prototype. Instead, the prototype should initially identify *major* window groups and the *overall* strategy for look and feel, and only at the end address issues of aesthetics.

Researchers have found that 60 percent of an application's usability can be traced to how well the user interface maps to the mental model of the user. Some people also refer to this as someone's mind map. Interaction accounts for 30 percent; presentation, for 10 percent. Surprisingly, developers usually first approach the task that has the lowest impact on usability.

In an effort to streamline the prototyping process, we will create screen structure charts before creating any actual screens. A structure chart is a low-technology way to storyboard the application flow, specifically the flow of pathways through the use-cases. The chart consists of various easy-to-use symbols. Figure 6-4 shows an example.

The symbols describe the major types of windowing activities in a graphical application:

- **Amodal (modeless) window:** Does not require a response from the user. For example, the window might be invoked and then minimized or bypassed in favor of another window within the application or another application entirely. Any Microsoft Office application is a good example of an amodal window.
- **Modal window:** Requires a response from the user. For example, the window might be invoked but will require that the user complete the dialog box or cancel out of it. (This statement actually is misleading because if you are a Microsoft Windows user, the **Alt+Tab** key combination can be used to invoke application toggle functionality on any other open applications.) The **Save As** dialog box in most applications is a good example of a modal window.
- **Direction of traversal:** Shows the pathway of window navigation. For example, suppose you are in a Java internal-frame setup

FIGURE 6-4 *Screen structure chart symbols*

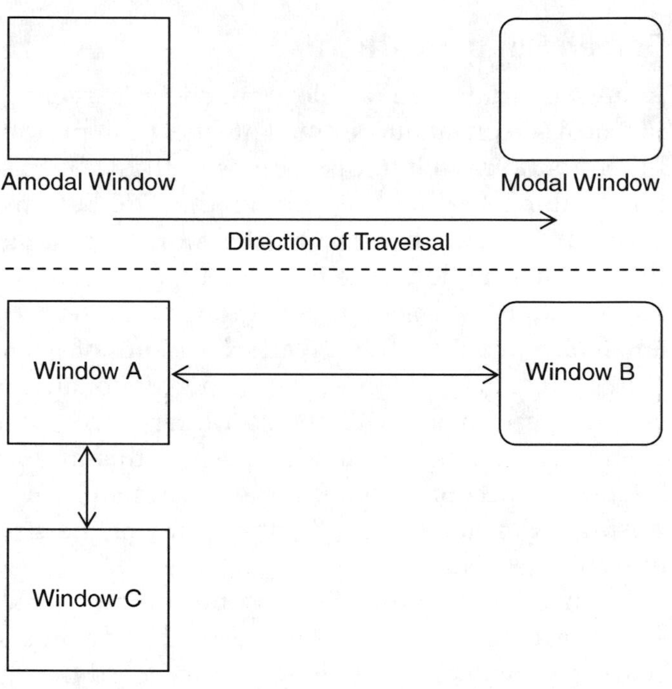

and a toolbar or menu item allows a transaction-based window to be opened, giving the user the option to return when that window is closed. Then the arrow will display as two-headed from the containing frame to the transaction window.

This low-technology approach can yield high rewards. We can also model some of the more often used controls, such as tabbed controls, as we will do for Remulak Productions. A tabbed control represents a form of logical paging and can be expressed with a focus block for a specific window, as shown in Figure 6-5.

The tabbed controls, shown as windows in the figure, are embedded on the physical window, but they actually represent separate navigational elements of the user interface. They also are often mutually exclusive. Sometimes just showing window navigation alone isn't sufficient. In the case of windows, which use tabbed dialogs or in some cases master detail grids, distinguishing them as separate logical enti-

FIGURE 6-5 *Logical paging using focus blocks*

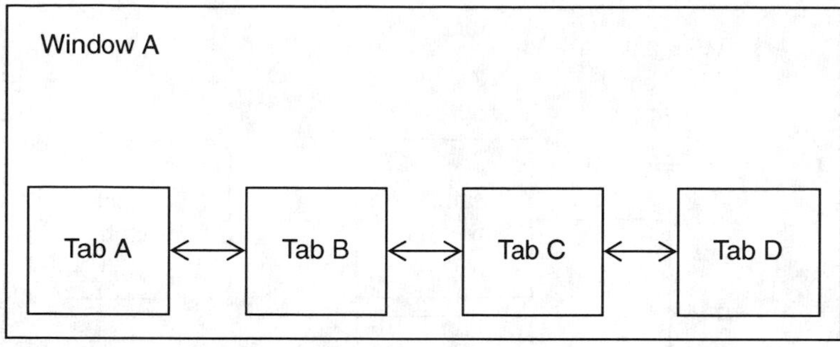

ties is important. Although these logical entities generally are layered onto one physical window, in some cases they are really user-driven navigational choices.

We create two structure charts for Remulak Productions in this chapter. Figure 6-6 depicts the overall screen structure chart for the order entry application. Figure 6-7 depicts the screen structure chart to support the *Process Orders* use-case.

Creating the Prototype

In the early days of Java, the creation of the visual portion for the application was excruciatingly slow and frustrating. The lack of visual development environments often prompted developers to use a different tool to visually prototype the application, perhaps Visual Basic or even Adobe FrameMaker or Microsoft Visio. This situation quickly changed with the introduction of integrated development environments (IDEs) for Java.

My next few comments will surely alienate some readers. This reaction is natural because of the religious nature and personal bias toward various vendors' IDE products. Many of you who learned Java did so in a classroom setting that didn't utilize an IDE. I am a big believer in this approach at the beginning of your Java education because it provides an excellent foundation for understanding the language. After the initial Java training, however, you're making a big mistake if you don't run out and buy an IDE to build your applications. These environments will save you hundreds if not thousands of hours of development time over the course of their usage.

FIGURE 6-6 *Remulak overall screen structure chart*

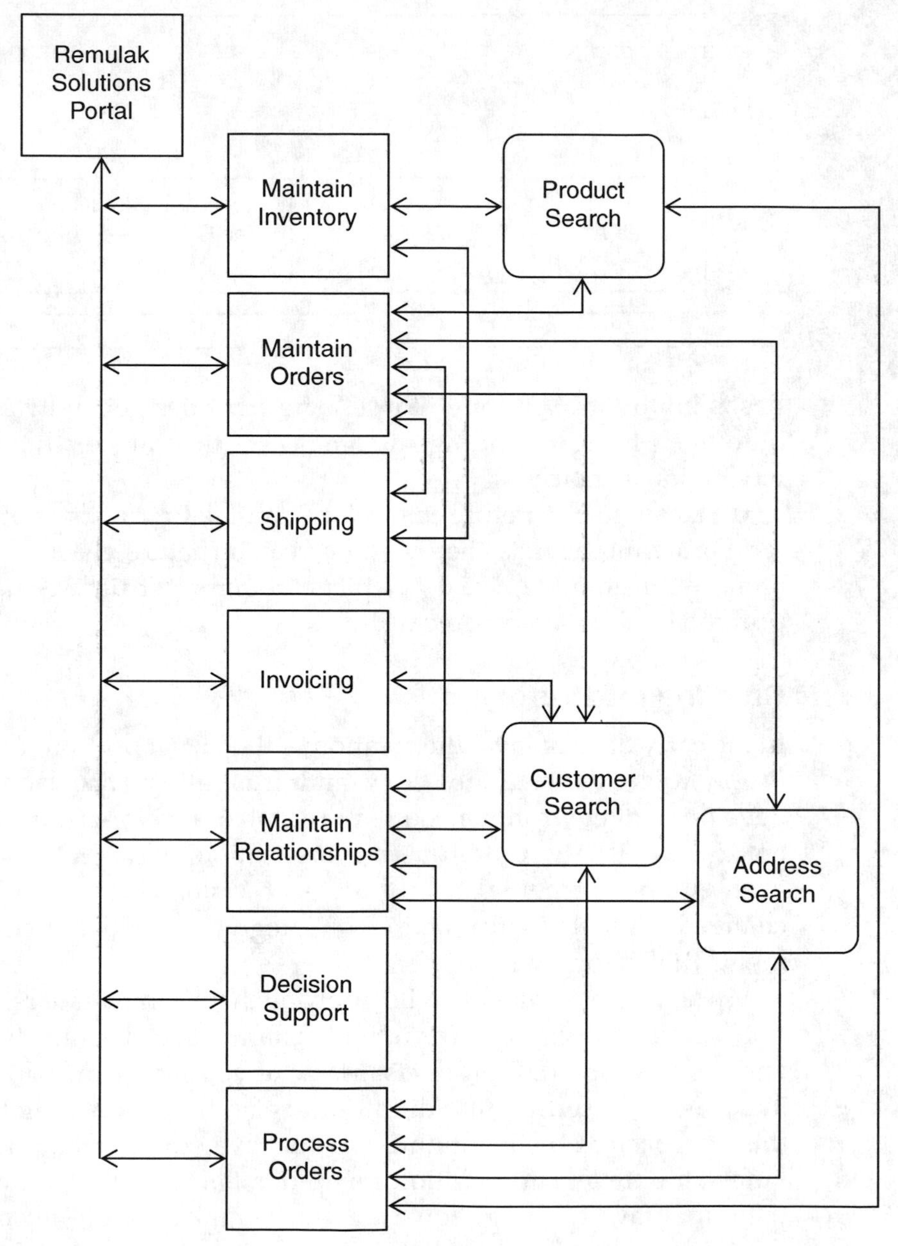

FIGURE 6-7 *Remulak* Process Orders *screen structure chart*

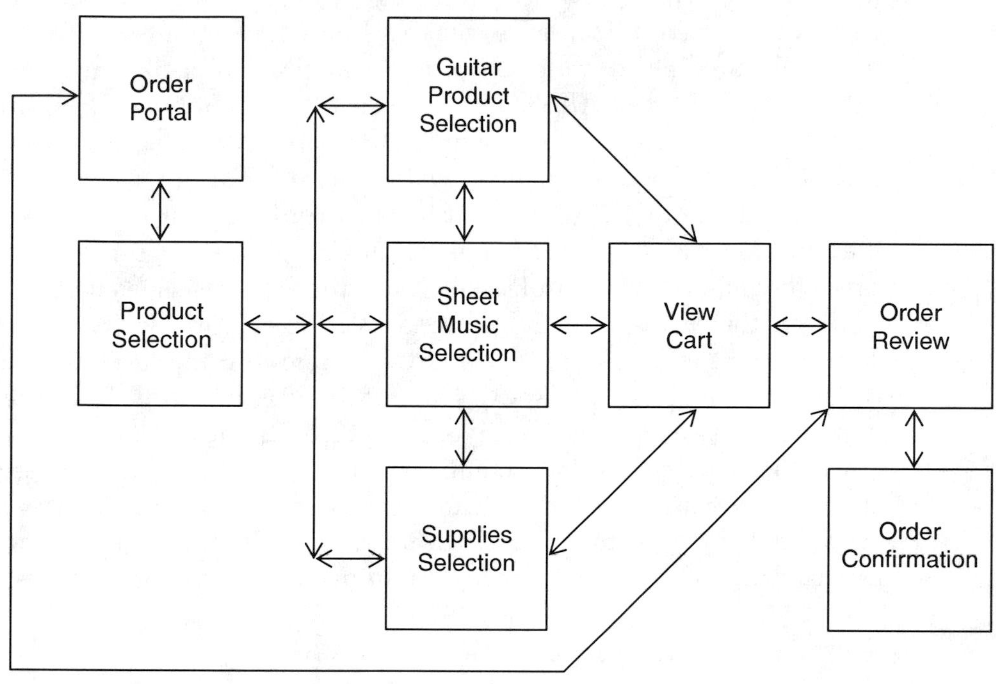

Other very esteemed individuals disagree, including James Gosling, the father of Java, who stated in an interview by SYS-CON Radio at the June 2001 JavaOne conference, "Real programmers don't use IDEs but instead stick with a good editor, since IDEs are too constraining." On occasion I still run across a development team that abides by this creed. My reply is simply, "Why?" I personally would rather have a root canal than use a line editor to build enterprise Java applications.

There are many IDE products on the market today, but three in particular are continually reviewed and compared together. Over the last several years, I have seen their rankings constantly shift, but they consistently are perceived as best-of-class IDE products. These products are JBuilder (by Inprise, formerly Borland), Visual Age for Java (by IBM), and VisualCafé (by WebGain). Yes, there are others out there, but the three mentioned here capture the lion's share of the Java IDE market.

As Java has evolved, and more recently with the release of the Java 2 Platform, Enterprise Edition (J2EE), the selection of the IDE has become even more contested. Clearly, one of the standouts of this latest release of Java is Enterprise JavaBeans (EJB). However, an effective EJB strategy requires an application server that implements the EJB infrastructure. All three IDE products either offer their own application server product (e.g., Inprise Application Server, IBM WebSphere Application Server) or are closely aligned with an application server provider (e.g., BEA WebLogic's strategic alliance with WebGain's VisualCafé). This isn't to say that you can't, for instance, build EJB applications and then deploy them on a different vendor's application server, but at times the integration is implemented in a more seamless fashion.

Given that bit of history, I intend to utilize Inprise's JBuilder for some of the examples in this book. I won't go into the nuances of the product but will use it to show some of the visual results. The beauty of Java is that all of the code that is available with the book will work in any of the vendor's products mentioned. To keep the playing field equal, and more importantly to provide more value-added information to readers so that they can pick their own tools for coding, I have purposely not used any of the vendor-provided unique classes or components.

Windowing Components

Using the structure chart presented in Figure 6-7, we can lay out some of the screen components. Keep in mind that these screens aren't "art fancy." They contain virtually no "eye candy." In practice you would probably want to employ the services of a graphic artist to make the screen designs really stand out. Figure 6-8 displays the Remulak initial Web page, which has no eye-candy.

The order portal allows for two branches in the screen dialog. One branch allows for the entry of a new order; the other, for a query on an existing order. Assuming a new order, we have the screen shown in Figure 6-9.

This screen allows the user to select a product category from which products will be chosen. In this case, if the user chooses **Guitars** as the product category, the screen in Figure 6-10 will pop up.

Figure 6-10 shows how a particular product is added to the shopping cart: by selection of the button **Add to Cart**. Pressing the **View Cart** button at this point will display the current shopping cart. Let's assume that we also added a sheet music item to our cart. Selecting **View Cart** would then display Figure 6-11.

FIGURE 6-8 *Remulak order portal*

http://mocha/RemulakJava/orderentry.html - Microsoft Internet Explorer

File Edit View Favorites Tools Help

Remulak Order Portal

Customer Number

abc1234 New Order

Order Number

Order Inquiry

Done Local intranet

FIGURE 6-9 *Product selection*

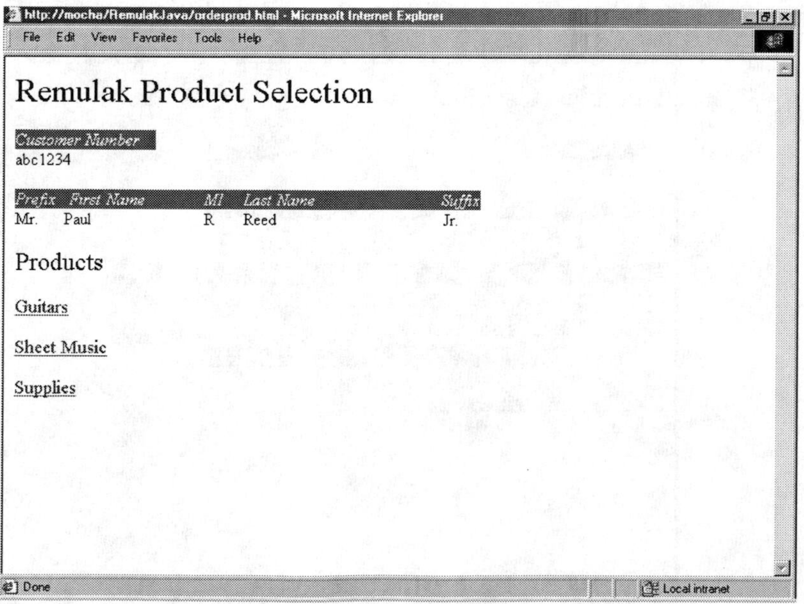

FIGURE 6-10 *Guitar selection*

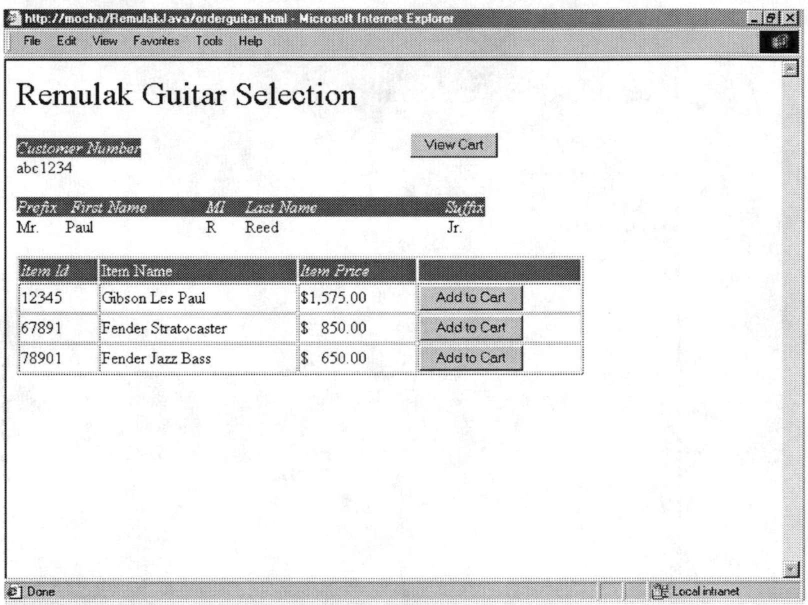

FIGURE 6-11 *Viewing the shopping cart*

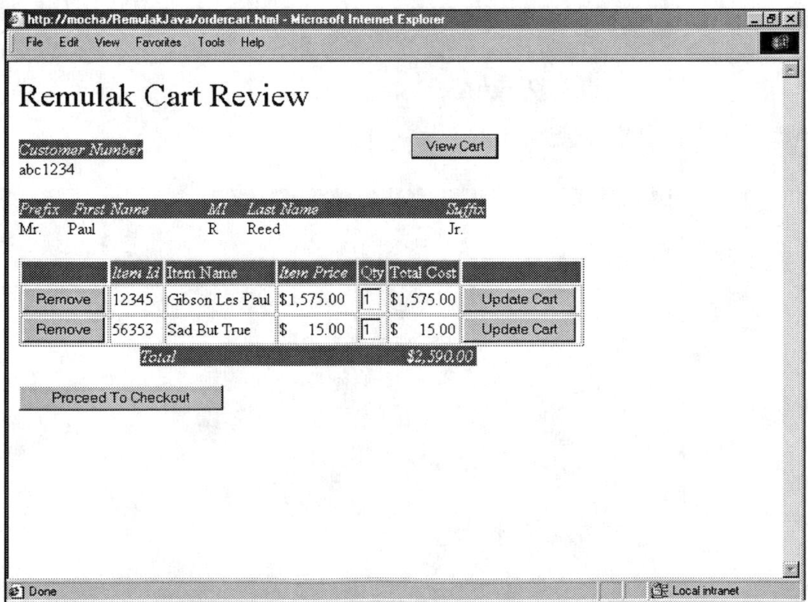

The **View Cart** screen offers several options. The user can change the **Qty** field and then press **Update Cart**. Note that this action does cause another screen to open; the same screen is simply displayed with the updated quantity now confirmed, along with a recalculated price.

The user may also remove any item by pressing the corresponding **Remove** button. Just as with **Update Cart**, this action will redisplay the same screen with updated pricing and line items. Assuming that all is well at this point, Figure 6-12 shows the screen that is displayed if **Proceed To Checkout** is pressed on Figure 6-11.

Note that at this stage the screen is the same as the one that is displayed if the user wishes to inquire about an order, as was made possible in Figure 6-8. Users who like what they see may confirm the order by pressing **Continue** on the screen depicted in Figure 6-12. The order confirmation screen is very basic and is merely meant to give users information, providing them with an order number as shown in Figure 6-13.

FIGURE 6-12 *Order review*

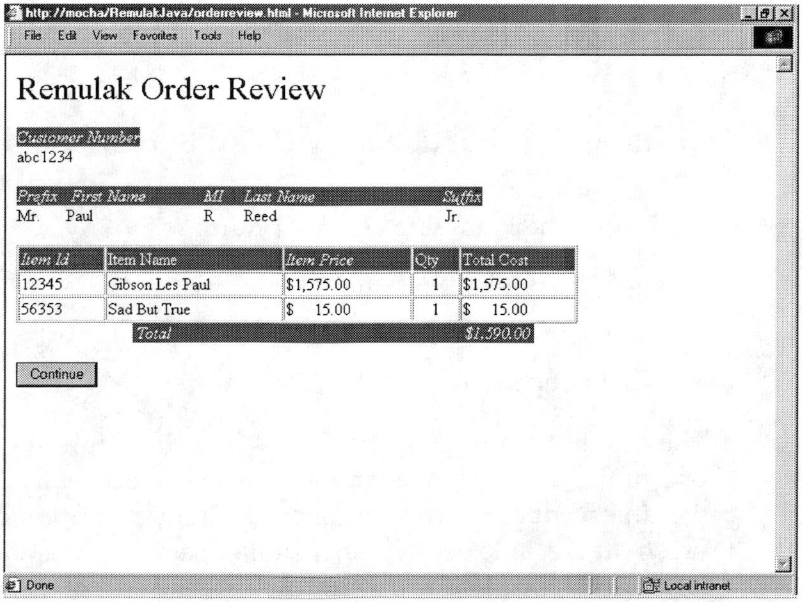

http://mocha/RemulakJava/orderreview.html - Microsoft Internet Explorer

File Edit View Favorites Tools Help

Remulak Order Review

Customer Number
abc1234

Prefix	First Name	MI	Last Name	Suffix
Mr.	Paul	R	Reed	Jr.

Item Id	Item Name	Item Price	Qty	Total Cost
12345	Gibson Les Paul	$1,575.00	1	$1,575.00
56353	Sad But True	$ 15.00	1	$ 15.00
	Total			$1,590.00

Continue

Done Local intranet

FIGURE 6-13 *Order confirmation*

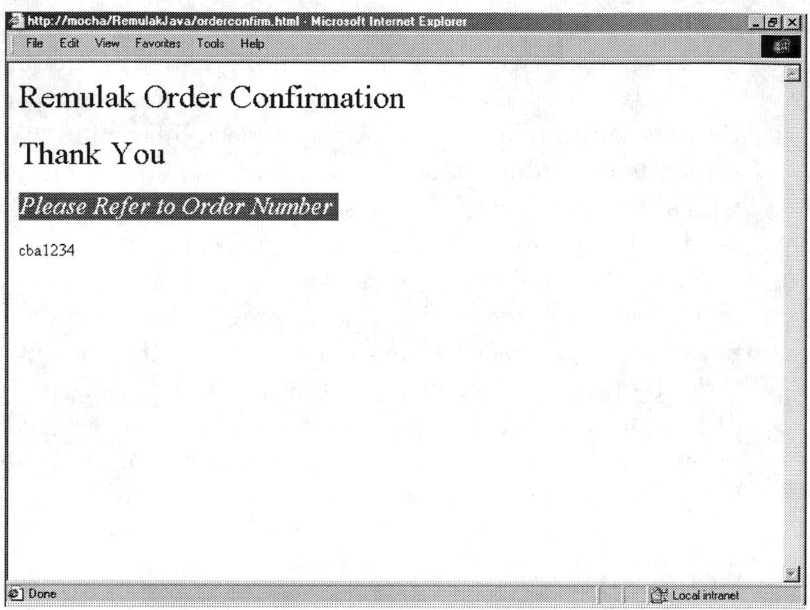

Collecting User Feedback by Using Screen Dialogs

User feedback about the screens benefits the prototype. This feedback should cover the following at a minimum:

- The logical function that is to be performed
- How the function is performed
- What happens as a result of the action

These might sound like the events identified in the earlier scoping efforts of the project; however, they concern the screens themselves. To gather this feedback, we follow a low-technology approach, by creating a screen dialog table below a snapshot of each screen image.

It is a good idea also to capture any special edit notes, as well as any special processing information. Table 6-3 shows such a table for the **Process Order** window, and Figure 6-14 shows the Special Edits/Notes section of the screen dialog for Process Order window.

TABLE 6-3 *Feedback Table for the **Process Order** Form*

Action to Perform	How It Is Done	What Happens
Select a customer for order entry.	Enter customer ID in the **Customer** field and click **New Order**.	Customer name appears along with demographic information. Screen should be positioned in preparation for product selection. Customer's terms are set. Date is defaulted to current system date.
Select a product type for the order.	Select one of three hyperlinks to advance to the appropriate product screen.	Product screen is displayed.
Select the product to purchase.	Press the **Add to Cart** button for the desired product.	Product should be added as an order line item for this order.
Review the current shopping cart contents.	Select **View Cart** in the window.	Screen displaying all current order line items is presented.
Change the quantity of a given item in the shopping cart.	Change the **Qty** field and select **Update Cart**.	Screen should be redisplayed showing the updated **Qty** field and a recalculated price and overall total.
Remove a given item from the shopping cart.	Press the **Remove** button next to the order line item to be removed.	The screen should redisplay showing the item now gone and the overall total adjusted.
Check out the shopping cart.	Select **Proceed to Checkout**.	Order is saved, and the order review screen is displayed.

FIGURE 6-14 *Special Edits/Notes section of screen dialog for **Process Order** window*

Special Edits

- Customer field ID contains a Mod10 check digit that allows an initial verification of correct syntax.

Special Features/Notes

The project team members typically perform the screen dialog exercise. It is approached from the user's perspective. Like the use-cases, the screen dialog focuses on the goals to be satisfied.

Learning from the Prototype

The final step is to review the static prototype with Remulak Productions' project sponsors and user team members. Suggestions for improving the user interface, as well as its functionality, always result from this step. If they don't, then either we are doing a very good job or we are dealing with very timid users.

It is important that we incorporate suggested changes, within reason, into the prototype as quickly as possible. This process is called **protocycling**. We must also separate user interface items from functional scope creep requirements and ensure that they go through some form of change control procedure. Many of the suggested changes are minor screen changes (e.g., to icons or tab ordering) that are easy to change and can be dealt with effectively without change control.

Remulak Productions' user team members have reviewed the screens and completed the screen dialogs, and they like what they see but want a few changes:

- No detailed product information on a given product is readily accessible to the order clerk. Although this feature is not considered a showstopper, users think that it would be nice to have this information in case the customer asks for it. In addition, products have associations with other products (i.e., certain guitars are associated with certain brands of strings and other supplies). Users want to be able to retrieve this information, if needed, from the **Process Order** screen.

  Solution: Provide a hyperlink on the item description to allow a more detailed product review.

- There is no predefined template order for special orders. Remulak Productions often has special offers that are handled by order clerks who take only those types of orders. Because calls go through a telephone response menu first, these special-offer sales can be routed accordingly. The users want predefined template orders that are retrievable and set as the default according to the order clerk and the clerk's immediate log-on session.

Solution: Allow for a template order dialog box and the ability to associate the template with a user session so that subsequent new orders invoke the previously associated template.

The first item is pretty straightforward. The second item might require a little additional work; it might not be a difficult change, but it is a potentially broad one because it expands the functionality to add additional pathways through three use-cases. Those use-cases and their impact on other UML artifacts are listed in Table 6-4.

The result of the change control process confirms that we should go ahead with the necessary changes in scope and functionality.

TABLE 6-4 *Impact Analysis and Report to Change Control Management*

Use-Case	Change to Be Made
Process Orders	Allow for the creation of template orders. Instead of accomplishing this with a separate `ModelOrder` class, do so with an attribute within the existing `Order` entity class. A more elegant solution is to employ some type of "factory" pattern that allows for the creation of template order objects, but that solution would be a bit of overkill for this change. Never associate template orders with a `Customer` object. This changes the multiplicity of the association between `Customer` and `Order`. An `Order` may now be associated with 0..1 `Customer` objects. Make entry of a template `Order` transparent, with only a confirmation at saving to verify that the user intends to create a template order. Provide user interface input of a template order and associate this with the duration of a user's log-on session. This template order will be invoked from the **Process Order** window and its context automatically carried forward from order to order for the duration of the user's log-on session. The source of the template/user association will be implemented within the security subsystem with the addition of a `Session` object (long term).
Maintain Orders	Allow for the ability to change an order that is in the template status and any associated business rules that might be violated for in-process orders.
Security	Add a `Session` class. This use-case is not scheduled until Increment 3 of the project. However, to support the session continuation feature for template orders, a `Session` class will be added in Increment 1. This class will be void of any authorization knowledge, as is envisioned for Increment 3.

This exhaustive example is included because it reflects real life. The changes discussed here represent the types of changes we expect to encounter, and we need to show how the impact analysis might be performed and provide traceability to the UML artifacts that require change.

As an aside, Figures 6-15, 6-16, and 6-17 are screenshots of the *Maintain Relationships* prototype.

The beauty of a process model such as the Unified Process, which supports iterative and incremental development, with UML as the artifact trail, is that all of the pieces hang together. The crucial point is that everything is tied back to the use-cases. If something isn't in the use-case, then it won't be in the final deliverable. Changes to use-cases should always go through change control.

We can learn a lot from the user interface prototype. The screen structure chart outlines logical flow (at a high level). The prototype itself gives the unique look-and-feel perspective of the application. And the screen dialog enables the user to offer feedback regarding logical actions, how to perform them, and the results they are expected to produce.

FIGURE 6-15 *Remulak relationship portal*

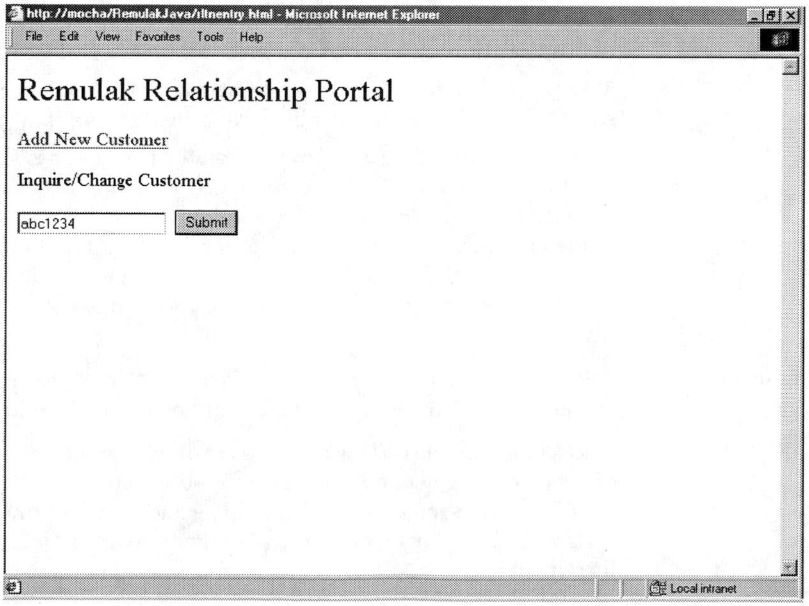

FIGURE 6-16 *Relationship inquiry*

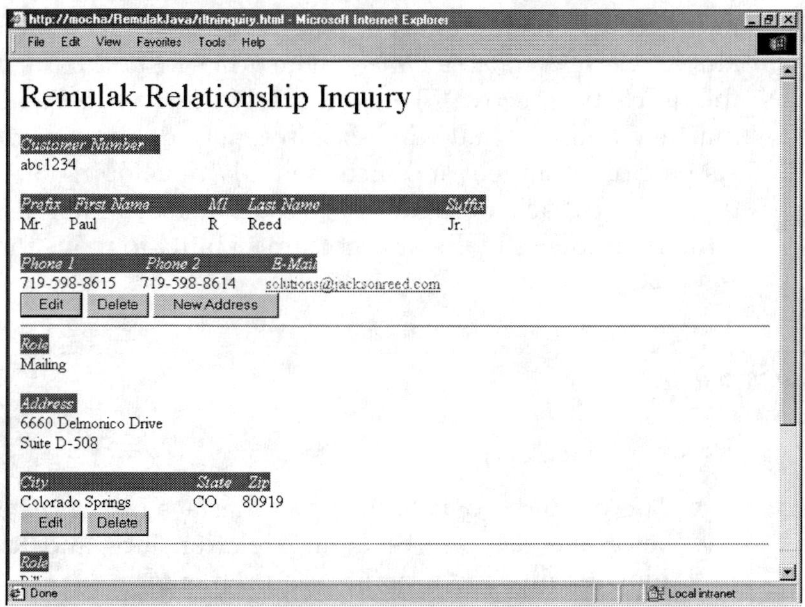

FIGURE 6-17 *Relationship maintenance*

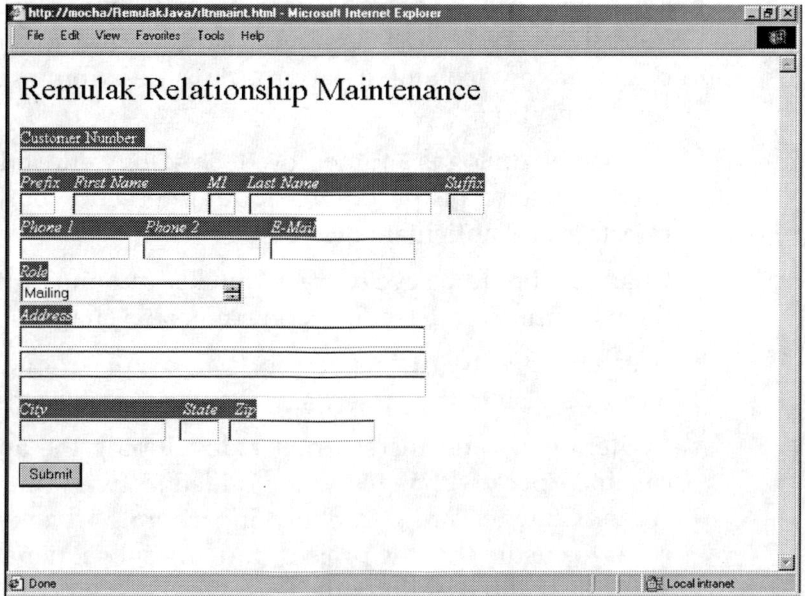

Next let's relate things to the UML deliverables produced thus far. The interaction begins with the actor's interface with the use-case in the form of an initial event that the actor wants to perform—for example, *Customer Places Order*—which is satisfied by a use-case (from the user's perspective). This ultimately must be realized in a human/machine interface that will assist in satisfying the goal of the use-case. As part of iteratively and incrementally developing applications, this type of feedback mechanism strengthens the final deliverable and builds confidence in the project team's ability to move forward.

Checkpoint

Where We've Been

- The primary goals of the user interface prototype are to confirm actor and use-case boundary relationships and to explore both functionality and usability requirements.
- Creating a user interface artifacts section for the use-cases enables better definition of the detail about the interaction required between actors and use-cases.
- Too often, project teams waste precious time creating a visual deliverable as the first step in the prototype. The screen structure chart is a low-technology approach to describing screen flow for the application.
- The screen dialog is another low-technology effort. It captures the user's perceived expectations about interaction between the user interface and anticipated results.
- Changes should be cycled back quickly into the prototype to give the user immediate feedback on suggested changes.
- Any changes to the use-cases that result from the prototype require a visit to the project's change control procedures.
- By iteratively and incrementally developing the application, we can incorporate changes while still effectively managing scope creep. Changes are iteratively incorporated back into the use-cases to ensure that the project, and any subsequent changes to its scope, leave traceability intact.

Where We're Going Next

In the next chapter we:

- Begin to explore the project's dynamic aspects.
- Synthesize the use-case pathway details into the two UML interaction diagrams: sequence and collaboration.
- Review the state diagram and its usefulness in exploring classes that exhibit interesting dynamic behavior, and explore the types of classes that might warrant the use of a state diagram to further our knowledge base.
- Discuss the activity diagram and how we might use it both for complex operations and to give a detailed description of the activities within use-cases.
- Create usage matrices to explore distributed loading characteristics of the Remulak Productions project.
- Conduct dynamic modeling and use what is learned from this exercise to enhance the class diagram.

CHAPTER 7

Dynamic Elements of the Application

IN THIS CHAPTER

In this chapter we become more specific regarding how the project will realize its ultimate goal: constructing an order entry application for Remulak Productions. For the project to accomplish this goal, we need to add to its dynamic aspects. More specifically, we must add a dynamic model view of the project that depicts the collaboration of objects, with the sole goal of satisfying the pathways through the use-cases. We already explored some of the dynamic aspects when we captured the detailed pathway task steps in Chapters 4 and 5.

GOALS

- To explore the mission of dynamic modeling and the perspective it brings to the project.
- To review the components of the sequence diagram and how to create them effectively from the use-case templates.
- To create sequence diagrams for Remulak Productions' happy pathways and alternate pathways.
- To discover how knowledge learned from the creation of sequence diagrams is transferred to the class diagram.

- To review the components of the collaboration, state, and activity diagrams.
- To learn when to use a specific type of diagram.
- To explore the need for usage matrices and the perspective that they provide that isn't directly conveyed in any of the base UML diagrams.

Next Steps of the Elaboration Phase

Before we explore the dynamic aspects of the project, let's revisit the Unified Process model. Figure 7-1 shows the model, with the Elaboration phase of the project highlighted.

FIGURE 7-1 *Unified Process model: Elaboration phase*

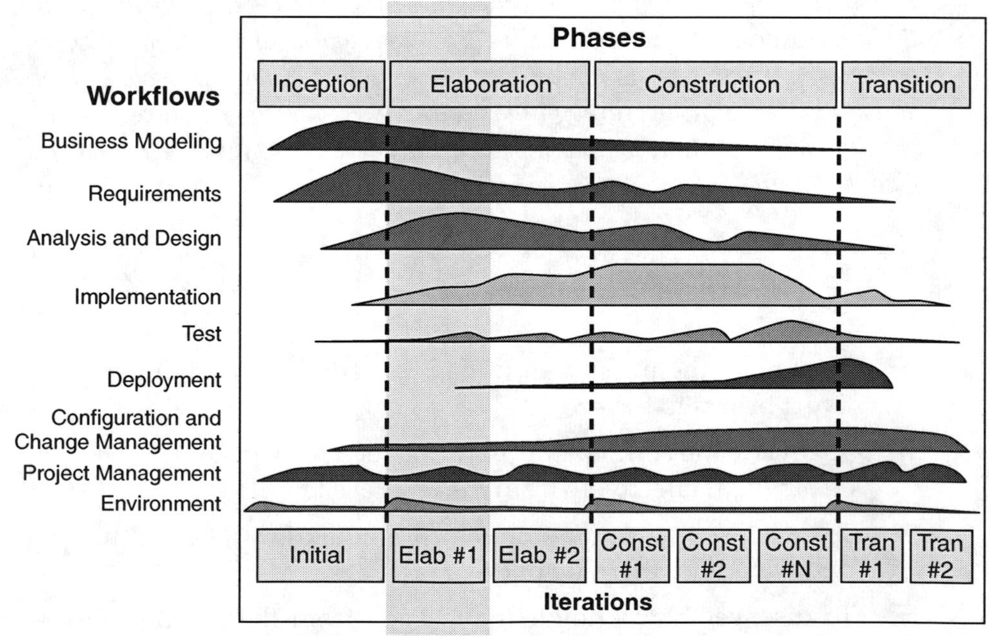

In this chapter the following Unified Process workflows and activity sets are emphasized:

- Requirements: Analyze the Problem
- Analysis and Design: Analyze Behavior
- Analysis and Design: Design Components
- Test: Design Test

Dynamic Modeling

The dynamic models focus on the interactions between objects—instances of the classes identified in prior chapters that work together to implement the detailed pathways through the use-cases. Dynamic models add considerable value to the project, as follows: For the first time we

- Bring together the classes and use-case pathways and demonstrate the ability to model the messaging necessary to implement them
- Transfer knowledge learned from the dynamic model to the class diagrams in the form of operations, attributes, and associations
- Incorporate knowledge learned from the use-case and class diagrams to model the volumetric and loading characteristics of the application through the creation of usage matrices

In our earlier work on the project, we explored the dynamic aspects of the Remulak Productions application. Many of the artifacts already captured add to the dynamic knowledge required to make the Remulak system a reality—for example, the following:

- The events identified during project scoping provide a clear picture of the external and internal stimuli to which the system must be prepared to respond.
- The pathways identified in the use-case templates are dynamic in that they explain the logical steps necessary to satisfy the goal of the use-case.
- The business rules capture the parameters and semantics that certain elements of the application must implement.

The dynamic models reviewed in this chapter provide a more formal approach to what has already been captured in various parts of the project's evolution. Chiefly, they reinforce the object-oriented concepts and principles to be used in the project.

Types of Dynamic Models

UML offers four dynamic models in the form of diagrams that offer different views of the dynamic perspectives of the application. Each diagram's view provides a unique focus and can be used in different instances depending on an application's needs.

- **Sequence diagram:** Often called one of the *interaction diagrams* (the other being the collaboration diagram), the sequence diagram, in my experience, is the most often used dynamic model. Applications will always produce sequence diagrams. A sequence diagram is time centered. Its focus is the linear flow of messages between objects. Time flows from the start of the diagram sequentially downward (see, for example, Figure 7-3).
- **Collaboration diagram:** Also often called one of the *interaction diagrams,* the collaboration diagram conveys the same meaning as the sequence diagram, except that it focuses on the individual objects and the messages that they send and receive. Collaboration diagrams are instance centered. Some of the visual modeling tools available (e.g., Rational Rose) will generate collaboration diagrams from sequence diagrams. If a particular design aspect of your application is multithreaded, collaboration diagrams do better than sequence diagrams at representing the application.

Note: The two interaction diagrams are the key link between the use-case pathways and the code that will be constructed to implement the pathways.

State diagram: A state diagram models the lifecycle of one class. More specifically, it models the various states in which an object can exist and the events and associated actions and activities that are performed when an object makes the transition to a new state or while it is in a particular state. State diagrams add value only when the class exhibits interesting and complex dynamic behavior. Many classes in the application (e.g., `Customer` and `Address`) are, well, uninteresting concerning state; others (e.g., `Order`) can be quite interesting, divulging additional requirements knowledge about the application. Most applications will have a low ratio of state diagrams to classes. Applications of a more real-time embedded nature (e.g., machine control, automotive, and telecommunications) typically have a higher ratio of state diagrams to classes.

- **Activity diagram:** An activity diagram models the steps in a complex operation. It can also be used to model the steps of a use-case pathway. Activity diagrams are as close to traditional flowcharts as one can get.

Figure 7-2 provides a view of the application artifacts as they change focus toward the dynamic elements of the project; the sequence diagram is shown here. The roots of this sequence diagram can be traced to both the use-case pathways and the class diagram.

The outlined steps or tasks necessary to implement a pathway through a use-case eventually must be transformed into messages between objects. The dynamic models, particularly the sequence and

FIGURE 7-2 *Artifact flow to yield the sequence diagram*

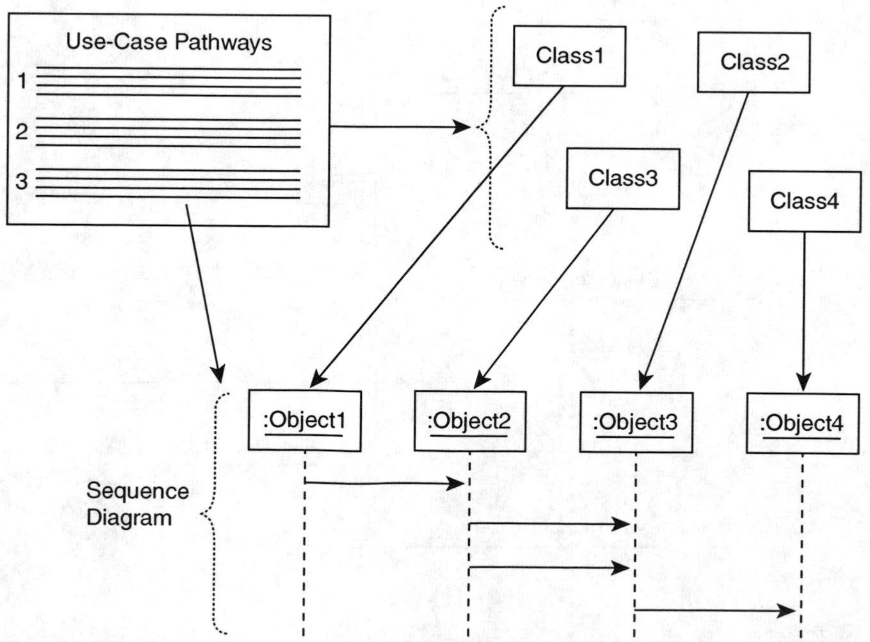

collaboration diagrams, always view the live instances of the classes—that is, the objects. The objects are doing the interacting in the dynamic models (*Micaela Reed Places an Order*). The classes define the rules regarding how each of their instances will change state. The following sections discuss the four diagrams in detail.

The Sequence Diagram

The sequence diagram is the most used of the dynamic models. It has a long and rich history tracing back to, among others, James Rumbaugh's OMT (Object Modeling Technique) methodology. The diagram begins with instances of classes—objects—organized in "swim lanes" across the top. Below each object is a "lifeline," as Figure 7-3 shows.

FIGURE 7-3 *Enterprise-level use of the sequence diagram*

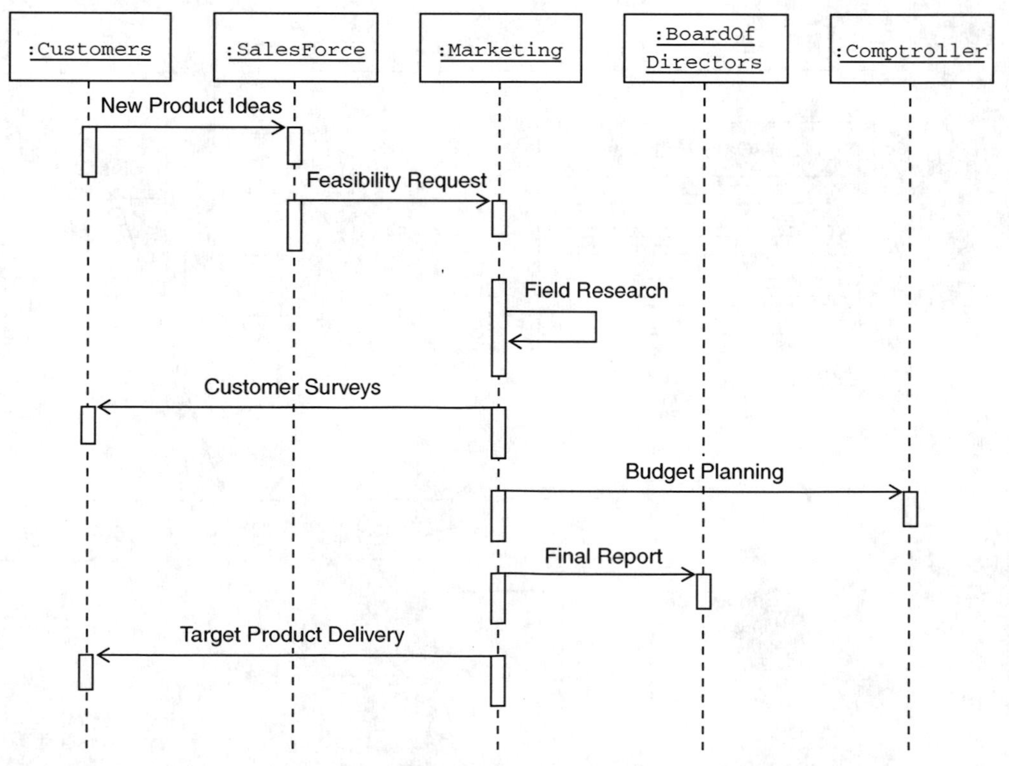

Objects are drawn as boxes, with the class name preceded by a colon and then the entire name underlined. This notation can be verbalized as, for example, "any old `Customer` object." If a specifically named object is desired, then the colon is preceded with the name of the object—for example, `Rene Becnel:Customer`, which, verbalized, means "the `Rene Becnel` object of class `Customer`." Figure 7-3 shows an example of objects interacting in a sequence diagram.

The sequence diagram often uses the **focus-of-control rectangle**. It appears as a rectangular box imposed on top of the swim lane. This optional adornment indicates that this object is orchestrating the messaging activity and has control of that particular messaging sequence. Indicating this control on the diagram, especially in multithreaded applications, can be helpful.

In this book we use the sequence diagram for a very specific purpose in the project's Elaboration phase. However, it may also be used for enterprise-level modeling—for example, in business process reengineering efforts or even during a project's scoping phase. Figure 7-3 is an example of a sequence diagram depicting the overall enterprise-level interactions of departments within Remulak Productions. Note that this is a much higher-level use of the sequence diagram than we require here and doesn't specifically model a concrete use-case pathway, at least not to the level at which we have defined our use-cases.

Additional adornments can be added to the sequence diagram, the most important of which are the following:

- **Script:** Script comments are aligned to the left of each message flow. Often a script gives a detailed description of a task taken directly from the pathway detail of the use-case.
- **Latency and timing:** Latency and timing allow us to designate time constraints on message send-and-receive semantics.
- **Guard condition:** The guard condition is a means to show condition checking. It allows us to introduce branching considerations.
- **Iteration:** Iteration allows us to note repetitive message sequences until a given guard condition is met.
- **Synchronization semantics:** Synchronization semantics allows us to identify messages that are nonblocking and that follow the "fire-and-forget" paradigm (asynchronous message—probably the most used). Other messages that fall into this category are classified as simple (the default), synchronous, timeout, and balking.

Sequence Diagram of the Happy Path

We begin our modeling by creating a sequence diagram of the use-case happy path. Recall that the happy path is the most commonly occurring pathway through the use-case (for the *Process Orders* use-case, the happy path is *Customer calls and orders a guitar and supplies, and pays with a credit card*). If this pathway is modeled first, the other sequence diagrams should simply be variations of the happy pathway's diagram. In this way we reduce the amount of work required, while adding the most artifacts (e.g., operations, attributes) to the class diagram in the shortest amount of time.

The class diagram benefits a lot from the dynamic modeling process because every message sent to an object results in an operation's being assigned to the target class. Figure 7-4 is the use-case diagram we de-

FIGURE 7-4 *Remulak use-case diagram*

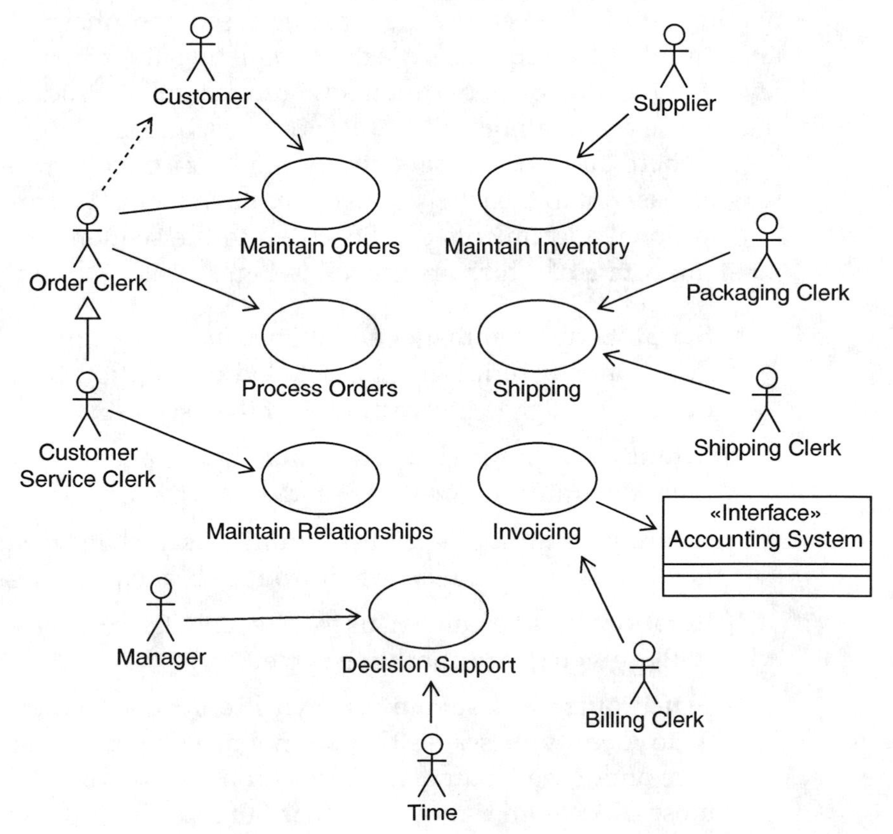

FIGURE 7-5 *Increment 1 package diagram*

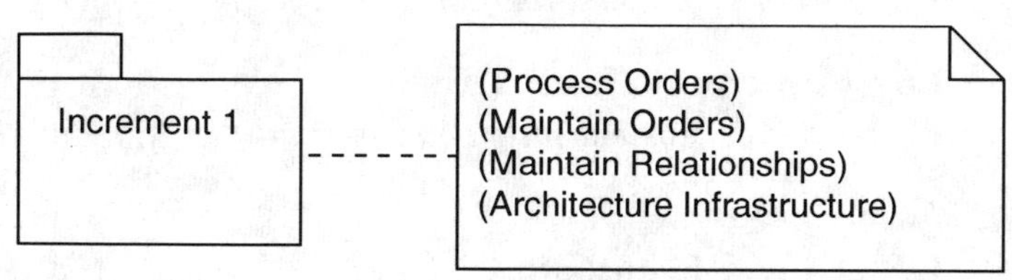

fined during project scoping in Chapter 4. In particular, we deal in this chapter with dynamic models for the use-cases that are part of Increment 1 of Remulak Productions' deliverable, as specified in the figure.

Recall from Figure 4-4 the *Architecture Infrastructure* shadow technical use-case. The first increment outlined with the package diagram is shown in Figure 7-5. This shadow use-case is not shown on the business view of the Remulak use-case diagram in Figure 7-4 because the use-case focuses on the infrastructure needed for communication to occur among the user interface, the Business Rule Services layer, and the Database Services layer of the application.

What follows is the completed use-case template (without pathway detail) for the *Process Orders* use-case. This is the same template that was introduced in Chapter 4.

Use-Case Template

1. Use-Case Description Information

1.1 Name

Process Orders.

1.2 Goal

This use-case satisfies all of the goals of setting up a new order. This applies for both new and existing customers. All aspects of the order entry process are covered, from initial entry to ultimate pricing.

1.3 Use-Case Team Leader/Members

Rene Becnel (team lead), Stan Young, Todd Klock, Jose Aponte.

1.4 Precondition

Order clerk has logged onto the system.

1.5 Postcondition

Order is placed, inventory is reduced.

1.6 Constraints/Issues/Risks

The new system might not be ready in time for the summer product promotions.

1.7 Trigger Event(s)

All events dealing with new and existing customers calling and placing an order.

1.8 Primary Actor

Order clerk.

1.9 Secondary Actor(s)

Customer.

2. Use-Case Pathway Names

2.1 Primary Pathway (Happy Path)

Customer calls and orders a guitar and supplies, and pays with a credit card.

2.2 Alternate Pathway(s)

- *Customer calls and orders a guitar and supplies, and uses a purchase order.*
- *Customer calls and orders a guitar and supplies, and uses the Remulak easy finance plan.*
- *Customer calls and orders an organ, and pays with a credit card.*
- *Customer calls and orders an organ, and pays with a purchase order.*

2.3 Exception Pathway(s)

- *Customer calls to place an order using a credit card, and the card is invalid.*
- *Customer calls with a purchase order but has not been approved to use the purchase order method.*
- *Customer calls to place an order, and the items desired are not in stock.*

3. Use-Case Detail

A Section 3 will exist for all use-case pathways that are detailed enough to warrant their own unique set of steps. In this case only the happy path and the payment variation are shown.

3.1 Pathway Name

Customer calls and orders a guitar and supplies, and pays with a credit card.

3.2 Trigger Event(s)

All events dealing with new and existing customers calling and placing an order.

3.3 Main Sequence of Steps

Step	Description
1	Customer supplies customer number.
2	Customer is acknowledged as current.
3	For each product that the customer desires:
3.1	- Product ID or description is requested.
3.2	- Product description is resolved with ID if necessary.
3.3	- Quantity is requested.
3.4	- Item price is calculated.
4	Extended order total is calculated.
5	Tax is applied.
6	Shipping charges are applied.
7	Extended price is quoted to customer.
8	Customer supplies credit card number.
9	Customer's credit card is validated.
10	Inventory is reduced.
11	Sale is finalized.

3.4 Variations

Step	Description
8.1	Customer may pay with purchase order or easy finance plan.

3.5 Extensions (optional)

None.

3.6 Business Rules (optional)

- *Customers may not order more than ten products at one time.*
- *Any sale over $50,000 requires supervisor approval.*
- *Any sale over $20,000 receives a five-percent discount.*

3.7 Constraints/Issues/Risks (optional)

Timeliness of the product is key to the next sales promotion.

4. Use-Case Tactical Information

4.1 Priority

Highest (#1).

4.2 Performance Target(s)

None indicated.

4.3 Frequency

- *Customer calls and orders a guitar and supplies, and pays with a credit card (800/day).*
- *Customer calls and orders a guitar and supplies, and uses a purchase order (120/day).*
- *Customer calls and orders a guitar and supplies, and uses the Remulak easy finance plan (25/day).*
- *Customer calls and orders an organ, and pays with a credit card (40/day).*
- *Customer calls and orders an organ, and pays with a purchase order (15/day).*

4.4 User Interface

This portion of the application will not use the Web as a form of entry because of the need for clerk assistance.

4.5 Location of Source

- *Newport Hills, Washington.*
- *Portland, Maine (in the future).*

We must determine the classes needed to build the first draft of the sequence diagram. We choose from the class diagram in Figure 7-6.

The following objects are selected:

- `Customer`
- `Invoice`
- `Order`
- `OrderLine`
- `Payment`
- `Product`

FIGURE 7-6 *Remulak class diagram: First draft*

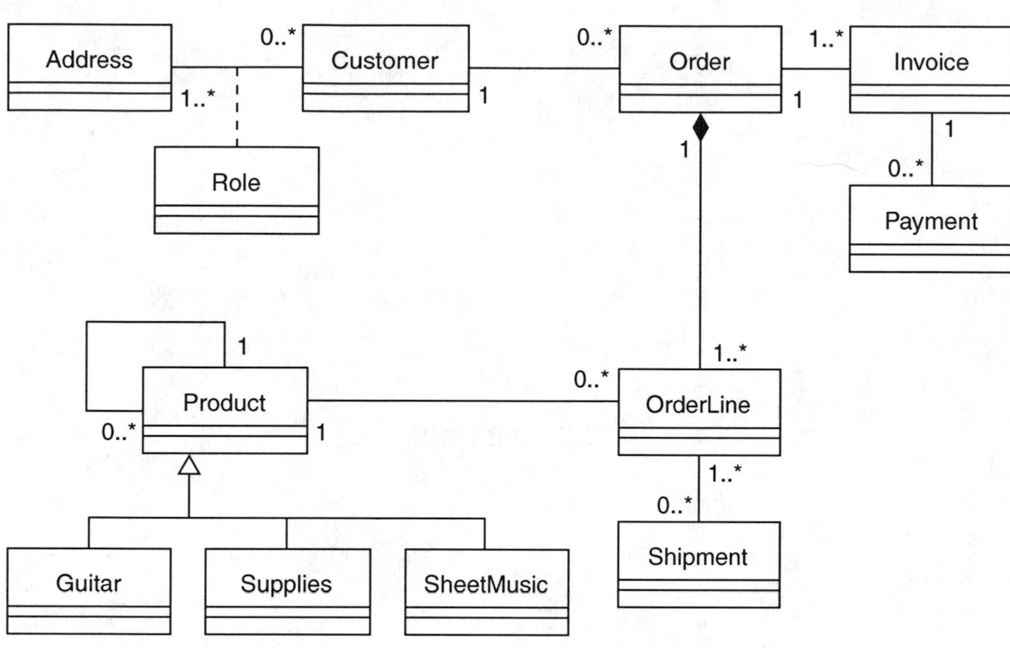

Figure 7-7 shows a first attempt at the sequence diagram for Remulak Productions and the happy path of the *Process Orders* use-case. In this view of the sequence diagram, sequence numbers are included to allow easier reference to specific messages. However, sequence numbers on a sequence diagram are optional because time flows from top to bottom in such diagrams.

The sequence diagram forces us to ask some serious questions about the other UML artifacts, especially the classes and associations between classes. A message cannot be sent between two objects unless an association is defined between the classes that represent the objects. If a use-case pathway requires communication between two objects whose classes have no such association, the class diagram is incorrect. In addition, early iterations of a sequence diagram might require that additional classes be created to satisfy the requirements specified in the pathways. These new classes may be any of the three types discussed in Chapter 5: entity, boundary, and control.

FIGURE 7-7 *Remulak sequence diagram: First attempt*

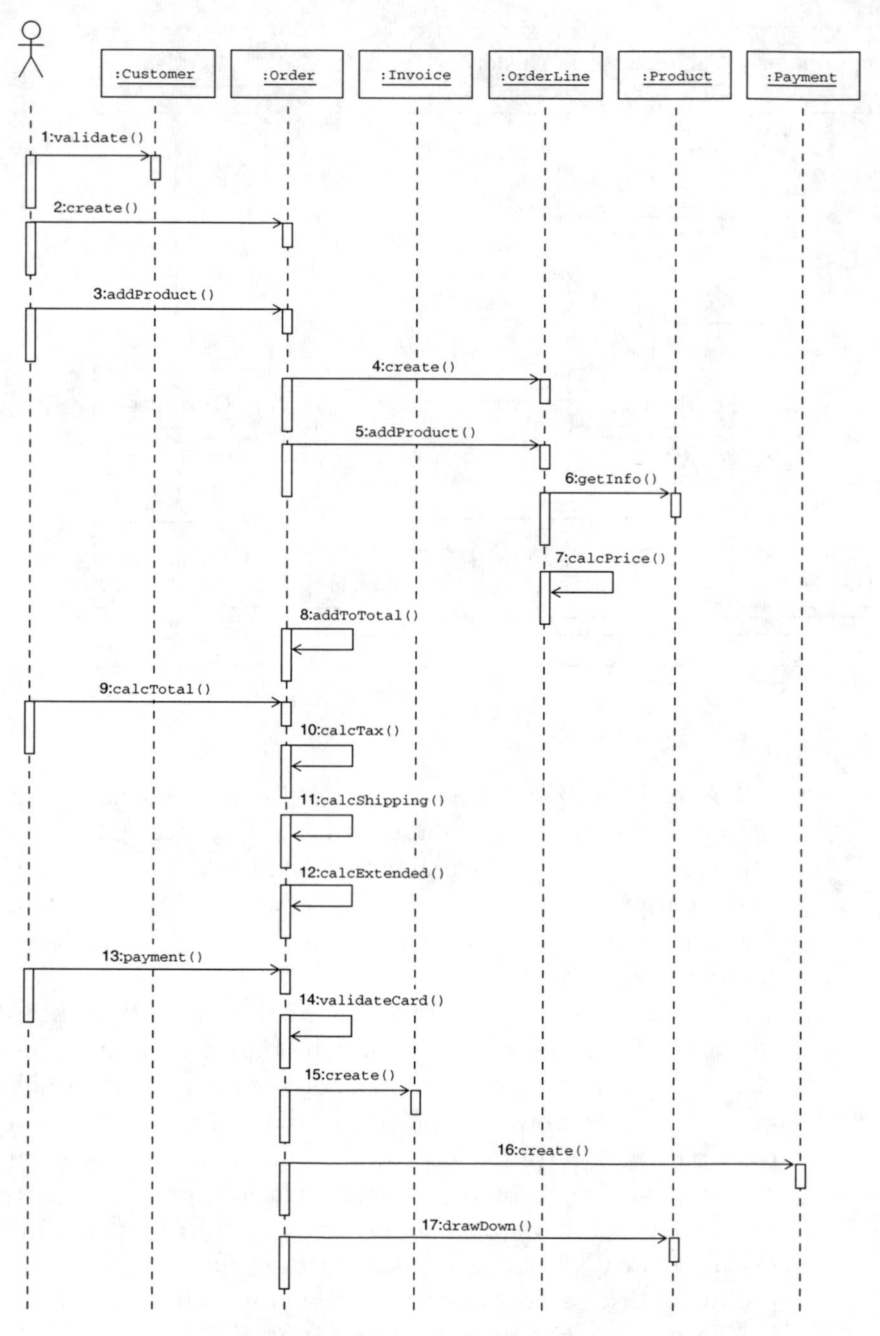

The sequence diagram also forces us to focus on good object-oriented design concepts. As messaging patterns begin to emerge, we will need to address some sound object-oriented design practices. One of these is the notion that classes in the solution set should be loosely coupled and highly cohesive.

Class Coupling and Cohesion

Classes are considered loosely coupled if generally the associations between them are minimal. This doesn't mean that we should skimp on associations. If an association is needed, then by all means we should add it to the model. However, if a new class, usually a control or boundary class, can be introduced to funnel messages, and thus reduce the overall number of associations, then going this route will make the design more resilient in the long run.

The reason is that every class association has eventual code ramifications in the form of references to other classes; these references are needed to allow messages to pass between the classes. Imagine the impact of a change to the domain and the resulting possible rippling to all of the associations. The amount of code that must be changed might be minimal, but if that code is in the interface, enormous amounts of regression testing might be necessary.

A good place to reduce class coupling is aggregation/composition associations. By nature these associations insulate their components from future changes. As an example, consider in the case of Remulak Productions the composition association between `Order` and `OrderLine`. `Order` is the "boss"; all messages should flow through the boss if at all possible. Nothing prevents our adding several associations to all of `Order`'s components. However, if the structure of an `Order` later changes, the impact of the change could be substantial.

In the sequence diagram in Figure 7-7, notice that any messages dealing with a component of `Order` are initially sent to the `Order` object. Message 4 (`create()`) could have originated from the order clerk actor, but it actually originates from `Order`. The same is true for message 5 (`addProduct()`). Although `Order` will have several "pass-through" shell operations that delegate work to its component parts, the solution is much more flexible.

You can also place classes that reduce coupling in the interfaces between packages (this will be required for Remulak Productions' security, audit, and archiving subsystems). These packages also happen to be use-cases. Recall from Chapter 5 that a control class was created for every use-case in Increment 1.

A class is considered highly cohesive if it adheres to the adage that "a class should do only one thing and do it well." Consider a class that does too many things. In our case, what if `Order` directly handled all of the responsibilities of its composite? Instead of two classes, we'd have just one. But `Order` would have taken on responsibilities that far exceed its original charter. The same issues that surfaced regarding coupling also show up with classes that are not highly cohesive. The design is improved by having each of the two classes continue to do one thing well. We can make this possible only by defining them as separate classes.

We learn as we go. In the case of Remulak Productions, some of the messaging didn't work, thereby requiring some changes. The issue here concerns tax calculation and shipping charges. The sequence diagram shows messages 10 and 11 (`calcTax()` and `calcShipping()`) being sent, privately, to the `Order` class. However, this raises the question about where to maintain the specific tax and shipping information. `Order` isn't a good solution. So we need to create a new class that manages not only the rates to charge but also the necessary algorithms for calculating the extended charges. For now, let's call this new class `Charge`. After further design of the class, we might find that `Charge` is an ancestor class to more specialized classes in the form of `Shipping` and `Tax`.

We also need to modify message 14 (`validateCard()`). The `Order` class isn't very smart regarding credit card validation—and it shouldn't be (remember: do one thing and one thing well). Thus the `Order` object should not receive the `validateCard()` message. Recall from Chapter 5 that we identified the boundary class `CreditCardInterface`. This is the object that should receive the `validateCard()` message.

One last observation about the sequence diagram: It does not reflect the iterative nature of buying multiple products. At present, the diagram applies to just one product. To make it more flexible, we add the ability to note iteration, simply by adding a note and then referencing the exact sequences that can repeat (see Figure 7-8).

FIGURE 7-8 *Remulak sequence diagram with iteration*

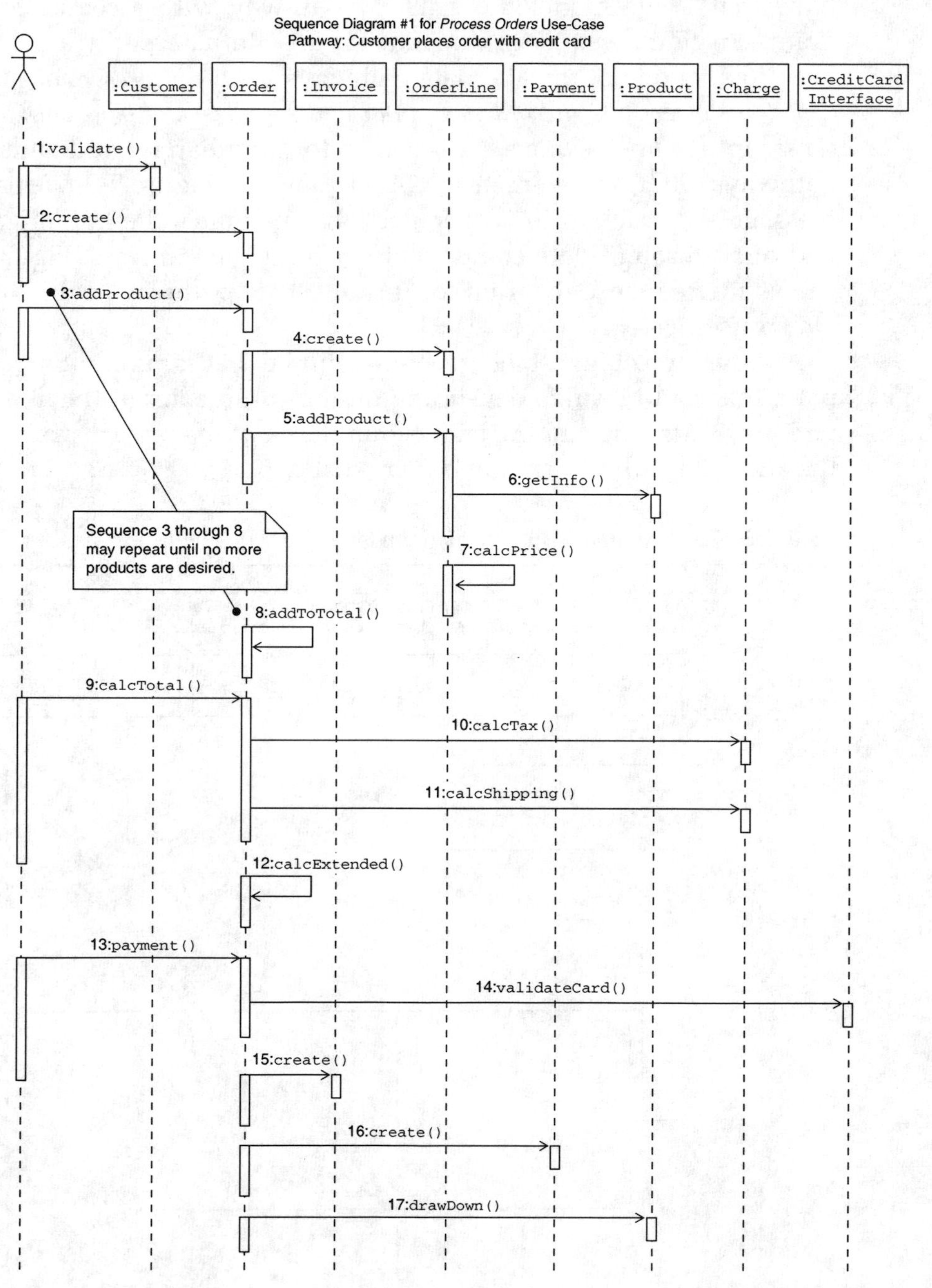

Sequence Diagram for an Alternate Pathway

Now that we've modeled the happy pathway with a sequence diagram, creating a sequence diagram for an alternate pathway is easy. Let's look at one of the alternate pathways for the *Process Orders* use-case (*Customer calls and orders a guitar and supplies, and pays with a purchase order*). The sequence diagrams for the happy and alternate pathways differ only in message 14, as shown in Figure 7-9. We need a message sent back to the order clerk that validates the authorization and good-through-date components of the `Payment` class. Figure 7-9 shows the sequence diagram for this alternate pathway of the *Process Orders* use-case.

Although our biggest job generally will be diagramming the happy path, this could change depending on the complexity of the alternate pathways. Also, depending on the granularity of the project's use-cases, the alternate pathways might be very distinct.

FIGURE 7-9 *Remulak sequence diagram for an alternate pathway*

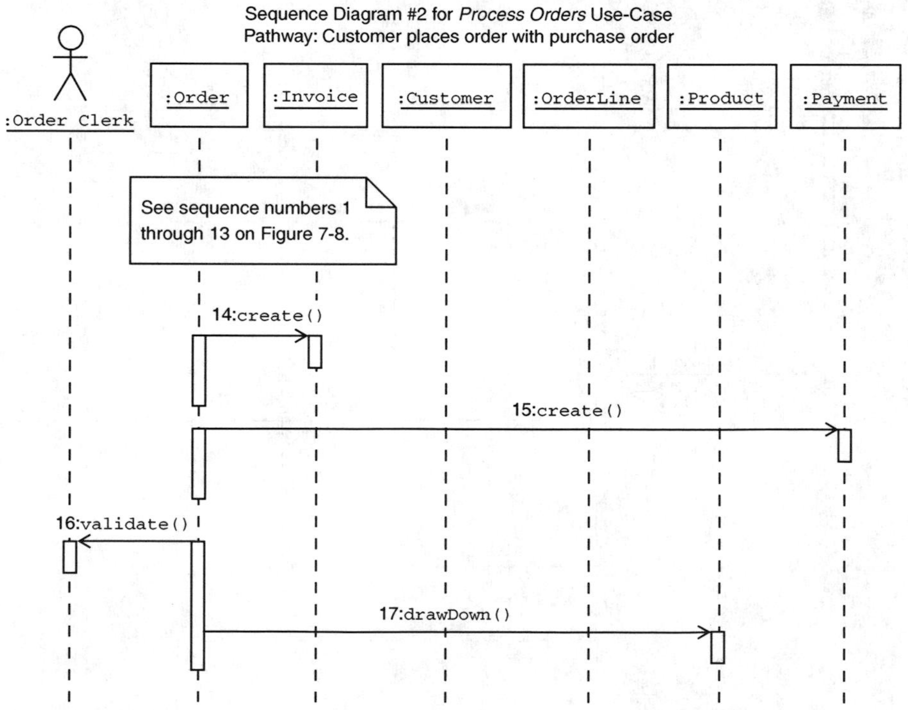

Transferring Knowledge to the Class Diagram

The power and benefits that result from using a visual modeling tool really become evident during the creation of sequence diagrams. Leading modeling products allow operations to be added dynamically to the classes represented by the objects on the diagram. This is fine, but the impact of this dynamic addition of operations enforces two key elements of good project management and software design:

1. As operations are added to the classes, subsequent messages to the same class instance will display the newly added operations, thereby allowing them to be selected from the list. This feature forces us to focus on reusing existing operations instead of working in a vacuum and duplicating work.
2. Most class operations will be defined just by diagramming of the happy pathway for each use-case. The speed with which we diagram can increase a lot as the first few sequence diagrams take shape.

Figure 7-10 shows the use of Rational Rose to add or select operations during the sequence diagramming process. We can add a new operation by clicking the **<new operation>** option, which opens the operation creation dialog box. Also under the **<new operation>** option is a list of operations already present in the `Order` class from which we can select.

Notice, too, the diagram's tree view pane in the upper left-hand corner of the window. The *Process Orders* use-case shows in the tree view; beneath it is a list of the associated sequence diagrams. The organization of the tree reinforces the steps taken in the Unified Process. What start out as events become pathways through a use-case. Those pathways eventually are rendered as sequence diagrams that show the dynamic interaction of objects necessary to realize the goal of the use-case.

Walking through the Sequence Diagram

We still need to create a sequence diagram that shows how the user interface will communicate with the essential use-case pathway of placing an order. We turn our attention now to using the sequence diagram to walk through the application to ensure its integrity. The sequence diagram is the primary vehicle for walk-throughs. Code walk-throughs become less of an issue when UML is used.

FIGURE 7-10 *Rational Rose visual modeling tool*

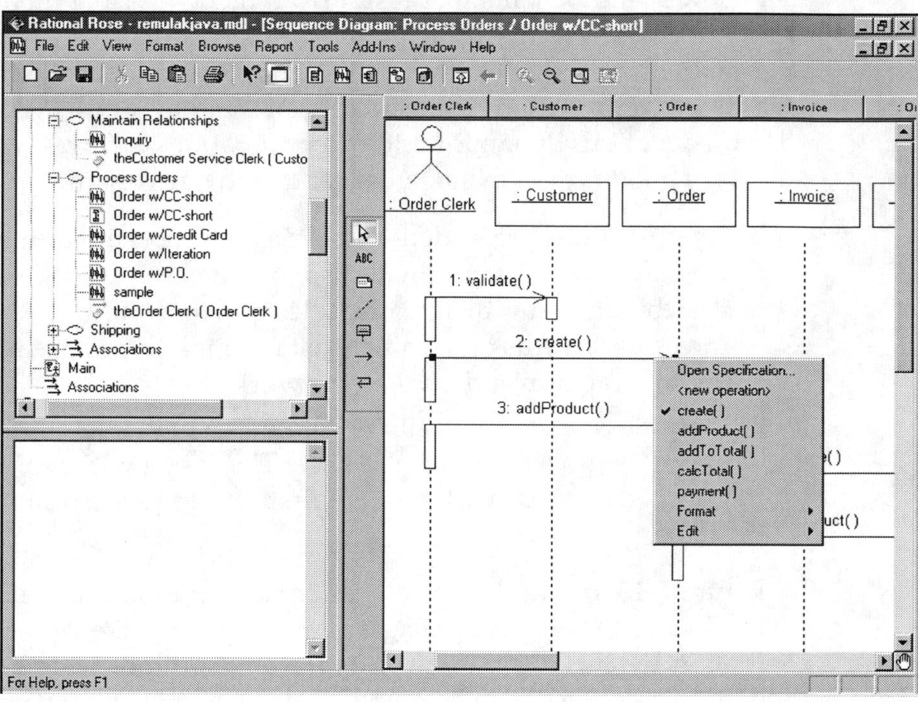

Although sound coding standards are still necessary (How will variables be defined? How are classes defined?), the integrity of the system is depicted through the perspective of the sequence diagram. Once the project team gets used to the idea, the creation of the sequence diagram will become an invaluable task on the project plan.

The Collaboration Diagram

The collaboration diagram is the direct cousin of the sequence diagram. The two differ only in their perspectives. The collaboration diagram has an "on top looking down" view of the interaction. It focuses more on the actual objects and their roles in the interaction than on the linear flow of time expressed in the sequence diagram. Figure 7-11 shows a collaboration diagram for the happy path of *Process Orders*.

FIGURE 7-11 *Collaboration diagram for the* Process Orders *happy path*

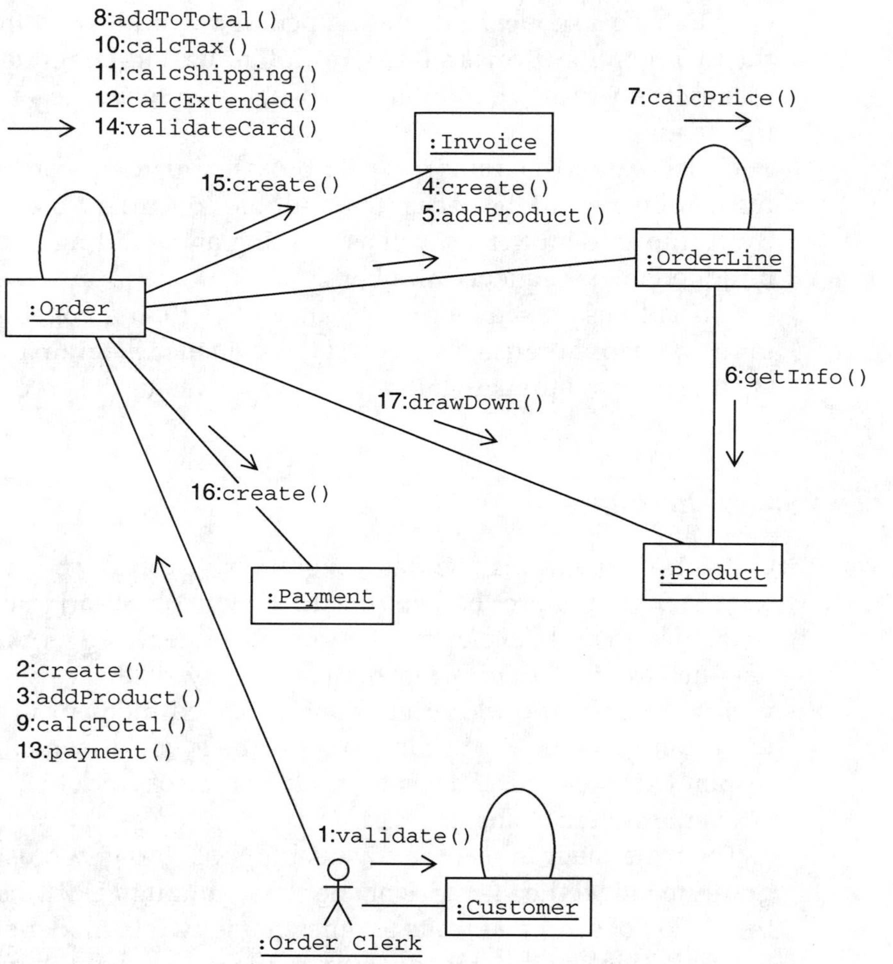

Here's where sequence numbers become important. Whereas the sequence diagram works fine without them, the collaboration diagram is useless without them because the order of the messages is lost. The collaboration diagram offers a perspective of just how busy certain objects can be: sending messages, receiving messages, or both. An object's being busy may mean that its lifecycle is interesting, and thus the project might benefit from a state diagram of that object. State diagrams are discussed in the next section.

Some visual modeling tools will create a collaboration diagram directly from a sequence diagram. When using Rational Rose, you need only to have a sequence diagram open in a window and then click on the menu option **Browse | Go To Collaboration Diagram**. Rose also makes it easy to toggle back and forth between sequence and collaboration diagrams.

Collaboration diagrams make it a bit easier to model complex branching conditions and the concept of multiple concurrent threads of activity. A thread identifier, as well as merging and splitting of control, can be added to the sequence number.

I usually use a sequence diagram rather than a collaboration diagram, perhaps because I have used the sequence diagram much longer. Also, however, I think that it's clearer to the casual observer.

The State Diagram

Of the UML diagrams, the state diagram has probably been around the longest. Its initial uses had nothing to do with object-oriented concepts. In the design and development of complex integrated circuits, a model was needed that minimized the complexity of the various states in which the system could exist at any specified moment in time. More importantly, the model needed to show the events to which the system responded when in a given state, and the type of work to be performed when the system changed states.

The state diagram can be a valuable tool. Today we use state diagrams to model the lifecycles of one class (although UML also supports the notion of sending events to other classes while modeling a class as to state). Think of the state diagram as the model that follows an object from birth to death (its final conclusion). As mentioned previously, many classes are uninteresting concerning state.

For example, most of Remulak Productions' classes are rather mundane regarding their various states. Consider `Customer`. What states could it be in? Maybe prospective, active, and inactive? Could we learn very much about the domain of `Customer` by modeling it in a state diagram and observing the work that the system needs to carry out as an object makes the transition from state to state? Probably not.

The `Order` class is a little different. An `Order` object will go through many different states in its lifetime and will be influenced by many different events in the system. In addition, quite a bit of work needs to be done as an `Order` arrives at a given state, stays in a given state, and finally moves on to another state. In this section, we create a state diagram for the `Order` class, modeled for Remulak Productions.

In its simplest form, a state diagram consists of a set of states connected by transition lines (the subtleties of nested states and concurrent models are outside the scope of this book). On each transition line are captured (usually) events that stimulate an object to move from one state to another. In addition, work also occurs during a transition (when the object enters or exits a state) and while the object stays in a given state. This work takes the form of actions (uninterruptible tasks) and activities (interruptible tasks). Finally, a state diagram can capture state variables that are needed for implementing the diagram (we don't do this for our example).

The steps for modeling the state of a class are quite straightforward:

1. Identify states.
2. Select the happy path of any use-case that utilizes the class.
3. Impose the context of the pathway on the state diagram.
4. Select another pathway from the same use-case or a different use-case until little additional knowledge remains to be learned.

Not all classes warrant a state diagram—for example, those in most business-oriented applications. (Although this conclusion is a very broad generalization, I have found it to be fairly consistent.) The following are some of the types of classes that usually warrant further exploration with a state diagram:

- A class that takes on the role of "controller" (it might be quite dynamic in nature)
- A class that appears to generate and/or receive high volumes of messages (as identified by the sequence or collaboration diagram)
- A class that takes on the role of "interface" (such as an interface that represents a facade to a complex subsystem)
- A class that has many different states that the domain is interested in capturing and that are relevant to the context of the application

Modeling the State Diagram of the Remulak Order Class

Figure 7-12 shows the state diagram for the Remulak Productions `Order` class. We can learn much from this state diagram. The event "Initiate order" gets the ball started. It then moves the `Order` object to the "Empty Order" state. Upon entry, the system must perform an action: "initialize order." Table 7-1 depicts the different types of work that can be performed and the different ways to model them.

As soon as the first line item has been added ("Add item(1)") the `Order` object moves to the "Adding Body" state. Notice that there is a self-transition back to the same state as additional items are added ("Add item(n)"). Next note that we use a guard condition: "[no more

FIGURE 7-12 *State diagram for the Remulak* `Order` *class*

Initiate Order
Empty Order
entry/initialize order
Add Item (1)
Adding Body
do/accumulate total
do/verify availability
do/allocate stock
[no more items]
Add item(*n*)
Confirmed Order
do/package for shipping
[credit passed]
Order Complete
do/check credit
[package complete]
[credit failed]^Customer.reject
Rejected Order
do/notify salesperson
do/update status
Fulfilled Order
do/print bill of lading
do/print invoice
[60 days since ship]/purge order

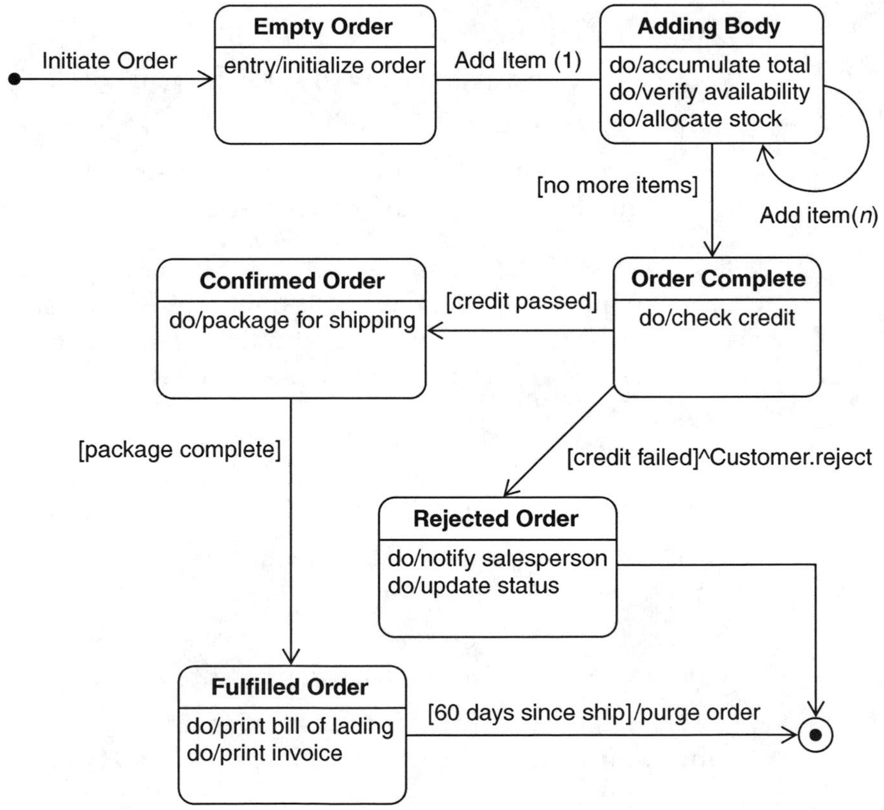

TABLE 7-1 *State Diagram Notation Elements*

Kind of Action/Activity	Purpose	Syntax
External transition	Action to be performed during the transition from one state to another	event/action
Internal transition	Action to be performed in response to an event but while in the current state with no resulting transition	event/action
Entry	Action to be performed upon entering a state	entry/action
Exit	Action to be performed upon leaving a state	exit/action
Idle	Activity to be performed while in a given state	do/activity

items]." Recall from the earlier discussion about the sequence diagram that a guard condition is a means to show condition checking and branching. The authors of UML kindly used similar syntax constructs across many of the models.

Next if the credit check fails ("[credit failed]"), a special format is used to communicate with another object: `^Customer.reject`. This is an event directed to the given `Order` object's `Customer` object. This is the UML mechanism for signaling other objects while modeling the state of another class.

Note, too, how the `Order` object eventually falls off the "radar screen"; that is, it reaches the final state, as noted by the bull's-eye in the figure. Assuming all goes well, once the guard condition is met (i.e., 60 days have transpired since shipment), the `Order` reaches its final state and will be purged. (The object also can reach its final state by being rejected because of bad credit.)

Modeling a class with a state diagram reveals the following:

- Many of the events will result in the modeling of operations in the class.
- All work (actions and activities) will result in the modeling of operations in the class. Many of the operations will be private to the class.
- All messages to other objects (`^Class.event`) will result in an operation's being defined on the target class.

- Any state variables identified will end up as member variables in the class that is being modeled. However, many of the variables will not be persisted during a single use of the system. Their purpose might be only to sustain a given state.

Alternative View of State Diagrams

A state diagram can be viewed in an alternative way: as a table. Although not an official UML view, the table represents the same information. Some practitioners prefer the table to a state diagram, especially when the state diagram is very complex and therefore becomes difficult to read. Table 7-2 is a table form of the state diagram in Figure 7-12.

The table form also is a great way to document the dynamic nature of the Java screens that will implement the user interface. The big difference is that the events are very user interface oriented (button-

TABLE 7-2 *State Information in Table Format*

Starting State	Event/Action	Ending State	Action/Activity
Null	Initiate order/Null	Empty Order	entry/initialize order
Empty Order	Add item(1)/Null	Adding Body	do/accumulate total do/verify availability do/allocate stock
Adding Body	No more items/Null	Order Complete	do/check credit
Adding Body	Add item(n)/Null	Adding Body	do/accumulate total do/verify availability do/allocate stock
Order Complete	Credit passed/Null	Confirmed Order	do/package for shipping
Order Complete	Credit failed/ `^Customer.reject`	Rejected Order	do/notify salesperson do/update status
Confirmed Order	Package complete/ Null	Fulfilled Order	do/print bill of lading do/print invoice
Rejected Order	"Automatic"	Final State	Null
Fulfilled Order	60 days since ship/ Purge order	Final State	Null

clicked) and the actions are geared to the user interface (e.g., load list box or disable text field).

The Activity Diagram

The activity diagram is the "new kid on the block," a special form of state diagram. Each state is considered an *activity state* that executes and then progresses to the next activity state. An activity diagram models workflows, computations, and complex operation steps.

Activity diagrams also are beneficial during the use-case definition process. Pathways within the use-cases can be easily modeled with an activity diagram (rather than an alternative outline format). Figure 7-13 shows an activity diagram for the `checkCredit()` operation in the Remulak Productions `Order` class.

FIGURE 7-13 *Activity diagram for the* `checkCredit()` *operation in the* `Order` *class*

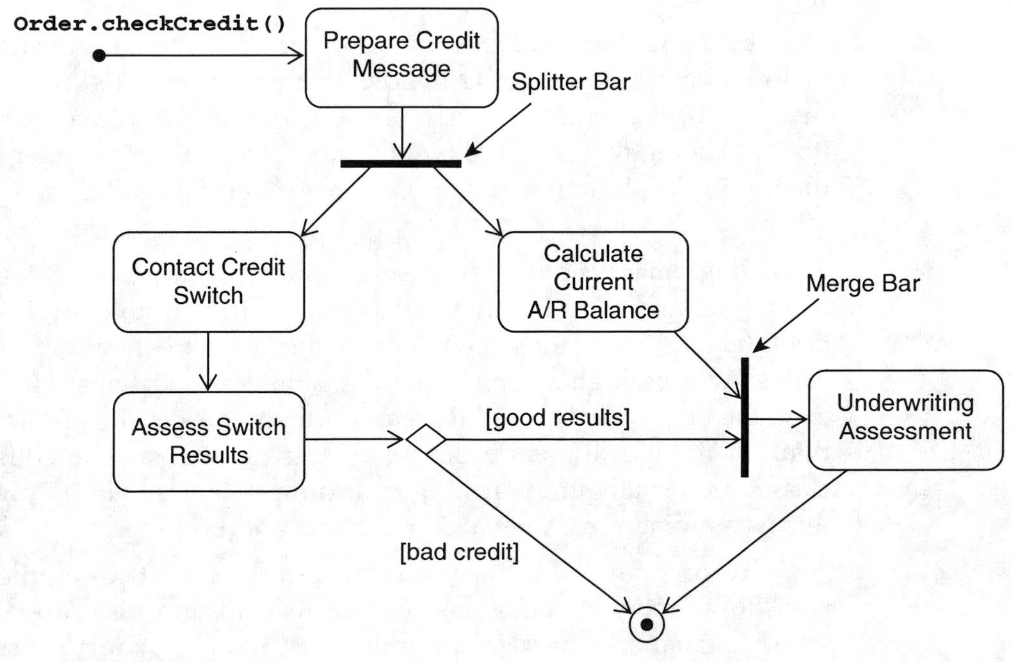

The activity diagram resembles a flowchart; notice that it includes a decision diamond. The presence of merge and splitter bars makes it very convenient to model concurrent activities and synchronization points.

Activity diagrams focus on the *what* of the flow, not the *how*. For example, the activity state of "Prepare Credit Message" on Figure 7-13 tells us what to do, but not how to do it.

Selecting the Right Diagram

The dynamic nature of the application domain can be viewed via the four diagrams just described: the two interaction diagrams (sequence and collaboration), the state diagram, and the activity diagram. When should you use which one?

1. **Sequence diagram:** Use this diagram for most dynamic modeling because it pertains to the use-case pathways. The big payback here is the creation of the operational signatures for the classes in the application.
2. **Collaboration diagram:** Use this diagram when the application includes complex branching dialogs that aren't rendered well in the sequence diagram. (I rarely produce collaboration diagrams, instead opting for the more familiar and more orderly sequence diagram.) Collaboration diagrams are also good for multithreaded scenarios.
3. **State diagram:** This diagram is useful only for a class that exhibits interesting and complex dynamic behavior. In real-time applications (e.g., embedded systems), the ratio of state diagrams to classes will be higher than in non-real-time applications. However, the exact number will depend on the nature of the application. Most applications do not need state diagrams. (The entity classes are usually uninteresting regarding state. Usually if I produce state diagrams, they are for control and boundary classes.)
4. **Activity diagram:** This diagram can clearly depict a complex workflow. Activity diagrams are easy to read and very understandable to the business community. (I use them a lot during use-case definitions. They sometimes produce a clearer picture than a verbal outline format in a use-case template.)

The sequence diagram is the most commonly used; the other three are used only as needed.

Non-UML Extensions in the Design: Usage Matrices

UML provides great artifacts that aid traceability from start to finish; however, they don't directly clarify the distributed or throughput requirements of the application. Although component and deployment diagrams can model the notion of "location," applications need a set of views that deal specifically with network and database loading and distribution. The good news is that the input to this effort comes directly from the use-cases, class diagram, and sequence diagrams; thus the project still weaves in traceability. These non-UML diagrams I call **usage matrices**. There are three types:

1. Event/frequency
2. Object/location
3. Object/volume

Event/Frequency Matrix

The **event/frequency matrix** applies volumetric analysis to the events the system will automate. It begins to establish a basis for what will become important decisions about the location of both program code and data. The matrix applies to any application, regardless of whether the requirements call for distributed elements. Even if only one location will be served, this form of matrix will present a network-loading picture to the operations staff.

The event/frequency matrix has as its input the event table created during the initial project scoping effort. Recall from Chapter 3, when we did project scoping for Remulak Productions, that we added more columns to the event table that attempted to capture the frequency information, albeit informally (see Table 3-3). The event/frequency matrix adds the element of location to the picture. The goal is to ask questions concerning throughput and growth spread over the dynamic spectrum of current and potential geographic locations.

Table 7-3 is an abbreviated event/frequency matrix for Remulak Productions. This is an incomplete list of events, so the growth percentage is specified as "per year."

TABLE 7-3 *Event/Frequency Matrix for Remulak Productions*

	Location			
	Newport Hills, Wash.		Portland, Maine (proposed)	
Event	Frequency	Growth (per year)	Frequency	Growth (per year)
Customer Places Order	1,000/day	20%	200/day	40%
Shipping Clerk Sends Order	700/day	20%	130/day	40%
Customer Buys Warranty	60/day	5%	10/day	10%
Customer Changes Order	200/day	20%	80/day	20%
Supplier Sends Inventory	10/day	10%	3/day	10%

Some of the information in Table 7-3 surfaced early during the project charter effort and by now has been refined and made more accurate. For example, early in the project the number of changed orders was much lower. Further research has caused that number to increase tremendously. Notice the column that represents a proposed East Coast location for Remulak Productions. Although this location isn't operational yet, we can take it into account when devising the final architecture solution and thereby improve the solution.

In a networked environment, an application's throughput is a function not so much of the media being used (fiber) or the data link layer being deployed (frame relay) but rather of the abuse that the application will inflict on the network technology. Granted, if the application will require subsecond response times to countries that have no communications infrastructure, the network technology itself will have a large impact. However, the very act of trying to collect these types of statistics might prove very difficult at best, and wrong information can be disastrous.

The operations element of the project might not care about 1,000 orders per day, but the occurrence of 90 percent of those orders between 8:00 A.M. and 9:00 A.M. would raise their curiosity as a potential problem to be addressed. So the application can be more effective by capturing the potential peak hour frequency—input that will be much more meaningful to the operations staff.

On the basis of the numbers and the anticipated growth rates, decisions will be made that affect the following:

- Where the processes (objects) that satisfy the events will reside
- The communications infrastructure that might need to be in place to satisfy the desired throughput levels
- Component granularity (the number of packages and classes)

Eventually we will be able to approximate just what the *Customer Places Order* event is in terms of the amount of information moving across the "pipe." This information is ultimately what the network staff will require. However, loadings can be simulated to anticipate potential bottlenecks much earlier than most project teams realize.

Object/Location Matrix

The **object/location matrix** focuses on the potential location at which various objects may need to reside to meet performance criteria. The matrix is really useful when multiple locations will require access to the application. For this matrix to be effective, we need information about not only the locations but also the kind of access the objects will require.

The object/location matrix captures two dimensions of the application concerning objects and locations:

1. Breadth of object access:
   - A = All object occurrences
   - S = Subset of object occurrences (the subset must be specified)
2. Pattern of object access:
   - R = Read-only (no operations require update activity)
   - U = Update (all types of operations are possible, including read)

In the current case, Remulak Productions wants the Newport Hills facility to have update access (U) to all objects in the system (A), including the proposed new location at Portland. The Portland location will need read-only access (R) to all objects in the system (A), but it will be able to update (U) only those objects that are serviced at Portland (S). An 800 number will enable customers to reach a dynamic call-routing system that is based on the calling area code and that will shuttle calls to the appropriate call center. Table 7-4 is an object/location matrix for Remulak Productions.

The object/location matrix quickly paints a picture of eventual object distribution in the system and the ultimate determination of how any

TABLE 7-4 *Object/Location Matrix for Remulak Productions*

	Location	
Object	**Newport Hills, Wash.**	**Portland, Maine (proposed)**
`Customer`	AU	AR, SU
`Order`	AU	AR, SU
`OrderHeader`	AU	AR, SU
`OrderLine`	AU	AR, SU
`OrderSummary`	AU	AR, SU
`Shipment`	AU	AR, SU
`Address`	AU	AR, SU
`Role`	AU	AR, SU
`Invoice`	AU	AR, SU
`Payment`	AU	AR, SU
`Product`	AU	AR, SU
`Guitar`	AU	AR, SU
`SheetMusic`	AU	AR, SU
`Supplies`	AU	AR, SU

AU = Update access to all object occurrences allowed
AR = Read access to all object occurrences allowed
SU = Update access to a subset of object occurrences allowed

database replication strategies might be laid out. Specifically, the object/location matrix influences decisions that will affect the following:

- Where physical objects will reside in the application. Unless the application will use an object-oriented database, which Remulak will not, this decision will affect the design of the underlying relational database.
- Data segmentation and distribution strategies, such as replication and extraction policies.

Common patterns found in the matrix will lead to specific solutions (or at least consideration of them). A classic pattern, which does not show up in Remulak Productions' object/location matrix, is one location having update access to all object occurrences (AU), and the remaining sites having read access to all object occurrences (AR). This pattern might be common when code tables, and in some cases inventory, are housed and managed centrally. It usually leads to some type of database snapshot extraction approach by which locations receive refreshed copies of a master database.

In another, similar, pattern one location has update access to all object occurrences (AU), and the remaining sites have read access to only their own unique subset (SR). Depending on the database technology being chosen, such as Oracle or Microsoft SQL Server, many of these issues can be handled with out-of-the-box solutions.

Object/Volume Matrix

The **object/volume matrix** is intended primarily to look at the number of objects used at specific locations and their anticipated growth rate over time. It is beneficial for single- or multiple-location application requirements. It uses the same x- and y-axes (object and location) as the object-location matrix. Table 7-5 is the object/volume matrix for Remulak Productions.

The object/volume matrix will affect several areas of the design, including the following:

- Server sizing, as it pertains to both the database server and the application server that might house the application's Business Rule Services layer. The sizing pertains not only to disk storage but also to memory and CPU throughput, and the quantity of CPUs per server.
- Database table size allocations, free space, and index sizing. Also affected will be the logging activities and how often logs are cycled, as well as backup and recovery strategies, considering the volumes expected at a given location.

Obviously, for any application many of these numbers will not be so exact that no changes will be made. They are approximations that allow for planning and implementation tactics for the application.

The usage matrices introduced in this section add additional perspective to the four dynamic UML diagrams. They enforce traceability because they get their input directly from the artifacts produced earlier in the chapter.

TABLE 7-5 *Object/Volume Matrix for Remulak Productions*

	Location			
	Newport Hills, Wash.		Portland, Maine (proposed)	
Object	**Volume (100s)**	**Growth (per year)**	**Volume (100s)**	**Growth (per year)**
`Customer`	750	20%	150	60%
`Order`	1,400	25%	275	25%
`OrderHeader`	60	5%	10	10%
`OrderLine`	3,400	35%	700	35%
`OrderSummary`	1,400	25%	275	25%
`Shipment`	2,200	10%	500	10%
`Address`	2,000	10%	450	20%
`Role`	2,600	10%	600	10%
`Invoice`	1,700	25%	500	25%
`Payment`	1,900	25%	400	25%
`Product`	300	15%	300	15%
`Guitar`	200	5%	200	5%
`SheetMusic`	50	5%	50	5%
`Supplies`	50	5%	50	5%

Checkpoint

Where We've Been

- UML offers four diagrams to model the dynamic view of the application domain.
- The interaction diagrams—sequence and collaboration—are used primarily to model the objects as they interact to satisfy the pathway of a given use-case.
- Sequence diagrams have a longer history than collaboration diagrams and are typically preferred over collaboration diagrams. The two relay the same message, but in different formats. Of all of

the UML dynamic diagrams, the sequence diagram is the most heavily used.

- The state diagram models the lifecycle of one class. State diagrams appear most often in applications that have a real-time element (e.g., an embedded system). Often control and boundary classes might contain interesting state information that can be described in further detail through state diagrams.
- An activity diagram models complex workflows, operations, or algorithms. Activity diagrams closely follow flowchart notation and can be used to model the pathways through a use-case.
- Usage matrices allow a dynamic view of the application as it deals with loadings from both a network and a database perspective.

Where We're Going Next

In the next chapter we:

- Explore the technology landscape as it pertains to projects being implemented today with Java as the solution set.
- Review the differences between logical and physical tiers and how an application can plan ahead to eventually take advantage of a multitier solution.
- Review the different mechanisms by which tiers can communicate.
- Explore issues concerning the management of transaction scope with and without a coordinator such as Enterprise JavaBeans.
- Examine how to leverage the Internet to migrate portions of Remulak Productions' application to the Web.

CHAPTER 8 *The Technology Landscape*

IN THIS CHAPTER

Keeping up with technology has always been a concern of Remulak Productions. Chapter 4 presented the preliminary execution architecture of the company's order-processing application, based on what was known at that point in the project. Much of that preliminary architecture still holds true. However, the architectural components set out then dealt more with the technical architecture—that is, the tools and product sets for building and implementing the solution. We have not yet determined the approaches to take for the application architecture and data access architecture. This chapter reconfirms the technology architecture selected earlier and explores options for the other two types of architectures.

GOALS

- To review the need for a sound technical architecture.
- To discuss the application architecture and why separation of services is so critical to the application's resiliency.
- To explore the issues concerning the selection of a data access architecture.

- To discuss the mechanisms available for enabling communication among the application's logical layers.
- To explore the use of Java servlets and JavaServer Pages (JSP) as a mechanism of the Web server to respond to HTML forms-based input.
- To cover how to manage transactions within the application via a framework such as Enterprise JavaBeans (EJB).

Next Steps of the Elaboration Phase

Before exploring the technology landscape of the project, let's revisit the Unified Process. Figure 8-1 shows the process model, with the focus on the Elaboration phase.

FIGURE 8-1 *Unified Process model: Elaboration phase*

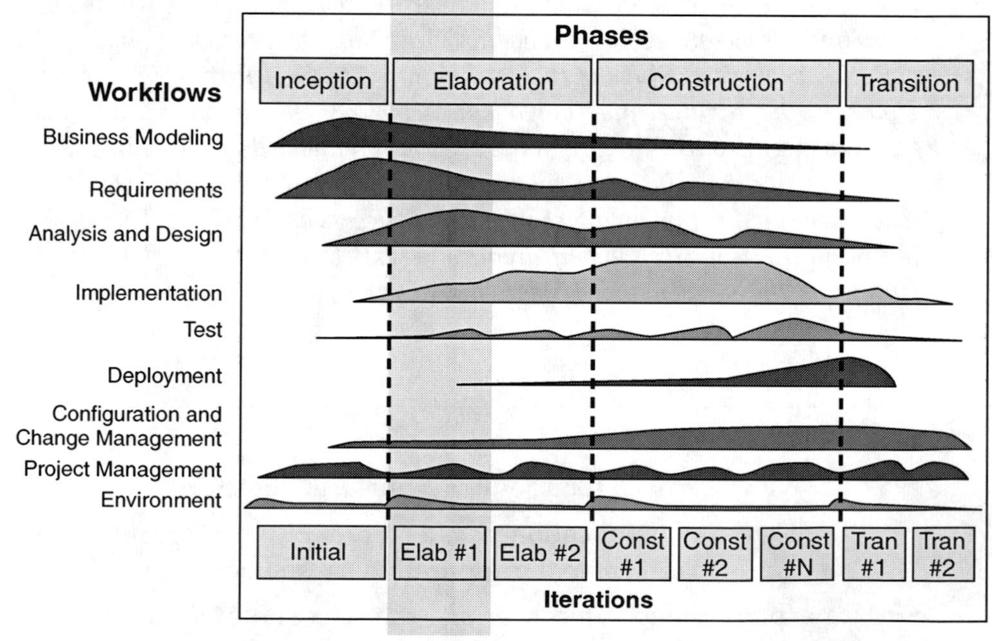

In this chapter we focus on the architecture activities within the Unified Process. In particular, the following workflows and activity sets are emphasized:

- Analysis and Design: Define Candidate Architecture
- Analysis and Design: Perform Architecture Synthesis
- Analysis and Design: Refine the Architecture
- Test: Design Test

A key artifact produced at this point in the project is the Software Architecture Document (SAD).

Architecture is a heavily used term in our industry. Many excellent studies have focused on effective architectures over the years, and using my own experiences, along with what I have learned from others, I categorize architecture into the following three areas:

1. **Technology:** This architecture deals with the many tools required to construct the application. These tools include the database technology, construction tools, source control, configuration management, transaction monitor software, and software distribution. Although going into the project we might know which tools to use, focusing on the technology architecture now will confirm that our choices are correct on the basis of what is currently known about the application.
2. **Data access:** This architecture deals with how the data will be accessed in the application, including the database replication technology and the data access infrastructure (JDBC in the case of our application).
3. **Application segmentation:** This architecture deals with how to segment the application, including the layering strategy that will separate the various layers of the application and how the layers will be managed.

These three architectures are assessed collectively with respect to known requirements, and the appropriate mix for the application is selected. This unique set of technology, product, and architecture choices is called the application's **execution architecture.**

Separating Services

Long before distributed applications and the Internet came to the forefront of technology, the layers of an application were thought best kept distinct and separate. Commingling of, for example, the data access and business logic led to "fragile" applications that were difficult to maintain and to understand. However, very few applications followed this approach—until the technology horizon changed and client/server and distributed computing became possible.

The term *legacy application* traditionally has been applied to mainframe-centric applications. However, many applications built in the past seven or eight years that wear the client/server and/or distributed label are also legacy applications because the logical layers of the applications were not separated in their design or implementation. Further exacerbating this situation is the nature of the unique graphical front end used to build many of these applications, which makes maintaining them more difficult. Again, who would have thought in 1996 that the predominant user interface of choice in the new millennium would be a Web browser? Even today we find the user interface choices still evolving as the advent of wireless devices such as cell phones and PDA (personal digital assistant) devices receives quite a bit of attention.

Although the concepts of layering functionality are easy to comprehend, we absolutely must make the application architecture extensible and isolate the logical layers of the application. There are three logical layers:

- Presentation Services
- Business Services
- Data Services

Table 8-1 lists the scope and objective of each one.

The Presentation Services layer traditionally has been graphical in nature (for the typical reader of this book), but it also may take the form of a report or even an external feed to a particular interface. The GUI (graphical user interface) layer evolves with time. If the Presentation Services layer supported by a given application had been separate from the Business Services layer when originally designed, snapping on a new front end would have involved minimal pain. Unfortunately, for

TABLE 8-1 *Scope and Objective of Each Logical Layer*

Layer	Scope	Objectives
Presentation Services	Data presentation	Ease of use
	Data acceptance	Natural, intuitive user interactions
	Graphical user interface	Fast response times
Business Services	Core business rules	Rigid enforcement of business rules
	Application/dialog flow control	Preservation of investment in code
	Data integrity enforcement	Reduced maintenance costs
Data Services	Durable data storage and retrieval	Consistent, reliable, secure database
	DBMS (database management system) accessed via API	Information sharing
	Concurrency control	Fast response times

most applications a better solution was to scrap what was there and start over, and that's what many organizations did.

The Business Services layer, and to some degree the Presentation Services layer, will likely be the most dynamic of all of the layers. Years of experience with software development have taught us that an application's rules and functionality change the most. And if the Business Services layer is isolated from the other two layers, changes to it will affect the application less. When possible, the Business Services layer should be void of all user interface and data access logic. I can't tell you how many lines of AWT (Abstract Windows Toolkit) and Swing code I have had to debug that were so intertwined with business logic that it was easier just to start over.

The Data Services layer often will be the most static aspect of the application. The data structures and their relationships are usually less effected by changes compared to the Business Services layer. Later in this chapter we explore the Data Access Services layer closely and segment it further, separating the logical request for data, such as a Structured Query Language (SQL) request, from the physical access technology, such as a Java Database Connectivity (JDBC). Constructing an application using good object-oriented design concepts can further insulate the layers. Note that the partitioning design presented in this chapter for the different layers relates to the shadow use-case called Architecture Infrastructure that was discussed in Chapter 4.

Logical versus Physical Tiers

The three services layers are often called *tiers,* or in this case, *three logical tiers.* They might be separated by well-defined interfaces, thereby allowing for less troublesome changes in the future, but they are considered logical because they may be implemented on only *two physical tiers.* Figure 8-2 depicts the notion of logical versus physical tiers.

This very common implementation scheme represents a logical three-tiered solution that is actually implemented on two physical tiers: the client and server. Called *fat-client* or *client-centric,* this solution initially served the push into distributed client/server computing quite well, but it soon began to show signs of wear and tear, as follows:

- Increased burden on an organization's infrastructure to distribute software to more and more clients when any part of the applica-

FIGURE 8-2 *Logical versus physical tiers*

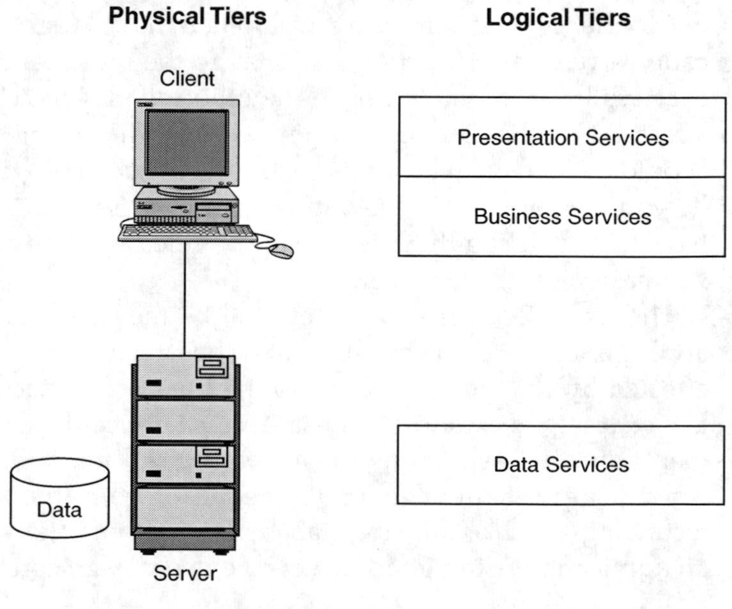

tion changed and to configure software on more and more clients when new distributions were made. The latter applies especially to the database access component and the troublesome nature of installing and configuring JDBC drivers on multiple machines.

- Nonoptimal transaction throughput as a result of poor resource pooling in the form of database connections. Depending on the physical database technology, the resulting increase in cost could be substantial because each client workstation required an access license to the database.
- Inappropriate resource utilization because some business service activities (e.g., complex mathematical calculations) might not be appropriate for the platform serving as the client; if placed there, they could result in poor performance.

Figure 8-3 depicts the same model presented in Figure 8-2, except that it implements the logical layers individually, as three separate

FIGURE 8-3 *Mapping logical to appropriate physical tiers*

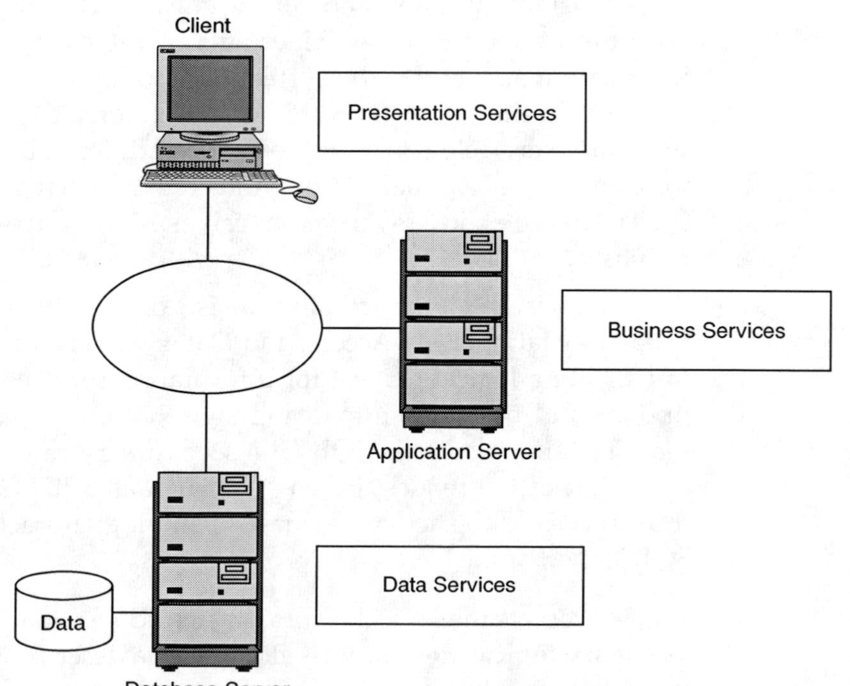

physical tiers rather than two. The figure illustrates the origin of the term *three-tier*. One needs to understand the context of the term when it is used because the user might be referring to logical rather than physical tiers. Actually, a better name is *multitier* (also called *N-tier*) because multiple physical tiers could be implementing the three logical tiers (multiple Business Services layer servers and multiple Data Services layer servers).

Tier Strategy

Many options are available to a project team that wants the best and most flexible design strategy. At a minimum, any application built today that is intended to be around longer than a year or two without experiencing a major reworking must implement a minimum of three logical tiers. This minimum is specified because the traditional three-tier model needs further categorizing, for the following reasons:

- The Business Services layer actually consists of two types of services: Business Context and Business Rule. The first type deals with the user interface as it pertains to filtering and cleansing information as it enters the system; for example, a value entered in one field limits the allowable values entered in another field. The other service deals with the more traditional business rules; for example, a Remulak Productions' customer that places over $10,000 in orders in a given year receives 10 percent off of the next purchase.
- The Data Services layer actually consists of three types of services: Data Translation, Data Access, and Database. The first deals with translating a logical request for information services (e.g., select, update, and/or delete) into a language that is compatible for the data repository, such as SQL. The second service deals with the execution of the request by an API, such as a JDBC driver. The third service is the actual database technology (Oracle, Microsoft SQL Server, or the like).

Figure 8-4 depicts the logical layers that could be used in any application—the **six-logical-tier model**—along with a description of the services provided at each layer.

FIGURE 8-4 *Six-logical-tier model*

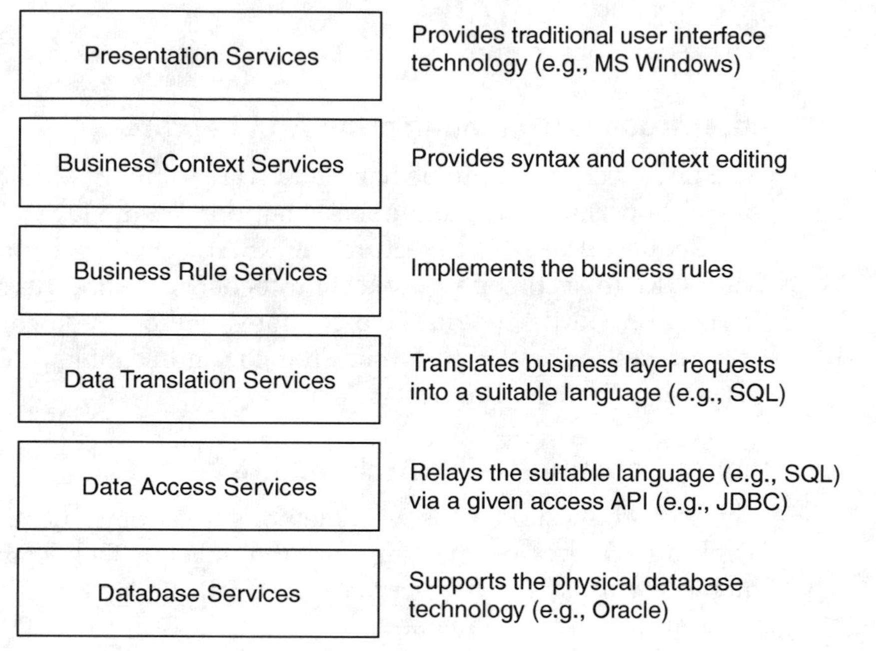

The Presentation Services and Database Services layers require the least amount of attention (although we have to build screens and design tables, of course). The remaining four layers must be very sound and well built to hold up for the other layers. If we do the job right, we should easily be able later to replace the Presentation Services and Database Services layers with different presentation services (such as the Internet) and different database technology (such as Oracle, to replace Microsoft SQL Server).

Communication among the Six Layers

We need to determine the most appropriate mechanism to enable communication among the six layers. To do so, we should first ask the following questions:

1. What interprocess communication (IPC) technology should be used among the layers?

2. What mechanism should be utilized to communicate among the layers when the IPC is used?

These two questions are addressed in the next two subsections.

Interprocess Communication Architecture

The IPC mechanism can be handled by any of many different technology options, including native socket support within Java, Common Object Request Broker Architecture (CORBA) technology and its Internet Inter-ORB (object request broker) Protocol (IIOP), and Remote Method Invocation (RMI) and its Java Remote Method Protocol (JRMP). In some cases for a Web front end, the communications IPC is actually HyperText Transfer Protocol (HTTP).

Layer Communication Architecture

The second question deals with methods for communicating, from the application's perspective, among the layers. This communication method will use the IPC services (RMI/JRMP, HTTP, CORBA/IIOP). Several choices are available:

- Pass individual attributes and objects, as needed, between each layer.
- Pass String arrays and attributes between each layer.
- Pass serialized versions of objects between each layer.
- Pass XML (eXtensible Markup Language) streams between each layer.

Managing Transaction Scope

An application that will interact with any type of data repository can face the somewhat daunting task of managing the **transaction scope**. Transaction scope is the entire process of establishing a database connection, communicating with the resource at the end of the connection, eventually committing any changes made, and then closing the connection.

Managing transaction scope is more difficult if the scope crosses physical database boundaries. For example, suppose that a transaction must update both an Oracle database and a Microsoft SQL Server database within the scope of one transaction and ensure that both servers are updated at the end of the transaction. This is difficult to do because talking to each database product (Oracle and SQL Server) requires a connection to each that must be managed individually with respect to their individual commit scope. Figure 8-5 depicts a transaction scenario between two database products.

One solution to this problem is to use a transaction monitor. A **transaction monitor**, such as BEA's Tuxedo, acts as a watchdog over any utilized resources and is delegated the task of monitoring transaction scope. However, transaction monitors are substantial overkill for small to medium-sized shops.

FIGURE 8-5 *Transaction scope with two databases*

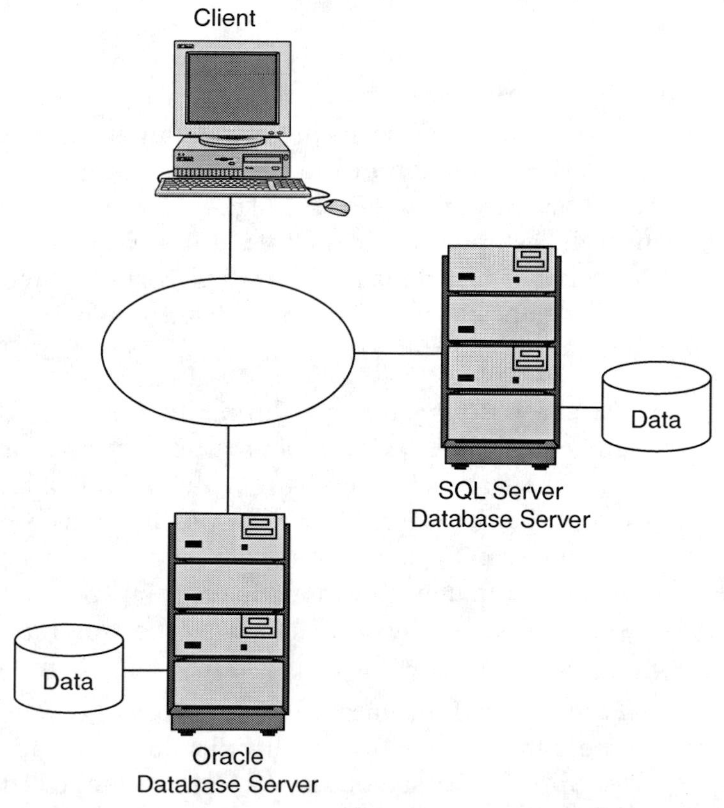

Another option is to utilize the services of plain JavaBeans coded to utilize JDBC and its ability to control transactions. In JDBC we can quite easily define a unit of work by beginning a transaction: that is, setting the `auto-commit` parameter of the JDBC connection to `false`, performing as many update-type transactions as desired, and then issuing a commit or rollback command on the connection. For Remulak Productions, this will be an initial solution that we present in a later chapter.

The final solution discussed here utilizes Enterprise JavaBeans running inside of an application server product. EJB is the framework offered by Sun Microsystems and implemented by many EJB vendors—such as BEA with its WebLogic product, and IBM with its WebSphere product—that provide for true enterprise-level transaction support. There are also open-source (i.e., free!) EJB servers, such as JBoss (found at *www.jboss.org*). For Remulak Productions, an EJB solution will be a second option that we present in a later chapter.

Enterprise JavaBeans

Two primary types of beans are at play in an EJB container. The first type consists of **session beans**, which can be thought of as workflow coordinators or utility services. The second type consists of **entity beans**, which represent the entity classes we have already discussed.

Managing transactions is just a small portion of what EJB can do for the application. EJB is reviewed in detail in Chapter 12. For now, the following are some of the many other problems that EJB addresses:

- **Database connection pooling:** EJB can pool database connections. Sadly, many developers write poor code and in the scope of just one transaction end up with several database connections open to a database. Not only does this waste precious memory resources on the client and server; it can also increase the project's cost if the database vendor is charging per connection. Pooling keeps used connections intact (to the programmer they appear closed), providing the ability to resurrect them as needed.
- **Thread pooling:** Each component can be written as if it were single-threaded. EJB actually disallows thread management by the application, so you may not use the keyword `synchronized;` EJB will take care of the rest. EJB also leaves threads open, pre-

allocated, to allow for quicker response to clients that request thread activation.

- **Reduction of transaction management logic:** Without EJB, each transaction must explicitly issue a "begin" transaction and an "end" transaction. In addition, the application must deal with a myriad of return code checks and error handling pertaining to the database with which it is interfacing. EJB takes care of this by virtually connecting transaction components via a common transaction context.

Note: If bean-managed transactions are used within EJB, the beans can still issue their own commit and rollback requests. With Remulak, however, we will use container-managed transactions.

- **Flexible security model:** EJB offers a flexible security model for the application's implementation via its deployment descriptor. Users can be assigned to roles, and then those roles can be assigned to components and interfaces within the components.
- **Container-managed persistence:** EJB versions 1.1 and 2.0 support container-managed persistence. Building and managing SQL statements and their interaction with the underlying database require quite a bit of effort on the part of the application team. Container-managed persistence (CMP) delegates the generation of SQL and the management of basic CRUD (create, read, update, delete) functionality to the EJB framework and the application server that implements the framework (e.g., BEA's WebLogic, IBM's WebSphere, Inprise's Application Server, to name a few). For Remulak we will show an EJB 2.0 implementation of CMP.

EJB can obviously assist the application in reducing the amount of overhead logic and transaction management plumbing. So to provide a perspective, Remulak will provide both a bean-managed persistence (BMP) implementation and a container-managed persistence (CMP) implementation. Both the BMP and the CMP examples will use container-managed transactions.

Once you have seen the additional advantages of using CMP in the EJB environment, it will be hard to use anything else. Just the simple fact of not having to write one line of SQL code is reason enough to jump on the CMP bandwagon. Unfortunately, at the time of this writing very few application server vendors support the EJB 2.0 specification. This is the primary reason why we have chosen BEA's WebLogic, because it was one of the early supporters. By the time this book reaches you, most vendors will be in compliance with the EJB 2.0 specification. The direction and emphasis in the Java community and the emphasis that Sun places on the technology attests to the fact that EJB will continue to be integrated into core product architectures.

Incorporating the Internet into the Solution

As stated early in the book, all of our implementation will utilize a light browser-based client front end:

- The Presentation Services layer will use a light Web-based front end that will use simple HTML and JavaScript communicating with a Web-based back end for all the pathways supported in the application. There will be a servlet on the Web server to act as a broker to both JavaBeans using native JDBC and JavaServer Pages, as well as an implementation using Enterprise JavaBeans and JavaServer Pages. Alternatively, we could use a Java applet or even a Java application to talk to the servlet (yes, you can send and receive information from a Java application to a servlet via a `DataOutputStream` object and an `InputStreamReader` object, respectively; however, the act of parsing the returned information from the servlet would be too cumbersome for our application).
- The Business Services layer will reside on the server and will use a servlet and JavaServer Pages as the intermediary for the Web client, as well as both JavaBeans and Enterprise JavaBeans to manage the entity classes (as described earlier). Our use-cases and their pathways will be implemented with control classes. In the servlet/JSP/JavaBean solution, the controller will be simply a JavaBean. In the servlet/JSP/EJB solution, the controller will be a session EJB.
- The Data Services layer will be implemented with both JavaBeans/JDBC and the EJB framework. Both CMP and BMP implementations will be explored for Remulak in Chapter 12. Prior to EJB 2.0, CMP implementations varied widely across EJB products, lead-

ing to less portability and perhaps resulting in fewer implementations utilizing this feature. EJB 2.0, among other features, vastly improved the capabilities of CMP, making it much more of a viable design alternative.

Remulak Productions, however, cannot dictate which Web browser a client will use, so we will test the application's functionality using the two most common browsers: Microsoft Internet Explorer and Netscape Navigator.

More about the Web Interface

A Web-based interface of some type will need to be positioned between the Web page and the Business Services layer. This interface will consist of a front-end component built as a servlet and JavaServer Pages (JSP) that will reside in a servlet container product. We will use both Apache Tomcat (at *jakarta.apache.org*) and the container services provided by BEA's WebLogic. However, the servlet and JSP architecture will support any Web server that can implement either their own implementation of servlets and JSP or a third-party JSP enabler (such as Allaire's JRun or the reference implementation from the Jakarta Project, Tomcat). The servlet and JSP will act as both the interface and controller of the process. The servlet will have to broker the request from the browser and then send the message to the appropriate beans, which in turn will allow the servlet to forward the appropriate JSP to return information suitable for building an HTML reply. Figure 8-6 is an overview of the Internet architecture.

In Chapter 2 we introduced the UML component diagram, which depicts software components and their relationships (dependencies). Figure 8-7 is a component diagram showing the software units that will implement the Remulak solution without using Enterprise JavaBeans.

Let's follow the stages of this architecture by referring to the circled numbers in Figure 8-7:

Step 1: The HTML form requests a resource. This resource request is mapped to a servlet.

Step 2: The servlet instantiates a control class that is a JavaBean. On the basis of the action requested by the HTML form, the servlet invokes a message on the controller bean.

FIGURE 8-6 *Remulak Internet strategy*

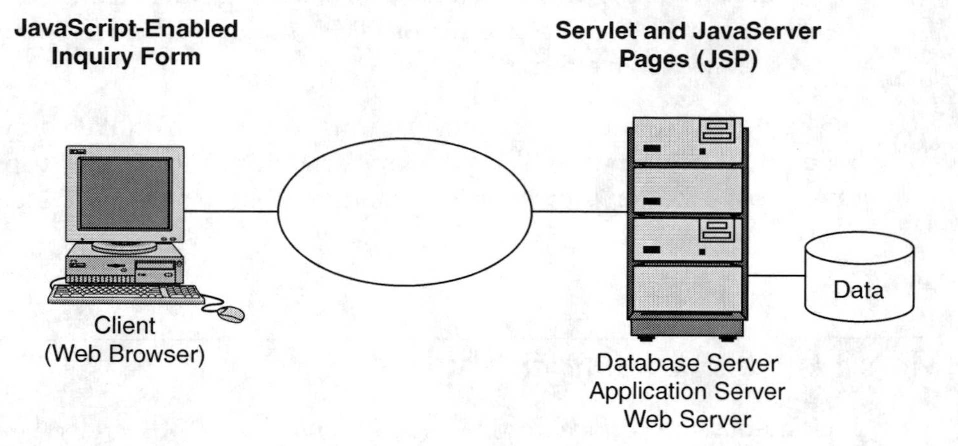

FIGURE 8-7 *Remulak component strategy without Enterprise JavaBeans*

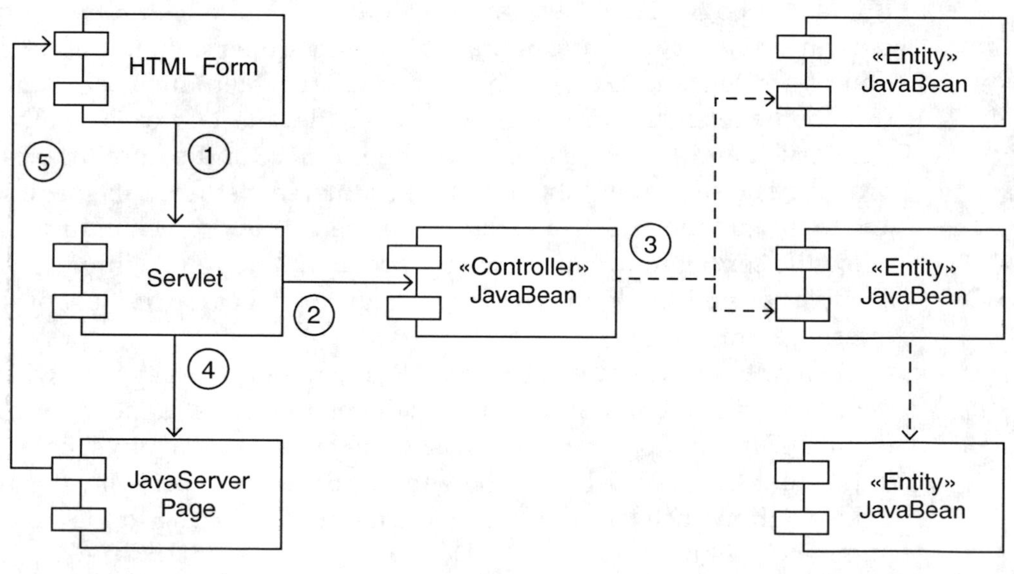

Step 3: The controller bean's sole mission is to implement the pathways of the use-case. There will be one control class for each use-case (how's that for traceability?). As an example, in the case of Remulak there will be a controller called `UCMaintainRltnshp` that contains an operation called `rltnCustomerInquiry()`. The sole mission of this operation is to send messages to other beans with the hopes of returning information about a customer.

Step 4: A value object (more on these in Chapter 9) eventually finds its way back to the servlet, where it is inserted into the request scope of the servlet. The servlet then forwards the request to the appropriate JavaServer Page.

Step 5: The Java Server page, using the object(s) recently placed in the servlet's request scope, formats a return page of HTML bound as a reply to the initiating browser.

The case of Enterprise JavaBeans as a solution is illustrated in Figure 8-8. There aren't too many differences.

FIGURE 8-8 *Remulak component strategy with Enterprise JavaBeans*

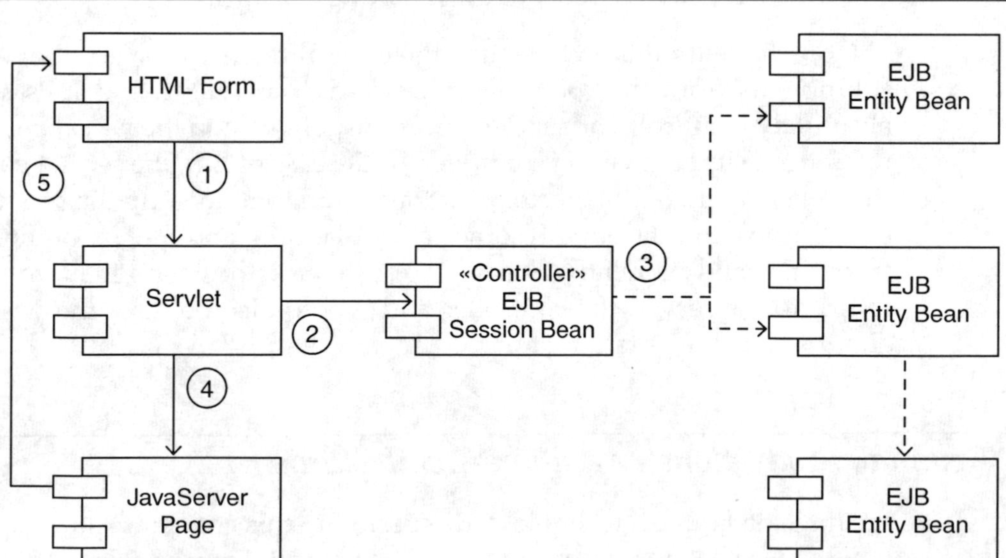

Let's follow the stages of this architecture by referring to the circled numbers in Figure 8-8:

Step 1: The HTML form requests a resource. This resource request is mapped to a servlet.

Step 2: The servlet instantiates a control class that is a session EJB. On the basis of the action requested by the HTML form, the servlet invokes a message on the controller bean.

Step 3: The controller bean's sole mission is to implement the pathways of the use-case. There will be one controller session bean for each use-case. As an example, in the case of Remulak there will be a controller called `UCMaintainRltnshp` that contains an operation called `rltnCustomerInquiry()`. The sole mission of this operation is to send messages to other entity EJBs with the hopes of returning information about a customer.

Step 4: A value object eventually finds its way back to the servlet, where it is inserted into the request scope of the servlet. The servlet then forwards the request to the appropriate JavaServer Page.

Step 5: The JavaServer Page, using the object(s) recently placed in the servlet's request scope, formats a return page of HTML bound as a reply to the initiating browser.

Note that with this architecture, the only difference between the two solutions is from the controller backward. The HTML and JSPs are absolutely identical. The servlet varies only slightly, in the way it gets a reference to its companion controller. In the case of EJB, the servlet uses the Java Naming and Directory Interface (JNDI) to look up the session bean's home interface. With some smart planning and the use of interfaces, it would be relatively easy to create a factory class that would return to the servlet the controller and would also be none the wiser about whom it was talking to.

Remulak Productions' Execution Architecture

We have had quite a technology discussion in this chapter. A summary of what we need to implement would be helpful. Figure 8-9 is the same diagram that was presented in Figure 8-4, except that it outlines the execution architecture specifically for Remulak Productions.

FIGURE 8-9 *Summary of the Remulak execution architecture*

Presentation Services	• HTML and scripted forms
Business Context Services	• Servlet and JavaServer pages (Internet) and Web server
Business Rule Services	• JavaBeans and Enterprise JavaBeans (session and entity beans)
Data Translation Services	• JavaBeans with native JDBC, as well as both BMP with native JDBC and CMP implemented by EJB-compliant application server
Data Access Services	• Implemented by JDBC and JDBC controlled by CMP and the persistence manager in the EJB-compliant application server
Database Services	• Microsoft SQL Server (production) • Oracle (investigation)

Checkpoint

Where We've Been

- After the requirements have been solidified and the design work has begun, three architectures must be considered. The final architecture selected for the application is called the execution architecture.
- To provide a technology-expansive set of choices, Remulak will present some solution aspects using servlets, JavaBeans, and JavaServer Pages. Other solution aspects will use servlets, Enterprise JavaBeans, and JavaServer Pages. In the first case, the open-source Tomcat server will be used. In the second, BEA's WebLogic application server will be used.

- Many mechanisms are available for communicating between the layers of the application. All have strengths and weaknesses. The one with the most appeal for Remulak Productions will be to use RMI and to pass objects and attributes between the layers.
- Transaction management is the ability of the application to ensure that changes are either committed to the database if all goes as planned, or rolled back and discarded otherwise. Both native JDBC transaction management services and an implementation with Enterprise JavaBeans (EJB) will be used.

Where We're Going Next

In the next chapter we:

- Explore the issues regarding the transition from the logical perspective offered by the design view of the class diagram to the physical persistence layer (which assumes the existence of a relational database).
- Review the issues concerning the use of a visual modeling tool such as Rational Rose to generate a Data Definition Language (DDL) from the class diagram.
- Discuss how to translate inheritance and aggregation/composition modeled on the class diagram to a table structure.
- Review how native JDBC data access and both container-managed persistence (CMP) and bean managed-persistence (BMP) within the Enterprise JavaBeans (EJB) application provide basic SQL support for Remulak.
- Explore how to keep the class diagram and tables in sync.
- Review the strengths and weaknesses of implementing the query access as stored procedures and triggers.

CHAPTER 9

Data Persistence: Storing the Objects

IN THIS CHAPTER

We have now reached a significant point in Remulak Productions' project lifecycle. In the next several chapters we will consider many traditional design issues. Iterative development fosters the notion of learning a little, designing a little, and then constructing a little. In this chapter we construct the necessary database components to implement the physical tables for the Remulak Productions solution.

Two alternative approaches will be presented. The first approach will be to use native JDBC calls from JavaBeans to gain access to the data. The second approach will use Enterprise JavaBeans and both container-managed persistence (CMP) and bean-managed persistence (BMP). Prior to those alternatives, the project must translate the class structure to a relational database schema. This is what we'll discuss first.

GOALS

- To review the issues encountered during mapping of the class diagram to a relational database management system (RDBMS).
- To discuss the mapping of simple associations to table structures.

- To explore the options for mapping generalization/specialization hierarchies to the table structures.
- To discuss the mapping of aggregation and composition to table structures.
- To explore how to select the proper key structure for tables and for normalization issues.
- To review how visual modeling tools generate Data Definition Language (DDL) statements for the database.
- To discuss how to improve the output from visual modeling tools to better approximate the final generated DDL.
- To discuss how to implement table access using native JDBC calls and JavaBeans.
- To review how container-managed persistence (CMP) works to provide much of our SQL support.
- To review the pros and cons of using stored procedures and triggers to implement aspects of the data layers.
- To examine the Data Translation Services and Data Access Services layers.

Next Steps of the Elaboration Phase

Before exploring the database persistence strategies, let's revisit the Unified Process. Figure 9-1 shows the process model, with the focus on the Elaboration Phase.

In this chapter we focus on the database activities within the Unified Process. In particular, the following workflows and activity sets are emphasized:

- Analysis and Design: Design Database
- Analysis and Design: Design Components
- Implementation: Structure the Implementation Model
- Implementation: Plan the Integration
- Implementation: Implement Components

FIGURE 9-1 *Unified Process model: Elaboration phase*

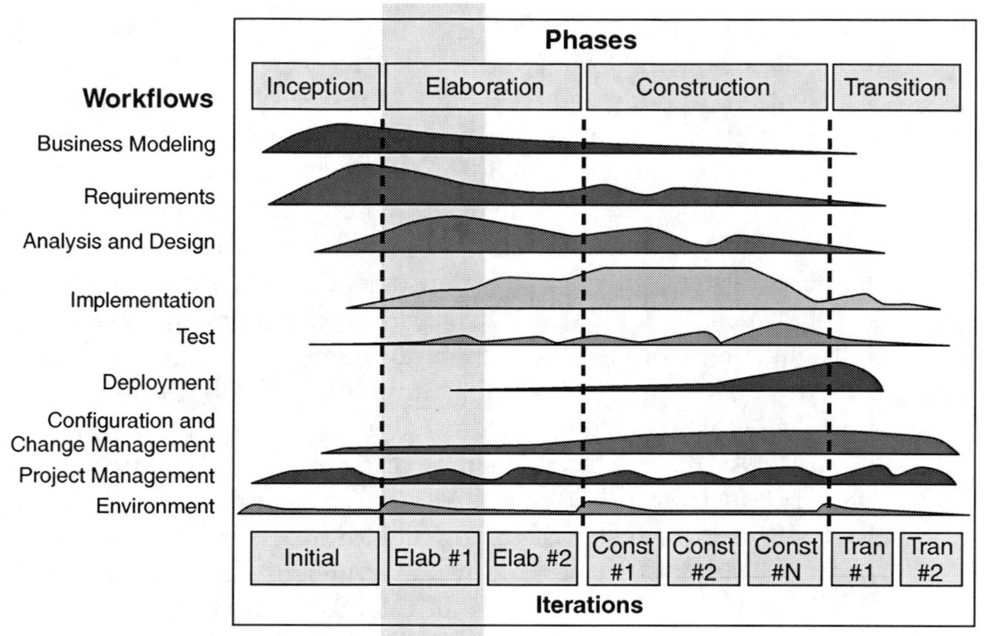

A key artifact that is further embellished in this chapter is the Software Architecture Document (SAD). The particular aspects addressed deal with making the transition from the class diagram created for Remulak Productions to a design that can support a relational database. Microsoft SQL Server is our initial target, but we will also test the database against an Oracle implementation.

The database design, along with its transformation from the class diagram, is critical not only to the other layers that will request the services of the database, but also to the performance of the database in a production environment. In addition, we will have to look at software component design strategies to deal with the passing of information from the Data Translation Services layer back to the Business Rule Services layer.

Object-Oriented Concepts and Translating to the Physical Design

Until now we haven't needed to translate what we modeled with UML into something that isn't object-oriented in order to implement the application. Making the transition from the class diagram to a relational view requires some additional analysis.

The next several sections deal with many aspects of this transition. We assume that the repository being used as the persistence layer is some type of RDBMS. Most issues addressed here don't come up if the persistence layer will be an object-oriented database management system (OODBMS). OODBMSs are still by far the minority (although I encounter them more and more often in my consulting practice). Most applications that utilize an OODBMS are also using C++, Java, or SmallTalk as their language implementation, primarily because OODBMS vendors usually directly support bindings between their products and those languages. We also find that the traditional RDBMS vendors are transforming their products to take on more object features. Many of these products are referred to as object-relational database management systems (ORDBMSs). However, the mainstream Java development being done today is against an RDBMS.

Before progressing down the translation path, we need to visit each class and ensure that we completely identify all of the attributes for each one, specifying their unique data types. We've already identified many along the way, but now we need to apply more rigor to the process because soon we will be generating relational tables to support them.

Mapping Classes to Tables

The easiest way to translate classes into tables is to make a one-to-one mapping (see Figure 9-2). I strongly recommend against this approach, yet it is done more often than you might realize. One-to-one mapping can lead to the following problems:

- **Too many tables:** Most object-to-relational translations done with one-to-one mapping produce more tables than are actually necessary.

- **Too many joins:** If there are too many tables, then logically there will be too many SQL join operations.
- **Missed tables:** Any many-to-many association (e.g., `Customer` and `Address`) will require a third relational table to physically associate particular objects (e.g., a given `Customer` with a given `Address`). At a minimum, the columns found in that table will be the primary identifier (primary key) from both classes.

In the Remulak Productions class diagram, outlined again in Figure 9-2, an association class, `Role`, is defined between `Customer` and `Address`. This class was defined because we want to capture important information about the association—namely, the role that `Address` serves (mailing, shipping, and billing) for a given `Customer/Address` pair. This class also conveniently handles the relational issue of navigating in either direction.

In the association between `OrderLine` and `Shipment`, however, no association class is defined. This is completely normal and common from the object viewpoint (this association has no

FIGURE 9-2 *Remulak class diagram*

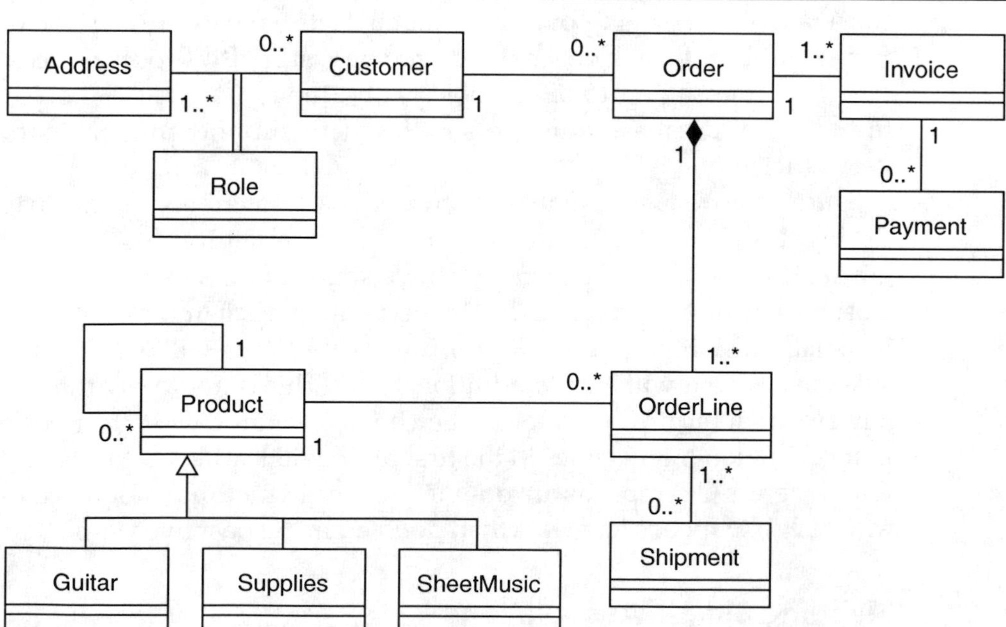

interesting information that we care to capture), but from the relational perspective an intersection table is necessary to implement the relationship.

- **Inappropriate handling of generalization/specialization (inheritance) associations:** Most often the knee-jerk reaction is to have a table for each class in the generalization/specialization association. The result can be nonoptimal solutions that impair performance. Later in this chapter we review specific implementation alternatives and rules of thumb for when to take which approach.
- **Denormalization of data:** Many applications are report intensive, and the table design might be directed to address their unique needs. For such applications, more denormalization of data might occur (i.e., the same data may be duplicated in multiple tables).

Rather than one-to-one mapping of classes to tables, a better approach is to revisit the pathways through the use-cases, especially how they manifest themselves as sequence diagrams. The class diagram, too, should be addressed. Other useful artifacts are the usage matrices created in Chapter 7.

James Rumbaugh once used the term *object horizon* when referring to the available messaging pathways that objects have in a given domain. For example, if the sequence diagrams suggest multiple occurrences of `Customer` messaging to `Order` objects and then to `OrderLine` objects, the physical database must be structured to support this navigation very efficiently.

The event/frequency matrix we created in Chapter 7 also is invaluable during this phase. Any action (event) will trigger a given sequence diagram into action. The frequency of these actions forces us to focus more closely on their performance. The biggest bottleneck in most applications is usually disk input/output (I/O). Too many tables will lead to excessive joins, which will lead to additional I/O. This is not to say that poor key selection (addressed later in the chapter) cannot also affect performance. But too many tables in the first place will lead to additional I/O. And whereas CPU speeds are doubling every 18 months (Moore's Law), raw disk I/O speeds have less than doubled in the past five years.

Mapping Simple Associations

Before we can begin transforming classes into relational entities, we must ask a question of each class: Does it even need to be persisted?

Some classes—for example, most boundary and control classes—will never be persisted to a physical repository. Classes that are not persisted are called *transient* because they are instantiated, typically used for the lifecycle of either a transaction or the actor's session (in which many transactions might be executed), and then destroyed. A good example of a transient class in the EJB environment would be a stateless session bean.

Visual modeling tools use this property of classes during generation of the SQL DDL for the database table structures to determine whether particular classes should be considered. Figure 9-3 shows the **Class Specification for Order** dialog box for Rational Rose. The **Detail** tab shows the specification of the persistence property of the class `Order`.

We have not yet addressed navigation. When creating the initial class diagram, we usually consider every association to be **bidirectional**, which means that it can be traversed in either direction of the

FIGURE 9-3 ***Class Specification for Order*** *dialog box for Rational Rose*

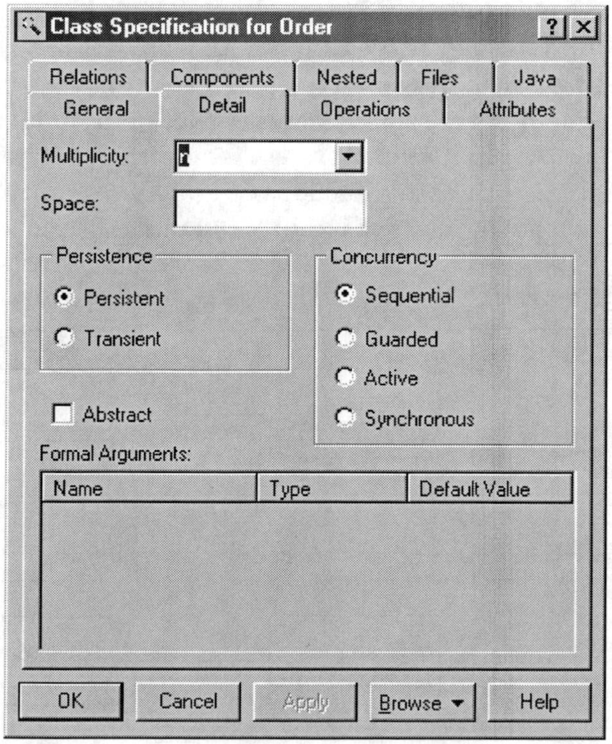

association (however, in my experience most associations are unidirectional). Treating every association as bidirectional is good policy because we momentarily cease to consider whether we actually need to be able to navigate from, say, `Customer` to `Order`, as well as from `Order` to `Customer`. This decision will affect the language implementation as well as the translation to the relational design.

Semantically, navigation in UML pertains to objects of a given class being able to send messages to other objects with which they might have an association. Nothing is said about the implications that navigation might impose on the supporting database table design. However, this is a very important consideration. On the surface we are referencing an object instance, but below that the ability to traverse an association will ultimately depend on the database technology (at least for classes that are persisted).

UML represents navigability as a stick arrowhead pointing in the direction of the navigation. Figure 9-4 illustrates a scenario involving the `Customer` and `Order` classes and the fact that `Customer` will navigate only in the direction of `Order` (each `Customer` object has a list of `Order` objects because the multiplicity can be infinite).

From this figure we can infer that an `Order` object does not know its associated `Customer` object. However, this scenario isn't very practical for our use and as such won't meet our navigational requirements (Remulak Productions' system requirements state that we must be able to navigate in both directions). Figure 9-5 shows `Customer` and `Order` taken from the class diagram for Remulak given in Figure 9-2.

FIGURE 9-4 `Customer` *and* `Order` *classes with explicit navigation*

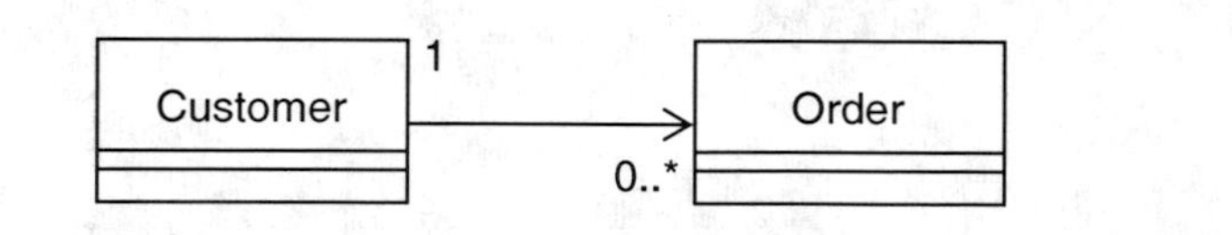

FIGURE 9-5 `Customer` *and* `Order` *classes with implied navigation*

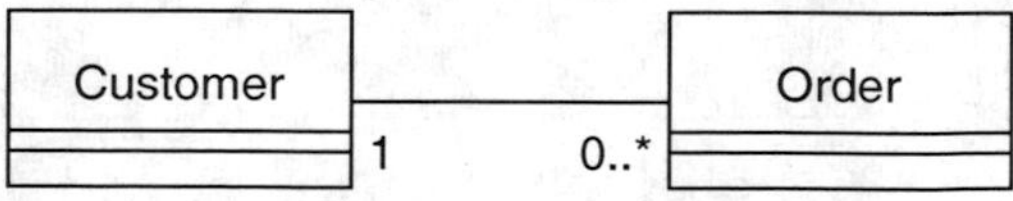

At this point you might be thinking that on the basis of our definition of navigation, we can't navigate in either direction. In UML, the navigational adornments may be omitted as a convenience and to manage clutter. A problem could result, however, if we did have an association that didn't have navigational requirements in either direction. Because this situation is highly unusual in practice, the navigational indicators are typically omitted. In the case of the class diagram for Remulak Productions, every relationship will be bidirectional and implied in the model (arrowheads omitted).

Suppose we want to translate the two classes, with their multiplicity and dual navigability, into relational tables. This process would require the following DDL (in ANSI SQL-92 format):

```
CREATE TABLE T_Customer (
        customerId INTEGER NOT NULL,
        customerNumber CHAR(14) NOT NULL,
        firstName CHAR(20),
        lastName CHAR(20),
        middleInitial CHAR(4),
        prefix CHAR(4),
        suffix CHAR(4),
        phone1 CHAR(15),
        phone2 CHAR(15),
        eMail CHAR(30),
        CONSTRAINT PK_T_Customer12 PRIMARY KEY (customerId),
        CONSTRAINT TC_T_Customer32 UNIQUE (customerNumber),
        CONSTRAINT TC_T_Customer31 UNIQUE (customerId));

CREATE TABLE T_Order (
        orderId INTEGER NOT NULL,
        customerId INTEGER NOT NULL,
        orderNumber CHAR(10) NOT NULL,
        orderDateTime DATE NOT NULL,
        terms VARCHAR(30) NOT NULL,
        salesPerson VARCHAR(20) VARCHAR NOT NULL,
        discount DECIMAL(17,2) NOT NULL,
        courtesyMessage VARCHAR(50) NOT NULL,
        CONSTRAINT PK_T_Order16 PRIMARY KEY (orderId),
        CONSTRAINT TC_T_Order37 UNIQUE (orderNumber),
        CONSTRAINT TC_T_Order36 UNIQUE (orderId));
```

Note: Class names in tables are prefaced by *T_* in accordance with the default-naming convention used by Rational Rose when generating a DDL from the class diagram, which can of course be changed if desired. Note that you don't need a visual modeling tool to do any of this. However, I am a firm believer that a visual modeling tool vastly improves the traceability and success of a project.

Notice in the preceding code fragment the other artifacts that are strictly relational in nature and that are not part of the class diagramming specifications (although they can all be handled as tagged values in UML). These artifacts include such items as data types for the relational database (e.g., `CHAR` and `DECIMAL`) and precision (e.g., `DECIMAL(17,2)`).

Notice also the absence of a reference in the `T_Customer` table to the `T_Order` table. The reason this reference is missing is that a `Customer` can have many `Order` objects but the database cannot handle multiple `Order` objects in the `T_Customer` table.

Note: Many relational databases today, including Oracle, support the concept of nested relationships. Database vendors are slowly crafting themselves as object relational in their ability to model more-complex relationship types.

A `Customer` object can find all of its `Order` objects simply by requesting them all from the `T_Order` table, in which the value of `customerId` is equal to a supplied number.

Table 9-1 explains the translation from multiplicity to the resulting database action. Keep in mind that this translation is done after the decision of whether or not to persist a table has been made.

Next we review the classes that have simple associations (including association classes such as `Role`) for Remulak Productions and apply the rules for translation. The result is shown in Table 9-2.

Other class-related tables are addressed in the next several sections.

Mapping Inheritance to the Relational Database

Creating generalization/specialization associations (inheritance) is one of the more interesting translation exercises during implementation of an object design in an RDBMS. Similar constructs that might have appeared in relational modeling are the subtype/supertype relationships. Figure 9-6 shows the generalization/specialization association portion of the Remulak Productions class diagram.

TABLE 9-1 *Mapping Multiplicity to Database Actions*

Multiplicity between Classes	Database Action
One to one	Creates a table for each class (Tables A, B). The primary key of each table (Tables A, B) is also a foreign key in the related table. If the relationship is actually one to *optionally* one, it might be beneficial to implement the association in the RDBMS as two separate tables. However, if there are many cases in which an association between the two exists or if the multiplicity is truly one to one, the best solution is to implement the association in the RDBMS as only one table.
One to many	Creates a table for each class (Tables A, B). The primary key of the table on the *one* side of the association (Table A) is a foreign key in the table on the *many* side of the association (Table B).
Many to many	Creates a table for each class (Tables A, B). Creates an additional intersection table (Table C). The primary keys of each class table (Tables A, B) are defined as foreign keys in the intersection table (Table C). The primary key of the intersection table may be a separate, unique column (surrogate primary key, which is generated). Or it may be the composite of the two foreign keys from the other tables (Tables A, B), along with a meaningful identifier (e.g., role, type).

TABLE 9-2 *Class-to-Table Translation: Simple Association*

Class	Table
`Address`	`T_Address`
`Locale`	`T_Locale`
`Customer`	`T_Customer`
`Invoice`	`T_Invoice`
`Payment`	`T_Payment`
`Shipment`	`T_Shipment`
	`T_OrderLineShipment` (intersection table for `OrderLine` and `Shipment`)

FIGURE 9-6 *Generalization/specialization and relational design*

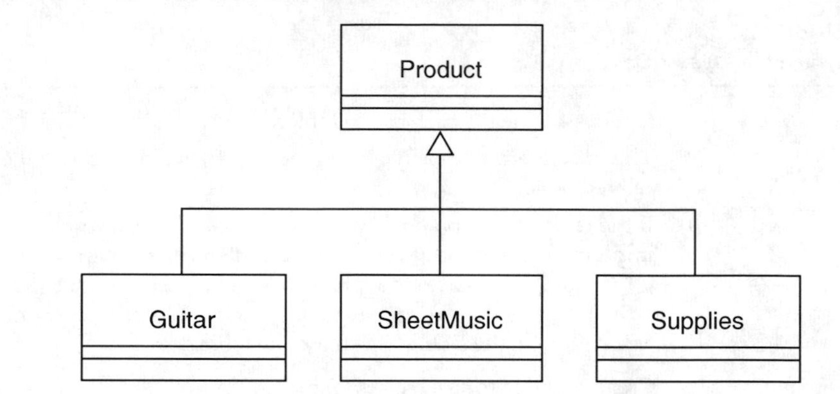

We can follow any of three alternatives when translating a generalization/specialization association to a relational design, as outlined in Table 9-3.

These choices might seem a bit overwhelming, but which one to choose is usually clear. Following are some sample scenarios to help you make the decision:

- If the number of rows is somewhat limited (in Remulak Productions' case, if the product database is small), the preference might be to insulate the application from future change and provide a more robust database design. Thus option 1 might be the most flexible. However, this option yields the worst performance (it involves lots of joins).
- If the number of attributes in the superclass is small compared to the number of its subclasses, option 3 might be the most prudent choice. The result would be better performance than that provided by option 1, and extending the model by adding more classes later would be easier.
- If the amount of data in the subclasses is sparse, option 2 might be best. This option enables the best performance, although it has the worst potential for future flexibility.

In the case of Remulak Productions, we use option 1 because the company later might want to expand its product line and would want

TABLE 9-3 *Three Options for Mapping Inheritance to a Relational Design*

Option	Benefits and Drawbacks
1. Create a table for each class and a SQL view for each superclass/subclass pair.	Results in a more flexible design, allowing future subclasses to be added with no impact on other classes and views. Results in the most RDBMS objects (in the case of Remulak Productions, seven separate objects: four tables and three views). Might hinder performance because each access will always require a SQL join through the view.
2. Create one table (of the superclass), and denormalize all column information from the subclasses into the one superclass table. Sometimes called the *roll-up method.*	Results in the least number of SQL objects (and in the case of Remulak Productions, only one table: `T_Product`). Typically results in the best overall performance because there is only one table. Requires table modifications and, if future subclassing is needed, possibly data conversion routines. Requires "dead space" in the superclass table, `T_Product`, for those columns not applicable to the subclass in question. This ultimately increases row length and could affect performance because fewer rows are returned in each physical database page access.
3. Create a table for each subclass and denormalize all superclass column information into each subclass table. Sometimes called the *roll-down method.*	When a change is required, results in somewhat less impact than option 2. If further subclassing is required, the other subclasses and the superclass will require no modifications. If the superclass later must be changed, each subclass table also must be changed and potentially undergo conversion. Results in adequate performance because in many cases fewer tables are needed (in the case of Remulak Productions, only three tables would be needed: `T_Guitar`, `T_SheetMusic`, and `T_Supplies`).

the least amount of disruption when that happened. As an implementation alternative, we will also present option 3 in the code you can download for this book.

Remember that this decision in no way changes the programmatic view of the business (except for the SQL statements). To the Java developer, the view of the business is still based on the class diagram.

Table 9-4 outlines classes and their associated tables.

TABLE 9-4 *Class-to-Table Translation: Inheritance Association*

Class	Table
Product	T_Product
Guitar	T_Guitar
	V_Product_Guitar (view of joined Product and Guitar)
SheetMusic	T_SheetMusic
	V_Product_SheetMusic (view of joined Product and SheetMusic)
Supplies	T_Supplies
	V_Product_Supplies (view of joined Product and Supplies)

Mapping Aggregation and Composition to the Relational Database

In a relational database, aggregation and composition are modeled in an identical fashion to simple associations. The same rules that apply to the entries in Table 9-4 also apply to aggregation and composition. Often aggregation and composition relationships involve many one-to-one relationships. Composition relationships almost always are implemented as just one relational table (the aggregation or composition class, such as T_Order for Remulak Productions). If the composition is implemented as separate tables, then the cascading of deletes must be addressed and implemented in the physical DBMS. Aggregation relationships, however, might end up as separate tables because the leaf classes (those being aggregated) can stand on their own.

For Remulak Productions, we create three composition associations as shown in Figure 9-7. We also create two relational tables: T_Order and T_OrderLine. Table 9-5 recaps the class-to-table translations for the Remulak Productions composition association.

TABLE 9-5 *Class-to-Table Translation: Composition*

Class	Table
Order	T_Order
OrderLine	T_OrderLine

FIGURE 9-7 *Composition and relational design*

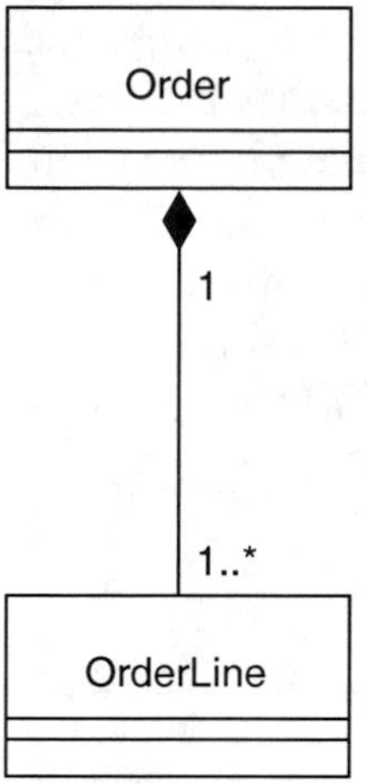

Mapping Reflexive Associations to the Relational Database

Remulak Productions' order entry application has one reflexive association—the `Product` class—as shown in Figure 9-8.

Recall that this association is necessary to support the requirement that products be related for cross-selling opportunities. A reflexive association, called a *recursive relationship* in relational modeling, results in the addition of columns that are themselves primary keys to another product. So each row in the `T_Product` table will have not only a `productId` column as its primary key, but also another `productId` column as a foreign key. This setup allows, for example, a specific set of strings (`Supplies`) to be related to a particular guitar (`Guitar`).

FIGURE 9-8 *Remulak reflexive association*

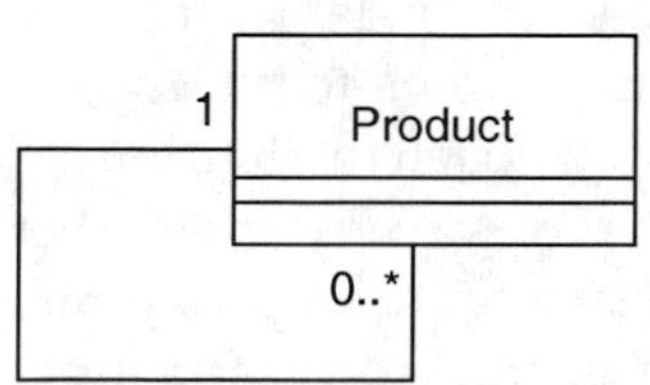

If the multiplicity for a reflexive association is one to many, no additional relational tables—but just an additional column in the `T_Product` table—are required for implementing the solution. However, let's assume a many-to-many multiplicity for the reflexive association. In this case the additional `productId` instance added to the `T_Product` table is moved to another table. This new table, perhaps called `T_Product_R`, would contain, at a minimum, two `productId` keys: one a parent product, the other a child product. The two keys are necessary because any given product could be both a parent and a child.

Key Structures and Normalization

You might have seen some column names such as `customerId` and `productId` in previous tables. These columns relate to keys and normalization. Every persistent object in the system must be uniquely identified; the nature of object design and implementation frees us, somewhat, from having to worry about object uniqueness. When an object of a given class is created, it is assigned a unique ID for its lifetime; this is done internally in the language subsystem. However, unique IDs are not assigned when the object is persisted to, for example, Microsoft SQL Server or Oracle. When making the transition from the object view to the relational view, we need to consider the primary identifiers, or keys, that will make every row in a table unique.

We can take either of two approaches to identifying keys in a relational database. The first is to select natural keys. A **natural key** is a meaningful column, or columns, that has a context and semantic relationship to the application. A good example is found in the DDL presented earlier in the chapter. The `T_Customer` table has a 14-character column called `customerNumber` (although this column contains both numbers and characters, it is still called a *number*). This column is an ideal, natural primary key for the `T_Customer` table because it is unique and has meaning to the application domain.

The second approach to identifying keys in a relational database is to pick keys that have no meaning to the application domain. This type of key is called a **surrogate**, or **programming**, **key**. Most often this type of key is a random integer or a composite creation of a modified time stamp. At first glance this approach might seem absurd. However, it can have some very positive ramifications for the design and performance of the system, as follows:

- The primary key of every table in the system is of the same data type. This promotes consistency, as well as speed in joins. Most database optimizers are much more efficient when joining on Integer-type columns. The reason is that the cardinality, or the distribution of possible values, is much smaller (a 14-byte character field versus a 4-byte Integer).
- Joins will be limited to single columns across tables. Often if the primary-key selection results in a compound composite key (i.e., more than one column is needed to uniquely identify the rows in the table), the ability to join on that key results in poorer performance and much more difficult SQL code.
- Storage needs are reduced. If the natural key of `customerNumber` is chosen as the primary key of `T_Customer`, the `T_Order` table will contain a `customerNumber` column as a foreign key to facilitate the join. This key will require 14 bytes in `T_Order`. However, if the primary key of `T_Customer` is a 4-byte Integer, the foreign key in `T_Order` will be only 4 bytes. This might not seem like much saved space, but for thousands or tens of thousands of orders the amount quickly adds up.
- More rows are returned in a physical page I/O. All databases fetch rows at the page level (at a minimum). They access pages ranging from 2K to 8K. Actually, in some cases, if a database vendor "senses" that you're reading sequentially, it might access pages in 32K and 64K increments. So the smaller the row size, the more rows will be on a page, resulting in more data being in memory when the next row is requested. Memory access is always faster than disk access, so if smaller primary keys exist, those same efficient keys will also be defined as foreign keys elsewhere. Overall, a physical page typically has more rows, thereby resulting in a few more rows being made available to the application at a much higher potential access rate.

Quite often I see implementations that use the surrogate key approach but use an automatically generated sequential number. Be careful with sequential integers as primary keys. The reason for caution here has to do with index management. If your index is not utilizing a hashing algorithm and being maintained in a typically B-tree structure, then a sequential integer will generate hot spots in your index data set. A hot spot means that you continually have to split the tree because your keys are continually increasing in sequence. Without going into the subtleties of B-tree performance, let me say that this scenario can kill applications that are insert intensive.

The Remulak Productions' relational design will use a surrogate key as the primary key of every relational table. The column names will be similar across tables, each using the mask of `tablenameId`, where *`tablename`* is the respective table in the system. This surrogate key will be stored as an Integer in the database and programmed as an Integer in Java. The next chapter introduces code that generates this surrogate key before the row is inserted into the table.

Figure 9-9 is an entity relationship diagram that shows the tables necessary to implement the Remulak Productions class diagram. The notation is in the industry-standard entity definition schema, the IDEF1X format.

FIGURE 9-9 *Entity relationship diagram for Remulak Productions*

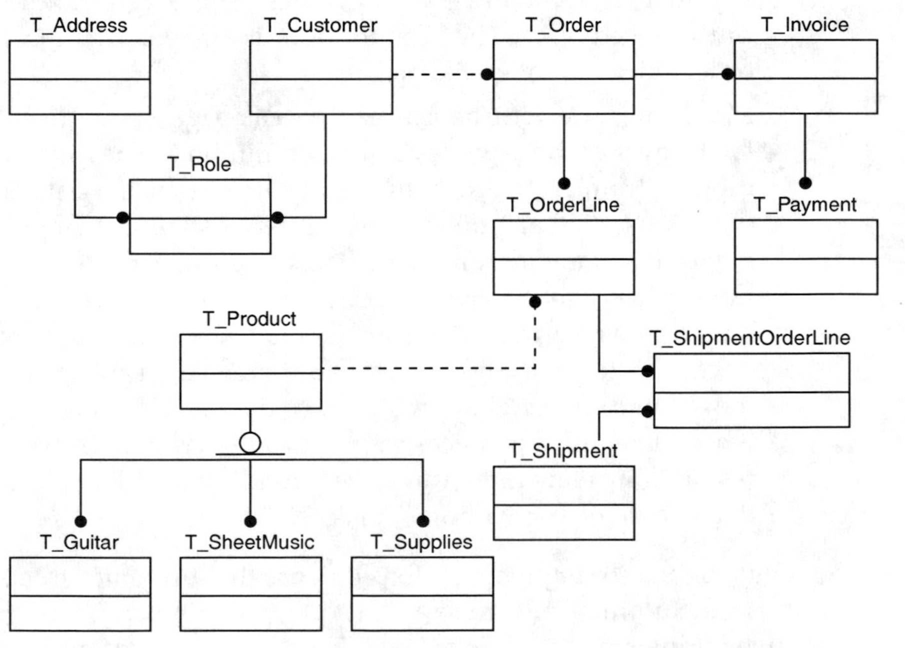

Using a Visual Modeling Tool to Generate the DDL

Visual modeling tools are a must for integrating UML with an implementation language. Chapter 10 will show that the iterative and incremental approach to building software relies on quick and accurate forward and reverse engineering. This approach to modeling and code generation is called **round-trip engineering.**

The quality of the SQL DDL to generate the table structures is just as critical as the quality of the Java code to implement the classes. As before, we use Rational Rose. With the enterprise version, Rose contains an add-in product called the Data Modeler. Again, I show this in the book because I find most project teams using some form of visual modeling not only to generate code but also to generate DDL. Visual modeling isn't a necessary part of the application, but it sure beats hand-editing the DDL.

When using Rose, we need to intervene manually in the area of transient attributes because although Rose supports transient classes, it does not support transient attributes. (Rose does have a transient attribute, but its usage pertains to Java and serialization). During DDL generation, each class attribute is given a corresponding column in the target relational table. Any attributes that are needed only at runtime and that we don't want persisted will require manual removal from the schema for the corresponding table. Figure 9-10 shows Rational Rose and the current class diagram for Remulak Productions.

DDL generation in Rose is very easy. Let's look at an example that generates DDL for the classes in the Remulak class diagram. We begin by defining the target database in Rose through the component view package located in the tree view on the left-hand side of the screen (see Figure 9-10).

1. Right-click on **Component View** in the tree view.
2. Select **Data Modeler** in the context menu.
3. Select **New** in the next context menu.
4. Select **Database** in the next context menu.

This sequence of commands will create a component in the component view that resembles a disk drive. Double-click on this component,

FIGURE 9-10 *The current Remulak class diagram in Rational Rose*

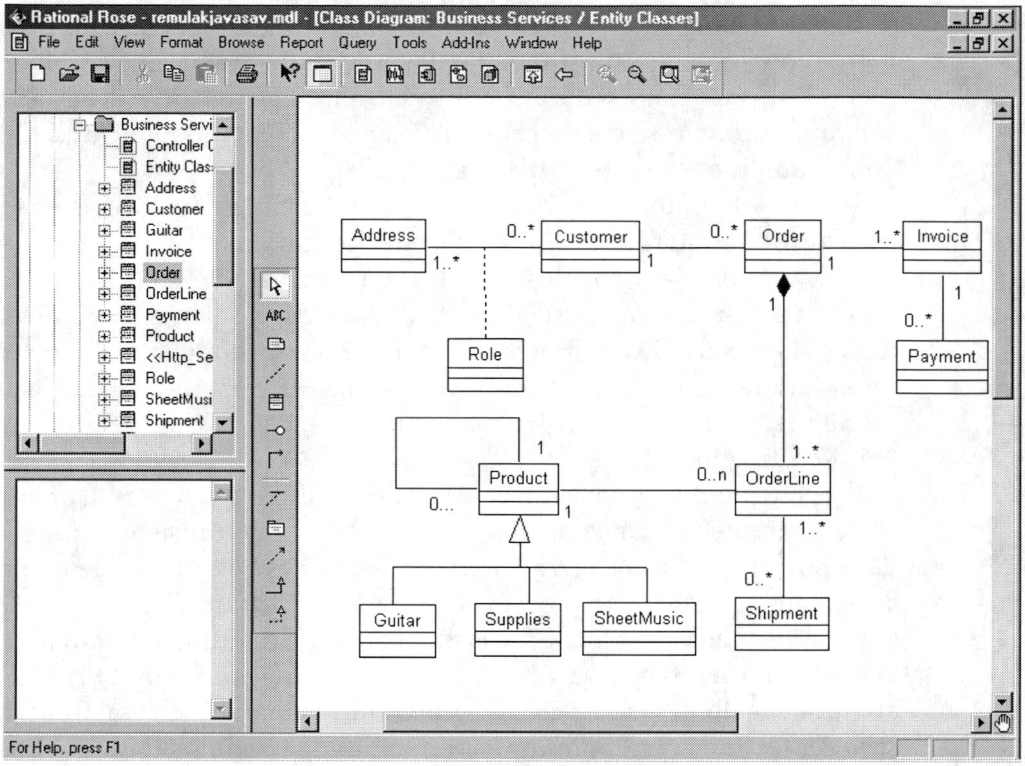

and a dialog box will appear (see Figure 9-11). This dialog allows you to select the type of database to which the specified component refers. This will be the component that we tie to the schema created in the next step (see Figure 9-12).

Next we must create an empty schema package to be the recipient of the relational entities. Keep in mind that this process creates only relational entities—fodder for an entity relationship diagram if you will. The step after this will be to forward-generate DDL from the schema we create here. So to create the schema, do the following:

1. Double-click on **Logical View** in the tree view.
2. Double-click on **Increment1** in the tree view.
3. Right-click on **Business Services.**

FIGURE 9-11 *Assigning a database type to a component in Rational Rose*

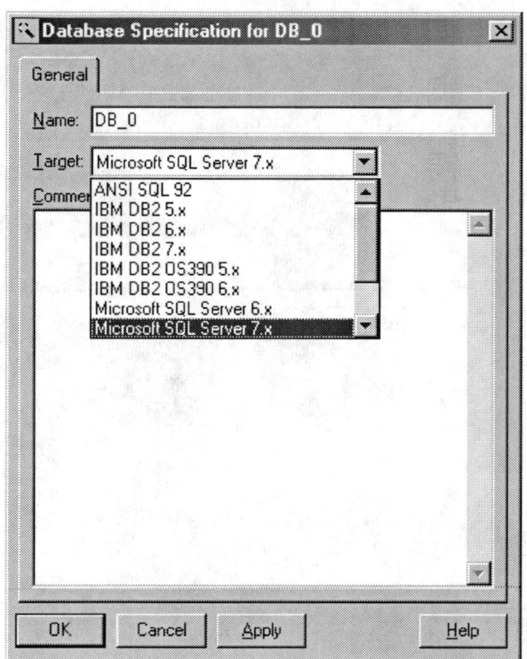

4. Select the **Data Modeler** context menu item.
5. Select **Transform To Data Model . . .**

This sequence will take you through a dialog to create a schema and the tables based on the classes found in the class diagram (see Figure 9-10).

Notice the **Target Database** drop-down list box in Figure 9-12. This is where a reference is made to the database component that was created in the previous step (see Figure 9-11). This level of abstraction for relating database components to schemas is quite powerful and reusable. For instance, The DB_0 component created in Figure 9-11 can be referenced by more than one schema. Why would we want more than one schema? There are two reasons: (1) Because each schema can refer to a unique table space (a physical container of sorts for tables), two different schemas are needed, but each one can refer to the same database component. (2) Perhaps some of your classes will be physically housed in a SQL Server database and others in an Oracle database. Remulak

FIGURE 9-12 *Rose schema/table creation dialog box*

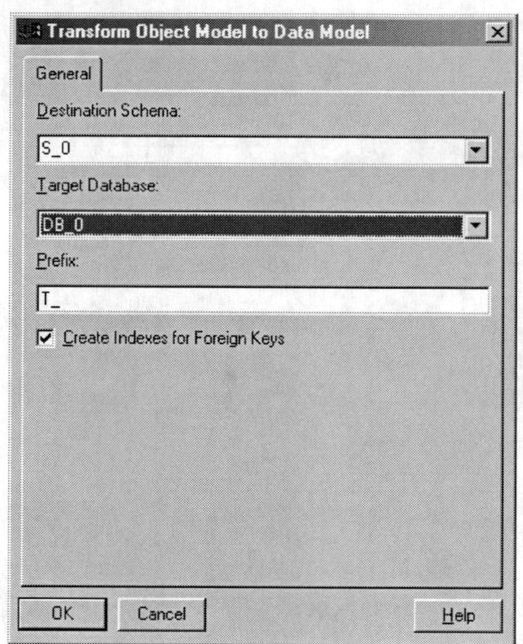

would then need two database components—DB_0 and DB_1—one referring to Microsoft SQL Server, the other to Oracle. This would allow each schema to refer to the appropriate database component.

Once the dialog in Figure 9-12 has been completed, there will be a new schema package containing another package that goes by the name of the schema assigned in the dialog outlined in Figure 9-12 (the default schema name is *S_0*). If you open up the S_0 schema (or whatever name you give it), several table names will be displayed. If you double-click on one—say, `T_Customer`—and select the **Columns** tab, a **Table Specification** dialog box will appear as in Figure 9-13.

Using the dialog outlined in Figure 9-13, you can make any necessary changes to the table definitions. To further reinforce the understanding of the relationship between the database component created in Figure 9-11 and the schema created in Figure 9-12, all of the column types displayed under the "Type" column in Figure 9-13 will be constrained to those supported by the database component specified when the schema was created. Additional dialogs support further definition of the columnar information.

FIGURE 9-13 *Rose* ***Table Specification*** *dialog box for the* `T_Customer` *table*

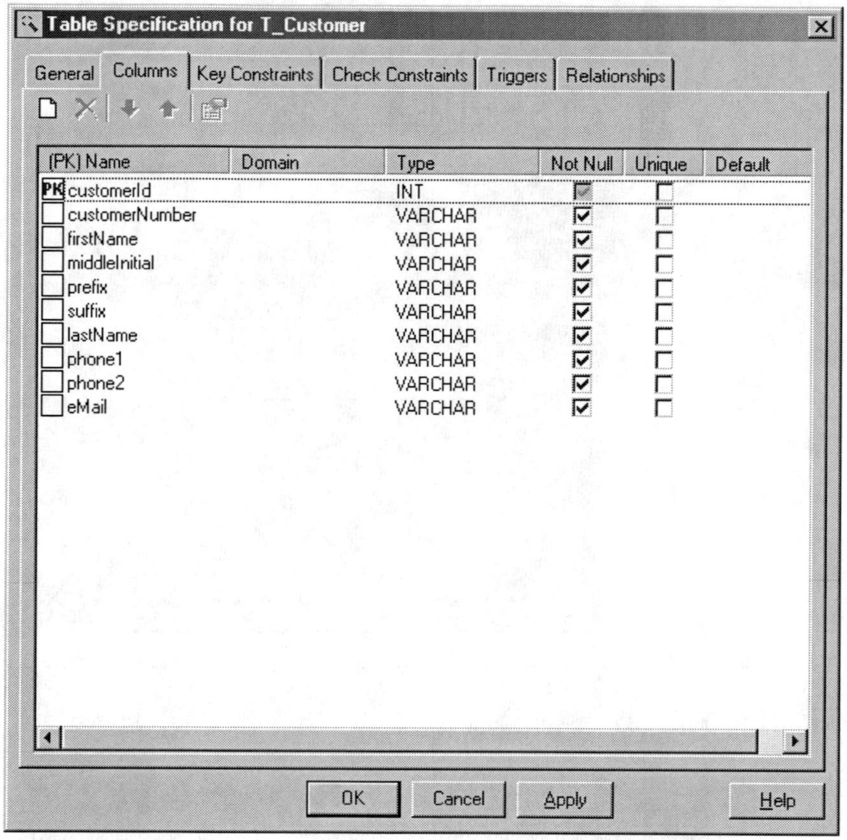

Table Specification for T_Customer

General | Columns | Key Constraints | Check Constraints | Triggers | Relationships

(PK) Name	Domain	Type	Not Null	Unique	Default
PK customerId		INT	☑	☐	
customerNumber		VARCHAR	☑	☐	
firstName		VARCHAR	☑	☐	
middleInitial		VARCHAR	☑	☐	
prefix		VARCHAR	☑	☐	
suffix		VARCHAR	☑	☐	
lastName		VARCHAR	☑	☐	
phone1		VARCHAR	☑	☐	
phone2		VARCHAR	☑	☐	
eMail		VARCHAR	☑	☐	

OK | Cancel | Apply | Help

Double-clicking on a column name—say, `customerNumber`—shows a dialog box like the one in Figure 9-14. It is here that items such as length and precision are specified for an individual attribute.

Now it's time to generate the DDL scripts for the schema. We can do this from two different locations: the schema package or the database component package. Here are the steps involved:

1. Right-click on the schema package created in Figure 9-12.
2. Select the **Data Modeler** context menu item.
3. Select the **Forward Engineer . . .** context menu item.
4. Select **Next** in the ensuing dialogs until a dialog appears as outlined in Figure 9-15.

FIGURE 9-14 *Rose **Columnar Specification** dialog box*

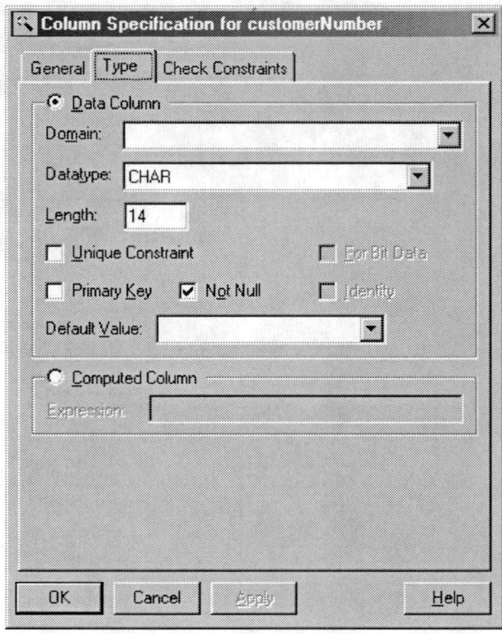

FIGURE 9-15 *Rose DDL script dialog box*

FIGURE 9-16 *Rose DDL script for Remulak's SQL Server tables*

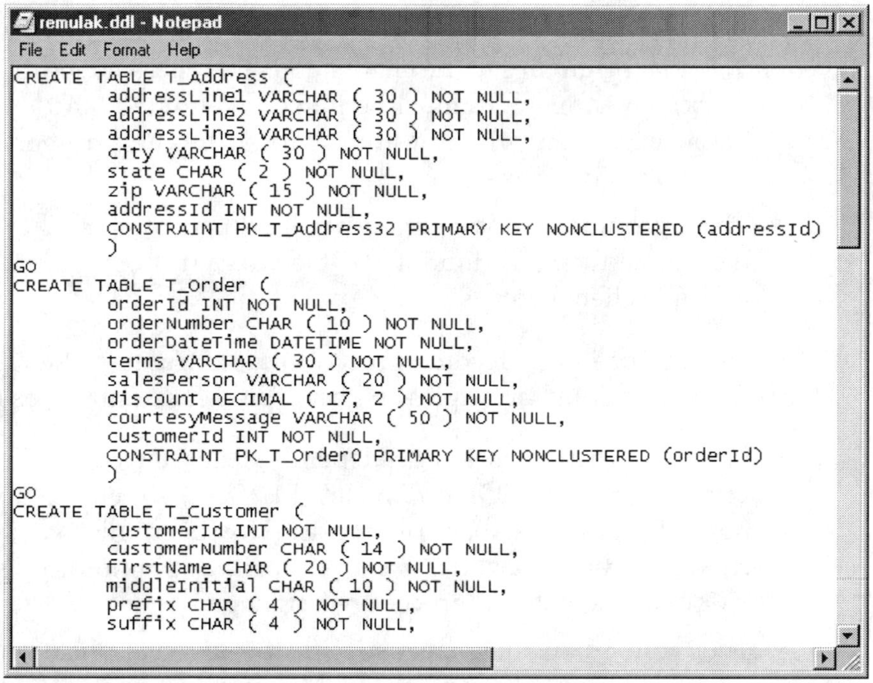

```
CREATE TABLE T_Address (
        addressLine1 VARCHAR ( 30 ) NOT NULL,
        addressLine2 VARCHAR ( 30 ) NOT NULL,
        addressLine3 VARCHAR ( 30 ) NOT NULL,
        city VARCHAR ( 30 ) NOT NULL,
        state CHAR ( 2 ) NOT NULL,
        zip VARCHAR ( 15 ) NOT NULL,
        addressId INT NOT NULL,
        CONSTRAINT PK_T_Address32 PRIMARY KEY NONCLUSTERED (addressId)
        )
GO
CREATE TABLE T_Order (
        orderId INT NOT NULL,
        orderNumber CHAR ( 10 ) NOT NULL,
        orderDateTime DATETIME NOT NULL,
        terms VARCHAR ( 30 ) NOT NULL,
        salesPerson VARCHAR ( 20 ) NOT NULL,
        discount DECIMAL ( 17, 2 ) NOT NULL,
        courtesyMessage VARCHAR ( 50 ) NOT NULL,
        customerId INT NOT NULL,
        CONSTRAINT PK_T_Order0 PRIMARY KEY NONCLUSTERED (orderId)
        )
GO
CREATE TABLE T_Customer (
        customerId INT NOT NULL,
        customerNumber CHAR ( 14 ) NOT NULL,
        firstName CHAR ( 20 ) NOT NULL,
        middleInitial CHAR ( 10 ) NOT NULL,
        prefix CHAR ( 4 ) NOT NULL,
        suffix CHAR ( 4 ) NOT NULL,
```

Supplying a DDL file name and selecting **Next** will create the DDL for all the tables in the schema. Figure 9-16 is a partial listing of the DDL. The entire DDL for the project can be found in Appendix D.

Stored Procedures and Triggers and the Object-Oriented Project

Client/server server technology really began to take shape in the late 1980s and early 1990s. One technology that boosted its credibility was the stored procedure and trigger. Initially offered by Sybase in its SQL Server product, the technology today is supported by most major database vendors.

Stored procedures and triggers gained wide acceptance for several reasons:

- They provide for the precompilation of SQL and procedural programming logic (`if . . . then . . . else`) into a tightly bound database object that can be invoked from a client or another server that is acting as a client to yet another server.

- They provide performance advantages over dynamic SQL (i.e., SQL that originates at the client and is then passed across the network). Dynamic SQL must be parsed, validated, and optimized before execution, whereas stored procedures and triggers wait to be invoked in an executable state.
- They provide a common, central repository for data access, thereby reducing redundant SQL code that might spread across multiple client sources.

Despite the promise of stored procedures and triggers, they fly in the face of object-oriented principles and concepts—for example, as follows:

- They are written in DBMS-dependent languages, such as SQL Server's Transact-SQL or Oracle's PL/SQL, which are not transportable across database platforms. (However, this is destined to change because most database vendors have announced support of Java as their stored procedure language.)
- They contain business rules specific to a given application and tie the rules not only to a specific DBMS language but also to the data access language (SQL).

This technology has both opponents and proponents. Developers who want an extensible design that is portable across database platforms oppose it. Proponents argue that if a stored procedure or trigger can make a poorly performing transaction really fast, then it doesn't matter what is used to meet the service-level agreement with one's clients.

I use stored procedures and triggers as the ultimate screwdriver to fine-tune the application. I initially approach my design without them. Then if I experience problems with performance, I use a stored procedure to perform the typical create, read, update, delete (CRUD) activities in SQL (i.e., insert, select, update, and delete). As a last resort, if a complicated business rule that requires access to many rows of information is simply not performing, I use a stored procedure or trigger. Keep in mind, however, that this migration from a program code solution to a database code solution is not trivial and will take some time.

With the advent of the thin-client computing model, most, if not all, of the business logic is being moved to the server. This makes not using a stored procedure more acceptable because the server that houses the business rules will probably be located in the same computing complex as the machine that houses the database. Furthermore, the network speeds that these machines can achieve are very fast, approaching gigabit throughput. These changes would remove many of the reasons for using stored procedures and triggers in the first place.

The key point is that the option exists. The bottom line in the decision process is meeting the performance goals of the application. Show me the last systems designer who was able to get away with ten-minute response times by saying, "We did it for object purity." (Don't laugh—I actually heard that line used once.)

The Data Translation Services and Data Access Services Layers

Recall that Chapter 8 discussed the six layers of an application, which are shown again in Figure 9-17. Also recall from Chapter 8 that for Remulak Productions the Data Translation Services layer will be implemented both for native JDBC calls made from JavaBeans and BMP entity beans and for CMP support within the EJB application server. We need to explore the architecture issues with these two approaches, so let's begin with the JavaBean/native JDBC approach.

JavaBeans with Native JDBC Support

Prior to the advent of container-managed persistence (CMP) in Enterprise JavaBeans, the only way to manage data access, with the exception of add-on persistence managers like TopLink for BEA/WebGain, was to craft them from scratch. This is still the option chosen today by many development groups. Until we see widespread support of the EJB 2.0 specification and CMP by application server vendors, it will be the favored choice. As we'll see, however, designing and building this solution represents a tremendous amount of work on the part of the development team.

JavaBeans and Native JDBC Data Management

JDBC (Java Database Connectivity) is still the technology that underlies our data translation and data access strategies. In our initial solution, we must craft it all ourselves. To do that we need an architecture that

FIGURE 9-17 *Six-logical-tier model*

Presentation Services	• HTML and scripted forms
Business Context Services	• Servlet and JavaServer pages (Internet) and Web server
Business Rule Services	• JavaBeans and Enterprise JavaBeans (session and entity beans)
Data Translation Services	• JavaBeans with native JDBC, as well as both BMP with native JDBC and CMP implemented by EJB-compliant application server
Data Access Services	• Implemented by JDBC and JDBC, controlled by CMP and the persistence manager in the EJB-compliant application server
Database Services	• Microsoft SQL Server (production) • Oracle (investigation)

represents a repeatable approach. When this type of solution is necessary, it is best to consider interfaces first. If your design appears to be potentially repeatable across many classes, an interface is the best approach. First we must consider what the data access layer must support. Every bean (e.g., `Customer` and `Order`) needs the ability both to retrieve itself from persistent storage and to persist itself back to the same storage device.

The Remulak design approach will be to create what are called **data access objects (DAOs)**. DAOs have been popular for many years. In my Visual Basic book, I had a similar construct called data translation classes. In Nicholas Kassem's popular book *Designing Enterprise Applications with the Java 2 Platform* (Addison-Wesley, 2000), the sample pet store application implements the concept of DAOs. The same DAOs will also be used for bean-managed persistence (BMP) in the Enterprise JavaBeans environment.

DAOs are meant to satisfy the data access requirements of our entity classes. Our design certainly could have implemented all the data access logic with embedded SQL statements in the entity classes themselves, but then we would have broken our motto of keeping the layers separate. Toward that end, our design will implement a DAO class for every entity class in the system. These classes will all follow the naming pattern of `classnameDAO`.

Next we must consider the functionality that these DAO classes should implement. This is where the idea of an interface would play quite nicely into a flexible design. These classes need to be able to retrieve information by their primary key. Because we have the luxury of every class being identified with the same surrogate key strategy, an Integer, this behavior can be common across all DAOs. These classes must also be able to insert, delete, and update themselves.

Finally, DAOs should be able to retrieve themselves by their natural identifiers if necessary. We have also ensured that this can be common because all top-level classes (e.g., `Customer`, `Order`) have a String by which they can be identified (e.g., "customer number," "order number"). This leads us to a potential set of operations that are common:

- **`insertObject()`**: This operation inserts records into the respective table. It requires an image of the object as input and returns nothing.
- **`updateObject()`**: This operation updates records of the respective table. It requires an image of the object as input and returns nothing.
- **`deleteObject()`**: This operation deletes records from the respective table. It requires the primary key identifier for the object as input and returns nothing.
- **`findByPrimaryKey()`**: This operation retrieves the persistent state of an object. It requires the primary key identifier as input and returns an image of the object retrieved.
- **`findByName()`**: This operation retrieves the persistent state of an object. It requires the natural String key of the object as input and returns an image of the object retrieved.

What follows here is the basis of the common interface that the Remulak project team calls `DataAccess`. Each DAO class will implement this interface.

```
package com.jacksonreed;
public interface DataAccess {
    public void insertObject(Object model) throws
                     DAOAppException, DAODBUpdateException,
                     DAOSysException;
    public void updateObject(Object model) throws
                     DAOAppException, DAODBUpdateException,
                     DAOSysException;
    public void deleteObject(Integer id) throws DAOSysException,
                     DAODBUpdateException;
    public Object findByPrimaryKey(Integer id) throws
    DAOSysException,
                     DAOFinderException;
    public Object findByName(String name) throws
                     DAOSysException, DAOFinderException;
}
```

In the interface description earlier, we stated that an object image is returned in the case of finders, and passed in in the case of insert and update operations. To make the interface generic, we must use the `Object` reference. It will then be the responsibility of the DAO class when receiving the object to cast it to the proper class. For instance, in the case of the `CustomerDAO` class, something like the following is necessary:

```
CustomerValue custVal = (CustomerValue) model;
```

A class that is receiving something back from a DAO, such as `CustomerBean`, would need a similar cast in its finder operation:

```
DataAccess custDAO = new CustomerDAO(transactionContext);
CustomerValue custVal = (CustomerValue)
          custDAO.findByName(customerNumber);
```

These object images being sent back and forth are also following a common design technique used to minimize network traffic. If the Java components accessing the entity bean components were on different machines, each get and set call to each attribute would be an expensive trip across the network. One way to reduce this overhead is to create an image of the object's state and pass it back and forth. With this approach, only one element is passed.

A class that does this contains nothing but attributes and get and set operations for these attributes. The format for naming such classes will be `classnameValue`. Here's the class definition for `CustomerValue`:

```
package com.jacksonreed;

import java.util.ArrayList;

public class CustomerValue implements java.io.Serializable {

   private Integer customerId;
   private String customerNumber;
   private String firstName;
   private String middleInitial;
   private String prefix;
   private String suffix;
   private String lastName;
   private String phone1;
   private String phone2;
   private String EMail;
   private ArrayList roleValue;
   private ArrayList orderValue;

   public CustomerValue() {
      roleValue = new ArrayList();
      orderValue = new ArrayList();
   }

   public Integer getCustomerId() {
      return customerId;
   }

   public void setCustomerId(Integer val) {
      customerId = val;
   }
   public String getCustomerNumber() {
      return customerNumber;
   }
   public void setCustomerNumber(String val) {
      customerNumber = val;
   }
   public String getFirstName(){
      return firstName;
   }
   public void setFirstName(String val){
      firstName = val;
   }
```

```
public String getMiddleInitial(){
   return middleInitial;
}
public void setMiddleInitial(String val){
   middleInitial = val;
}
public String getPrefix(){
   return prefix;
}
public void setPrefix(String val){
   prefix = val;
}
public String getSuffix(){
   return suffix;
}
public void setSuffix(String val){
   suffix = val;
}
public String getLastName(){
   return lastName;
}
public void setLastName(String val){
   lastName = val;
}
public String getPhone1(){
   return phone1;
}
public void setPhone1(String val){
   phone1 = val;
}
public String getPhone2(){
   return phone2;
}
public void setPhone2(String val){
   phone2 = val;
}
public String getEMail(){
   return EMail;
}
public void setEMail(String val){
   EMail = val;
}
public ArrayList getRoleValue(){
   return roleValue;
}
```

```
    public void setRoleValue(ArrayList val){
       roleValue = val;
    }
    public ArrayList getOrderValue(){
       return orderValue;
    }
    public void setOrderValue(ArrayList val){
       orderValue = val;
    }
}
```

So just what does a DAO class that implements the `DataAccess` interface look like? Let's look at a few snippets of `CustomerDAO` and in particular the operations that realize the interface. Here we show only the class definition and the `updateObject()` operation:

```
package com.jacksonreed;

import java.io.*;
import java.sql.*;
import java.text.*;
import java.util.*;
import javax.sql.*;

public class CustomerDAO implements Serializable, DataAccess {
    private transient TransactionContext globalTran = null;
    private transient CustomerValue custVal    = null;

    public CustomerDAO(TransactionContext transactionContext) {
          globalTran = transactionContext;
    }
    public void updateObject(Object model) throws
                   DAOSysException, DAODBUpdateException {

        CustomerValue custVal = (CustomerValue) model;
        PreparedStatement stmt = null;
        try {
            String queryStr = "UPDATE " + "T_Customer" +
              " SET " + "customerNumber = ?, " +
              "firstName = ?, " +
              "middleInitial = ?, " +
              "prefix = ?, " +
              "suffix = ?, " +
              "lastName = ?, " +
              "phone1 = ?, " +
```

```
                "phone2 = ?, " +
                "eMail = ? " +
                "WHERE customerId = ?";

            stmt =

    globalTran.getDBConnection().prepareStatement(queryStr);

            int i = 1;
            stmt.setString(i++, custVal.getCustomerNumber());
            stmt.setString(i++, custVal.getFirstName());
            stmt.setString(i++, custVal.getMiddleInitial());
            stmt.setString(i++, custVal.getPrefix());
            stmt.setString(i++, custVal.getSuffix());
            stmt.setString(i++, custVal.getLastName());
            stmt.setString(i++, custVal.getPhone1());
            stmt.setString(i++, custVal.getPhone2());
            stmt.setString(i++, custVal.getEMail());
            stmt.setInt(i++, custVal.getCustomerId().intValue());

            int resultCount = stmt.executeUpdate();
            if ( resultCount != 1 ) {
                 throw new DAODBUpdateException ("ERROR updating
                           Customer in"
          + " Customer_TABLE!! resultCount = " + resultCount);
            }
        } catch(SQLException se) {
            throw new DAOSysException("Unable to update item " +
                 custVal.getCustomerId() + " \n" + se);
        } finally {
            globalTran.closeStatement(stmt);
            log("CustomerDAO: closeStatement");
        }
    }
}
```

Here we see that native JDBC calls are being made to execute the SQL statement `stmt.executeUpdate()`. Notice also in the signature of the constructor for `CustomerDAO` that there is an object of type `TransactionContext` being passed in from the caller, `CustomerBean`. This object allows coordination of the many database activities and is the unifying element that allows unit-of-work transaction management. Chapter 11 will say more about transaction management and

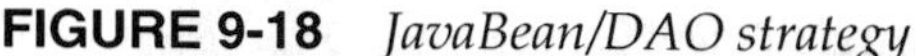

FIGURE 9-18 *JavaBean/DAO strategy*

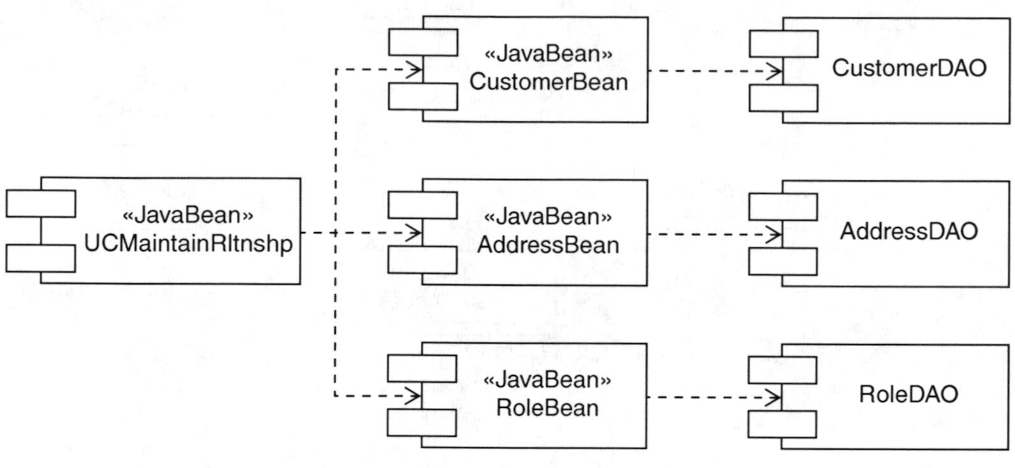

`TransactionContext`. Figure 9-18 is a component diagram of the data access architecture for our JavaBean/DAO strategy.

Figure 9-19 is a class diagram representing the interface and its relationship to the DAO classes. Again, this would apply to all entity beans for Remulak; we are showing only those that relate to the *Maintain Relationships* use-case.

Remember how to interpret this class diagram? `DataAccess` is an interface and it is realized, or implemented, by the three DAO classes. The three JavaBean classes all depend on this interface.

Enterprise JavaBeans and Data Management

EJB offers two varieties of data management: bean-managed persistence (BMP) and container-managed persistence (CMP). All Enterprise JavaBeans implement a callback model to allow the container product to manage the state of the bean. This is necessary because the container in which they run must be able to communicate with the bean at various times within the bean's lifecycle. Although we will learn more about these callback mechanisms later, it is the responsibility of the container to invoke the necessary operations—for example, `ejbCreate()`—on the basis of how clients of the bean interact with it.

In the case of BMP, you still must write SQL code. However, the good news is that we are able to use the same DAO strategy and modules

FIGURE 9-19 *UML class diagram depicting the* `DataAccess` *interface*

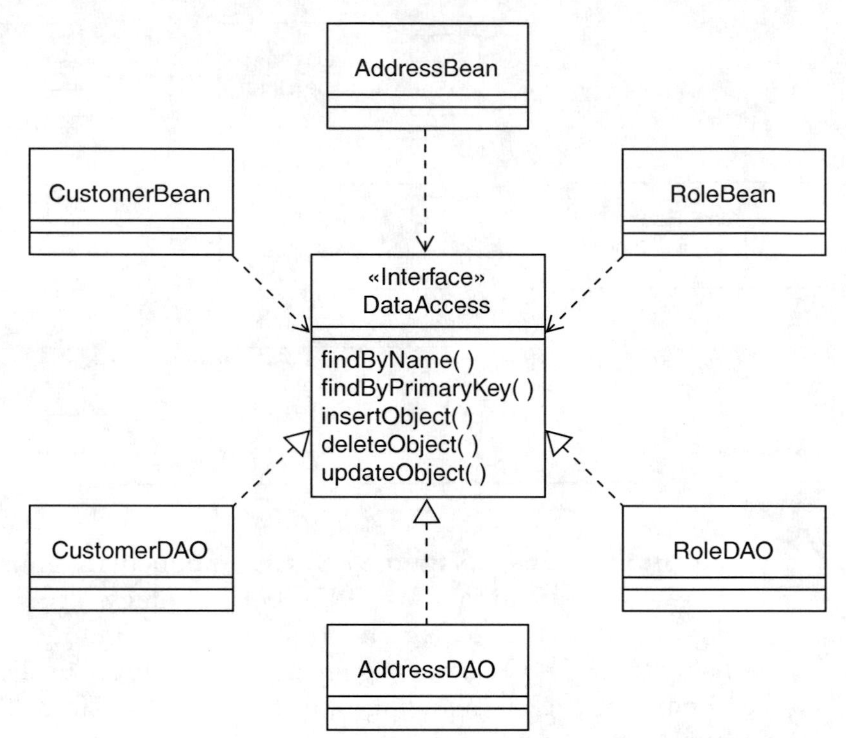

with very few changes over what was built to work for the non-EJB environment. So with the exception of ensuring that we place the proper calls to the DAO objects in the right callback operations implemented in our EJBs, the EJB strategy is very similar in functionality to what we have already built. Figure 9-18 would apply for BMP as well; the only difference would be that instead of plain JavaBeans interfacing with the DAO classes, they would be entity EJBs implementing bean-managed persistence. We will see more of BMP using our DAO objects when we build the EJB solution in Chapter 12.

Things are really different with the next data management strategy: container-managed persistence (CMP). Because the folks at Sun needed to greatly improve the consistency of their CMP message with EJB 1.1, they decided to totally revamp how CMP works with EJB 2.0. EJB 2.0 is not backward compatible with EJB 1.1. Although the two can still coexist, once you have experienced CMP under EJB 2.0, you won't even think about going back to EJB 1.1 CMP. I will even go a step further and say that once you experience CMP, it will be very difficult to go back to BMP.

My review of CMP will be cursory here, although in later chapters we will see quite a bit of application code using it. I would highly recommend that you read a book devoted to EJB application architectures, such as *Enterprise JavaBeans* by Richard Monson-Haefel (published by O'Reilly, 2000). For the inquisitive mind, however, the brief review I present here will, I think, provide a good overview as it relates to Remulak.

First, it is important to understand that with CMP, *you write absolutely no SQL code.* This will take some getting used to. The closest thing to SQL you will write is something called EJB-QL, and only then if you have specific select requests of your entity beans (e.g., "Show me all orders over a certain dollar amount"). For simple CRUD activities, CMP handles it all. Of particular importance, it handles the relationships between beans such as one to one, one to many, and many to many. There is no fiddling with foreign keys once the application server is aware of the relationships. The simple act of an entity bean, such as `Order`, storing `OrderLine` objects in its own `ArrayList` object will result in rows being inserted into both the `T_ORDER` and `T_ORDERLINE` tables with all the appropriate foreign key information being set.

Figure 9-20 is an overview of an EJB container (in our case BEA's WebLogic) and some of its components. A key link between your Java code and the resulting RDBMS activity is formed by the deployment descriptors. The descriptors describe what Sun calls an *abstract persistence schema.* This schema maps physical columns in the tables to operations and relationships in your code. Other EJB vendors will have more or less the same descriptors, but what goes into the descriptors as pertains to the RDMBS components is specified by the EJB 2.0 specification, not the EJB vendor.

Schemas are just XML that describes the data aspects of your beans. The following snippet of the `ejb-jar.xml` file for Remulak describes the persistent view of the `OrderBean` object (for space reasons I have removed the other objects). The descriptor also takes into account the relationships they may have with other beans, as well as transaction requirements. This descriptor is the pivotal component that ties your beans to the back-end persistence mechanisms.

FIGURE 9-20 *Deployment descriptors and bean relationships*

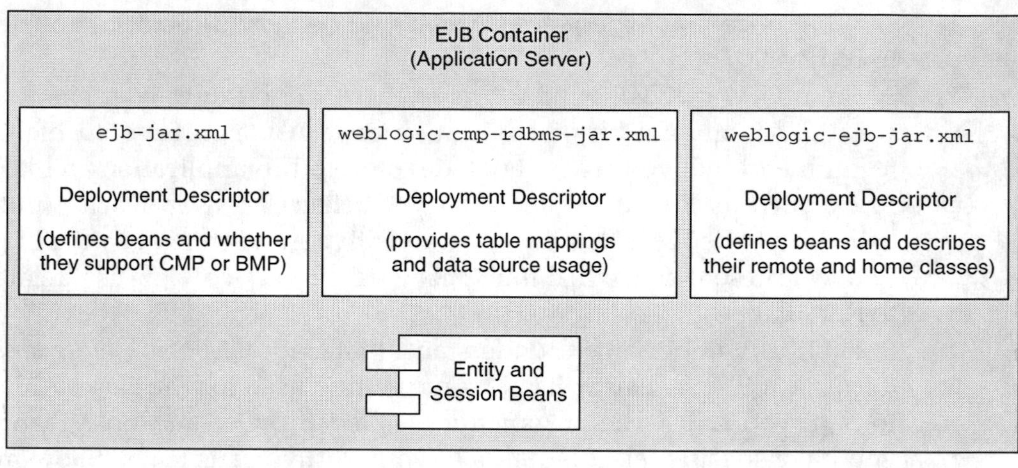


```
<ejb-jar>
   <enterprise-beans>
      <entity>
         <ejb-name>OrderBean</ejb-name>
         <home>com.jacksonreed.OrderHome</home>
         <remote>com.jacksonreed.Order</remote>
         <ejb-class>com.jacksonreed.OrderBean</ejb-class>
         <persistence-type>Container</persistence-type>
         <prim-key-class>java.lang.Integer</prim-key-class>
         <reentrant>False</reentrant>
         <cmp-version>2.x</cmp-version>
         <abstract-schema-name>OrderBean</abstract-schema-name>
         <cmp-field>
            <field-name>orderId</field-name>
         </cmp-field>
         <cmp-field>
            <field-name>orderNumber</field-name>
         </cmp-field>
         <cmp-field>
            <field-name>orderDateTime</field-name>
         </cmp-field>
         <cmp-field>
            <field-name>terms</field-name>
         </cmp-field>
         <cmp-field>
            <field-name>salesPerson</field-name>
```

```
    </cmp-field>
    <cmp-field>
       <field-name>discount</field-name>
    </cmp-field>
    <cmp-field>
       <field-name>courtesyMessage</field-name>
    </cmp-field>
    <primkey-field>orderId</primkey-field>
    <query>
       <query-method>
          <method-name>findAllOrders</method-name>
          <method-params/>
       </query-method>
       <ejb-ql><![CDATA[ WHERE orderId IS NOT NULL]]>
       </ejb-ql>
    </query>
    <query>
       <query-method>
          <method-name>findByOrderNumber</method-name>
          <method-params>
             <method-param>java.lang.String</method-param>
          </method-params>
       </query-method>
       <ejb-ql><![CDATA[ WHERE orderNumber = ?1]]>
       </ejb-ql>
    </query>
 </entity>
 <ejb-relation>
    <ejb-relation-name>Order-OrderLine</ejb-relation-name>
    <ejb-relationship-role>
       <ejb-relationship-role-name>OrderLineBean-Has-
       OrderBean</ejb-relationship-role-name>
       <multiplicity>many</multiplicity>
       <role-source>
          <ejb-name>OrderLineBean</ejb-name>
       </role-source>
    </ejb-relationship-role>
    <ejb-relationship-role>
       <ejb-relationship-role-name>OrderBean-Has-
       OrderLineBean</ejb-relationship-role-name>
       <multiplicity>one</multiplicity>
       <role-source>
          <ejb-name>OrderBean</ejb-name>
       </role-source>
       <cmr-field>
```

```
            <cmr-field-name>orderLines</cmr-field-name>
            <cmr-field-type>java.util.Collection</cmr-
            field-type>
         </cmr-field>
      </ejb-relationship-role>
   </ejb-relation>
   <ejb-relation>
      <ejb-relation-name>Customer-Order</ejb-relation-name>
      <ejb-relationship-role>
         <ejb-relationship-role-name>OrderBean-Has-
         CustomerBean</ejb-relationship-role-name>
         <multiplicity>many</multiplicity>
         <role-source>
            <ejb-name>OrderBean</ejb-name>
         </role-source>
         <cmr-field>
            <cmr-field-name>customer</cmr-field-name>
         </cmr-field>
      </ejb-relationship-role>
      <ejb-relationship-role>
         <ejb-relationship-role-name>CustomerBean-Has-
         OrderBean</ejb-relationship-role-name>
         <multiplicity>one</multiplicity>
         <role-source>
            <ejb-name>CustomerBean</ejb-name>
         </role-source>
         <cmr-field>
            <cmr-field-name>orders</cmr-field-name>
            <cmr-field-type>java.util.Collection</cmr-field-
            type>
         </cmr-field>
      </ejb-relationship-role>
   </ejb-relation>
   <ejb-relation>
      <ejb-relation-name>Product-OrderLine</ejb-relation-
      name>
      <ejb-relationship-role>
         <ejb-relationship-role-name>OrderLineBean-Has-
         ProductBean</ejb-relationship-role-name>
         <multiplicity>many</multiplicity>
         <role-source>
            <ejb-name>OrderLineBean</ejb-name>
         </role-source>
         <cmr-field>
            <cmr-field-name>product</cmr-field-name>
         </cmr-field>
```

```
            </ejb-relationship-role>
            <ejb-relationship-role>
               <ejb-relationship-role-name>ProductBean-Has-
               OrderLineBean</ejb-relationship-role-name>
               <multiplicity>one</multiplicity>
               <role-source>
                  <ejb-name>ProductBean</ejb-name>
               </role-source>
               <cmr-field>
                  <cmr-field-name>orderLines</cmr-field-name>
                  <cmr-field-type>java.util.Collection</cmr-
                  field-type>
               </cmr-field>
            </ejb-relationship-role>
         </ejb-relation>
      </enterprise-beans>
      <assembly-descriptor>
         <container-transaction>
            <method>
               <ejb-name>OrderBean</ejb-name>
               <method-intf>Remote</method-intf>
               <method-name>*</method-name>
            </method>
            <trans-attribute>Required</trans-attribute>
         </container-transaction>
      </assembly-descriptor>
   </ejb-jar>
```

Notice that the tags define the table to which the entity bean is persisted, as well as relationships that this bean has with other entity beans. Multiplicity is also specified with the `<multiplicity>` tag, as well as the Java variable and its type for storing the relationships in the `<cmr-field>` and subordinate tags. The other two descriptors contain information such as the data source to use when accessing the application's data.

Regardless of the EJB vendor, today with the EJB 2.0 specification it is much more feasible to transport CMP beans between vendor containers. The only changes would be to replace the descriptors with the new target vendor's descriptors and redeploy the application.

Commercial Persistence Layers

It is worth mentioning that other commercial products are available that provide excellent implementation layers for translating the object model to a relational database support infrastructure. These layers include, among other services, the generation of SQL and execution of the necessary JDBC calls to read, update, insert, and delete data from the relational database of choice, much as we described here with CMP beans in EJB. These products can save quite a bit of time in the development lifecycle. One such product is TopLink from BEA/WebGain. In some cases, as with TopLink, they can work with an EJB vendor's implementation of EJB CMP, such as with BEA WebLogic, to provide even more functionality.

Checkpoint

Where We've Been

- We must consider several issues when mapping an object view of the system to a relational database design. The early inclination is to create one-to-one mappings, but this approach usually results in too many tables.
- Most one-to-one class associations can be collapsed into one relational table. This might not be the case if the association is optional.
- Three common approaches to mapping inheritance to the relational model are available. One is to create a table for each class involved and a view for each subclass. Another is to collapse all of the attributes from the subclasses into a table matched to the superclass. The last is to take the attributes found in the superclass and duplicate them in each table for each of the subclasses.
- Aggregation and composition associations are mapped in the same way as simple associations.
- We have many options for identifying primary keys. A common approach that offers significant flexibility is to use surrogate, or programming, keys.

- A visual modeling tool is a must for any project team that is serious about building object-oriented systems. Such tools can generate code, as well as SQL DDL.
- The Rational Rose modeling tool can be customized to add additional flexibility to the DDL generation process.
- Stored procedures and triggers should be viewed as the ultimate screwdriver for fine-tuning the application. If they are commingled with the business logic, the application becomes more dependent on the product architecture choices.
- The Enterprise JavaBeans (EJB) specification and its support for container-managed persistence (CMP) will be used to handle the data translation and data access features for Remulak.

Where We're Going Next

In the next chapter we:

- Explore the needs of the infrastructure layers as a whole, and establish layer communication mechanisms and an error-handling process.
- Review the identified classes and assess all attributes that have been defined to ensure completeness.
- Build a template for applying the layered code.
- Begin to generate code components from the class diagram.

CHAPTER 10 *Infrastructure and Architecture Review*

IN THIS CHAPTER

The previous chapter introduced some of the elements of the infrastructure necessary to support our design, dealing primarily with the back end and the database technology. That discussion stressed the need to separate business rules from the physical access technologies, such as SQL construction and eventual execution of the query. The same message will be emphasized in this chapter, but the focus will be broader and serve as a means to assess our architecture one more time and it will be a bit more specific, through the creation of a sequence diagram.

A good way to show this back-to-front process is to start with the user interface, such as an HTML form, and follow its path through all the layers. This chapter will also begin to explore the means of our presentation in the form of servlets and JavaServer Pages.

GOALS

- To review the infrastructure issues in communicating from the user interface all the way to the persistence layer at the back end.
- To explore the layers not defined in the previous chapter (Presentation Services and Business Services) and assign them to components.

- To review the importance of keeping the user interface as simple as possible.
- To apply the three types of classes (boundary, control, and entity) to the layered architecture for Remulak Productions.
- To review the final component infrastructure to support all the use-cases and related pathways.

Next Steps of the Elaboration Phase

Before exploring the user interface and implementation strategies, let's revisit the Unified Process. Figure 10-1 shows the process model, with the focus on the Elaboration phase.

In this chapter we focus on both the user interface and its ultimate interaction with all the layers in the application. It will be a good time

FIGURE 10-1 *Unified Process model: Elaboration phase*

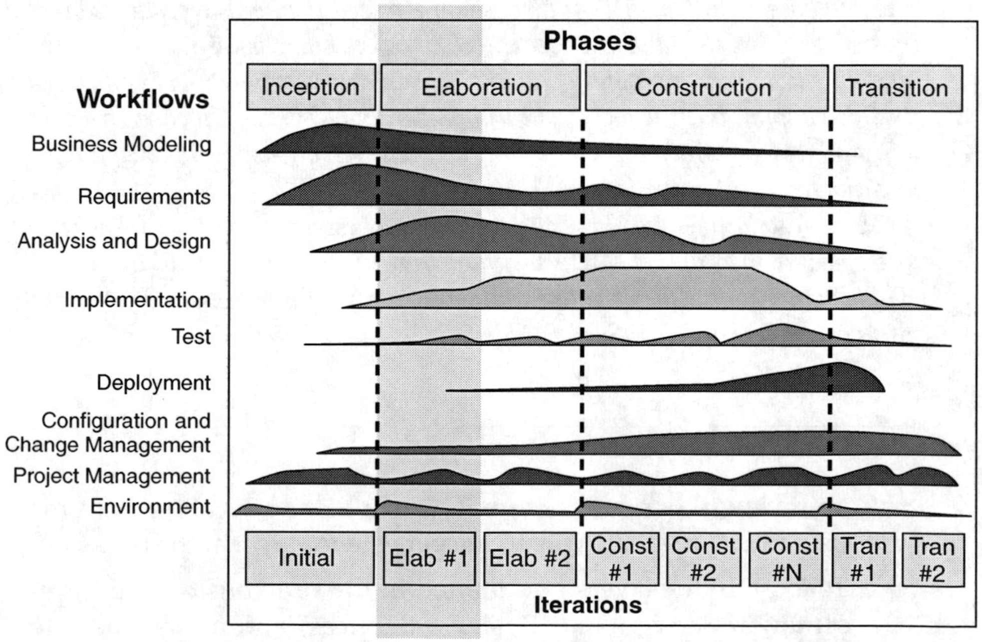

to assess our architecture one more time before the coding portion begins in earnest. The following Unified Process workflows and activity sets are emphasized:

- Implementation: Structure the Implementation Model
- Implementation: Plan the Integration
- Implementation: Implement Components

A key artifact that is finally completed in this chapter is the Software Architecture Document (SAD). Once the final architectural components are in place, we can continue with and finish our first architectural prototype. This process will culminate with the completion of Chapter 11, where we implement the non-EJB solution, and Chapter 12, where we implement the EJB solution.

Infrastructure Issues and Communicating with All Layers

Figure 10-2 shows the layered architecture that was introduced earlier in the book and then reintroduced in Chapter 9 in the context of databases. Again, these layers are logical and, in some cases, physical as well.

Remember that even though they are individual layers, many may run together on the same machine. At least one of them, Presentation Services, will be on the client in the form of a browser. Figure 10-3 focuses on the layers to be reviewed in this chapter, giving a more in-depth review of the roles that they will serve.

The Presentation Services Layer

The Presentation Services layer will be the most volatile layer in the entire application. The project must be able to take advantage of new technologies that arise. For instance, the client could just as easily be a cell phone or a PDA device. In addition, as time passes the project sponsors will want to see information in different ways that the project must be able to accommodate quickly and easily.

One way to facilitate the ever changing presentation requirements, and to provide a better design for extensibility, is to implement a **model-view-controller** (**MVC**) framework. MVC got its start in the SmallTalk world and has been used extensively in many commercial

FIGURE 10-2 *Service layers*

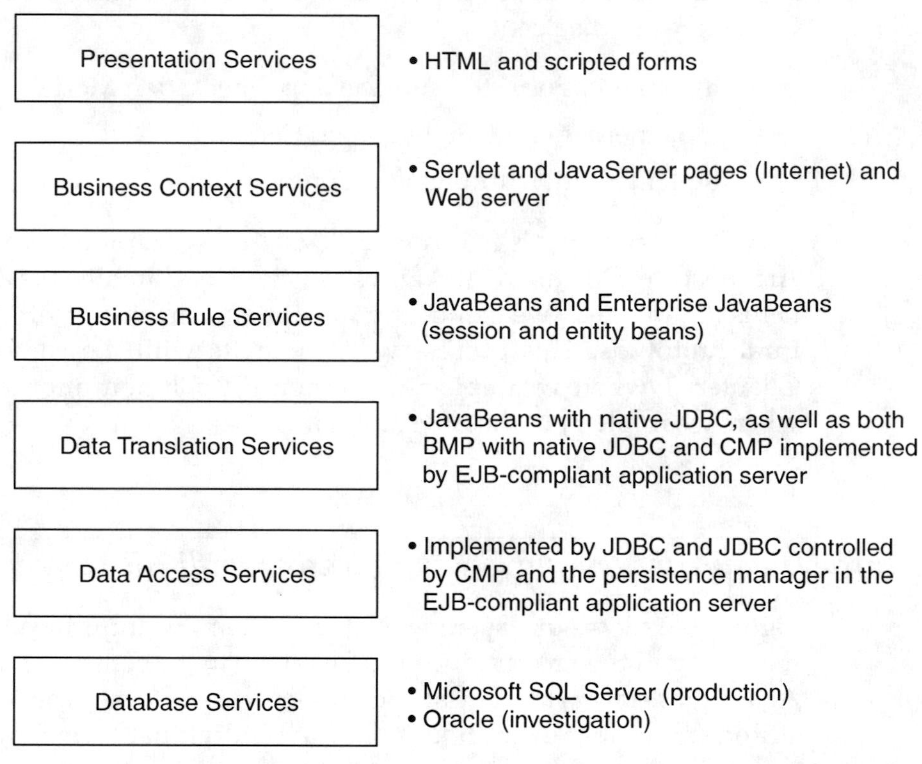

frameworks (Java's Swing architecture for one). Before we finalize the Remulak architecture, some discussion of terminology is in order.

- **Model** in the MVC framework is the entity class (e.g., `Customer`, `Order`). The goal of the model is to keep the framework pure, void of any user interface knowledge. The value classes introduced in Chapter 9 would be a proxy of sorts for the model layer.
- **View** in the MVC framework is the rendered interface that will be delivered to the client. The view can know about both the controller and the model. In the Remulak system the view is actually two things: the HTML form and the JavaServer Page (JSP).
- **Controller** in the MVC framework is the service that most often acts as the go-between for the model and the view. Two types of classes will implement the controller in the Remulak system. The

FIGURE 10-3 *Presentation, Business Context, and Business Rule Services layers*

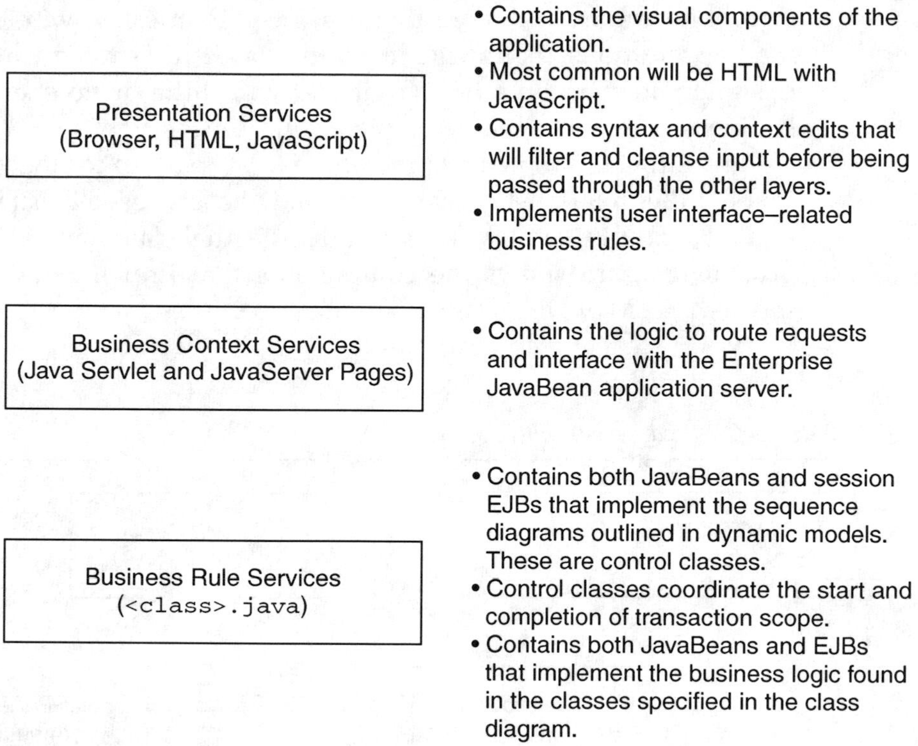

Presentation Services (Browser, HTML, JavaScript)	• Contains the visual components of the application. • Most common will be HTML with JavaScript. • Contains syntax and context edits that will filter and cleanse input before being passed through the other layers. • Implements user interface–related business rules.
Business Context Services (Java Servlet and JavaServer Pages)	• Contains the logic to route requests and interface with the Enterprise JavaBean application server.
Business Rule Services (`<class>.java`)	• Contains both JavaBeans and session EJBs that implement the sequence diagrams outlined in dynamic models. These are control classes. • Control classes coordinate the start and completion of transaction scope. • Contains both JavaBeans and EJBs that implement the business logic found in the classes specified in the class diagram.

first is the servlet. The servlet acts as the user interface controller, a router, that both instantiates and routes messages to the next type of class, the use-case controller. The use-case control classes were discussed in both Chapters 8 and 9. In the non-EJB solution, one JavaBean will play the role of use-case controller for every use-case. In the EJB solution, one session EJB will play the role of use-case controller for every use-case.

One benefit of letting the controller broker requests between the view (screen) and the model (entity class) is that it keeps the user interface light. Although there is nothing to prevent the user interface from calling into the entity classes to retrieve information, by keeping the HTML forms relatively uninformed, we end up with service layers that are highly cohesive and less coupled to other service layers. In addition, as the presentation technology changes over time, the ability to snap off one in favor of another becomes much easier. Today the Web is popular, but we hear more and more about the need to interface wireless clients into applications. Following a sound layering strategy allows the designers to snap on a new front end with little or no change to the business rules packaged in the EJB application server.

Figure 10-4 is a representation of the MVC pattern for the Web client that handles relationship management. It closely resembles Figures 8-7 and 8-8, except that now we have added actual class names. This component diagram shows the components that implement a pathway through the *Maintain Relationships* use-case.

FIGURE 10-4 *Model-view-controller framework*

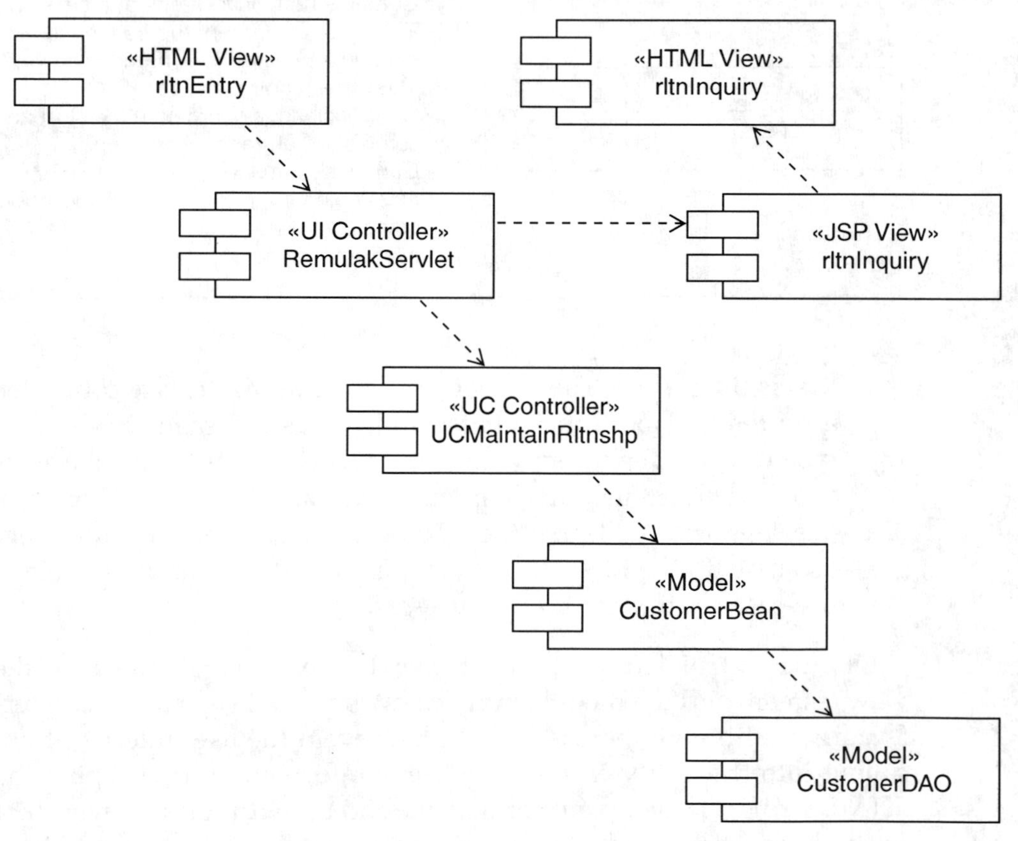

The dependency relationship between `RemulakServlet` and the `rltnInquiry` JSP is on the return trip back to the browser. Note that with a well-designed MVC architecture, simply changing the outbound JSP page to something else, perhaps one that returns Wireless Markup Language (WML) bound for a wireless PDA, would require absolutely no changes to the controller or the model components. They are none the wiser. Their role is simply to return a display-neutral object representing the customer. It is the role of the view to transform that object into something desired by the user.

Notice that there are two types of controllers in our architecture: a user interface controller and a use-case controller. The user interface controller is responsible for dealing with unique interface architecture (e.g., Web, wireless, voice response unit). The use-case controller is responsible for implementing the pathways defined in the use-cases and eventually modeled by sequence diagrams. The use-case controller doesn't care who requests its services or what technology ultimately delivers it.

A key component of the architecture used for Remulak is that there is a one-to-one mapping between a use-case and a use-case control class. Think of a use-case controller as a traffic cop of sorts, a facilitator for the sequence diagrams, which are realizations of the use-cases created. Every use-case will have a unique session bean.

There is also a one-to-one mapping of pathways (happy and alternate) in a use-case to operations in its related JavaBean or EJB session bean. Exception pathways are usually handled in the course of the happy or alternate pathway. This relationship should further reinforce the importance of traceability that was introduced at the beginning of this book. Too often there is no way to trace back from code to the requirement that brought us to a particular point in the project. With this design pattern we have such traceability.

Figure 10-5 provides a context for how we go from a use-case all the way to the JavaBean or EJB session bean that realizes that use-case's pathways. In this diagram we show the use-case controller as a session EJB; in the non-EJB solution, however, our design will implement controllers as just JavaBeans.

As Figure 10-5 shows, there is an order to the progression of mapping to components: (1) From use-cases we find our domain classes (2). (3) From the use-cases we create dynamic models (e.g., sequence/collaboration) that model our classes now acting as living objects

FIGURE 10-5 *Traceable lifecycle of deliverables*

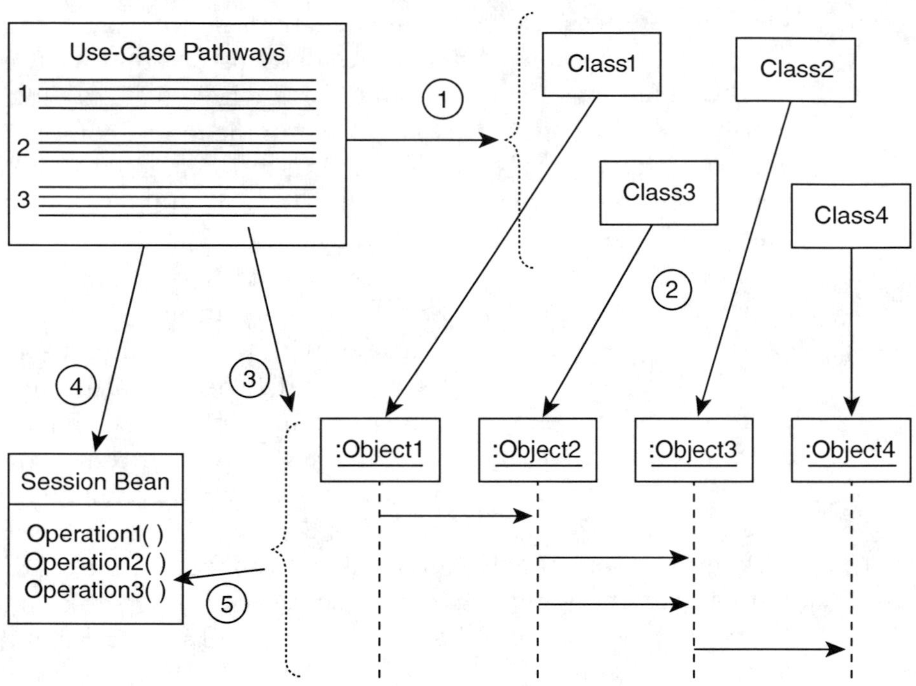

sending messages to one another with the sole purpose of accomplishing the goal of the use-case pathway. (4) For each use-case, a use-case controller will be implemented as either a JavaBean (non-EJB) or a session bean (EJB). This use-case controller bean will contain operations (5) that implement the orchestration logic to carry out an individual sequence diagram. Again, these map directly to the use-case pathways.

The Business Context Services Layer

The Business Context Services layer of the application works very closely with the specific presentation technology. It is responsible for much of the editing that transpires during the user interface interaction. Some of these logical services are split between the actual form-level code (packaged in either HTML or JavaScript) and the business rule component (classes implemented as either JavaBeans or EJBs).

This logical layer focuses on what is happening during a given interaction between the system and the application and in particular on syntax and context edits. These various edits perform as follows for the application:

- **Syntax edits** focus on formatting and cleansing information before it ever leaves the user interface. These edits can range from numeric range checks to valid date formatting.
- **Context edits** focus more on the business aspect of the information. For instance, if someone selects a payment type of finance and has a credit score below 50, approval by a finance officer is required for a sale. Quite often what is a context-type edit should be an operation in one of the entity classes.

Some would argue that we should not have any type of syntax or context editing going on in the form-level code. The reason is that these types of edits would apply whether the user interface was a Java application or a Web-based front end. Some designs actually package the edits as a single method inside of the user interface control class and pass all the screen information to the edit operation to perform the edit. This would allow some level of reusability if the front end changed to a Web-based solution. However, depending on the technology selected for a Web-based front end, something as simple as preventing the entry of a field on the basis of the value entered in another field (context edit) may require a trip all the way back to the Web server for editing. This is clearly a case where purity and performance will butt heads.

The Business Rule Services Layer

Because the industry overuses the term *business rule,* let's clarify how we will use it. What really resides in the Business Rule Services layer? We have used the term *entity class* quite a bit in this book, and this layer is where those classes will live. Initially, the implementation constructs of each will mirror the attributes defined in the class diagram. There will also be get and set operations for each attribute because all attributes will be declared as private. The same is true for the rules to be considered a bean. Each entity class will provide certain services, such as a way to request the retrieval of information about itself for eventual use by a particular aspect of the system. The classes will also have to be able to respond to update requests, thereby resulting in some form of persistence.

The logical layer of Business Rule Services actually has a dual spirit. The business rules physically implemented in an entity class are very workflow oriented. Other business rule services deal with the business aspect of data management, which will be implemented in what we referred to in the previous chapter as data access objects (DAOs).

Cooperating Classes: Boundary, Control, and Entity

Let's now map a simple interaction, the retrieval of customer information via the *Maintain Relationships* use-case, into the layers of the application. This exchange of messages will be initially mapped out at a high level and then will become much more concrete (as to full operation signatures) as you move through your design. Figure 10-6 outlines the UML sequence diagram depicting the interaction.

FIGURE 10-6 *Customer inquiry sequence diagram*

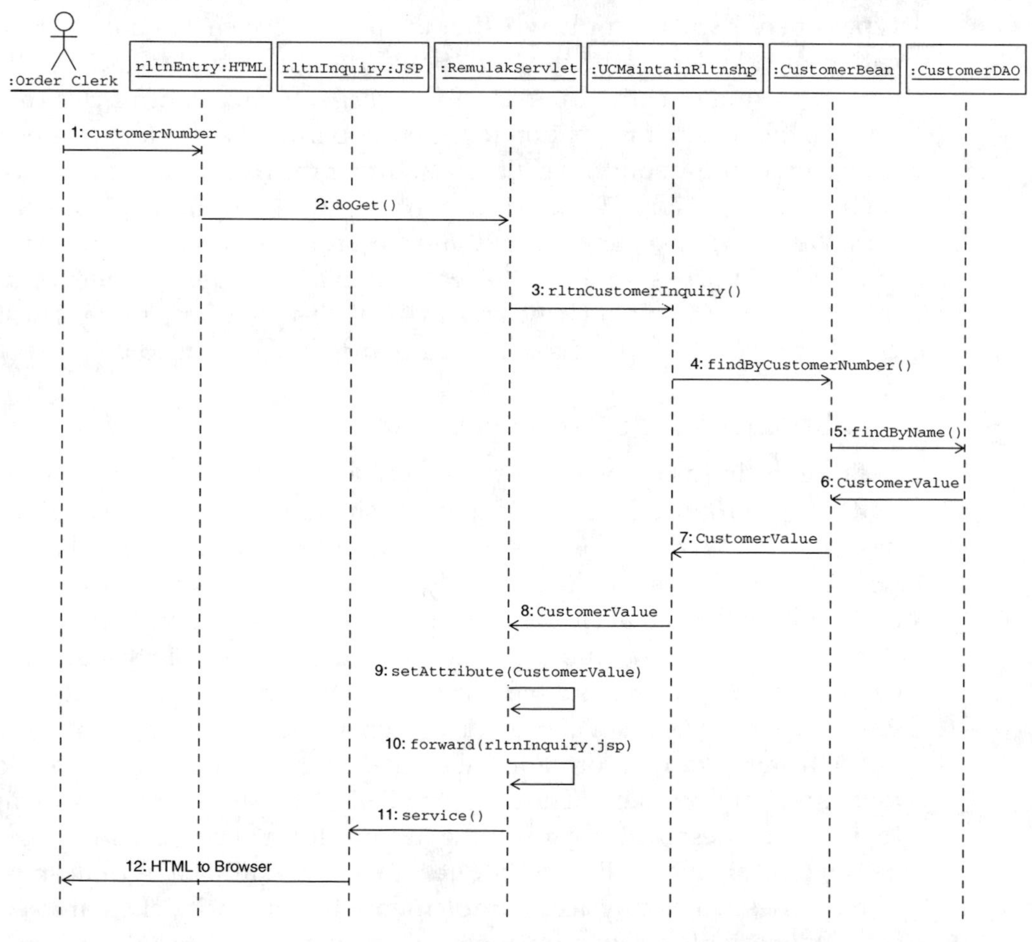

Let's walk through the messaging. I have placed sequence numbers on the diagram for readability; as stated in Chapter 7, however, they are unnecessary for sequence diagrams because the order flows from top to bottom. I have also left a few classes off of the diagram but will explain where they would be placed in reality.

1. The clerk interacts with the Web server by requesting a Web page. This Web page has entry space for a customer number. The Web server is not shown on this sequence diagram, but you certainly could include it if you wished.

   Because of the `Action` statement in the HTML page and the servlet mapping tags supported in the container product (in this book either Apache Tomcat or BEA WebLogic), a specific servlet is invoked on the Web server; in our case it is `RemulakServlet`.

2. Because this is an HTTP get request, the `doGet()` operation is invoked in the servlet. As we'll see in Chapter 11, `doGet()` simply calls `doPost()`. In this operation we find the servlet requesting the customer number from the `Request` object.
3. `RemulakServlet` instantiates and then sends a message to the use-case controller, `UCMaintainRltnshp`, and invokes its `rltnCustomerInquiry()` operation. The `UCMaintainRltnshp` class is just a Java Bean in the non-EJB implementation, and a session EJB in the EJB implementation.
4. The use-case controller asks `CustomerBean` to call `findByCustomerNumber()`, passing in the customer number.
5. `CustomerBean` asks `CustomerDAO`, using the interface `DataAccess`, which was presented in Chapter 9, to invoke `findByName()`, and the result is a newly created `CustomerValue` object. I have left the `CustomerValue` class off the sequence diagram for space reasons, but it is created within the `findByName()` operation.
6. The `findByName()` operation returns `CustomerValue` to `CustomerBean`. `CustomerBean` then sets its internal state from `CustomerValue`.
7. `CustomerBean` returns to `UCMaintainRltnshp` with `CustomerValue`.
8. `UCMaintainRltnshp` returns to `RemulakServlet` with `CustomerValue`.

9. `RemulakServlet` sets the `CustomerValue` object into the `Request` scope of the servlet with the `setAttribute()` operation. The `Request` object could also have been shown on the sequence diagram.
10. `RemulakServlet` gets a reference to the servlet's `Request Dispatcher` object and then issues the `forward()` operation on it, passing the parameter `rltnInquiry.jsp`. This causes the container product to compile the `rltnInquiry.jsp` page into a servlet (if it isn't already compiled; remember that JSP pages are nothing more than servlets in disguise).
11. This process forces the `service()` operation of the now compiled JSP/servlet to be invoked. The JSP/servlet creates HTML output destined for the browser.
12. The HTML form arrives at the browser.

This interaction is very typical of all the interactions on which Remulak Productions' system will be based. It is a framework that can be applied time and time again.

Deployment Architecture View

For Remulak Productions, the probable deployment strategy is straightforward. The client will be browser based, and the remaining components will run on the server. Figure 10-7 depicts the likely deployment strategies using UML component and deployment diagrams.

Remember that to cover as many technical bases as we can, we will present phases of two different solutions: one using just a servlet/JSP/JavaBean container (Apache Tomcat), the other using a commercial EJB container (BEA's WebLogic). The database server, EJB container, and servlet container are shown as components that are active objects. Active objects in UML are components that run in their own process space and have their own threads of control.

FIGURE 10-7 *Remulak's deployment strategy using an EJB or servlet container*

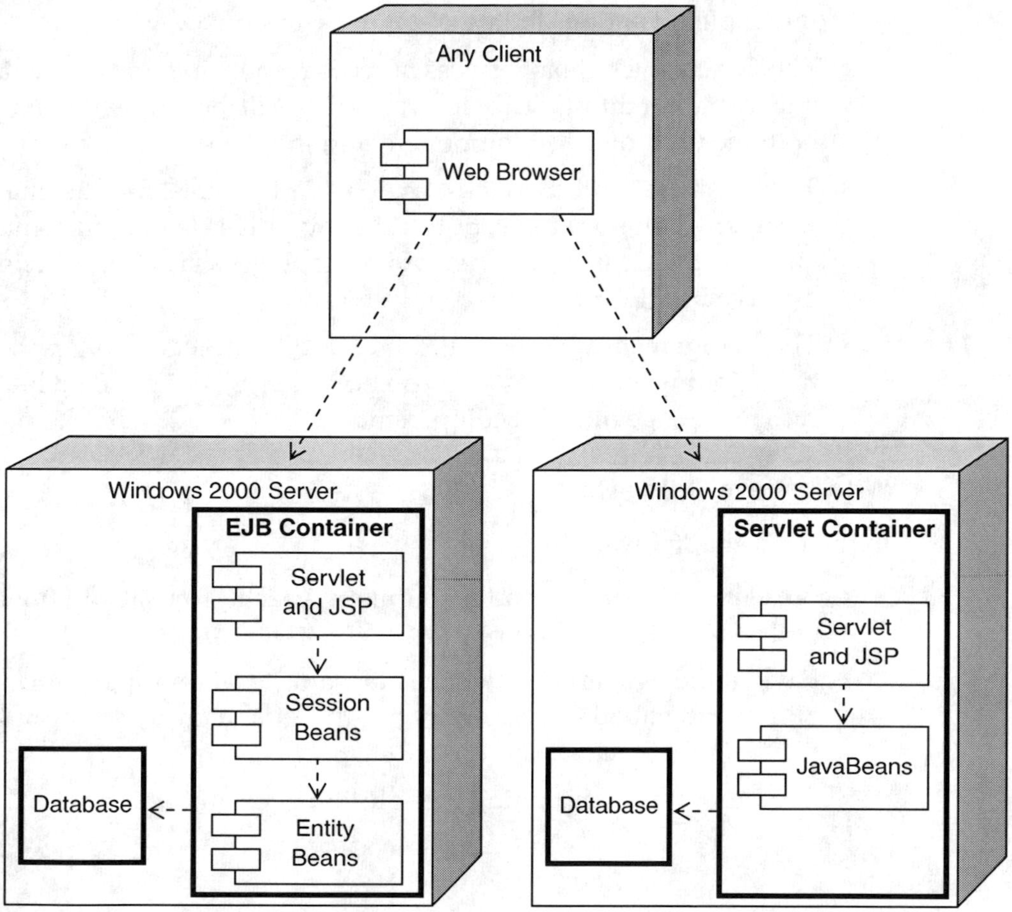

Checkpoint

Where We've Been

- A well-designed application requires that the logical layers be treated with care during the physical implementation to ensure that as the business evolves, a shift in either the business model or the technology framework won't leave the application in the legacy bin.

- The Presentation Services layer will change often in the life span of an application. It is crucial to separate the user interface from the implementation. Today, Web forms; tomorrow, wireless.
- The Business Context Services layer is responsible for the syntax and context editing. This logical layer will be implemented in both the user interface component and the Web server.
- The Business Rule Services layer is responsible for the many workflow issues that the application faces. This layer will contain all the entity classes, and they can be deployed on either the client or server platform.
- The deployment options could be varied (applets, Java applications), but we have chosen to use both non-EJB and EJB architecture to manage our Java components.

Where We're Going Next

In the next chapter we:

- Present some background material on Apache Tomcat and how it will be used in our example.
- Lay out the remaining sequence diagrams for the simple pathway of inquiring about a customer and updating a customer through the *Maintain Relationships* use-case.
- Explore ways of improving the solution over time.

CHAPTER 11 *Constructing a Solution: Servlets, JSP, and JavaBeans*

IN THIS CHAPTER

In the last chapter we gave our user interface strategy a final review and then traced the communication from front to back as a means to solidify our architecture via a sequence diagram. This chapter focuses on pulling together the various technology puzzle pieces we have presented over the last three chapters and building the first round of our architectural prototype.

This portion of the Remulak solution will present both simple inquiry and update pathways through the Maintain Relationships *use-case. The architecture will consist of Apache Tomcat as the servlet/JSP container and JavaBeans as the implementation for the entity classes. The JSPs will be identical between the two implementations, and the servlets will require only a small change to function in either environment.*

GOALS

- To review the services that Apache Tomcat has to offer and the role played in this phase of the solution.
- To explore the user interface control class and how it brokers calls to the use-case control class.

- To review the role of entity beans and how they implement the business rules of the application.
- To look at the DAO classes in more depth and how they carry out the create, read, update, delete (CRUD) services of the entity beans.

Next Steps of the Elaboration Phase

Before constructing the first portion of the Remulak solution, let's revisit the Unified Process. Figure 11-1 shows the process model, with the focus on the Elaboration phase.

In this chapter we will specifically focus on building code. This code will lead to the first attempt at an architectural prototype. The architectural prototype will be complete at the conclusion of the next chapter, in which we present an EJB solution. Now is also a good time to stress

FIGURE 11-1 *Unified Process model: Elaboration phase*

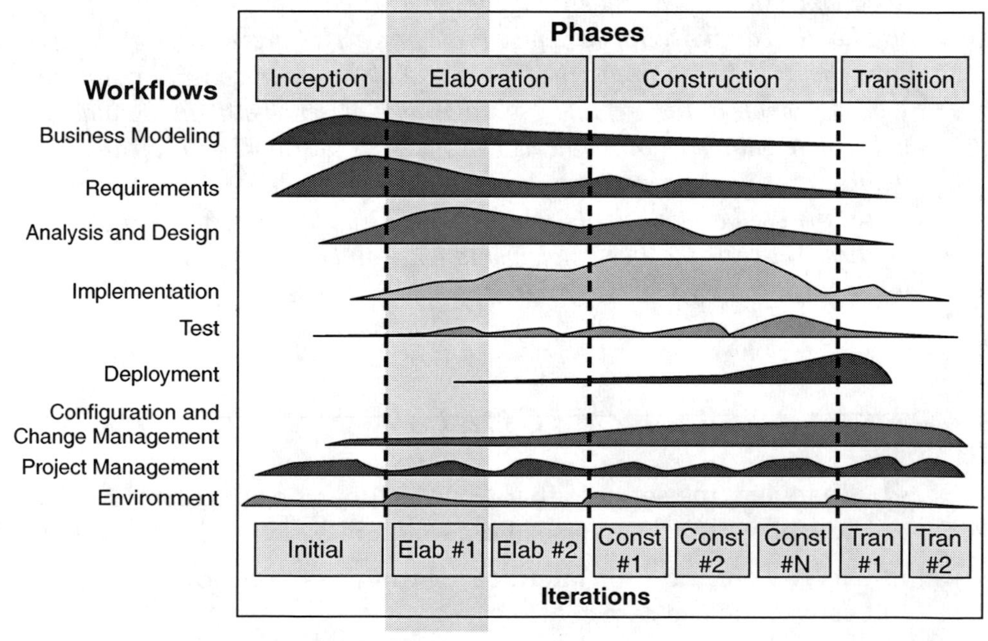

that there should be very few surprises, from an architecture and construction perspective, as we move through the remaining iterations in the Elaboration phase and then into Construction and Transition. Tasks will focus more on deployment and support as we move into Construction and Transition, but the real software architecture challenge happens early in Elaboration.

The following Unified Process workflows and activity sets are emphasized:

- Analysis and Design: Design Components
- Implementation: Implement Components

The emphasis now is to test our design strategies for how the code comes together.

Building the Architectural Prototype: Part 1

Part 1 of building the architectural prototype for our non-EJB solution covers the setup of the environment and the front components of the servlet and JSPs.

Baselining the Environment

Without the benefit of a commercial servlet/JSP container, we must turn to a solution that will be both flexible and able someday to migrate to a commercial product. The good news here is that the reference implementation for servlet/JSP containers was handed over by Sun Microsystems to the nonprofit Apache Software Foundation (*jakarta.apache.org*). Since that time, Tomcat has evolved at a rapid pace and is used by many organizations not only as a testing environment but in production settings as well. The features that commercial equivalents offer that are not offered by Tomcat tend to focus more on performance and less on functionality.

The first thing we must do is download the Tomcat binary from the Jakarta Project Web site (*jakarta.apache.org*). The instructions are very easy, so I won't bother describing the install process. If it takes more than five minutes, you're doing something wrong. After installing Tomcat and testing the install to see if it works, we are ready to begin our adventure into setting up the first part of the architectural prototype.

The next thing we'll need is both the latest version of the Java Development Kit (this project was built with JDK 1.3), as well as the latest version of the Java 2 Software Development Kit (this project was built with Java 2 SDK 1.2.1). To run the code from this chapter should require no classpath changes on your system because after you install Tomcat, you will copy the classes into the proper directories within Tomcat.

Personally, I wouldn't bother typing in the examples in this chapter and the next. What helps me the most is to get the source code and examine it, run it a little, then examine it some more. Just looking at these pages while you type the code is much less of a learning experience. As mentioned in the front of the book, you can get the code from two locations. The first is my Web site, at *www.jacksonreed.com*. The second is Addison-Wesley's Web site, at *www.awl.com*. Download the code and unzip it into folders within the contained zip directory or put it into another, higher-level directory.

Setting Up the Environment

The implementation we are about to undertake would run just as well in IBM WebSphere or BEA WebLogic. The only difference is that we wouldn't be using the EJB features of these products. However, each is equally adept at running servlets, compiling JSPs, and managing JavaBeans. The EJB part of the commercial offerings is sometimes sold as an add-on component.

Where Tomcat is installed you will find a directory called `webapps`. On my machine it looks something like this:

```
C:\tomcat\Jakarta-tomcat-3.2.1\webapps
```

Under this directory we want to add a new collection of directories. The first level will represent the application. I have called this one `RemulakWebApp`. Under this directory we create two subdirectories: `images` and `WEB-INF`. Under the `WEB-INF` directory we create two more subdirectories: `classes` and `lib`. The result should be something like this:

```
C:\tomcat\Jakarta-tomcat-3.2.1\webapps\RemulakWebApp\images
C:\tomcat\Jakarta-tomcat-3.2.1\webapps\RemulakWebApp\WEB-INF
C:\tomcat\Jakarta-tomcat-3.2.1\webapps\RemulakWebApp\
   WEB-INF\classes
C:\tomcat\Jakarta-tomcat-3.2.1\webapps\RemulakWebApp\
   WEB-INF\lib
```

The steps just described are not necessary if you want to just install the software from the book after the download. On a windows system, type in the following:

```
C:\javauml> xcopy /s /I RemulakWebApp %TOMCAT_HOME%\webapps\
    RemulakWebApp
```

On a UNIX system, type in

```
[username /usr/local/javauml] cp -R RemulakWebApp $TOMCAT_
HOME/webapps
```

Now start your Tomcat server and type in

```
http://localhost:8080/RemulakWebApp/
```

You should see something that looks like Figure 11-2 to confirm that the installation of Remulak was successful.

FIGURE 11-2 *Initial default Web page for Remulak's* Maintain Relationships *use-case*

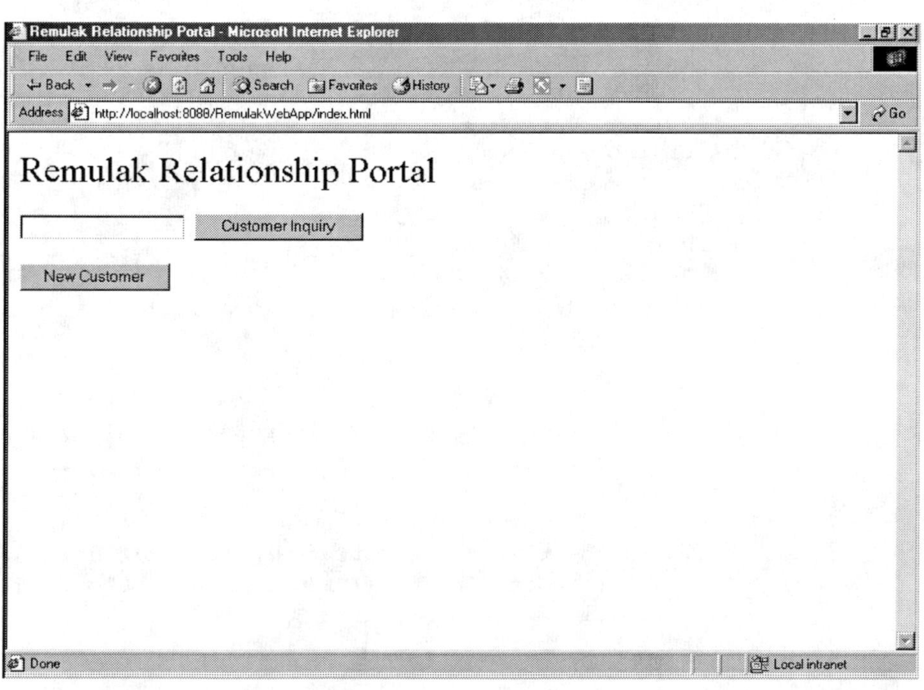

Invoking Servlets

Servlets can be invoked in different ways. Actually, you can invoke a servlet from a Java application (non-browser-based client) running on a client machine if you so desire. We will use the standards set down in the Java specification and implemented not only in Tomcat but in all commercial servers, using a descriptor file. In the case of Web applications, this file is `web.xml`, and it resides in the root directory of your Web application. In the case of Remulak, the root directory would be `RemulakWebApp`.

```
<?xml version="1.0" encoding="ISO-8859-1"?>
<!DOCTYPE web-app PUBLIC "-//Sun Microsystems, Inc.//DTD Web
 Application 2.2//EN"
  "http://java.sun.com/j2ee/dtds/web-app_2_2.dtd">
<web-app>
   <display-name>Remulak Web Application</display-name>
   <servlet>
      <servlet-name>RemulakServlet</servlet-name>
      <servlet-class>com.jacksonreed.RemulakServlet</servlet-
       class>
   </servlet>
   <servlet-mapping>
      <servlet-name>RemulakServlet</servlet-name>
      <url-pattern>/rltnInquiry</url-pattern>
   </servlet-mapping>
   <servlet-mapping>
      <servlet-name>RemulakServlet</servlet-name>
      <url-pattern>/rltnUpdate</url-pattern>
   </servlet-mapping>
   <welcome-file-list>
      <welcome-file>index.html</welcome-file>
   </welcome-file-list>
   <taglib>
      <taglib-uri>/WEB-INF/struts-bean.tld</taglib-uri>
      <taglib-location>/WEB-INF/struts-bean.tld</taglib-
       location>
   </taglib>
   <taglib>
      <taglib-uri>/WEB-INF/struts-form.tld</taglib-uri>
      <taglib-location>/WEB-INF/struts-form.tld</taglib-
       location>
   </taglib>
   <taglib>
```

```
        <taglib-uri>/WEB-INF/struts-logic.tld</taglib-uri>
        <taglib-location>/WEB-INF/struts-logic.tld</taglib-
         location>
    </taglib>
    <taglib>
        <taglib-uri>/WEB-INF/struts-template.tld</taglib-uri>
        <taglib-location>/WEB-INF/struts-template.tld</taglib-
         location>
    </taglib>
</web-app>
```

Initially Remulak will use only one servlet, RemulakServlet. First find the <welcome-first> tag in the web.xml file. This tag indicates to the service running on the Web server the HTML page that it should send back if a specific page is not requested. In our case, we have indicated index.html.

The next piece of the XML file, which is by far the most important, consists of the <servlet-mapping> and <servlet-name> tags:

```
<servlet-mapping>
        <servlet-name>RemulakServlet</servlet-name>
        <url-pattern>/rltnInquiry</url-pattern>
    </servlet-mapping>
    <servlet-mapping>
        <servlet-name>RemulakServlet</servlet-name>
        <url-pattern>/rltnUpdate</url-pattern>
</servlet-mapping>
```

The <url-pattern> tag is used to identify, from the query string that comes from the browser, what servlet to invoke to process the request. In our case any string that contains */rltnInquiry/* or */rltnUpdate/* will be mapped to the servlet specified in the respective <servlet-name> tag. These two types of statements happen to map to the same servlet. The beauty of abstracting to the descriptor the name specified in the URL, as well as its mapping to the servlet, is that we can change the flow of the application for perhaps performance tuning or security without touching any code.

Any servlet that is specified in the <servlet-name> tag must also have a corresponding <servlet> tag. This tag specifies the class that implements the servlet. In our case it is the RemulakServlet class, which resides in the com.jacksonreed package.

```
<servlet>
      <servlet-name>RemulakServlet</servlet-name>
      <servlet-class>com.jacksonreed.RemulakServlet</servlet-
       class>
</servlet>
```

If more servlets were desired, they would need to be reflected in the descriptor. A good design strategy might be to have a unique servlet for each use-case. When we explore our JSPs, I will mention the other tags in the `web.xml` file, especially the `<taglib>` tags.

The Servlet for Remulak: Broker Services

Remulak's servlet, `RemulakServlet`, was explored a bit in the sequence diagram presented in Chapter 10. We will now explore some of the code components of the servlet, starting initially with the main processing engine that is behind every servlet: the `doGet()` and `doPost()` operations:

```
package com.jacksonreed;

import javax.servlet.*;
import javax.servlet.http.*;
import java.io.*;
import java.util.*;

import java.util.Properties;
import javax.naming.Context;
import javax.naming.InitialContext;
import javax.naming.NamingException;

public class RemulakServlet extends HttpServlet {
    private String url;

    public void init() throws ServletException {
        url = "";
    }
    public void destroy() {
    }

    public void doGet(HttpServletRequest request,
        HttpServletResponse response)
```

```
        throws IOException, ServletException {

        doPost(request, response);
    }

    public void doPost(HttpServletRequest request,
        HttpServletResponse response)
        throws IOException, ServletException {

        String action = request.getParameter("action");

        // Check which action to do and forward to it
        if ("Customer Inquiry".equals(action)) {
            doRltnCustomerInquiry(request, response);
          }
        else if ("New Customer".equals(action)) {
            doRltnCustomerNew(request, response);
          }
        else if ("Edit Customer".equals(action)) {
            doRltnCustomerEdit(request, response);
          }
        else if ("Delete Customer".equals(action)) {
            doRltnCustomerDelete(request, response);
          }
        else if ("Add/Update Customer".equals(action)) {
            doRltnCustomerAdd(request, response);
          }
        else if ("Edit Address".equals(action)) {
            doRltnAddressEdit(request, response);
          }
        else if ("Delete Address".equals(action)) {
            doRltnAddressDelete(request, response);
          }
        else if ("Add/Update Address".equals(action)) {
            doRltnAddressAdd(request, response);
          }
        else if ("Add Address".equals(action)) {
            doRltnAddressNew(request, response);
          }
        else {
            response.sendError(HttpServletResponse.SC_NOT_
            IMPLEMENTED);
        }
    }
}
```

The `doPost()` method is the main driver of `RemulakServlet`. Notice that the `doGet()` method simply calls `doPost()` where all the activity is. The `request.getParameter("action")` call retrieves the value of the `action` parameter that comes in as part of the query string, and on the basis of this value we branch to the appropriate operation to process this unique request. For instance, the query string that would come in after a customer number was entered into the form in Figure 11-2 would look like this:

```
". . . /RemulakWebApp/rltnInquiry?action=Customer+Inquiry&
customerNumber=abc1234"
```

This structure serves our purposes well and allows for easy branching to support different functions of the application. However, it does make for additional maintenance, should you want to add more actions in the future. Although I have chosen this route to show you the semantics of the whole application interaction and to avoid more complicated abstractions, I encourage you to look at some of the interesting alternatives offered by other authors and practitioners.

The first one I direct you to is Hans Bergsten's *Java Server Pages* (published by O'Reilly, 2001). This book introduces the notion of "action" classes that are driven by an XML descriptor. These action classes deal with the unique processing necessary for each request. So to add more actions, you write the action class and update the XML descriptor. There is no need to recompile the servlet.

The second source is from the same folks who gave us Tomcat—that is, the Apache group's Struts framework (*jakarta.apache.org*). Struts covers many aspects of the management of user interface editing, including brokering calls within the servlet. Struts also uses action objects just as in Bergsten's approach. We will use Struts in Chapter 12 to provide a looping capability to our JSPs.

The Servlet for Remulak: Responding to an Action Request

The next aspect of the servlet to explore is how it responds to the action requests. We have already shown how the servlet determines which action to carry out. The following code deals with carrying out the request:

```
private void doRltnCustomerInquiry(HttpServletRequest
request, HttpServletResponse response)
```

```
        throws IOException, ServletException {
  String customerNumber = request.getParameter("customerNumber");

        if (customerNumber == null) {
              throw new ServletException("Missing
              customerNumber info");
        }

        UCMaintainRltnshp UCController = new
        UCMaintainRltnshp();

        // Call to method in controller bean
        CustomerValue custVal =
              UCController.rltnCustomerInquiry(customerNumber);

        // Set the custVal object into the servlet context so
        // that JSPs can see it
        request.setAttribute("custVal", custVal);

        // Remove the UCMaintainRltnshp controller
        UCController = null;

        // Forward to the JSP page used to display the page
        forward("rltnInquiry.jsp", request, response);
     }
```

The `doRltnCustomerInquiry()` method is a heavily requested pathway through the *Maintain Relationships* use-case. Once invoked from the `doPost()` method, it first retrieves the `customerNumber` attribute that came in with the query string via the `getParameter()` message to the servlet's `Request` object. The next step is to instantiate the use-case control class: `UCMaintainRltnshp`. Now with an instance of the controller available, the servlet can send messages to the `rltnCustomerInquiry()` operation in the controller. Remember from the sequence diagram that the result of this message brings back the proxy object that represents the state of a `Customer` object: `CustomerValue`. Later in this chapter we will explore the details of the control, bean, and DAO classes involved. The `CustomerValue` object is inserted into the servlet's `Request` object so that it can be accessed by our JSPs. Then a message is sent to a `forward()` operation that is common across all the requests that the servlet processes:

```
private void forward(String url, HttpServletRequest request,
        HttpServletResponse response)
        throws IOException, ServletException {

        RequestDispatcher rd = request.getRequestDispatcher
        (url);
        rd.forward(request, response);
    }
```

The `forward()` request retrieves the submitted JSP and then processes the results, which look like Figure 11-3.

Let's now look at the operation that handles adding and updating of a `Customer` object:

```
private void doRltnCustomerAdd(HttpServletRequest request,
    HttpServletResponse response)
    throws IOException, ServletException {

    UCMaintainRltnshp UCController = new UCMaintainRltnshp();
    CustomerValue custVal = setCustomerValueFromForm(request);

    if (request.getParameter("customerId").length() == 0) {
        UCController.rltnAddCustomer(custVal); //Add
    }
    else {
        UCController.rltnUpdateCustomer(custVal); //Update
    }

    custVal = UCController.rltnCustomerInquiry
         (custVal.getCustomerNumber());

    UCController = null;

    request.setAttribute("custVal", custVal);

    forward("rltnInquiry.jsp", request, response);
}
```

This operation has many similarities to the `doRltnCustomerInquiry()` operation. It also sends messages to the control class, `UCMaintainRltnshp`, to get its work done. But before doing that, it must transfer the values from the `Request` object into a proxy `CustomerValue` object to be sent through layers, resulting in some type of database

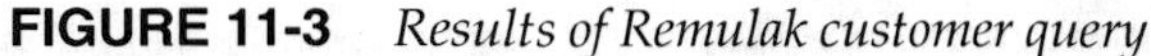

FIGURE 11-3 *Results of Remulak customer query*

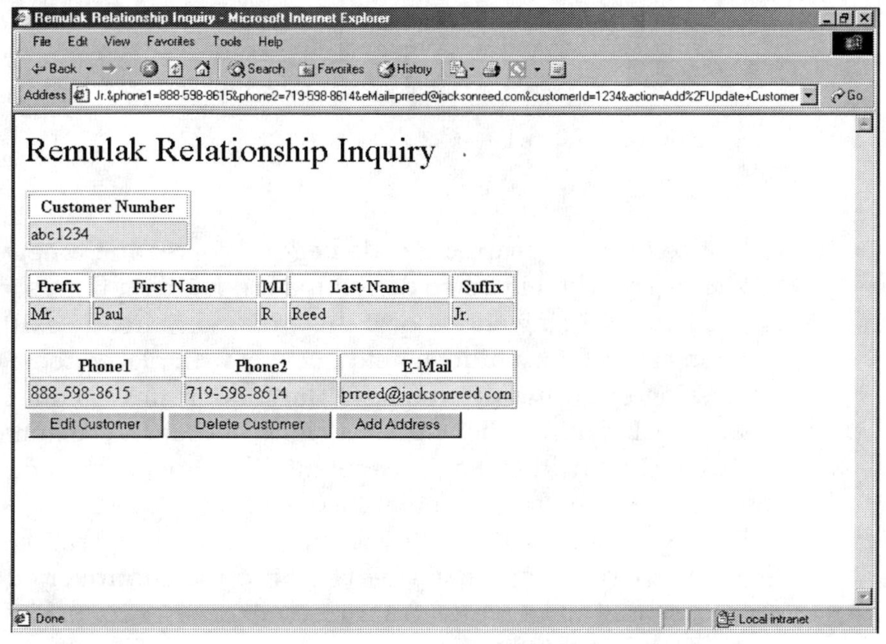

update (insert or update). The `setCustomerValuesFromForm()` operation does this for us:

```
private CustomerValue setCustomerValueFromForm
      (HttpServletRequest request)
      throws IOException, ServletException {

   CustomerValue custVal = new CustomerValue();

   if (request.getParameter("customerId").length() > 0) {
      Integer myCustId = new Integer
            (request.getParameter("customerId"));
      custVal.setCustomerId(myCustId);
   }
   custVal.setCustomerNumber
      (request.getParameter("customerNumber"));
   custVal.setPrefix(request.getParameter("prefix"));
   custVal.setFirstName(request.getParameter("firstName"));
   custVal.setMiddleInitial
      (request.getParameter("middleInitial"));
```

```
    custVal.setLastName(request.getParameter("lastName"));
    custVal.setSuffix(request.getParameter("suffix"));
    custVal.setPhone1(request.getParameter("phone1"));
    custVal.setPhone2(request.getParameter("phone2"));
    custVal.setEMail(request.getParameter("eMail"));

    return custVal;
}
```

Notice that this mapping code begins by creating a new `CustomerValue` object. Then it has to determine if it is doing this as a result of a new customer being added or if this customer already exists. The distinction is based on a hidden field in the HTML placed there during the processing of an inquiry request. The hidden field is `customerId`. A customer ID will not have been assigned yet if the customer is being added, so this field is the determinant. The remaining code just cycles through the form fields populating `CustomerValue`.

Let's go back to the `doRltnCustomerAdd()` operation. After the fields are populated, a message is sent to the controller either asking for a customer to be added (`rltnAddCustomer()`) or asking for a customer to be updated (`rltnUpdateCustomer()`). The customer is then queried again through the `rltnCustomerInquiry()` operation of the controller, and the customer is displayed via the `rltnInquiry()` JSP. Figure 11-4 is a screen shot of the form used both to update an existing customer and to add a new customer; it is the output from the `rltnCustomer()` JSP.

The remaining operations within `RemulakServlet` follow. For the sake of brevity, I have stripped out the comments that exist in the code because they look very similar to the comments in `doRltnCustomerInquiry()`:

```
private void doRltnCustomerNew(HttpServletRequest request,
    HttpServletResponse response)
    throws IOException, ServletException {

    CustomerValue custVal = new CustomerValue();

    request.setAttribute("custVal", custVal);

    forward("rltnCustomer.jsp", request, response);
}
```

FIGURE 11-4 *Results of Remulak customer add/update request*

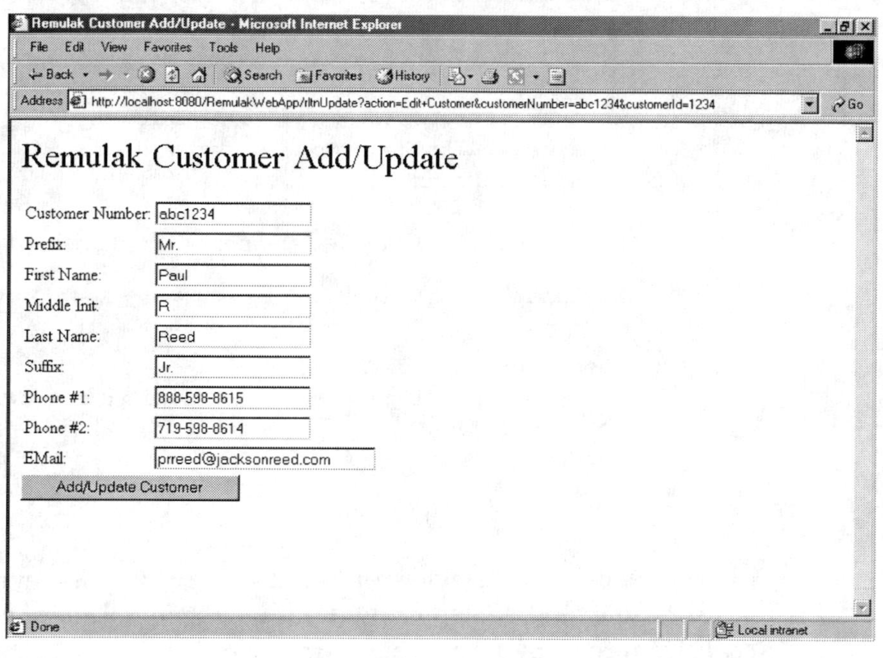


```
  private void doRltnCustomerEdit(HttpServletRequest request,
     HttpServletResponse response)
     throws IOException, ServletException  {

     String customerNumber = request.getParameter
     ("customerNumber");

     UCMaintainRltnshp UCController = new UCMaintainRltnshp();

     CustomerValue custVal =
          CController.rltnCustomerInquiry(customerNumber);
     request.setAttribute("custVal", custVal);

     UCController = null;

     forward("rltnCustomer.jsp", request, response);
 }
 private void doRltnCustomerDelete(HttpServletRequest
 request,
```

```
        HttpServletResponse response)
        throws IOException, ServletException {

        String custId = request.getParameter("customerId");

        Integer customerId = new Integer(custId);
        UCMaintainRltnshp UCController = new
        UCMaintainRltnshp();

        UCController.rltnDeleteCustomer(customerId);

        UCController = null;

        response.sendRedirect
             ("http://localhost:8080/RemulakWebApp/rltnEntry.
             html");
        return;

  }
```

This is a fairly concise view of `RemulakServlet`. However, it is only for strictly the `Customer` portion of the *Maintain Relationships* use-case. Recall from the `doPost()` operation reviewed earlier that there were operations such as `doRltnAddressAdd()` and `doRltnAddressDelete()`. We will review this aspect of the *Maintain Relationships* use-case and inquire on all its related objects when we visit the EJB solution in Chapter 12.

JavaServer Pages for Remulak

Before moving toward the back end in our review of the use-case control classes and DAO classes, it's a good idea to talk about how the user interface, or the view, is handled. Remember that JSPs serve the role of our view in the MVC framework. JSPs operate on objects placed into the `Request` scope by the servlet. By separating the very volatile view from the more stable model, we insulate the application from future maintenance and technology changes. This combination of servlets and JSPs has a name: *Model 2.* (Model 1 applications are just JSPs playing both the role of broker and output page formatting.)

At first glance, JavaServer Pages seem like a hodge-podge of elements: scripting, HTML, Java code, and tag library references. After working with them, however, you will appreciate them not just for their speed but also for their flexibility. Again, my coverage of JSP can't do the entire topic justice. So I refer you to the previously mentioned JSP book by Hans Bergsten for exhaustive coverage.

Let's start by jumping right into a JSP for Remulak, the `rltn Inquiry` JSP:

```
<%@ page language="java" contentType="text/html" %>
<jsp:useBean id="custVal" scope="request"
       class="com.jacksonreed.CustomerValue" />
<HTML>
<HEAD>
<TITLE>Remulak Relationship Inquiry</TITLE>
</HEAD>
<BODY >
<form action="rltnUpdate" method="post">
<P><FONT size=6>Remulak Relationship Inquiry</FONT></P>
<table border="1" width="20%"  >
  <tr>
    <th align="center">
      Customer Number
    </th>
  </tr>
  <tr>
    <td align="left" bgColor="aqua">
      <%= custVal.getCustomerNumber() %>
    </td>
  </tr>
</table>
<p><p>
<table border="1" width="60%"  >
  <tr>
    <th align="center" width="10%">
      Prefix
    </th>
    <th align="center" width="25%">
      First Name
    </th>
    <th align="center" width="2%">
      MI
    </th>
    <th align="center" width="25%">
      Last Name
    </th>
    <th align="center" width="10%">
      Suffix
```

```
      </th>
    </tr>
    <tr>
      <td align="left" width="10%" bgColor="aqua">
        <jsp:getProperty name="custVal" property="prefix"/>
      </td>
      <td align="left" width="25%" bgColor="aqua">
        <%= custVal.getFirstName() %>
      </td>
      <td align="left" width="2%" bgColor="aqua">
        <%= custVal.getMiddleInitial() %>
      </td>
      <td align="left" width="25%" bgColor="aqua">
        <%= custVal.getLastName() %>
      </td>
      <td align="left" width="10%" bgColor="aqua">
        <%= custVal.getSuffix() %>
      </td>
    </tr>
  </table>
  <p><p>
  <table border="1" width="60%"  >
    <tr>
      <th align="center" width="25%">
        Phone1
      </th>
      <th align="center" width="25%">
        Phone2
      </th>
      <th align="center" width="25%">
        E-Mail
      </th>
    </tr>
    <tr>
      <td align="left" width="25%" bgColor="aqua">
        <%= custVal.getPhone1() %>
      </td>
      <td align="left" width="25%" bgColor="aqua">
        <%= custVal.getPhone2() %>
      </td>
      <td align="left" width="25%" bgColor="aqua">
        <%= custVal.getEMail() %>
      </td>
    </tr>
  </table>
  <!--Buttons for Customer -->
```

```
<table border="0" width="30%"  >
  <tr>
    <th align="left" width="33%">
      <INPUT type=submit value="Edit Customer" name=action >
    </th>
    <th align="left" width="33%">
      <INPUT type=submit value="Delete Customer" name=action >
    </th>
    <th align="left" width="33%">
      <INPUT type=submit value="Add Address" name=action>
    </th>
  </tr>
</table>
<INPUT type="hidden" name="customerNumber"
       value='<%= custVal.getCustomerNumber() %>' >
<INPUT type="hidden" name="customerId"
       value='<%= custVal.getCustomerId() %>' >
</form>
</BODY>
</HTML>
```

A JavaServer Page consists of three types of elements: directives, actions, and scripts. **Directives** are global definitions that remain constant across multiple invocations of the page. Items such as the scripting language being used and any tag libraries are common directives found in most JSPs. Directives are always enclosed by `<%@ . . . %>`. In the `rltnInquiry()` page above, the `page` directive is a good example of a directive.

Actions, or action elements, are uniquely processed for each page request. A good example would be the `CustomerValue` object mentioned previously that is placed into the `Request` scope by the servlet. The ability to reference the attributes within the page during execution is an action. There are several standard actions, such as `<jsp:useBean>`, that are always found in JSPs. In the `rltnInquiry` JSP, the `useBean` action tag is defining a reference item, `custVal`, that is implemented by the `com.jacksonreed.CustomerValue` class. If you look down about forty lines in the JSP, you will run across a `<jsp:getProperty>` tag for the prefix field for the customer. This tag is referencing the element defined by the `useBean` tag.

Scripts, or scripting elements, let you add actual Java code, among other things, to the page. Perhaps you need a branching mechanism or a looping arrangement; these can be created with scripts. Scripts are easy to identify because they are enclosed by `<% . . . %>`, `<%= . . . %>`, or `<%! . . . %>`, depending on what you're trying to do. If you revisit the `rltnInquiry` page above, right after the prefix action reference you will see a script displaying the first name field. The `<%= custVal.getFirstName()%>` scripting element contains an actual line of Java code that is executing the getter for the first name.

As powerful as scripting elements are, they should be avoided. They make maintenance more difficult, and they clutter up the JSP. It is much better today to use tag libraries, such as Struts, which encapsulate most of the logic for you. Your motto should be to have as little scripting as possible in your JSPs.

The `rltnInquiry` page is simply utilizing the information in the `CustomerValue` object, which was inserted by the servlet, to build a table structure with returned values. Notice the hidden fields at the bottom of the page. These are used to facilitate some of the action processing in the servlet. When we explore the EJB solution for *Maintain Relationships,* more will be added to this page to facilitate looping through all the `Role/Address` combinations for the `Customer` object. That's where we will use some of the features of Struts.

The `rltnCustomer` page is used to both add and update a `Customer` object. Here's the JSP behind the screen display in Figure 11-4:

```
<%@ page language="java" contentType="text/html" %>
<jsp:useBean id="custVal" scope="request"
       class="com.jacksonreed.CustomerValue" />
<HTML>
<HEAD>
<TITLE>Remulak Customer Add/Update</TITLE>
</HEAD>
<BODY >
<P><FONT size=6>Remulak Customer Add/Update</FONT></P>

<%--Output form with submitted values --%>
<form action="rltnUpdate" method="get">
  <table>
    <tr>
      <td>Customer Number:</td>
      <td>
        <input type="text" name="customerNumber"
                value="<jsp:getProperty name="custVal"
                property="customerNumber"/>">
      </td>
```

```
</tr>
<tr>
  <td>Prefix:</td>
    <td>
      <input type="text" name="prefix"
        value="<jsp:getProperty name="custVal"
        property="prefix"/>">
    </td>
</tr>
<tr>
  <td>First Name:</td>
    <td>
      <input type="text" name="firstName"
             value="<jsp:getProperty name="custVal"
             property="firstName"/>">
    </td>
</tr>
<tr>
  <td>Middle Init:</td>
    <td>
      <input type="text" name="middleInitial"
             value="<jsp:getProperty name="custVal"
             property="middleInitial"/>">
    </td>
</tr>
<tr>
  <td>Last Name:</td>
    <td>
      <input type="text" name="lastName"
        value="<jsp:getProperty name="custVal"
        property="lastName"/>">
    </td>
</tr>
<tr>
  <td>Suffix:</td>
    <td>
      <input type="text" name="suffix"
        value="<jsp:getProperty name="custVal"
        property="suffix"/>">
    </td>
</tr>
<tr>
  <td>Phone #1:</td>
    <td>
      <input type="text" name="phone1"
        value="<jsp:getProperty name="custVal"
```

```
                property="phone1"/>">
            </td>
        </tr>
        <tr>
          <td>Phone #2:</td>
            <td>
              <input type="text" name="phone2"
                value="<jsp:getProperty name="custVal"
                property="phone2"/>">
            </td>
        </tr>
        <tr>
          <td>EMail:</td>
            <td>
              <input type="text" name="eMail" size=30
                value="<jsp:getProperty name="custVal"
                property="EMail"/>">
            </td>
        </tr>
      </table>
    <INPUT type="hidden" name="customerId"
           value="<jsp:getProperty name="custVal"
           property="customerId"/>">
    <INPUT type=submit value="Add/Update Customer" name=action>
    </form>
    </BODY>
    </HTML>
```

Both JSP pages—`rltnInquiry()` and `rltnCustomer()`—have all three types of elements: directives, actions, and scripts.

Building the Architectural Prototype: Part 2

Part 2 of building the architectural prototype for our non-EJB solution covers the use-case control class and the issues of transaction management.

Remulak Controllers and Initial Operations

The Remulak software architecture uses two types of controllers: user interface and use-case. In the previous section we covered the user interface aspects that the controller handles for us—namely, the servlet.

In this section we cover the use-case control class: `UCMaintainRltnshp`. To reemphasize our strategy, each use-case will have a use-case control class. Each use-case control class will have an operation for each happy and alternate pathway in the use-case. Occasionally, depending on the granularity of the use-case, some of the alternates may be handled in the course of either the happy path or one of the other alternates. Exceptions are always handled in the course of another pathway.

`UCMaintainRltnshp` is a JavaBean in this first analysis of use-case controllers. In Chapter 12 the same class will be made into a session EJB. However, the operation names and what they do will remain identical. Let's review, as we did with `RemulakServlet`, the various parts of the use-case control class, starting with the class definition and the `rltnCustomerInquiry()` operation referred to in the previous section:

```
package com.jacksonreed;

import java.util.Enumeration;
import java.util.Random;
import javax.naming.InitialContext;
import javax.naming.NamingException;
import javax.naming.NamingException;

public class UCMaintainRltnshp implements
java.io. Serializable {

  private static Random generator;
  private static TransactionContext transactionContext;

  public UCMaintainRltnshp() {
      transactionContext = new TransactionContext();
  }

  public CustomerValue rltnCustomerInquiry(String
  customerNumber){

      CustomerValue customerValue = new CustomerValue();
      CustomerBean customerHome = new CustomerBean();

      try {
          transactionContext.beginTran(false);
          customerValue = CustomerHome.findByCustomerNumber
              (transactionContext, customerNumber);
          transactionContext.commitTran();
```

```
        } catch (RemulakFinderException fe) {
        } catch (TranCommitException ce) {
        } catch (TranSysException se) {
        } catch (TranBeginException be) {
        } catch (TranRollBackException re) {
        } catch (Exception e) {
        } finally {
          customerHome = null;
        }
        return customerValue;
    }
  }
```

The `rltnCustomerInquiry()` operation begins by instantiating a `CustomerBean` object. This step is necessary because, as you may recall, the use-case controller is akin to the conductor of an orchestra; in this case the orchestra is the use-case, and the musicians are the individual objects involved in the score. A use-case controller may send messages to only one bean or to many beans, depending on the needs of the use-case pathway. The operation then invokes `beginTran()` on an object called `TransactionContext` (more on this shortly). The `CustomerBean` object is sent a `findByCustomerNumber()` message, with both the `TransactionContext` object and the `customerNumber` attribute passed in. The result returned from this operation is our populated `CustomerValue` object.

The last thing that happens in this use-case pathway operation is that the `TransactionContext` object receives a `commitTran()` request. The rest continues with what we saw in the previous section: `RemulakServlet` now has the `CustomerValue` object, and the JSP does its work, filling the screen with information for the user. However, the `TransactionContext` object needs more discussion.

Remulak Transaction Management: Roll Your Own

Transaction management is key to any software application today. In particular, it is vital for update activity when more than one set of updates is occurring, all part of a package of updates. This package of updates is called a **unit of work** in transaction terminology. How does transaction management work and how do we code for it? Here's one of the big drawbacks to not using a commercial container product that implements the EJB framework. If the application is using just native JDBC, the software developer is responsible for all transaction management activities.

Where to put the transaction logic is a problem. However, the beauty of the design strategy we are following (a controller for each use-case and an operation for each pathway) is that management of the unit of work must begin in the use-case control class. We can't put the begin/commit logic in the DAO classes because many DAO classes may be involved in one unit of work. We also can't put the begin/commit logic in the entity bean classes because they are in the same boat as the DAO classes: They represent just one musician playing in the orchestra of the use-case pathway. So figuring out where to manage the transaction seems logical, but the architecture of it isn't.

We need a class that can load JDBC drivers, manage connection pools, and open database connections. We need a class that can begin a transaction as well as commit it. This is what the `TransactionContext` class will do for us. To be able to roll back a transaction, all SQL activity must happen on the same connection. The connection's life span is usually parallel to that of the unit of work. So the `TransactionContext` object must be passed into the entity bean classes and then into the DAO classes. This same requirement applies to all entity beans involved in a unit of work.

Let's examine the `TransactionContext` class:

```
package com.jacksonreed;

import java.io.*;
import java.sql.*;
import java.text.*;
import java.util.*;
import javax.sql.*;

public class TransactionContext implements Serializable {
    private Connection dbConnection = null;
    private DataSource datasource   = null;
    private CustomerValue custVal   = null;
    private boolean unitOfWork = false;

    public TransactionContext() {
      try {
        // This is where we load the driver
```

```
          Class.forName("sun.jdbc.odbc.JdbcOdbcDriver");
        }
        catch (ClassNotFoundException e) {
          System.out.println("Unable to load Driver Class");
          throw new TranSysException(e.getMessage());
        }
      }
```

Note first that the constructor is where the driver is loaded for our database. Again, wanting to stick with the semantics of what is happening versus additional abstractions, I'll say simply that it is done in a very manual way. A better solution would be to use JNDI or perhaps a *.properties* file to look up the driver name instead of hard-coding it in the constructor.

```
  public Connection getDBConnection() {
        log("TransactionContext: in get connection");
        if (dbConnection == null)
           throw new TranSysException
                      ("no database connection established
                       yet");
        return dbConnection;
  }

  public void beginTran(boolean supportTran)
        throws TranBeginException, TranSysException {

    unitOfWork = supportTran;
    getConnection();
    try {
        if (supportTran) {
           dbConnection.setAutoCommit(false);
        }
        else {
           dbConnection.setAutoCommit(true);
        }
    }
    catch (SQLException e) {
        throw new TranBeginException(e.getMessage());
        }

  }
```

The `beginTran()` operation receives a `boolean` input parameter. This `boolean` tells the operation if a unit of work is necessary, meaning that updates are going to occur. The next element of `beginTran()` is to call its `getConnection()` operation:

```
public void getConnection() throws TranSysException {
     try {
          dbConnection = DriverManager.getConnection
               ("jdbc:odbc:remulak-bea","", "");
     } catch (SQLException se) {
          throw new TranSysException("SQLExcpetion while
          getting" +
                                        " DB Connection : \n" + se);
     }
 }
```

A `getConnection()` call to the `DriverManager` object created in the constructor establishes a connection with the driver loaded previously, by use of the data source name necessary to talk to the database. Again, it would be an added benefit to load this driver with JNDI.

Back to `beginTran()`, if a unit of work is necessary, `false` is passed to the `setAutoCommit()` method; otherwise each individual update request would be committed as it occurred. If this is a read-only type of request, `true` (the default) is passed to `setAutoCommit()`.

```
public void commitTran()
    throws TranCommitException, TranSysException,
              TranRollBackException {

    if (unitOfWork) {
      try {
           dbConnection.commit();
      }
      catch (SQLException e) {
           rollBackTran();
           throw new TranCommitException("Can't commit
           transaction");
           }
    }
    closeConnection();
}
```

When committing work, `TransactionContext` knows from the initial call to `beginTran()` whether a unit of work is under way; if so, a commit is issued on the connection and the connection is closed. If no unit of work is under way, the connection is simply closed.

The remaining operations in the `TransactionContext` class follow. Some of the operations, such as `closeResultSet()` and `closeStatement()`, will be used by the DAO classes that will be reviewed later in this chapter.

```
public boolean rollBackTran()
        throws TranRollBackException, TranSysException {
    boolean returnValue = false;
    try {
        dbConnection.rollback();
        closeConnection();
        returnValue = true;
    }
    catch (SQLException e) {
        throw new TranRollBackException("Can't roll back
        transaction");
    }
    return returnValue;
 }

 public void closeResultSet(ResultSet result)
     throws TranSysException {
      try {
          if (result != null) {
              result.close();
          }
       }
       catch (SQLException se) {
          throw new TranSysException("SQL Exception while
          closing " + "Result Set : \n" + se);
      }
 }

 public void closeStatement(Statement stmt)
     throws TranSysException {
      try {
          if (stmt != null) {
              stmt.close();
          }
      } catch (SQLException se) {
          throw new TranSysException("SQL Exception while
          closing " + "Statement : \n" + se);
      }
 }
```

```
    public void closeConnection() throws TranSysException {
        try {
            if (dbConnection != null && !dbConnection.isClosed()) {
                dbConnection.close();
                log("TransactionContext: closing connection");
            }
        } catch (SQLException se) {
            throw new TranSysException("SQLException while closing"
            + " DB Connection : \n" + se);
        }
    }
}
```

The `TransactionContext` class allows us to encapsulate all the transaction management logic in one place. It also makes it convenient because each controller pathway operation can use the same syntax. It is true that read-only operations don't begin and commit transactions, but we have abstracted out the underlying functionality by simply indicating the intent with the `beginTran()` call at the beginning of the interaction.

Remulak Controllers and Subsequent Operations

Let's continue with the `UCMaintainRltnshp` control class by looking at the `rltnAddCustomer()` operation. For add operations, a primary key must be assigned. The relevant code follows, but it simply uses the `Random` class out of the `java.util` package. You can build more industrial-strength generators, but this one will serve our purpose.

```
public void rltnAddCustomer(CustomerValue custVal) {

        // Seed random generator
        seedRandomGenerator();

        // Generate a random integer as the key field
        custVal.setCustomerId(generateRandomKey());

        CustomerBean customerHome = new CustomerBean();

        try {
            transactionContext.beginTran(true);
            customerHome.customerInsert(transactionContext,
            custVal);
```

```
            transactionContext.commitTran();
          } catch (RemulakFinderException fe) {
          } catch (TranCommitException ce) {
            try {
              transactionContext.rollBackTran();
            }
            catch (TranRollBackException ree) {
            }
          } catch (TranSysException se) {
              try {
              transactionContext.rollBackTran();
            }
            catch (TranRollBackException ree) {
            }
          } catch (TranBeginException be) {
          } catch (TranRollBackException re) {
          } catch (Exception e) {
              try {
              transactionContext.rollBackTran();
            }
            catch (TranRollBackException ree) {
            }
          } finally {
            customerHome = null;
          }
      }

      private static void seedRandomGenerator() {
        generator = new Random(System.currentTimeMillis());
      }

      private Integer generateRandomKey() {
        Integer myInt = new Integer(generator.nextInt());
        return myInt;
      }
```

The fact that `beginTran()` is now passed a value of `true` indicates that there is a unit-of-work requirement for this transaction. In the `try/catch` blocks we see how `rollBackTran()` is called within `TransactionContext` if there are problems along the way.

The remaining operations of the `UCMaintainRltnshp` class follow. In Chapter 12 we'll see that this class also covers the pathways of adding roles and addresses.

```
public void rltnUpdateCustomer(CustomerValue custVal) {

      CustomerBean customerHome = new CustomerBean();

      try {
          transactionContext.beginTran(true);
          customerHome.customerUpdate(transactionContext,
          custVal);
          transactionContext.commitTran();
      } catch (RemulakFinderException fe) {
      } catch (TranCommitException ce) {
        try {
          transactionContext.rollBackTran();
        }
        catch (TranRollBackException ree) {
        }
      } catch (TranSysException se) {
          try {
          transactionContext.rollBackTran();
        }
        catch (TranRollBackException ree) {
        }
      } catch (TranBeginException be) {
      } catch (TranRollBackException re) {
      } catch (Exception e) {
          try {
          transactionContext.rollBackTran();
        }
        catch (TranRollBackException ree) {
        }
      } finally {
        customerHome = null;
      }
  }

  public void rltnDeleteCustomer(Integer customerId) {
      CustomerBean customerHome = new CustomerBean();

      try {
          transactionContext.beginTran(true);
          customerHome.customerDelete(transactionContext,
          customerId);
          transactionContext.commitTran();
      } catch (RemulakFinderException fe) {
      } catch (TranCommitException ce) {
```

```
          try {
            transactionContext.rollBackTran();
          }
          catch (TranRollBackException ree) {
          }
        } catch (TranSysException se) {
            try {
            transactionContext.rollBackTran();
          }
          catch (TranRollBackException ree) {
          }
        } catch (TranBeginException be) {
        } catch (TranRollBackException re) {
        } catch (Exception e) {
            try {
            transactionContext.rollBackTran();
          }
          catch (TranRollBackException ree) {
          }
        } finally {
          customerHome = null;
        }
    }
```

Building the Architectural Prototype: Part 3

Part 3 of building the architectural prototype for our non-EJB solution covers the entity bean and DAO classes.

Entity Beans

The entity beans are where the business logic lies in our application. This logic implements the Business Rule Services layer from our architecture. It also represents the state of the attributes of the entity. At a minimum, entity classes will have attributes as well as accessors for those attributes. There are also value classes that are proxies for the entity beans. Previously we stated that these proxies insulate the application from future distributed architecture migrations and reduce network chatter. Today everything may be running on one machine, but tomorrow that may change.

Let's continue with our progression and introduce the `CustomerBean` class:

```
package com.jacksonreed;

import java.io.Serializable;
import java.util.Enumeration;
import java.util.Vector;
import java.util.Collection;

import javax.naming.InitialContext;
import javax.naming.NamingException;
import java.util.List;
import java.util.Iterator;
import java.util.ArrayList;

public class CustomerBean implements java.io.Serializable {

   private Integer customerId;
   private String customerNumber;
   private String firstName;
   private String middleInitial;
   private String prefix;
   private String suffix;
   private String lastName;
   private String phone1;
   private String phone2;
   private String EMail;
   private ArrayList roleBean;
   private ArrayList orderBean;
```

All attributes of the bean are declared private. Notice that the relationships to other classes, as specified in the class diagram, are represented as `ArrayList` objects. These lists would hold `RoleBean` and `OrderBean` objects, respectively.

```
   public void CustomerBean() {
      RoleBean = new ArrayList();
      OrderBean = new ArrayList();
   }
   public Integer getCustomerId() {
      return customerId;
   }
   public void setCustomerId(Integer val) {
       customerId = val;
```

```
}
public String getCustomerNumber() {
    return customerNumber;
}
public void setCustomerNumber(String val) {
    customerNumber = val;
}
public String getFirstName(){
    return firstName;
}
public void setFirstName(String val){
    firstName = val;
}
public String getMiddleInitial(){
    return middleInitial;
}
public void setMiddleInitial(String val){
    middleInitial = val;
}
public String getPrefix(){
    return prefix;
}
public void setPrefix(String val){
    prefix = val;
}
public String getSuffix(){
    return suffix;
}
public void setSuffix(String val){
    suffix = val;
}
public String getLastName(){
    return lastName;
}
public void setLastName(String val){
    lastName = val;
}
public String getPhone1(){
    return phone1;
}
public void setPhone1(String val){
    phone1 = val;
}
public String getPhone2(){
    return phone2;
}
```

```
public void setPhone2(String val){
    phone2 = val;
}
public String getEMail(){
    return EMail;
}
public void setEMail(String val){
   EMail = val;
}
```

These are the accessors for the beans related to `CustomerBean`:

```
public ArrayList getRoleBean(){
    return roleBean;
}
public void setRoleBean(ArrayList val){
    roleBean = val;
}
public ArrayList getOrderBean(){
    return orderBean;
}
public void setOrderBean(ArrayList val){
    orderBean = val;
}
```

Some of the code below we saw as a preview in Chapter 9 when we reviewed the data access architecture. Here the `findByCustomerNumber()` operation, which has been called by the use-case control class, is presented in a more complete form:

```
public CustomerValue findByCustomerNumber
     (TransactionContext transactionContext, String
      customerNumber)
      throws RemulakFinderException, Exception {

      try {
        // Initiate and get the information from the DAO
        DataAccess custDAO = new CustomerDAO (transactionContext);
        CustomerValue custVal = (CustomerValue)
               custDAO.findByName(customerNumber);

        // Sets the values of the bean with the DAO results
        setCustomerValue(custVal);
        custDAO = null;
        return custVal;
```

```
        }
        catch (DAOSysException se) {
          throw new Exception (se.getMessage());
        }
        catch (DAOFinderException fe) {
          throw new RemulakFinderException (fe.getMessage());
        }
}
```

The operation first must get a reference to the `CustomerDAO` class that carries out its `findByName()` request. Notice that the type of the `custDAO` attribute is `DataAccess`. `CustomerDAO` implements the `DataAccess` interface presented in Chapter 9. This ensures, or enforces, that all DAOs implemented in Remulak adhere to the same behavioral contract. The return of the `CustomerValue` object must be cast because the return type of the interface is `Object`.

```
public void customerUpdate
      (TransactionContext transactionContext, CustomerValue
       custVal)
       throws RemulakFinderException, Exception {

       try {
         setCustomerValue(custVal);
         DataAccess custDAO = new CustomerDAO
         (transactionContext);
         custDAO.updateObject(custVal);

         custDAO = null;
       }
       catch (DAOSysException se) {
         throw new Exception (se.getMessage());
       }
       catch (DAODBUpdateException ue) {
         throw new Exception (ue.getMessage());
       }
}
```

In the case of `customerUpdate()` above and `customerInsert()` below, the `CustomerValue` object is passed in to the appropriate DAO operation.

```
public void customerInsert
      (TransactionContext transactionContext, CustomerValue
       custVal)
```

```
        throws RemulakFinderException, Exception {

        try {
          setCustomerValue(custVal);
          DataAccess custDAO = new
          CustomerDAO(transactionContext);
          custDAO.insertObject(custVal);

          custDAO = null;
        }
        catch (DAOSysException se) {
          throw new Exception (se.getMessage());
        }
        catch (DAODBUpdateException ue) {
          throw new Exception (ue.getMessage());
        }
  }
```

The `customerDelete()` operation passes to the `CustomerDAO deleteObject()` operation the `customerId` parameter:

```
    public void customerDelete
         (TransactionContext transactionContext, Integer
          customerId)
          throws RemulakFinderException, Exception {

          try {
            DataAccess custDAO = new CustomerDAO
            (transactionContext);
            custDAO.deleteObject(customerId);

            custDAO = null;
          }
          catch (DAOSysException se) {
            throw new Exception (se.getMessage());
          }
          catch (DAODBUpdateException ue) {
            throw new Exception (ue.getMessage());
          }
    }

    public void setCustomerValue(CustomerValue val)
    {
      log("Setting Customer Value");

      setCustomerId(val.getCustomerId());
```

```
      setCustomerNumber(val.getCustomerNumber());
      setFirstName(val.getFirstName());
      setMiddleInitial(val.getMiddleInitial());
      setPrefix(val.getPrefix());
      setSuffix(val.getSuffix());
      setLastName(val.getLastName());
      setPhone1(val.getPhone1());
      setPhone2(val.getPhone2());
      setEMail(val.getEMail());
    }

    public String toString() {
      return "[CustomerBean " + getCustomerId() + ", " +
            getFirstName() + ", " + getLastName() + "]";
    }

    private void log(String s) {
      System.out.println(s);
    }
  }
```

Data Access Objects

Data access objects (DAOs) were introduced in Chapter 9 as the mechanism that Remulak uses to gain access to and update data about beans. We shall see that the DAOs also use the `TransactionContext` object to do much of their work. The `TransactionContext` object has been passed in from the use-case control class so that it can control the scope of the unit of work. Let's begin our analysis by looking at the `CustomerDAO` class and the `findByName()` operation.

```
package com.jacksonreed;

import java.io.*;
import java.sql.*;
import java.text.*;
import java.util.*;
import javax.sql.*;

public class CustomerDAO implements Serializable, DataAccess {
   private transient TransactionContext globalTran = null;
   private transient CustomerValue custVal = null;

   public CustomerDAO(TransactionContext transactionContext) {
```

```
        globalTran = transactionContext;
}
```

Notice that the constructor takes in a `TransactionContext` object as a parameter and assigns it to a local copy.

```
public Object findByName(String name)
    throws DAOSysException, DAOFinderException {

      if (itemExistsByName(name)) {
         return custVal;
         }
      throw new DAOFinderException ("Customer Not Found = "
              + name);
}

private boolean itemExistsByName(String customerNumber)
      throws DAOSysException {
    String queryStr ="SELECT customerId, customerNumber,
    firstName " +
      ",middleInitial, prefix, suffix, lastName, phone1,
       phone2 " +
      ",eMail " + "FROM T_Customer " +
      "WHERE customerNumber = " + "'" + customerNumber.
       trim() + "'";

     return doQuery(queryStr);
}
```

The `findByName()` operation, part of the `DataAccess` interface, works with a private operation, `itemExistsByName()`, to retrieve the `CustomerBean` state information. First the SQL query must be built. For variety, I show an unprepared statement here and later will present a sample prepared statement.

```
private boolean doQuery (String qryString) throws
DAOSysException {
    Statement stmt = null;
    ResultSet result = null;
    boolean returnValue = false;
    try {
        stmt = globalTran.getDBConnection().
        createStatement();
        result = stmt.executeQuery(qryString);
```

```
            if ( !result.next() ) {
                returnValue = false;
            }
            else {
                custVal = new CustomerValue();

                int i = 1;
                custVal.setCustomerId(new Integer(result.getInt
                (i++)));
                custVal.setCustomerNumber(result.getString(i++));
                custVal.setFirstName(result.getString(i++));
                custVal.setMiddleInitial(result.getString(i++));
                custVal.setPrefix(result.getString(i++));
                custVal.setSuffix(result.getString(i++));
                custVal.setLastName(result.getString(i++));
                custVal.setPhone1(result.getString(i++));
                custVal.setPhone2(result.getString(i++));
                custVal.setEMail(result.getString(i++));

                returnValue = true;
            }
        } catch(SQLException se) {
            throw new DAOSysException("Unable to Query for item " +
                                      "\n" + se);
        } finally {
            globalTran.closeResultSet(result);
            globalTran.closeStatement(stmt);
        }
        return returnValue;
    }
```

The `doQuery()` operation takes in the query previously built and executes it. Notice that it gets a `Statement` object by referencing the connection stored in the local copy of the `TransactionContext` object. The query is executed via the `executeQuery()` operation and if there is something found, a new `CustomerValue` object is created and its values set. At the end, both the `ResultSet` and the `Statement` objects are closed. These close operations are part of the services offered by the `TransactionContext` object.

```
    public Object findByPrimaryKey(Integer id)
        throws DAOSysException, DAOFinderException {

        if (itemExistsById(id)) {
              return custVal;
```

```
        }
        throw new DAOFinderException ("Customer Not Found = " +
        id);
}

private boolean itemExistsById(Integer customerId)
        throws DAOSysException {
    String queryStr ="SELECT customerId, customerNumber,
    firstName " +
        ",middleInitial, prefix, suffix, lastName, phone1,
         phone2 " + ",eMail " + "FROM T_Customer " +
                   "WHERE customerId = " + customerId;

    return doQuery(queryStr);
}
```

The `findByPrimaryKey()` operation, also part of the `DataAccess` interface, works very much like `findByName()`. They both use the same private `doQuery()` operation. The only difference between the two is that one uses the secondary access mechanism of name (customer number in our case) and the other uses the primary key (customer ID in our case).

```
public void deleteObject(Integer id) throws
            DAOSysException, DAODBUpdateException {

    String queryStr = "DELETE FROM " + "T_Customer" +
            " WHERE customerId = "
                + id;

    Statement stmt = null;
    try {
        stmt = globalTran.getDBConnection().
        createStatement();
        int resultCount = stmt.executeUpdate(queryStr);
        if ( resultCount != 1 )
            throw new DAODBUpdateException
             ("ERROR deleting Customer from" +
             " Customer_TABLE!! resultCount = " +
              resultCount);

    } catch(SQLException se) {
        throw new DAOSysException("Unable to delete for
        item " +
```

```
                    id + "\n" + se);
        } finally {
            globalTran.closeStatement(stmt);
        }
    }
```

The `deleteObject()` operation simply deletes a row from the `T_Customer` table on the basis of the primary key of `customerId` being passed in.

```
    public void updateObject(Object model) throws
                    DAOSysException, DAODBUpdateException {

        CustomerValue custVal = (CustomerValue) model;

        PreparedStatement stmt = null;
        try {
            String queryStr = "UPDATE " + "T_Customer" +
              " SET " + "customerNumber = ?, " +
              "firstName = ?, " +
              "middleInitial = ?, " +
              "prefix = ?, " +
              "suffix = ?, " +
              "lastName = ?, " +
              "phone1 = ?, " +
              "phone2 = ?, " +
              "eMail = ? " +
              "WHERE customerId = ?";

            stmt = globalTran.getDBConnection().
                      prepareStatement(queryStr);

            int i = 1;
            stmt.setString(i++, custVal.getCustomerNumber());
            stmt.setString(i++, custVal.getFirstName());
            stmt.setString(i++, custVal.getMiddleInitial());
            stmt.setString(i++, custVal.getPrefix());
            stmt.setString(i++, custVal.getSuffix());
            stmt.setString(i++, custVal.getLastName());
            stmt.setString(i++, custVal.getPhone1());
            stmt.setString(i++, custVal.getPhone2());
            stmt.setString(i++, custVal.getEMail());
            stmt.setInt(i++, custVal.getCustomerId().intValue());

            int resultCount = stmt.executeUpdate();
            if ( resultCount != 1 ) {
```

```
            throw new DAODBUpdateException
                    ("ERROR updating Customer in" +
                    " Customer_TABLE!! resultCount = " +
                    resultCount);
        }
    } catch(SQLException se) {
        throw new DAOSysException
            ("Unable to update item " +
            custVal.getCustomerId() + " \n" + se);
    } finally {
        globalTran.closeStatement(stmt);
    }
}
```

In the case of the `updateObject()` operation, I chose to use a prepared statement. Prepared statements generally perform better and are easier to build.

```
public void insertObject(Object model) throws
                 DAOSysException, DAODBUpdateException {

    CustomerValue custVal = (CustomerValue) model;

    PreparedStatement stmt = null;
    try {
        String queryStr = "INSERT INTO " +
          "T_Customer" + " (" +
          "customerId, " +
          "customerNumber, " +
          "firstName, " +
          "middleInitial, " +
          "prefix, " +
          "suffix, " +
          "lastName, " +
          "phone1, " +
          "phone2, " +
          "eMail) " +
          "VALUES " +
          "(?, ?, ?, ?, ?, ?, ?, ?, ?, ?)";

        stmt = globalTran.getDBConnection().
                   prepareStatement(queryStr);

        int i = 1;
        stmt.setInt(i++, custVal.getCustomerId().intValue());
        stmt.setString(i++, custVal.getCustomerNumber());
```

```
            stmt.setString(i++, custVal.getFirstName());
            stmt.setString(i++, custVal.getMiddleInitial());
            stmt.setString(i++, custVal.getPrefix());
            stmt.setString(i++, custVal.getSuffix());
            stmt.setString(i++, custVal.getLastName());
            stmt.setString(i++, custVal.getPhone1());
            stmt.setString(i++, custVal.getPhone2());
            stmt.setString(i++, custVal.getEMail());

            int resultCount = stmt.executeUpdate();
            if ( resultCount != 1 )
                throw new DAODBUpdateException
                       ("ERROR inserting Customer in" +
                       " Customer_TABLE!! resultCount = " +
                       resultCount);
        } catch(SQLException se) {
            throw new DAOSysException
                 ("Unable to insert item " + custVal.
                  getCustomerId() +
                        " \n" + se);
        } finally {
            globalTran.closeStatement(stmt);
        }
    }
```

The `insertObject()` operation is virtually identical to `updateObject()`, with the difference of the actual SQL statement. The remaining operations are private and used locally by the DAO to clean up resources used in the SQL calls.

```
    private void closeResultSet(ResultSet result)
        throws DAOSysException {
        try {
            if (result != null) {
                result.close();
            }
        } catch (SQLException se) {
            throw new DAOSysException
                 ("SQL Exception while closing " +
                      "Result Set : \n" + se);
        }
    }

    private void closeStatement(Statement stmt)
```

```
            throws DAOSysException {
            try {
                if (stmt != null) {
                    stmt.close();
                }
            } catch (SQLException se) {
                throw new DAOSysException
                     ("SQL Exception while closing " +
                         "Statement : \n" + se);
            }
        }
        private void log(String s) {
            System.out.println(s);
        }
    }
```

Front to Back in One Package

We have built quite a bit of logic for our non-EJB solution. When you download all the code, you will find similar constructs for all aspects of the application, including the order entry part. However, if you understand how this flow worked and how the software architecture is laid out, you will find that the other components are identical.

Checkpoint

Where We've Been

- Applications built today without the services of Enterprise JavaBeans require quite a bit of overhead code, particularly in the area of transaction management and SQL execution. The open-source container used in the Remulak example is the Apache Tomcat product.
- Servlets and JavaServer Pages working together are called the Model 2 approach to the MVC pattern. Servlets act as the first line of defense to the browser and route all the traffic. They play the role of user interface controller. The container knows to execute a given servlet via the `web.xml` descriptor. All container products, whether commercial or open source, use the `web.xml` descriptor.

- The use-case control class has a one-to-one mapping to a use-case. Each pathway in the use-case will have an operation in the control class. The logic found in these individual operations maps to the sequence diagrams created during the dynamic modeling activities of the project.
- To coordinate the transactional aspects of the use-case control classes, a `TransactionContext` class is used to manage the unit-of-work control. This object is passed through the entity beans and eventually into the DAO classes, giving them the ability to work on the same connection before a commit or rollback decision is made in the use-case controller.
- Entity bean classes and DAO classes work hand in hand to insulate the outside world from the persistence mechanics of the system. There is a one-to-one mapping between entity classes and DAO classes. All DAO classes implement the same `DataAccess` interface.

Where We're Going Next

In the next chapter we:

- Explore the second iteration of the architectural prototype using Enterprise JavaBeans.
- Review how additional functionality is added to the *Maintain Relationships* use-case and how both roles and addresses are handled.
- Discuss how both bean-managed persistence and container-managed persistence, along with container-managed transactions, alleviate the extra burden of controlling the unit-of-work activity of the use-case pathways.

CHAPTER 12 *Constructing a Solution: Servlets, JSP, and Enterprise JavaBeans*

IN THIS CHAPTER

In the last chapter we finally saw the fruits of our hard analysis and design efforts. We crafted a slice of our architectural prototype using a collection of components that had one requirement: not to rely on a commercial container product or use Enterprise JavaBeans. In this chapter we move forward and take the same slice of the architectural prototype created in the last chapter, add additional functionality, and implement it using Enterprise JavaBeans.

We will do things a bit differently in our approach in this chapter. In the last chapter we didn't use the benefits that a visual modeling tool has to offer code generation; in this chapter we will use a visual modeling tool to generate much of our code. But don't worry. Code generation gives us only the embryo of the code; we still have to do the hard part: filling in between the lines.

Our focus in this chapter will be to generate initial skeleton code from the class diagram that we built in Rational Rose. From there, we have to begin filling in the code to make the skeleton do something for us.

GOALS

- To review the mission of the visual modeling tool as it pertains to program code generation.
- To review the setup issues in preparing to generate program code.
- To review what to watch out for after code generation is complete.
- To explore the code necessary to add additional functionality to the *Maintain Relationships* use-case and to implement the solution in a commercial EJB container.

Next Steps of the Elaboration Phase

Before constructing the first portion of our Remulak solution, let's revisit again the Unified Process. Figure 12-1 shows the process model, with the Elaboration phase highlighted.

FIGURE 12-1 *Unified Process model: Elaboration phase*

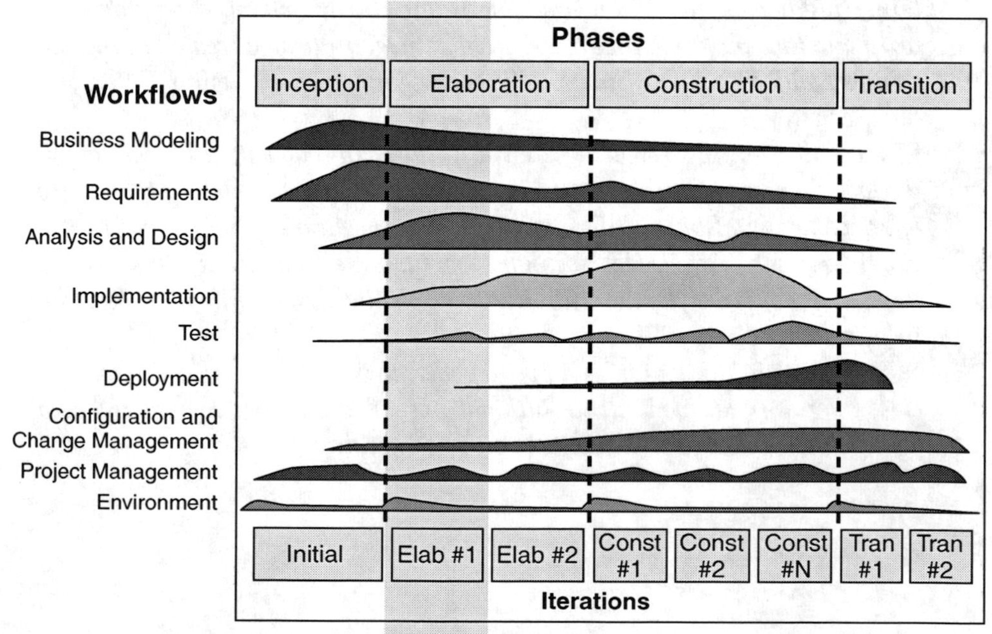

In this chapter we will again specifically focus on building code. This code will lead to the second attempt at an architectural prototype. The architectural prototype will be complete at the end of this chapter. At that point the architecture itself should also be considered complete, and we will have reached the Lifecycle Architecture milestone within the Unified Process.

Even at the end of this chapter it may seem as though we haven't reached the Construction phase as the Unified Process defines it. Remember, however, that each phase slices through all the workflows. The Implementation workflow deals with building code, and we have most definitely been building code. The focus, once the Construction phase is entered, will be to incorporate all the exception handling of every use-case as defined in each package for Remulak. All the business rules must be implemented as well. Construction is a manufacturing process that leverages what we have built in the Elaboration phase.

In the Unified Process, the following workflows and activity sets are emphasized:

- Analysis and Design: Design Components
- Implementation: Implement Components

The emphasis now is on testing our design strategies for how the code comes together with Enterprise JavaBeans.

Building the Architectural Prototype: Part 1

Part 1 of building the architectural prototype for our EJB solution covers the setup of the environment and the use of a visual modeling tool to facilitate the early aspects of code generation.

Baselining the Environment

Our environment in this evolution of the prototype will be BEA's WebLogic application server. Note that the BMP and CMP implementations will work on any commercial or open-source EJB container that complies with the EJB 2.0 specification. Toward that end, I will show little of anything that is unique to WebLogic. In the appendices I will review the console monitor that BEA provides, as well as a unique deployment descriptor.

As in the previous chapter, you should be able to install the EJB solution right from the download. It is packaged in a standard Enterprise Archive (EAR) file, thus complying with the EJB 2.0 specification. EAR files contain both Web Archive (WAR) files and Enterprise JavaBean Java Archive (JAR) files. The name of the file for Remulak is `ejb20_remulak.ear`.

Visual Modeling: Its Mission for the Project

Let me stand on my soapbox once again: Too many Java projects fail because the developers' desire to produce code far outweighs the importance of sound project planning and a precise understanding of the application's requirements.

To reemphasize what was stated earlier, if you have come this far in the book and have not seen the benefit of using a visual modeling tool, this chapter either will finally convince you or merely cement your already positive conclusion. Besides the obvious benefits of having a repository of artifacts and a consistent approach to creating them, the visual modeling tool really excels in getting the programming effort started. It also gets high marks for the ongoing evolution of the application by bringing code artifacts back into the model.

In this book we have used Rational Rose as the visual modeling tool. Note, however, that many excellent visual modeling tools on the market support Java code generation, in particular for the EJB environment. Another tool I like a lot—Together Control Center—is produced by TogetherSoft. But be forewarned: These products are quite expensive.

Note: This chapter will benefit you greatly even if you don't choose to use a visual modeling tool because I review all of the code in any case.

Like its many competitors in the marketplace, this generation of Computer-Aided Software Engineering (CASE) tools is a skeleton-generation product. Modeling tools are focused on analysis, design, or a combination of the two. Unfortunately, I have been the victim, in a previous life, of being "welded" to my modeling tool, always forced to take the code output it produced and forced again to get it to run in a production environment. These integrated CASE tools demanded that the user learn a new language that would eventually translate into code (e.g., COBOL, C, or C++)—usually not a pretty picture.

The current generation of skeleton-generation tools provides both the analysis and the design transition support, but only the code structure and framework are generated from the model. I really like this approach. It allows the project to apply the rigor of keeping true to the structure of the application design, while not dictating the solution for the *how*. For instance, it will put in place the class structures, operation signatures, and available message paths to calculate an order discount but not force me to tell it how to calculate the discount. My once negative opinion of integrated modeling tools has been swayed into the positive. In summary, you need a visual modeling tool that generates code in your language of choice.

Visual Modeling: Its Mission for Program Code Generation

Rational Rose generates code strictly from the information found in the class diagram, along with some physical attributes that we give the UML component that has been assigned to realize, or implement, the class.

There is a completed Rose model that you can use if you have a copy of Rational Rose. You can enter each class by hand, along with all of its support material (attributes, operations), or you can use my model as a start to generate your code. I highly recommend the latter.

Reviewing the Setup Issues

We need to revisit the class diagram for Remulak Productions and see how some of the components have been arranged. This review will facilitate how we work with the diagram, and it will help us better manage all aspects of the code generation. Figure 12-2 shows Remulak Productions' model, `remulakjava.mdl`.

On the right-hand side of Figure 12-2 is the overall package diagram broken down by the increments, with a note attached describing the use-cases that are being realized. In the browser tree view on the left-hand side, there are now packages under each increment that weren't there before. These packages reflect the physical layering decided on in Chapters 10 and 11.

I reemphasize here that in practice you shouldn't worry about being totally accurate with your signature layouts. The model delivered with the book is complete. Just remember that in reality this knowledge will grow with the code. Actually, I find the best source for the signatures are the programmers themselves. Because we will reengineer our code

FIGURE 12-2 *Rose model organization*

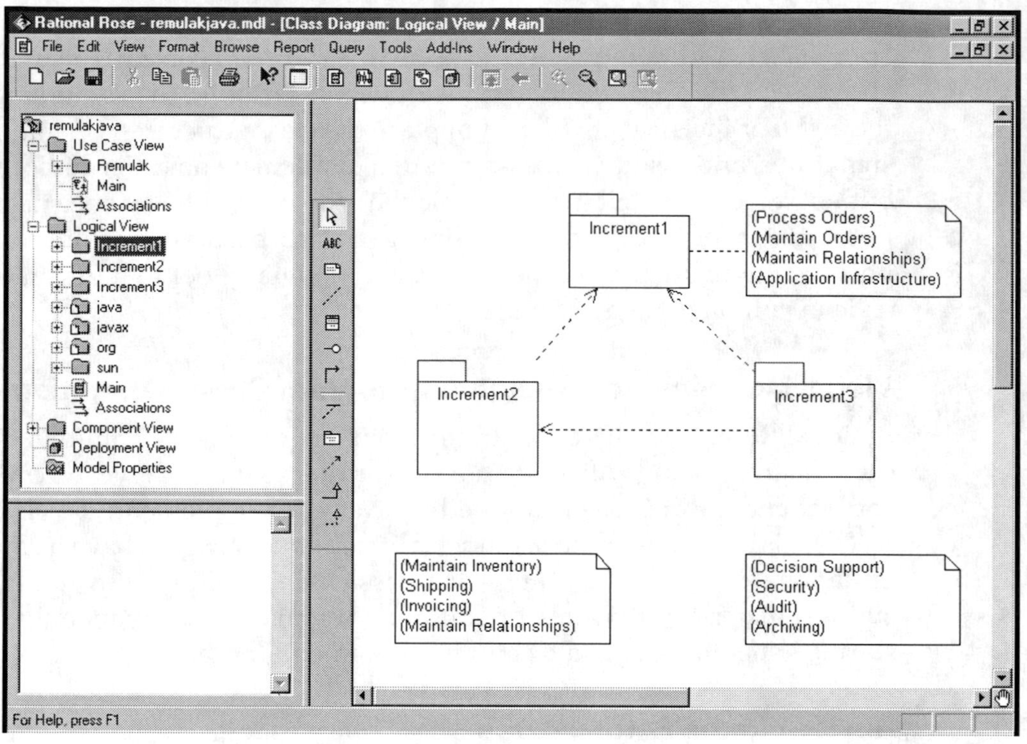

back into the model, everything will eventually be in sync. For instance, when adding input parameters for operations, you can specify their data types. However, don't bother to add them to the class diagram because when we reverse-engineer the code, Rose will fill in that information for us. We want to get to the code as soon as we can.

Modifying the Code Generation Parameters

With Rose we will generate the code to implement our solution using container-managed persistence (CMP). Before we tell our tool to generate code, we need to tweak some of the Java code generation options that Rose provides. Figure 12-3 shows the **Options** dialog box for Remulak Productions' model.

FIGURE 12-3 *Changing the code generation properties*

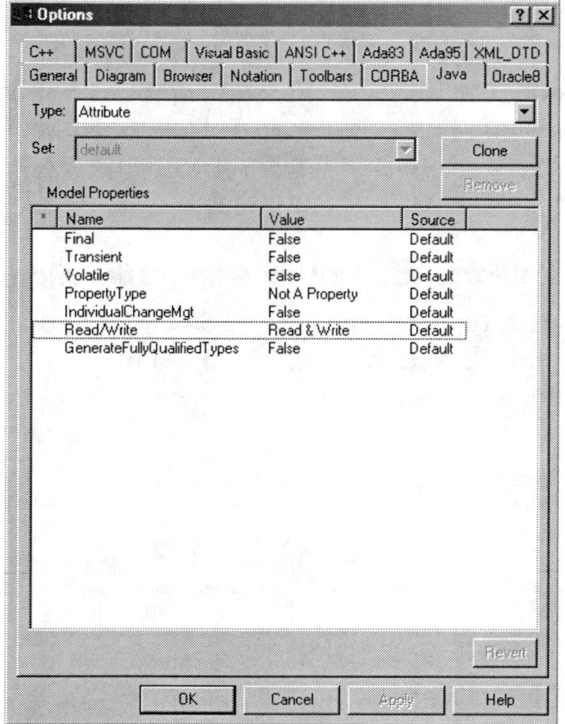

To get to this screen, do the following:

1. Select **Tools** from the menu.
2. Select **Options** from the drop-down list box.
3. Select the **Java** tab.

Note that the drop-down menu in Figure 12-3 for **Type** indicates several things (class, role, and so on). These are all the default options defined at these various levels. We first want to change an option for the type of attribute. To do this we change the `PropertyType` attribute from **Not A Property** to **Simple**. This action will result in get and set operations being defined for each of the class attributes. We'll do the same thing for the type of role, changing its `PropertyType` attribute as well.

While on the role type, we want to add an item value for `Container Class`. This attribute defines what type of container to use when dealing with one-to-many or many-to-many relationships between classes. Let's use `java.util.ArrayList` instead of `Vector`. Although `Vector` would work just fine, all the operations that it supports are synchronized and the `synchronized` keyword is not allowed in Enterprise JavaBeans. So for the type of role, your screen should look something like what you see in Figure 12-4.

A Final Pass at Attributes and Operations

Before actually generating code for Remulak, we need to make a pass through our target classes and tie up any loose ends in the areas of attributes and operations. As mentioned in the previous section, the

FIGURE 12-4 *Changing type properties for role*

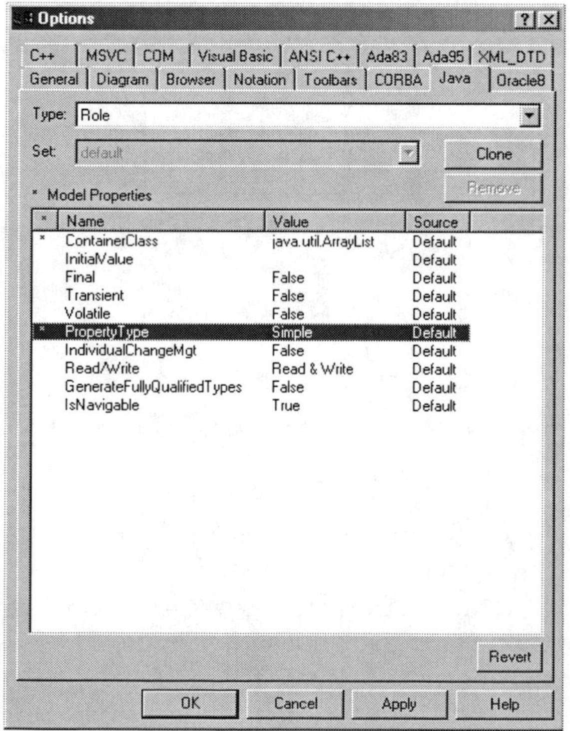

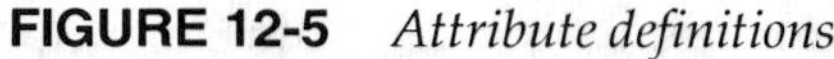

FIGURE 12-5 *Attribute definitions*

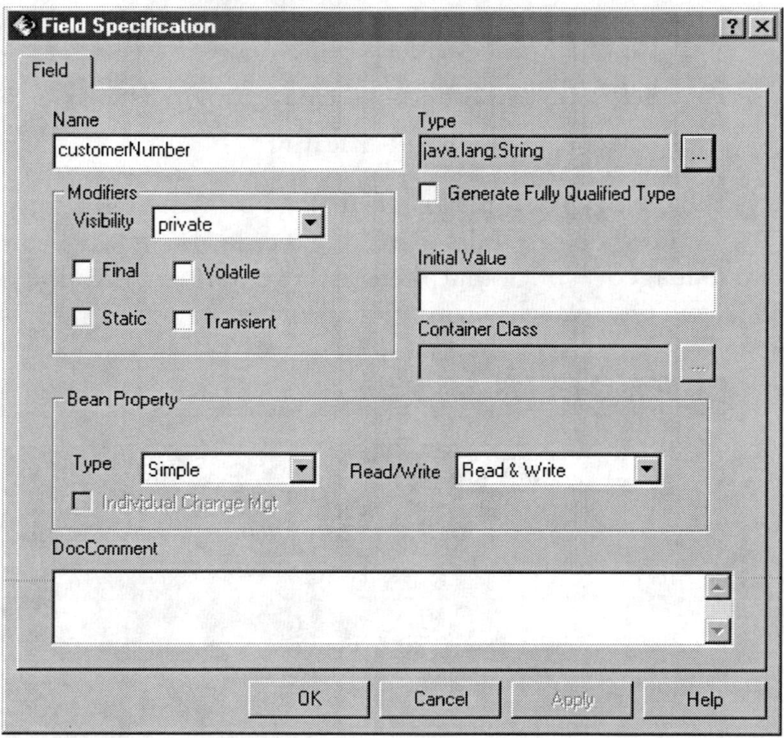

signature issues are not as great a concern as having good coverage of our attributes is. Figure 12-5 shows the Rose attribute dialog box. Here I'm setting the properties for the `customerNumber` attribute found in the `Customer` class. For the **Type** attribute I have selected `java.lang.String` from the drop-down list. Notice also that the **Bean Property** type has defaulted to **Simple** in accordance with the changes made in Figure 12-3.

Converting Classes to Enterprise JavaBeans

It's now time to move beyond our logical view of the class diagram and begin to transform it into more of a design view. Because we are implementing our beans in an EJB container, we need to take a class, such as `Address`, and convert it into an EJB-compliant class.

To do this, first we need to open the class diagram and select a class—say, `Address`. After selecting the class, we do the following:

1. Right-click on the class.
2. Select **Java / J2EE** from the drop-down list box.
3. Select **EJB: Open Specification.**

What will appear next is the dialog box shown in Figure 12-6.

The dialog defaults to making the class an entity bean and container-managed. Notice that there is an option to make it a session bean as well. Our use-case control classes will be session beans, but we'll say

FIGURE 12-6 *EJB dialog box in Rose*

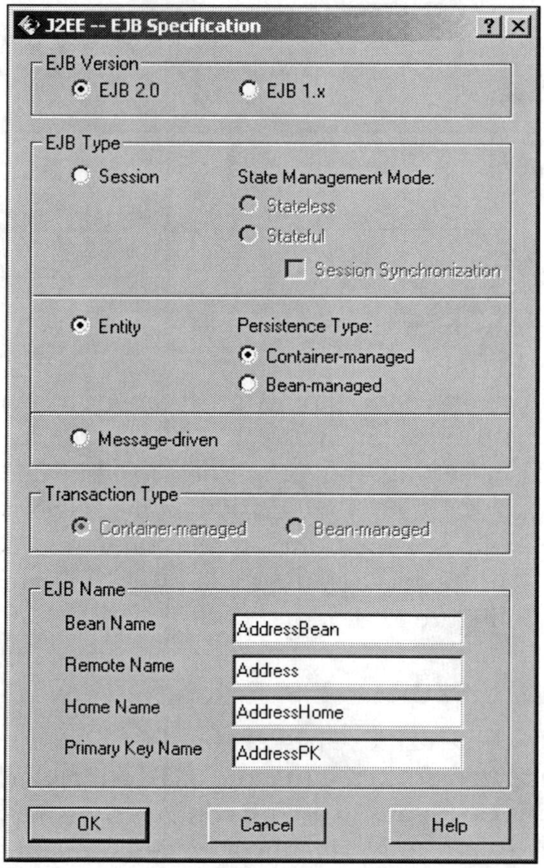

more about that later. I also changed the default bean name. Rose takes the class name and adds *EJB* to the end. I changed the name to `AddressBean`.

After you have selected **OK**, the class will be converted to an entity-type EJB. Three classes are created as a result of the Rose dialog. In the case of the `Address` class, these classes are `AddressBean`, `Address`, and `AddressHome`. An `AddressPK` class will be created as well, but it will be needed only if the class is identified, from the relational perspective, as having a compound primary key or if it is of a complex type, such as another object. Figure 12-7 is a view of the `Address` class after it has been converted to an EJB.

EJBs are completely lifecycle driven, meaning that most of the operations that are generated by the conversion wizard are operations that are called, on your behalf, by the EJB container. Our mission in this

FIGURE 12-7 `Address` *class after invocation of EJB configuration dialog*

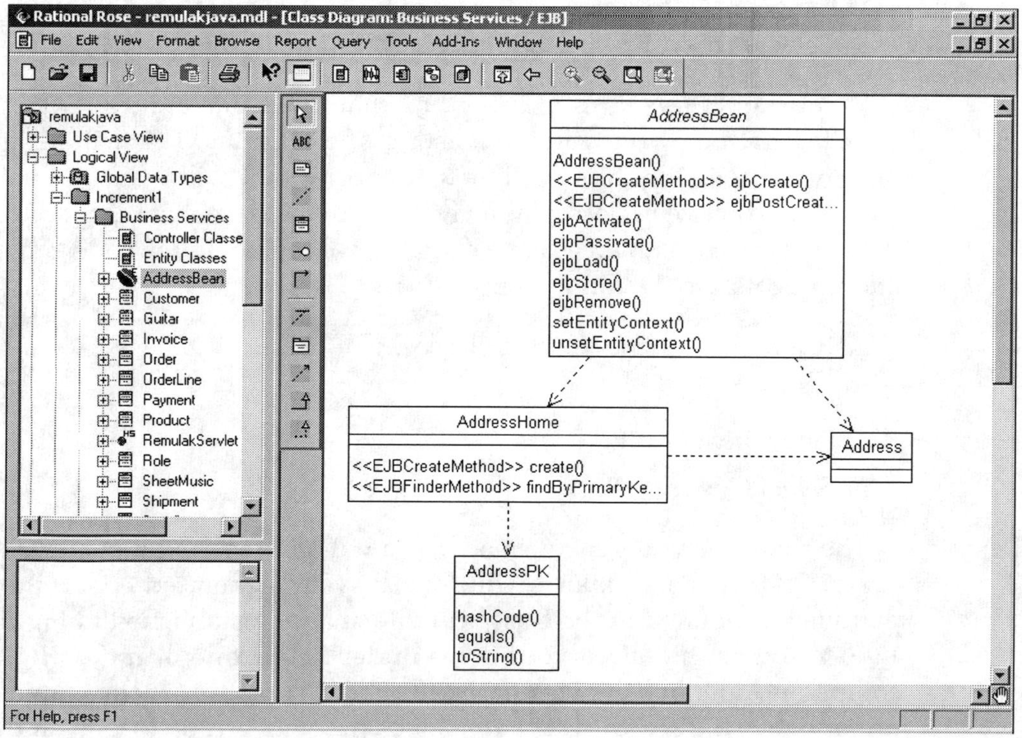

chapter is to be able to query on a `Customer` object and display `Role` and `Address` objects. As a result, we need to perform this same function on the `Customer` and `Role` classes. I won't cover those here, but they follow the same procedure as `Address`.

Generating Code

Now it's time finally to generate some code out of our modeling tool. The process is relatively easy and straightforward. We begin by opening the class diagram and highlighting the classes that the EJB conversion wizard created for each of the three classes `Address`, `Role`, and `Customer`. The total should be nine classes (twelve if you count the three primary-key classes, which we won't use). Now do the following:

1. Select **Tools.**
2. Select **Java / J2EE.**
3. Select **Project Specification. . . .**

What should appear is a dialog box that looks like Figure 12-8. For the **Classpath** tab you will find a listing of classpaths. This will be important because a prompt will appear shortly that will want to know how to map between classes and where to put the code that is generated.

Once the classpath areas have been set, we can begin the code generation process. Do the following:

1. Right-click on the selected classes.
2. Select **Tools.**
3. Select **Java / J2EE.**
4. Select **Generate Java.**

The first time you generate code, you will get the dialog box in Figure 12-9. This dialog allows you to map your generated code into a pathway as defined in the classpath information established in Figure 12-8. You must highlight your items under **Select one or more pkgs / comps** and identify the classpaths to which you want them mapped under **Select a CLASSPATH entry**. Click the **Map** button to kick off the code generation process; at the end you will have your first forward-engineered code from the class diagram.

FIGURE 12-8 *Setting the classpath in the **Project Specification** dialog*

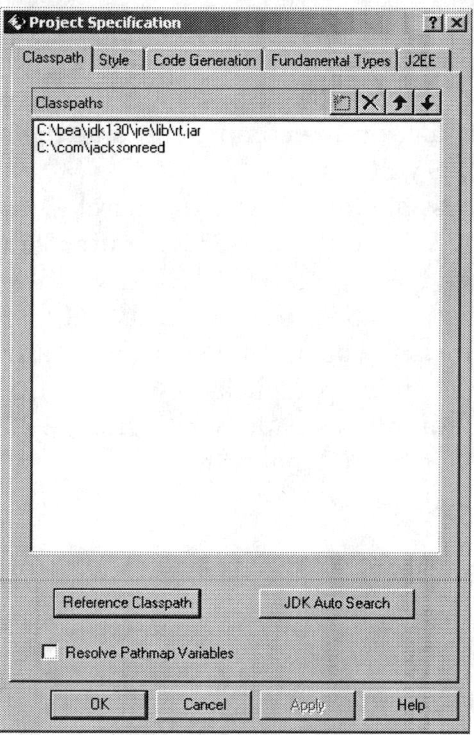

FIGURE 12-9 *Classpath to package-mapping screen*

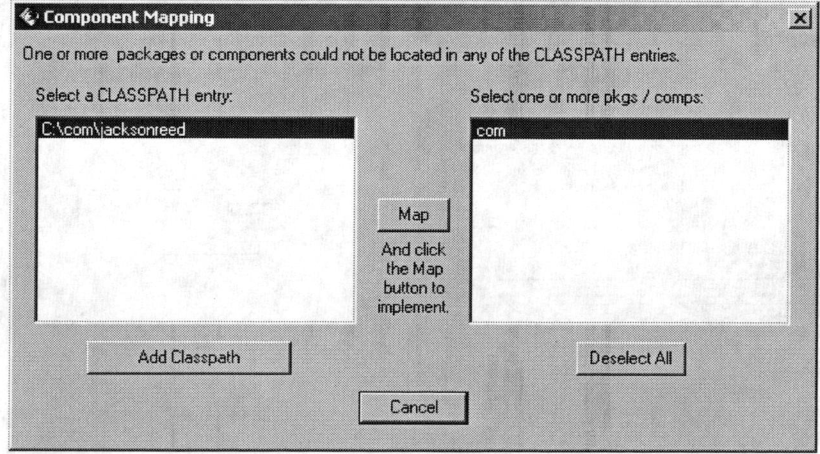

Along with the code generation process, behind the scenes Rational Rose creates components for each class for which code was generated. In Figure 12-10 I have pulled out `CustomerBean`, `RoleBean`, and `AddressBean` from the tree view on the left and placed them on a component diagram. You can generate code from this view, as well as by right-clicking on the component, and the same dialog as outlined in Figure 12-9 will ensue.

It is possible to look at the generated code within Rose. As Figure 12-8 shows, there is a **Code Generation** tab. Selecting this tab invokes the dialog box in Figure 12-11. Notice that the **IDE** drop-down menu allows you to select from several of the top integrated development environments, which can be very handy. If you don't have an IDE or just want to pop up a quick browser window of your code, the built-in internal editor does a nice job. Figure 12-12 shows the recently generated code in the internal editor.

FIGURE 12-10 `CustomerBean`, `RoleBean`, *and* `AddressBean` *components*

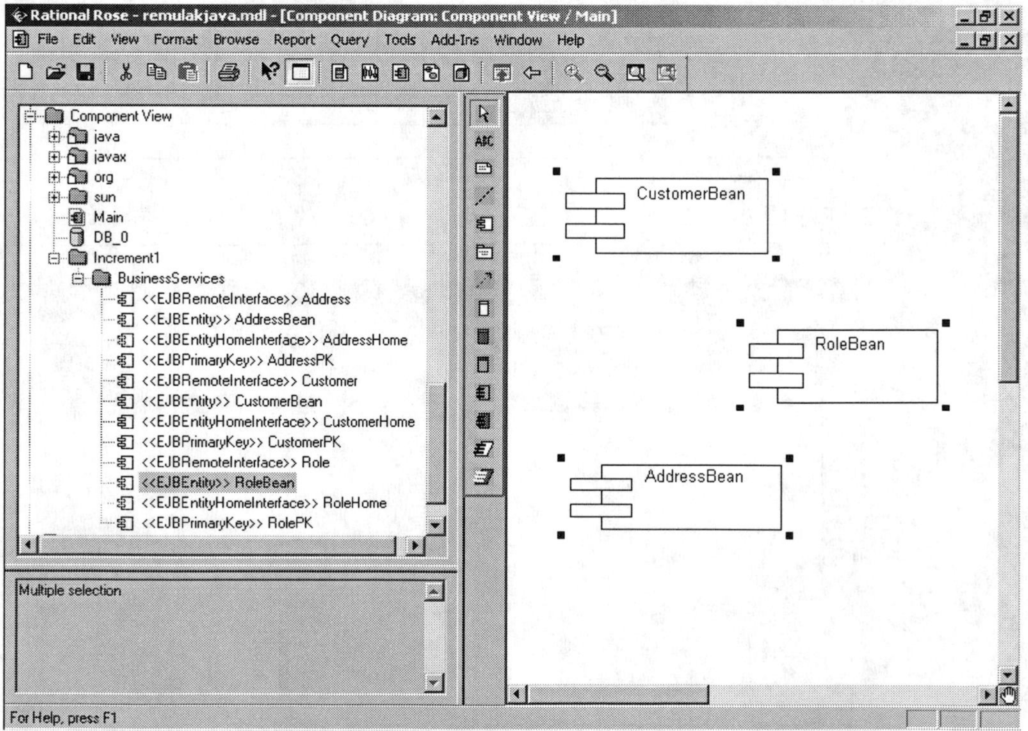

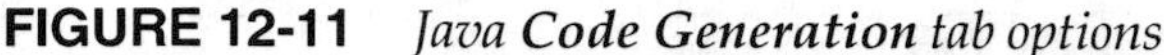

FIGURE 12-11 *Java Code Generation tab options*

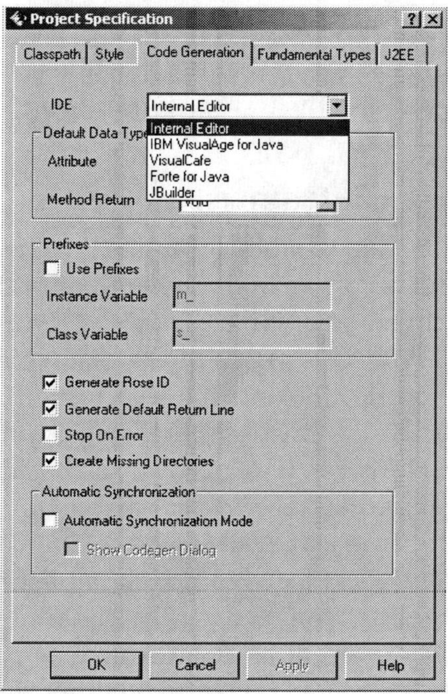

FIGURE 12-12 *Java code displayed in the internal editor*

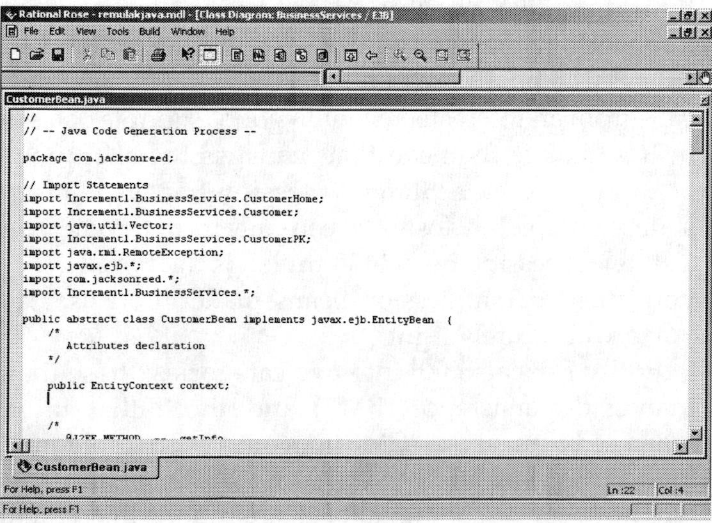

Building the Architectural Prototype: Part 2

Part 2 of building the architectural prototype for our EJB solution presents a primer on EJB that reviews the callback mechanism, interfaces to the clients, and the transaction support available.

A Primer on Enterprise JavaBeans

As mentioned in Chapters 9 and 11, we need to discuss the lifecycle of the EJB and become a bit more familiar with its architecture. As I stated with the coverage of JSP in Chapter 11, this book can't cover the entire topic, so I refer you to one of the many excellent books on the market today covering EJB for a more thorough presentation (earlier I mentioned Richard Monson-Haefel's *Enterprise JavaBeans,* published by O'Reilly). However, we can cover the basics here, and most of the readers will get the message.

An Enterprise JavaBean is a component that runs within a container that follows the lifecycle model published in the EJB specification. This lifecycle is managed by the container product that is purchased or downloaded from an open-source organization. There are two different lifecycles, depending on whether the bean is a session EJB or an entity EJB.

Session EJBs are typically used to house utility services and coordination logic in dealing with the entity EJBs. Session beans can do anything they like, even make database calls; however, that is not their intent. There are two types of session EJBs, stateful and stateless. **Stateful session beans** are guaranteed to have their state persisted between calls from an interested client. A good example of a stateful session bean in Remulak is the bean that manages the shopping cart for an order, `UCMaintainOrder`. **Stateless session beans** are just the opposite; their state is completely lost between calls from the client. A good example of a stateless session bean in Remulak is the `UCMaintainRltnshp` bean. If you guessed that session beans make good use-case control classes, you are absolutely right.

Entity EJBs also fall into two categories: those that implement bean-managed persistence (BMP) and those that implement container-managed persistence (CMP). An entity EJB implemented with BMP will look somewhat similar to what we did in Chapter 11. The bean classes will have several of the callback operations that I mentioned previously (and will cover shortly), but the DAO classes will be almost identical. In the case of an entity EJB that implements CMP, as you will see in the first major coding section in this chapter, the landscape will be drastically different. By *different*, I mean much smaller. First of all, most callback operations in the beans will be empty. The best part is that there will be absolutely no DAO classes; you can throw them away.

EJB Callback Mechanism

We have mentioned the callback mechanism already; now it's time to describe it a bit more. The EJB container must have strict control over how your beans behave, both session and entity. This one right that you must give up is payback for the container's being able to manage your transactions and the lifecycle of the bean.

Session beans implement four callback operations that are specified in the `SessionBean` interface:

1. **`ejbActivate()`**: This operation is called by the container when the bean has been deserialized from passive storage on the server. It allows the bean to reclaim any resources freed during passivation.
2. **`ejbPassivate()`**: This operation is called by the container just before the bean is to be serialized and stored in passive storage on the server. It allows the bean to release any nonserializable resources.
3. **`ejbRemove()`**: This operation is called just before the bean is to be removed from the container and made available for garbage collection.
4. **`ejbCreate()`**: This operation is called whenever a complementary create operation is called on the bean's home interface. It can be used to retrieve values that may apply for the duration of the bean's lifetime.

With session beans, depending on what they are being used for, there may be no implementation code in these required operations of the `SessionBean` interface. In the case of the `UCMaintainRltnshp` class, all four will be empty. In the case of the `UCMaintainOrder` session bean, however, because it is stateful, it has logic in both the `ejbCreate()` and `ejbRemove()` operations.

Entity EJBs implement seven different callback operations that are specified in the `EntityBean` interface:

1. **`ejbActivate()`**: This operation is called by the container when the bean has been deserialized from passive storage on the server. It allows the bean to reclaim any resources freed during passivation.
2. **`ejbPassivate()`**: This operation is called by the container just before the bean is to be serialized and stored in passive storage on the server. It allows the bean to release any nonserializable resources.
3. **`ejbRemove()`**: This operation is called just before the bean is to be removed from the container and made available for garbage collection. In the case of BMP, this is where a SQL delete operation would take place. In the case of CMP, the method is typically empty.
4. **`ejbCreate()`**: This operation is called whenever a complementary create operation is called on the bean's home interface. It can be used to retrieve values that may apply for the duration of the bean's lifetime. In the case of BMP, this is where a SQL insert operation would take place. In the case of CMP, this is where the information originating from the client would be assigned to attributes defined in the bean as `abstract public`.
5. **`ejbPostCreate()`**: This operation is called immediately after the related `ejbCreate()` method and is the last place to do initialization work before the client has access to the bean. In the case of BMP and CMP, the methods are typically empty.
6. **`ejbLoad()`**: This operation is called when the container deems it necessary to synchronize the state of the database with the state of the bean. The primary key is taken from the `EntityContext` object of the bean and not its local attribute. In the case of BMP, this is where a SQL select statement is called. In the case of CMP, the method is typically empty.
7. **`ejbStore()`**: This operation is called when the container deems it necessary to synchronize the state of the bean with the database. In the case of BMP, this is where a SQL update statement is called. In the case of CMP, the method is typically empty.

It should be even more clear now after seeing all the callback method descriptions that with the exception of `ejbCreate()`, CMP entity beans usually have only business methods. Whether an entity bean is implemented with BMP or CMP can mean the difference of hundreds of lines of codes.

Working with an EJB

For clients to be able to access an EJB, it must work with two interfaces. One is called the home interface, the other the remote interface. Each bean we create then will have three Java classes: *`classname`*`Bean`, *`classname`*`Home`, and *`classname`*. The remote interface is just the class name. All of our hard coding work lives in the *`classname`*`Bean` class.

Both of the interfaces eventually obtain access to the bean for the client. Clients may absolutely never directly access the bean. If this were possible, the container would have lost control of the lifecycle of the bean, rendering all the callback mechanisms useless.

The home interface contains operation stubs to both create and find a bean. These operations are implemented in the bean class. The remote interface is where all the business operation stubs are found. All of these concepts can be made clearer with a few sequence diagrams, as we do next.

EJB Sequence Diagrams

The sequence diagram in Figure 12-13 shows the creation and removal of an entity EJB implementing BMP.

The sequence diagram in Figure 12-14 shows CMP creation and removal. In both cases, the remote interface is referenced by `EJBObject`. In addition, the `EJBHome`, `EJBObject`, and `Container` objects are all part of the EJB container. In UML terms, the EJB container is a component that is an active object.

Notice again that the bean instance in the CMP world doesn't do much more than satisfy business method requests.

EJB Transaction Management

Another big advantage to an application's using an EJB container is transaction management. Although you can "roll your own" transaction scheme in the EJB world, it is better if you rely on the container

FIGURE 12-13 *Sequence diagram of BMP creation and removal*

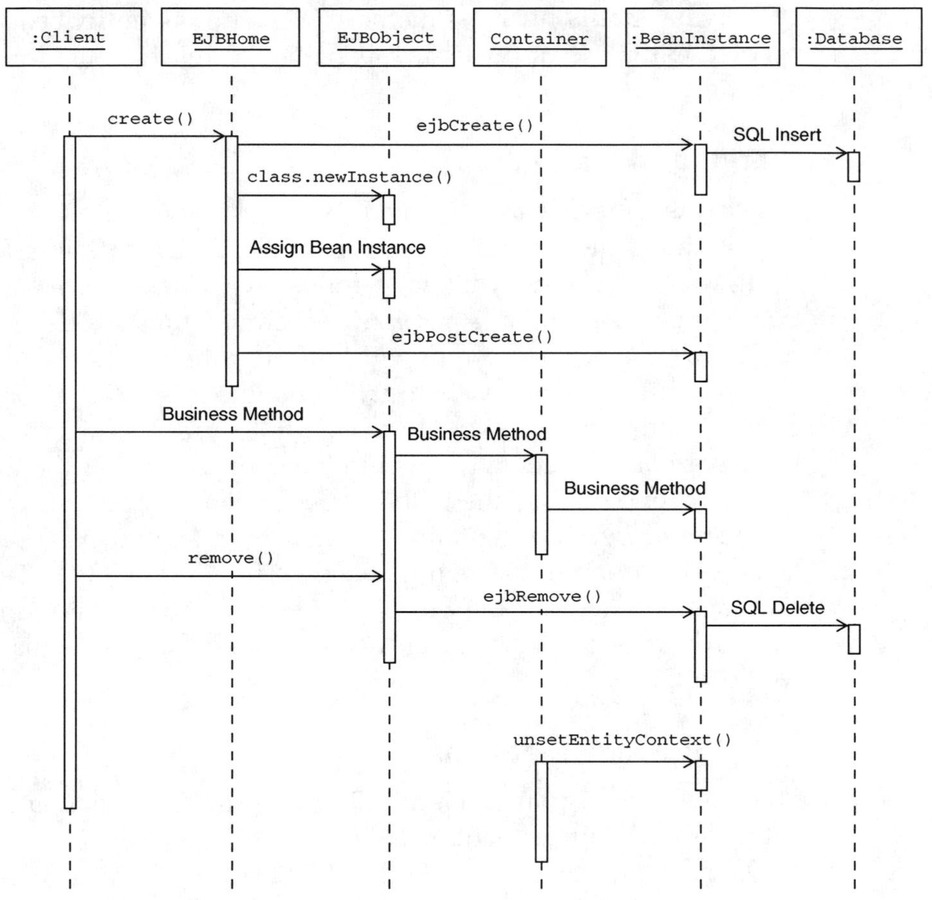

to do it for you. First, it reduces the amount of code that has to be written. Second, it is less error prone.

As with everything else in the EJB environment, transaction control is handled by deployment descriptors. We call this *declarative transaction management*. Unlike EJB competitors such as Microsoft's COM+ and Component Services framework, the transaction scope can be set at both the bean and the method levels. This is more important than it sounds. Remember that a bean can have both inquiry-type operations and update-type operations. It would be very inefficient to have to

FIGURE 12-14 *Sequence diagram of CMP creation and removal*

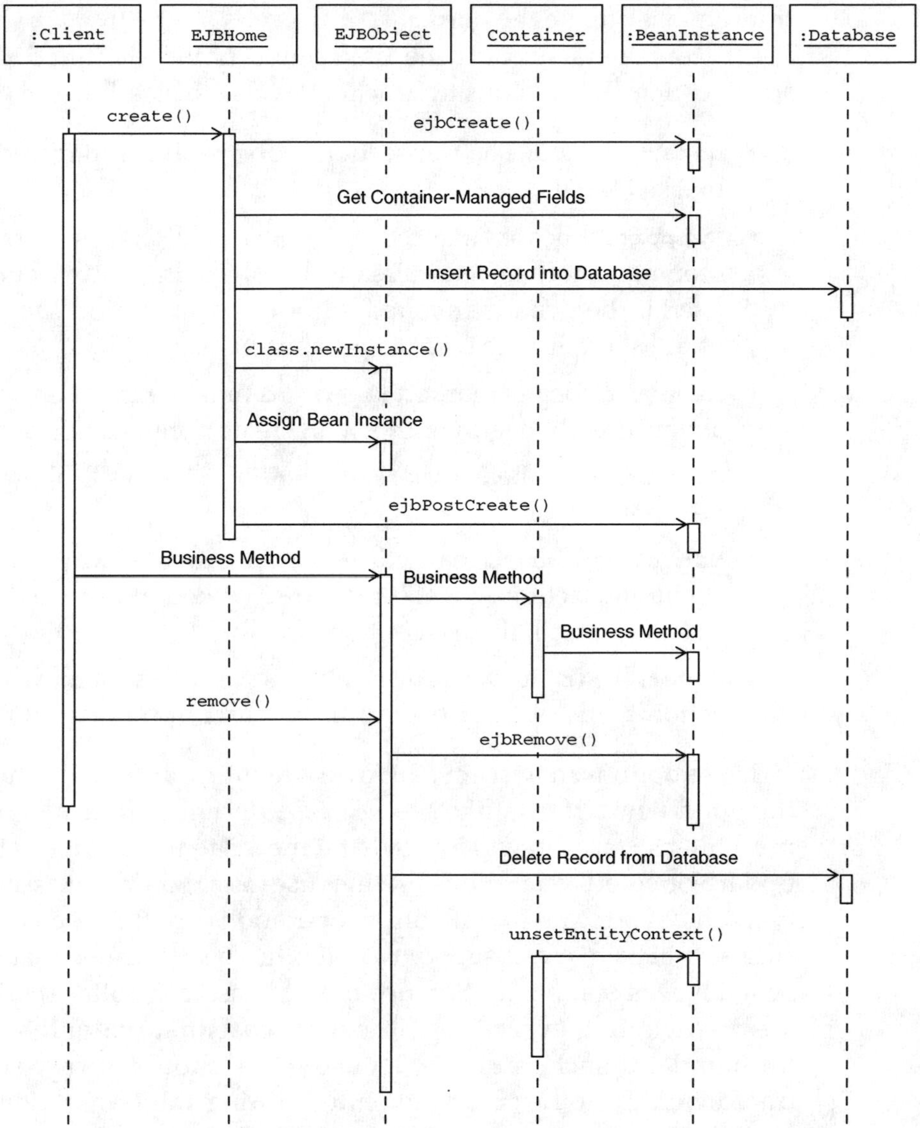

:Client
EJBHome
EJBObject
Container
:BeanInstance
:Database

create()
ejbCreate()
Get Container-Managed Fields
Insert Record into Database
class.newInstance()
Assign Bean Instance
ejbPostCreate()
Business Method
Business Method
Business Method
remove()
ejbRemove()
Delete Record from Database
unsetEntityContext()

establish all the overhead of beginning a transaction just to read information from the database. In all cases with Remulak, container-managed transactions will be the norm.

EJB containers support the transaction types identified in the EJB specification. The various transaction levels are as follows:

- **`NotSupported`**: The transaction scope is not propagated to beans marked `NotSupported`.
- **`Supports`**: Beans marked `Supports` will join the transaction scope of another bean already involved in a transaction. However, if the bean is invoked without a transaction scope already established, it runs without a transaction.
- **`Required`**: Beans marked `Required` must be invoked with transaction already begun or they will create a transaction scope.
- **`RequiresNew`**: Beans marked `RequiresNew` will always start a new transaction.
- **`Mandatory`**: Beans marked `Mandatory` must always be part of a client transaction scope. If they are invoked without a transaction already started, the transaction will fail.
- **`Never`**: Beans marked `Never` must never be invoked with a transaction scope already begun. If they are, the transaction will fail.

These options may seem a bit overwhelming at first, but here comes the good news. If you like the use-case design pattern we have been preaching so far, you will love what it means to transaction settings. All update-oriented operations in the use-case control classes will be marked `RequiresNew`. All other operations in the use-case control classes will be marked `Supports`. All other beans can be marked at the bean level as `Supports`. Because the use-case controller session beans are orchestrating everything, it makes sense that operations that perform updates, such as `rltnAddCustomer()`, should always start a new transaction. All other beans executed during the transaction just join with the transaction scope that the controller starts. The following is a snippet of the `<assembly-descriptor>` tag that is part of the `ejb-jar.xml` file that must be packaged with each deployment:

```
<assembly-descriptor>
   <container-transaction>
      <method>
```

```
            <ejb-name>UCMaintainRltnshp</ejb-name>
            <method-intf>Remote</method-intf>
            <method-name>*</method-name>
        </method>
        <trans-attribute>RequiresNew</trans-attribute>
    </container-transaction>
    <container-transaction>
        <method>
            <ejb-name>UCMaintainRltnshp</ejb-name>
            <method-intf>Remote</method-intf>
            <method-name>rltnCustomerInquiry</method-name>
        </method>
        <trans-attribute>Supports</trans-attribute>
    </container-transaction>
    <container-transaction>
        <method>
            <ejb-name>UCMaintainRltnshp</ejb-name>
            <method-intf>Remote</method-intf>
            <method-name>rltnAddressInquiry</method-name>
        </method>
        <trans-attribute>Supports</trans-attribute>
    </container-transaction>
    <container-transaction>
        <method>
            <ejb-name>UCMaintainRltnshp</ejb-name>
            <method-intf>Remote</method-intf>
            <method-name>rltnRoleInquiry</method-name>
        </method>
        <trans-attribute>Supports</trans-attribute>
    </container-transaction>
```

The `<container-transaction>` tag tells the EJB container how to manage the transaction. The `<ejb-name>` tag identifies the bean, and the next two important tags are `<method-name>` and `<trans-attribute>`. Luckily, the EJB specification allows us to indicate a wild-card character—in this case an asterisk (*)—for the method name. This character tells the container to treat all methods of the bean in the same way.

Notice also that we have three additional blocks of `<container-transaction>` tags. These override the first one. So in effect the tags just mentioned together indicate that all methods in `UCMaintainRltnshp` will be set to `RequiresNew`, but `rltnCustomerInquiry()`, `rltnAddressInquiry()`, and `rltnRoleInquiry()` will be set to `Supports`. Following the advice already given, the remaining beans in the *Maintain Relationships* use-case should be marked `Supports`, as shown here:

```
    <container-transaction>
      <method>
        <ejb-name>CustomerBean</ejb-name>
        <method-intf>Remote</method-intf>
        <method-name>*</method-name>
      </method>
      <trans-attribute>Supports</trans-attribute>
    </container-transaction>
    <container-transaction>
      <method>
        <ejb-name>AddressBean</ejb-name>
        <method-intf>Remote</method-intf>
        <method-name>*</method-name>
      </method>
      <trans-attribute>Supports</trans-attribute>
    </container-transaction>
    <container-transaction>
      <method>
        <ejb-name>RoleBean</ejb-name>
        <method-intf>Remote</method-intf>
        <method-name>*</method-name>
      </method>
      <trans-attribute>Supports</trans-attribute>
    </container-transaction>
  </assembly-descriptor>
```

With container-managed transactions (not to be confused with container-managed persistence), we don't explicitly commit a unit of work and we don't explicitly roll back a unit of work. The container determines what to do according to the exceptions that are thrown. If no exceptions are thrown, then upon completion of the method that started a transaction (all use-case control classes that are update oriented, in Remulak's case), the transaction will commit.

Anytime `RuntimeException`, `RemoteException`, or any exception that inherits from either of these exceptions occurs, a rollback will result. The exception called `DAOSysException` that was introduced in Chapter 11 inherits from `RuntimeException`. The other exceptions all inherit from `DAOAppException`, which inherits from `Exception`. These are all application errors and won't cause a rollback. A common approach taken to force a rollback when an application exception occurs is to throw `EJBException`, which inherits from `RuntimeException`. This is a smart strategy because many application-level exceptions may be able to be corrected, allowing for a recovery.

Building the Architectural Prototype: Part 3

Part 3 of building the architectural prototype for our EJB solution covers the addition of CMP code to the skeleton code generated out of Rose. It also covers the changes necessary to the JSPs, servlet, and use-case control classes.

Adding Logic to the Generated Code

It's time to make our initial code generation effort bear some fruit. By itself it won't buy us much. We will start out easy and take the simple pathway of asking for all customers, their addresses, and the role each address plays. Let's begin by reviewing some of the key components of the `CustomerBean` class. Remember that bean classes implement all the business logic of our application, but they are even more instrumental in the part of the application that implements container-managed persistence (CMP). It is CMP that eliminates the need to write SQL code, and CMP is a major productivity boost to anyone building EJB applications today.

The following accessor methods are the `cmp` fields for the `Customer` bean:

```
abstract public Integer getCustomerId();
abstract public void setCustomerId(Integer val);

/**
 * @cmp-field customerNumber
 * @business-method
 */
abstract public String getCustomerNumber();
abstract public void setCustomerNumber(String val);

/**
 * @cmp-field firstName
 * @business-method
 */
abstract public String getFirstName();
abstract public void setFirstName(String val);

/**
 * @cmp-field middleInitial
 * @business-method
 */
```

```
abstract public String getMiddleInitial();
abstract public void setMiddleInitial(String val);

/**
 * @cmp-field prefix
 * @business-method
 */
abstract public String getPrefix();
abstract public void setPrefix(String val);

/**
 * @cmp-field suffix
 * @business-method
 */
abstract public String getSuffix();
abstract public void setSuffix(String val);

/**
 * @cmp-field lastName
 * @business-method
 */
abstract public String getLastName();
abstract public void setLastName(String val);

/**
 * @cmp-field phone1
 * @business-method
 */
abstract public String getPhone1();
abstract public void setPhone1(String val);

/**
 * @cmp-field phone2
 * @business-method
 */
abstract public String getPhone2();
abstract public void setPhone2(String val);

/**
 * @cmp-field eMail
 * @business-method
 */
abstract public String getEMail();
abstract public void setEMail(String val);
```

These fields represent the attributes that will be persisted to and retrieved from the database. The modeling tool (e.g., Rational's Rose, TogetherSoft's Together Control Center) generates these accessors for you on the basis of the input provided to the modeling tool. In EJB 2.0, unlike prior versions, the accessors are declared abstract because the persistence engine implemented by the container vendor's product (i.e., BEA's WebLogic, or IBM's WebSphere) is what actually implements the accessor. The selling point that beans can be transported between different container vendor products is now finally moving closer to reality. You may have noticed comments with some tag indicators between the methods; I will discuss those comments at the end of this code section.

The next important fields to look at in the `CustomerBean` class are the container-managed relationship, or `cmr`, fields. These are instrumental in implementing the relationships between beans. This information comes from the relationships that are drawn in the modeling tool between the beans:

```
s  /**
    * Syntax:
    *   cmr          source ejb-name          multiplicity
    *  ==========================================================
    * @cmr-field   CustomerBean   one
    * @business-method
    */
   abstract public Collection getRoles();
   abstract public void setRoles(Collection Role);
   /**
    * Syntax:
    *   cmr          source ejb-name          multiplicity
    *  ==========================================================
    * @cmr-field   CustomerBean   one
    * @business-method
    */
   abstract public Collection getOrders();
   abstract public void setOrders(Collection Role);
```

Remember that there were two one-to-many relationships in which `Customer` was involved: one with `Order` and one with `Role` (via the association relationship between `Customer` and `Address`). Again, just as with the attribute accessors, the `cmr` accessors are declared abstract because it is up to the persistence engine implemented by the container to handle how relationships are physically traversed. Notice that these accessors return `Collection` objects because a `Customer` object can have many `Role` objects and many `Order` objects.

Let's look at the `Role` class next. I won't review `Address` here because it looks very similar to `Customer`, except it doesn't have a relationship with `Order`. `Role` is interesting because it contains relationships to both a single `Customer` and a single `Address`. Remember that the `Role` class defines the involvement between a `Customer` object and an `Address` object. `Role` is easy from an attribute standpoint, having only its primary key and `roleName`:

```
 /**
 * @cmp-field roleId
 * @primkey-field
 * @business-method
 */
abstract public Integer getRoleId();
abstract public void setRoleId(Integer val);

 /**
 * @cmp-field roleName
 * @business-method
 */
abstract public String getRoleName();
abstract public void setRoleName(String val);
```

The two `cmr` accessors look like this:

```
/**
 * Syntax:
 *   cmr        source ejb-name        multiplicity
 *  ===========================================================
 * @cmr-field   RoleBean   many
 * @business-method
 */
abstract public Customer getCustomer();
abstract public void setCustomer(Customer Customer);
/**
 * Syntax:
 *   cmr        source ejb-name        multiplicity
 *  ===========================================================
 * @cmr-field   RoleBean   many
 * @business-method
```

```
    */
   abstract public Address getAddress();
   abstract public void setAddress(Address Address);
```

Notice that unlike the `cmr` fields for `Customer`, the `cmr` fields for `Role` return actual objects of the `Address` and `Customer` classes.

There is quite a bit of power in what we have constructed so far. When we build a client to gain access to the services of our beans, you will see code that somewhat resembles this:

```
role.getAddress().getPrimaryKey()
```

Although these look like just methods being invoked, they are handled by the persistence implementation in the container and will generate SQL access code to retrieve the desired objects (unless they are already cached from previous access). In the case illustrated here, the `Address` object is retrieved and then the primary key of `Address` is returned.

A Bit of Magic in Those Tags

As I mentioned earlier, you may have noticed some funny-looking Javadoc-like tags in the comments above each accessor. These tags are not put there by the modeling tool but are another alternative to help you with generating code. Most of the visual modeling vendors do a decent job of generating deployment descriptors, but depending on your container vendor, you have other options, particularly if you are using BEA's WebLogic product. Don't worry, though; if you included these tags and you use another product, such as IBM's WebSphere, it will still enhance your productivity immensely.

If you are not using a modeling tool (which is a big mistake in my opinion), then a gentleman named Cedric Beust is potentially a hero to you. Beust developed a marvelous "free" tool called EJBGen, which is a doclet. It uses the little-known ability of the `javadoc` utility to override the standard document engine with your own parser. EJBGen takes in your bean classes and generates not only the corresponding home, remote, and primary-key classes but also the deployment descriptors. This is where the tags (e.g., `@cmp-field`, `@business-method`) come into play.

Actually you can use this tool regardless of your container engine product, but you will have to play a bit with the vendor-specific deployment descriptors if you are using something other than

WebLogic. Remember that there is one common descriptor that all vendors must implement: `ejb-jar.xml`. All the XML descriptors go into the `META-INF` directory in your implementation. The descriptors are the real workhorse in the EJB implementation and they are standard across all vendors. Other descriptor tags, depending on your particular vendor, will also be required. I won't spend more time on EJBGen, other than to refer you to Beust's Web site, at *http://beust.com/cedric/ejbgen*, for more information.

Compiling the EJB Code

Once the code has been written and the deployment descriptors created, a few steps are required. Note that step 3, running the EJB compiler, will vary slightly with each vendor:

1. All the Java components must be compiled, including the remote, home, and bean classes for each entity bean:

```
c:\>javac -d %classdirectory% Customer.java
    CustomerHome.java CustomerBean.java Role.java
    RoleHome.java RoleBean.java
Address.java AddressHome.java AddressBean.java
```

2. An EJB JAR file must be created that contains the result of the previous compile and the XML deployment descriptors that reside in the `META-INF` directory:

```
jar cv0f remulak.jar %metadirectory% %classdirectory%
```

3. The EJB compiler must be run against the JAR file created in step 2:

```
c:\>java -classpath %WL_HOME%/lib/weblogic_sp.jar;
    %WL_HOME% /lib/weblogic.jar  weblogic.ejbc
    -compiler javac Remulak.jar
ejb20_Remulak.jar
```

The `ejb20_Remulak.jar` file can now be deployed and tested by the client. In WebLogic we do this by placing the JAR file in the `applications` directory of the deployment target.

Building a Simple Client to Test the Beans

Later in this chapter we will make our client much more appealing and flexible by enhancing the beans and JSPs created in Chapter 11. In this chapter, however, we will build a very rudimentary client that we will invoke from the command line to test the `Customer`, `Role`, and `Address` beans.

For a client to access a bean managed by an EJB container, it must first obtain a reference to the bean via the bean's home interface. The Java Naming and Directory Interface (JNDI) accomplishes this task for the client. Our client, which we will call `ClientRemulak`, will implement the initial bean-testing logic. To begin the process, we must first obtain a context to the JNDI services as implemented by our container product. This logic will be unique to the individual container product; however, all container products operate in the same fashion (with a few exceptions). The following logic obtains a JNDI context from the BEA WebLogic server:

```
/**
 * Get an initial context into the JNDI tree
 *
*/
private Context getInitialContext() throws NamingException {

  try {
    // Get an initial context
    Properties h = new Properties();
    h.put(Context.INITIAL_CONTEXT_FACTORY,
        "weblogic.jndi.WLInitialContextFactory");
    h.put(Context.PROVIDER_URL, url);
    return new InitialContext(h);
  } catch (NamingException ne) {
    throw ne;
  }
}
```

After obtaining the context, we can obtain the address of a home interface. In our case we need access to the `CustomerHome` interface, as shown here:

```
package com.jacksonreed;

import javax.ejb.CreateException;
import javax.ejb.EJBHome;
import javax.ejb.FinderException;
```

```
import java.rmi.RemoteException;
import java.util.Collection;

public interface CustomerHome extends EJBHome {

  public Customer findByPrimaryKey(Integer primaryKey)
    throws FinderException, RemoteException;

  public Collection findAllCustomers()
    throws FinderException, RemoteException;

  public Customer findByCustomerNumber(String customerNumber)
    throws FinderException, RemoteException;

  public Customer create(Integer CustomerId, String
  CustomerNumber,
       String FirstName, String MiddleInitial, String Prefix,
       String Suffix, String LastName, String Phone1, String
       Phone2,
       String EMail)
    throws CreateException, RemoteException;
}
```

We specifically want to access the `findAllCustomers()` method in the `CustomerHome` interface. The logic to get the reference to `Customer Home` uses the context retrieved earlier. Notice that the first method called in `lookupCustomerHome()` is `getInitialContext()`:

```
/**
 * Look up the customer bean's home interface using JNDI
 */
private CustomerHome lookupCustomerHome()
  throws NamingException
{
  Context ctx = getInitialContext();

  try {
    Object home = (CustomerHome) ctx.lookup("remulak.
    CustomerHome");
    return (CustomerHome) PortableRemoteObject.narrow(home,
           CustomerHome.class);

  } catch (NamingException ne) {
    throw ne;
  }
}
```

As reviewed in Chapter 9, the key ingredient to the Enterprise JavaBean framework and the flexibility gained at deployment time consists of the deployment descriptors. The deployment descriptor allows, among other things, the ability to express in a query-neutral fashion, the logic executed by finder methods, such as `findAllCustomers()`. This neutral query logic is called EJB-QL and is an EJB 2.0 standard. EJB-QL statements are parsed and turned into SQL queries by the persistence manager implemented by the EJB container. What follows is a snippet from the `ejb-jar.xml` file produced by either the visual modeling tool vendor (Rational, TogetherSoft) or as a result of a utility like EJBGen:

```
<query>
   <query-method>
      <method-name>findAllCustomers</method-name>
      <method-params/>
   </query-method>
   <ejb-ql><![CDATA[ WHERE customerId IS NOT NULL]]>
   </ejb-ql>
</query>
<query>
   <query-method>
      <method-name>findByCustomerNumber</method-name>
      <method-params>
         <method-param>java.lang.String</method-param>
      </method-params>
   </query-method>
   <ejb-ql><![CDATA[ WHERE customerNumber = ?1]]>
   </ejb-ql>
</query>
```

The `findAllCustomers()` method specified by the `<method-name>` tag maps directly to the method implemented in the `CustomerBean` class. The information between the `<ejb-ql>` tags represents the generic query that the container converts to SQL at runtime. There is also a `findByCustomerNumber()` method that provides a similar implementation but returns only a `Customer` matching a given customer number. The following is the `CustomerHome` interface, which reflects the create and find methods:

```
package com.jacksonreed;

import javax.ejb.CreateException;
import javax.ejb.EJBHome;
```

```
import javax.ejb.FinderException;
import java.rmi.RemoteException;
import java.util.Collection;

public interface CustomerHome extends EJBHome {
  public Customer findByPrimaryKey(Integer primaryKey)
    throws FinderException, RemoteException;

  public Collection findAllCustomers()
    throws FinderException, RemoteException;

  public Customer findByCustomerNumber(String customerNumber)
    throws FinderException, RemoteException;

  public Customer findByCustomerId(Integer customerId)
    throws FinderException, RemoteException;

  public Customer create(com.jacksonreed.CustomerValue custVal)
    throws CreateException, RemoteException;

}
```

Remember that the client engages with both the home and the remote interfaces, and they, in turn, work with the bean instance.

Let's now turn our attention back to our client, `ClientRemulak`. The `findAllCustomers()` method will select rows from the database and, in turn, instantiate objects in our code. The `customerHome` variable was returned from the `lookupCustomerHome()` method shown earlier. After retrieving the collection of `Customer` objects with the `findAllCustomers()` method, we use an `Iterator` object to cycle through the collection and retrieve the related `Role` objects and associated `Address` objects:

```
private void findAllCustomers()
    throws RemoteException, FinderException {

    Integer addrKey;

    log("Querying for all customers\n");
    Collection custCol =
customerHome.findAllCustomers();

    Iterator custIter = custCol.iterator();
    if(! custIter.hasNext()) {
```

```
        log("No customers were found with a null customerId");
        return;
      }

      while (custIter.hasNext()) {
        Customer cust = (Customer) custIter.next();
        log("customer id is " + cust.getPrimaryKey() +
           "  customer number is " + cust.getCustomerNumber() +
              " last name is " + cust.getLastName() );

        Collection roleCol = cust.getAllRoles();

        Iterator roleIter = roleCol.iterator();
        if(! roleIter.hasNext()) {
          log("  No roles for this customer");
        }
        else {
          while (roleIter.hasNext()) {
            Role role = (Role) roleIter.next();
            log("  role id is " + role.getPrimaryKey() +
                "  role name is " + role.getRoleName() );
            log("     address id is " + role.getAddress().
            getPrimaryKey() +
                "  address line 1 is " + role.getAddress().
                   getAddressLine1() +
                "\n" );
          }
        }
      }
    }
```

It's time to run `ClientRemulak` from the DOS command prompt:

```
C:\> java com.jacksonreed.ClientRemulak

Beginning com.jacksonreed.ClientRemulak . . .

Querying for all customers

customer id is 1234  customer number is abc1234 last name is
Reed
  role id is 3456  role name is Billing
     address id is 1234  address line 1 is 6660 Delmonico Drive
  role id is 1234  role name is Shipping
     address id is 1234  address line 1 is 6660 Delmonico Drive
```

```
customer id is 2345  customer number is abc2345 last name is
Becnel
  role id is 2345  role name is Mailing
     address id is 2345  address line 1 is 2323 Happy Boy
     Lane

customer id is 3456  customer number is abc3456 last name is
Young
  No roles for this customer

Ending com.jacksonreed.ClientRemulak . . .
```

The foundation has been laid. It is amazing how little code has to be written when the container-managed persistence support offered by the EJB specification is being used.

Enhancing the CMP Implementation

Adding More Use-Case Pathways

In Chapter 11 we demonstrated the ability to inquire about a `Customer` object, as well as to insert, update, and delete one. However, the *Maintain Relationships* use-case has quite a few more pathways. These relate to adding, updating, and deleting roles and addresses for that customer. The next section covers those changes.

In the CMP implementation we have no DAO classes, and we have already seen most of the CMP beans in action. However, we will present other changes that are required of these beans later in this chapter. Obviously we can't use the DOS-based client presented in the preceding section; it was just a means to test the EJB implementation of our three entity beans. This client was really playing the role that our use-case controller needs to play. We saw the use-case controller in action in Chapter 11. However, it will need a few changes.

We will also require some additions to the JSP `rltnInquiry.jsp` to be able to handle the display of multiple role/address combinations for a customer. The last changes we need to make are to the servlet, and these changes are meant only to support how we instantiate the controller. Let's start at the front this time with the changes necessary for the JSP side of Remulak.

Changes to the JSPs

The JSPs presented earlier require just a few changes. Actually, the only JSP that must be modified is `rltnInquiry.jsp`, and we have to add a new JSP, `rltnAddress.jsp`. In Chapter 11, the JSP for displaying a `Customer` object was rather straightforward. Now, however, we have to deal with a `CustomerValue` object having not only `Customer` information but also `Role` and `Address` information. In addition, the `CustomerValue` object was created in `CustomerDAO` in the non-EJB solution. The whole DAO layer is gone with CMP. We will have to make the bean do this for us now. Before we dive into the JSP, we should review how `CustomerValue` is created because this will make the additions to `rltnInquiry.jsp` more straightforward.

In `CustomerBean`, the result of the `findByCustomerNumber()` method, which we saw previously in the home interface, causes a `CustomerBean` object to be created for us. To get the proxy image of this bean, we will invoke its `getCustomerValue()` operation. We will see this in action a bit later. For now let's explore the `getCustomerValue()` operation in `CustomerBean`:

```
public CustomerValue getCustomerValue()
    throws RemoteException {

    CustomerValue myCustVal = new CustomerValue();

    myCustVal.setCustomerId(getCustomerId());
    myCustVal.setCustomerNumber(getCustomerNumber());
    myCustVal.setFirstName(getFirstName());
    myCustVal.setMiddleInitial(getMiddleInitial());
    myCustVal.setPrefix(getPrefix());
    myCustVal.setSuffix(getSuffix());
    myCustVal.setLastName(getLastName());
    myCustVal.setPhone1(getPhone1());
    myCustVal.setPhone2(getPhone2());
    myCustVal.setEMail(getEMail());

    // Get the RoleValue objects by iterating over the Roles
       collection
    ArrayList returnList = new ArrayList();
    Iterator roleIter = getRoles().iterator();
    if(! roleIter.hasNext()) {
      log("  No roles for this customer");
    }
```

```
        else {
            while (roleIter.hasNext()) {
              Role role = (Role) roleIter.next();
              RoleValue roleValue = role.getRoleValue();
              roleValue.setCustomerValue(myCustVal);
              returnList.add(roleValue);
            }
        }
        myCustVal.setRoleValue(returnList);

        return myCustVal;
    }
```

Notice that in addition to setting the base attributes from `Customer`, `getCustomerValue()` iterates over the beans contained in the collection of `RoleBean` objects. Each instance of `RoleBean` in the `ArrayList` object is sent a `getRoleValue()` message. Let's follow the trail to the `RoleBean` now and look at the `getRoleValue()` operation within that bean:

```
public RoleValue getRoleValue()
    throws RemoteException {

    RoleValue myRoleVal = new RoleValue();

    myRoleVal.setRoleId(getRoleId());
    myRoleVal.setRoleName(getRoleName());
    myRoleVal.setAddressValue(getAddress().getAddressValue());

    return myRoleVal;

  }
```

For the `RoleBean` object in the contained `ArrayList` within `CustomerBean`, we are setting the local value as well. The last assignment is then to send a `getAddressValue()` message to the contained `AddressBean` reference that exists in the `RoleBean` object. Let's follow the trail to the `AddressBean` object and look at its `getAddressValue()` operation:

```
public AddressValue getAddressValue()
  {
    AddressValue myAddrVal = new AddressValue();

    myAddrVal.setAddressId(getAddressId());
    myAddrVal.setAddressLine1(getAddressLine1());
```

```
        myAddrVal.setAddressLine2(getAddressLine2());
        myAddrVal.setAddressLine3(getAddressLine3());
        myAddrVal.setState(getState());
        myAddrVal.setCity(getCity());
        myAddrVal.setZip(getZip());

        return myAddrVal;

    }
```

The `getAddressValue()` operation also gets the related `Address` object's internal values. So to recap, by the `getCustomerValue()` operation's iteration over its collection of roles, the `RoleValue` object that now exists in the `CustomerValue ArrayList` of `RoleValue` also contains its related `AddressValue` object.

The reason for these proxy objects is to reduce expensive network trips and to decouple the use of the beans from the beans' states. However, it also raises the question of just how far you should chase the object graph. The graph could consist of all possible relationships to the very bottom leaf. Clearly this would be overkill for someone who wanted only specific information. Much thought has been devoted to this issue; the possibilities range from fully chasing the object graph to initiating a lazy loading strategy. Lazy loading entails only loading the other related objects in the graph on request. Floyd Marinescu, with the Middleware Company (*www.middleware-company.com*), has written some excellent articles on this very topic. His thoughts can be found on the portal he manages at *www.theserverside.com*.

The work that must happen on `rltnInquiry.jsp` should make a bit more sense. The JSP must not only extract information about the `Customer` object from `CustomerValue`, but it also needs to iterate through all the `RoleValue` objects and the `AddressValue` object within each `RoleValue` object. Figure 12-15 is the result of the modifications that follow:

```
<%@ page language="java" contentType="text/html" %>
<%@ taglib uri="/WEB-INF/struts-bean.tld" prefix="bean" %>
<%@ taglib uri="/WEB-INF/struts-html.tld" prefix="html" %>
<%@ taglib uri="/WEB-INF/struts-logic.tld" prefix="logic" %>
<jsp:useBean id="custVal" scope="request"
 class="com. jacksonreed.CustomerValue" />
<bean:define id="custOther" name="custVal"/>
```

FIGURE 12-15 *A customer with more than one address*

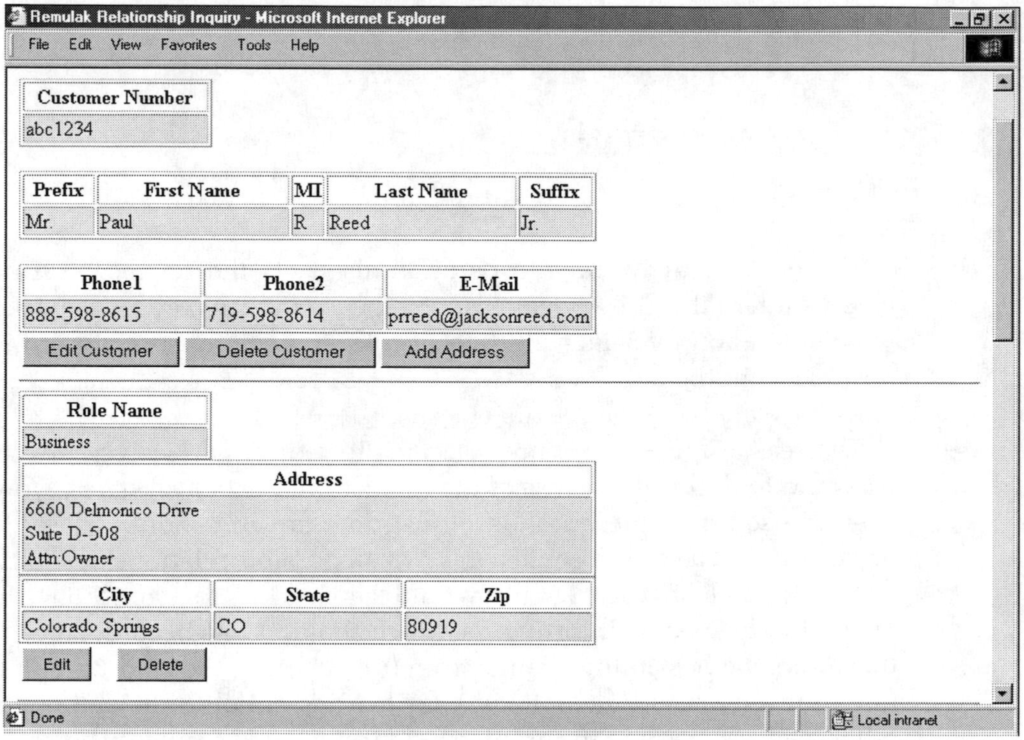

The heading of the JSP has changed. The biggest difference is the inclusion of the `taglib` directives. This is where we will utilize some excellent work by the folks from Apache on the Struts framework. Without Struts and other `taglib` directives on the market today, JSPs would be bloated with scripting elements. The `<bean:define>` tag makes a copy of the `CustomerValue` object for Struts so that it can work its magic. Everything is the same as in Chapter 11, until we reach the next set of comments:

```
<HTML>
<HEAD>
<TITLE>Remulak Relationship Inquiry</TITLE>
</HEAD>
<BODY >
<form action="rltnUpdate" method="get">
<P><FONT size=6>Remulak Relationship Inquiry</FONT></P>
```

```
<table border="1" width="20%"  >
  <tr>
    <th align="center">
      Customer Number
    </th>
  </tr>
  <tr>
    <td align="left" bgColor="aqua">
      <%= custVal.getCustomerNumber() %>
    </td>
  </tr>
</table>
<p><p>
<table border="1" width="60%"  >
  <tr>
    <th align="center" width="10%">
      Prefix
    </th>
    <th align="center" width="25%">
      First Name
    </th>
    <th align="center" width="2%">
      MI
    </th>
    <th align="center" width="25%">
      Last Name
    </th>
    <th align="center" width="10%">
      Suffix
    </th>
  </tr>
  <tr>
    <td align="left" width="10%" bgColor="aqua">
      <jsp:getProperty name="custVal" property="prefix"/>
    </td>
    <td align="left" width="25%" bgColor="aqua">
      <%= custVal.getFirstName() %>
    </td>
    <td align="left" width="2%" bgColor="aqua">
      <%= custVal.getMiddleInitial() %>
    </td>
    <td align="left" width="25%" bgColor="aqua">
      <%= custVal.getLastName() %>
    </td>
    <td align="left" width="10%" bgColor="aqua">
      <%= custVal.getSuffix() %>
```

```
        </td>
      </tr>
    </table>
    <p><p>
    <table border="1" width="60%"  >
      <tr>
        <th align="center" width="25%">
          Phone1
        </th>
        <th align="center" width="25%">
          Phone2
        </th>
        <th align="center" width="25%">
          E-Mail
        </th>
      </tr>
      <tr>
        <td align="left" width="25%" bgColor="aqua">
          <%= custVal.getPhone1() %>
        </td>
        <td align="left" width="25%" bgColor="aqua">
          <%= custVal.getPhone2() %>
        </td>
        <td align="left" width="25%" bgColor="aqua">
          <%= custVal.getEMail() %>
        </td>
      </tr>
    </table>
    <!--Buttons for Customer -->
    <table border="0" width="30%"  >
      <tr>
        <th align="left" width="33%">
          <INPUT type=submit value="Edit Customer" name=action >
        </th>
        <th align="left" width="33%">
          <INPUT type=submit value="Delete Customer" name=action >
        </th>
        <th align="left" width="33%">
          <INPUT type=submit value="Add Address" name=action>
        </th>
      </tr>
    </table>
```

In the next block of code notice the `<logic:iterate>` tag. This is one of the features offered by Struts through its logic `taglib`. The `name` parameter points to the copy of the `CustomerValue` bean. The `property` parameter points to the `RoleValue ArrayList` that is sitting in `Customer Value`.

```
<!--This is the Struts iterator that will cycle over our
    RoleValue -->
<logic:iterate id="role" name="custOther" property="roleValue">
<!--Role Name -->
<hr>
<table border="1" width="20%"  >
  <tr>
    <th align="center">
      Role Name
    </th>
  </tr>
  <tr>
    <td align="left" bgColor="aqua">
      <bean:write name="role" property="roleName"
         filter="true"/>
```

The `<bean:write>` tag points to the `getRoleName()` operation in the `RoleValue` object. Notice that we don't have to reference the actual accessor, just the property. This reference causes the accessor's value to be displayed.

In the code that follows, the `<bean:write>` tag is performing the same function as described with `roleName`; however, note how Struts makes the syntax so much easier to write than scripting does. The statement `property="addressValue.addressLine1"` inside the tag is the equivalent of writing `GetAddressValue().getAddressLine1()` in a scripting element.

```
    </td>
  </tr>
</table>
<!--Address Lines -->
<table border="1" width="60%"  >
  <tr>
    <th align="center" width="10%">
      Address
    </th>
  </tr>
  <tr>
    <td align="left" width="60%" bgColor="aqua">
      <bean:write name="role" property="addressValue.
       addressLine1" filter="true"/>
```

```
        <br>
        <bean:write name="role" property="addressValue.
         addressLine2" filter="true"/>
        <br>
        <bean:write name="role" property="addressValue.
         addressLine3" filter="true"/>
      </td>
```

The following snippet of code shows the placement of the remaining attribute elements of the `AddressValue` object:

```
    </tr>
  </table>
  <!--City, State, ZIP -->
  <table border="1" width="60%"  >
    <tr>
      <th align="center" width="25%">
        City
      </th>
      <th align="center" width="25%">
        State
      </th>
      <th align="center" width="25%">
        Zip
      </th>
    </tr>
    <tr>
      <td align="left" width="25%" bgColor="aqua">
        <bean:write name="role" property="addressValue.city"
         filter="true"/>
      </td>
      <td align="left" width="25%" bgColor="aqua">
        <bean:write name="role" property="addressValue.state"
         filter="true"/>
      </td>
      <td align="left" width="25%" bgColor="aqua">
        <bean:write name="role" property="addressValue.zip"
         filter="true"/>
      </td>
    </tr>
  </table>
```

The next portion of code in the JSP associates a hyperlink with the buttons that display beneath the address (**Edit** and **Delete**), as shown in Figure 12-15. We can't simply create a button with an `<INPUT>` tag because we have to customize the query string when the button is pushed. This is necessary because if someone wants to edit the second of three role/address elements on the form, you must indicate to the servlet which ones they want to change.

```
<!--Buttons for Address -->
<table border="0" width="30%"  >
  <tr>
    <th align="left" width="33%">
      <a href="rltnUpdate?action=Edit+Address&roleId=<bean:
       write name="role" property="roleId" filter="true"/>
       &addressId=<bean:write name="role" property=
       "addressValue.addressId" filter="true"/>
       &customerNumber=<%= custVal.getCustomerNumber()
       %>&customerId=<%= custVal.getCustomerId() %>"><img
       src=images/edit.gif border="0" alt="Update Role or
       Address">
      </a>
    </th>
    <th align="left" width="33%">
      <a href="rltnUpdate?action=Delete+Address&roleId=<bean:
       write name="role" property="roleId" filter="true"/>
       &addressId=<bean:write name="role" property=
       "addressValue.addressId" filter="true"/>
       &customerNumber=<%= custVal.getCustomerNumber()
       %>&customerId=<%= custVal.getCustomerId() %>"><img
       src=images/delete.gif border="0" alt="Delete Role and
       Address">
      </a>
    </th>
    <th align="left" width="33%">
       
    </th>
  </tr>
</table>
</logic:iterate>
```

The tag that signals the end of the iteration, `</logic:iterate>`, causes the loop to cycle again until there are no more `RoleValue` objects in the `CustomerValue` `ArrayList`.

```
<INPUT type="hidden" name="customerNumber" value='<%=
 custVal.getCustomerNumber() %>' >
<INPUT type="hidden" name="customerId" value='<%= custVal.
 getCustomerId() %>' >
```

```
</form>
</BODY>
</HTML>
```

Many tag libraries are in circulation today. However, the Struts framework, from the Apache Software Foundation at *jakarta.apache.org*, is both free and quite complete in its implementation. In addition, Struts is constructed with components, so you can use only what you want. As of this writing, Sun is working on formulating a standard tag library that will be made part of a JDK release in the future. It is thought that much of what we see in Struts will end up in that effort. Whatever the case, tag libraries are essential for reduced maintenance and accelerated application development.

Adding an Address JSP

As described already, the client can now view a `Customer` object and its associated `Role` and `Address` objects. The mechanism to pass that information back to the servlet has also been reviewed. Now we need `rltnAddress.jsp` to allow us to both add and update `Role/Address` pairs and assign them to a `Customer` object. Figure 12-16 shows what the `Address` JSP would look like in the browser if the client had depressed the **Edit** button for the first address related to customer abc1234.

The `rltnAddress` JSP is straightforward:

```
<%@ page language="java" contentType="text/html" %>
<jsp:useBean id="addrVal" scope="request"
         class="com.jacksonreed.AddressValue" />
<jsp:useBean id="roleVal" scope="request"
         class="com.jacksonreed.RoleValue" />
<jsp:useBean id="custVal" scope="request"
         class="com.jacksonreed.CustomerValue" />
```

The heading is a bit different from the heading for the `rltnInquiry` and `rltnCustomer` JSPs. There are no Struts tag library references because we aren't using its features on this page. However, because we are addressing elements from both `RoleValue` and `AddressValue`, we must reference those items with `<jsp:useBean>` tags.

In the next example I have once again used a combination of both action elements (`<jsp:getProperty>`) and scripting elements (`<% %>`) just to show the variety.

FIGURE 12-16 *JSP to add and update addresses*

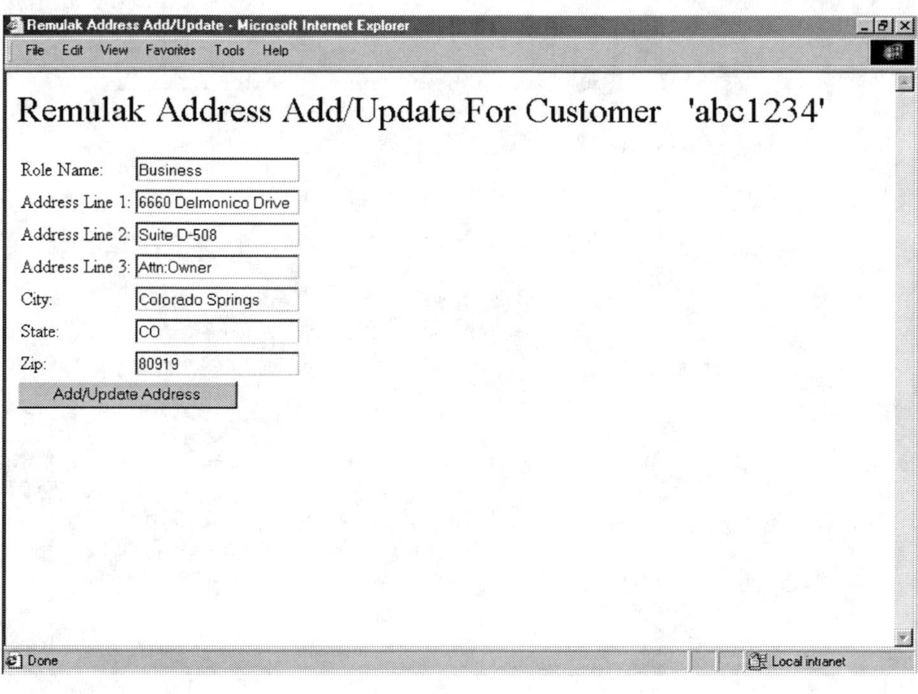


```
<HTML>
<HEAD>
<TITLE>Remulak Address Add/Update</TITLE>
</HEAD>
<BODY >

<P><FONT size=6>Remulak Address Add/Update For Customer  
    '<%= custVal.getCustomerNumber() %>'
</FONT></P>

<%--Output form with submitted values --%>
<form action="rltnUpdate" method="get">
  <table>
    <tr>
      <td>Role Name:</td>
      <td>
        <input type="text" name="roleName"
                 value="<jsp:getProperty name="roleVal"
                 property="roleName"/>">
      </td>
```

```
      </tr>
      <tr>
        <td>Address Line 1:</td>
        <td>
          <input type="text" name="addressLine1"
              value='<%= addrVal.getAddressLine1() %>' >
        </td>
      </tr>
      <tr>
        <td>Address Line 2:</td>
        <td>
          <input type="text" name="addressLine2"
              value='<%= addrVal.getAddressLine2() %>' >
        </td>
      </tr>
      <tr>
        <td>Address Line 3:</td>
        <td>
          <input type="text" name="addressLine3"
              value='<%= addrVal.getAddressLine3() %>' >
        </td>
      </tr>
      <tr>
        <td>City:</td>
          <td>
            <input type="text" name="city"
              value='<%= addrVal.getCity() %>' >
          </td>
      </tr>
      <tr>
        <td>State:</td>
          <td>
            <input type="text" name="state"
              value='<%= addrVal.getState() %>' >
          </td>
      </tr>
      <tr>
        <td>Zip:</td>
          <td>
            <input type="text" name="zip"
              value='<%= addrVal.getZip() %>' >
          </td>
      </tr>
    </table>
  <INPUT type="hidden" name="customerNumber"
   value='<%= custVal.getCustomerNumber() %>' >
```

```
<INPUT type="hidden" name="customerId"
         value='<%= custVal.getCustomerId() %>' >
<INPUT type="hidden" name="roleId"
         value='<%= roleVal.getRoleId() %>' >
<INPUT type="hidden" name="addressId"
         value='<%= addrVal.getAddressId() %>' >
<INPUT type=submit value="Add/Update Address" name=action>
</form>
</BODY>
</HTML>
```

Notice that in the hidden fields at the bottom of the page we now have the primary key of all three value objects: `customerId`, `roleId`, and `addressId`.

Changes to the Servlet

To accommodate the enhanced *Maintain Relationships* use-case support, changes are required to the work that was done in Chapter 11 with regard to both the user interface controller (`RemulakServlet`) and the use-case controller (`UCMaintainRltnshp`). The Remulak `CustomerBean`, `AddressBean`, and `RoleBean` objects are working fine as entity EJBs, but as of yet, the only client accessing them is the DOS-based client built to test the deployment. We have the JSPs in place, but now they need something to talk to, and that is our servlet.

The changes necessary to the servlet are quite small—so small, in fact, that I will merely point out the differences. The primary change is how we find the use-case controller. In Chapter 11 the use-case controller was just a JavaBean. The use-case controller in this enhanced architectural prototype will be a stateless session EJB. The only way for a client to talk to the EJB container is to get the home interface of the bean, in this case `UCMaintainRltnshpHome`. Once the home interface is available to `RemulakServlet`, the door is wide open for us to work with the container and the beans within. Let's start by examining the changes necessary to one of the servlet operations, `doRltnCustomerInquiry()`:

```
private void doRltnCustomerInquiry(HttpServletRequest request,
    HttpServletResponse response)
    throws IOException, ServletException, RemoveException,
    CreateException, NamingException, FinderException {
```

```
String customerNumber = request.getParameter
("customerNumber");

if (customerNumber == null) {
      throw new ServletException("Missing customerNumber
      info");
}

UCMaintainRltnshpHome home = lookupHome();

UCMaintainRltnshp UCController =
     (UCMaintainRltnshp) PortableRemoteObject.narrow(home.
     create(), UCMaintainRltnshp.class);
```

The first difference to point out is how we obtain the reference to `UCMaintainRltnshp`. A private `lookupHome()` operation, which we will look at in this section, is called to get a reference to our home interface for `UCMaintainRltnshp`. The next statement calls `create()` on the home interface, which returns a reference to the remote interface. Remember that it isn't the bean, but the remote interface, that acts as the proxy to the bean sitting in the container.

```
// Call to controller method in session bean
CustomerValue custVal =
      UCController.rltnCustomerInquiry(customerNumber);

// Set the custVal object into the servlet context so that
// JSPs can see it
request.setAttribute("custVal", custVal);

// Remove the UCMaintainRltnshp controller
UCController.remove();

// Forward to the JSP page used to display the page
forward("rltnInquiry.jsp", request, response);

   }
```

The remainder of the servlet is identical to the non-EJB solution. The only other notable difference is how we remove the reference to the controller when the servlet is done with it. In Chapter 11 we set the reference to `null`. In the case of our session bean, we call `remove()`. I won't review the other operations in `RemulakServlet` because the changes to be made are identical. However, let's look at the `lookup Home()` operation that returns the home interface:

```
private UCMaintainRltnshpHome lookupHome()
      throws NamingException {

    // Look up the bean's home using JNDI
    Context ctx = getInitialContext();

    try {
      Object home = ctx.lookup("remulak.UCMaintainRltnshpHome");

      return (UCMaintainRltnshpHome) PortableRemoteObject.narrow
                (home, UCMaintainRltnshpHome.class);

      } catch (NamingException ne) {
          logIt("The client was unable to lookup the EJBHome." +
                "Please make sure ");
          logIt("that you have deployed the ejb with the JNDI
          name " + "UCMaintainRltnshpHome" +
                    " on the WebLogic server at ");
          throw ne;
      }
    }
```

The lookup starts with getting the `Context` reference for the container. The `getInitialContext()` operation returns the necessary string to be used by JNDI to prepare for the home interface lookup. The `ctx.lookup()` call takes the JNDI name of the `UCMaintainRltnshpHome` interface and returns a reference:

```
private Context getInitialContext() throws NamingException {
    try {

      // Get an initial context
      Properties h = new Properties();

      h.put(Context.INITIAL_CONTEXT_FACTORY,
        "weblogic.jndi.WLInitialContextFactory");

      h.put(Context.PROVIDER_URL, url);

      return new InitialContext(h);
    } catch (NamingException ne) {
      logIt("We were unable to get a connection to the " +
          " WebLogic server at ");
      logIt("Please make sure that the server is running.");
      throw ne;
    }
  }
```

The `getInitialContext()` operation is the only place where differences will be found, because of the unique needs of the EJB container in use. However, this operation is very isolated and could be separated out in a factory class that holds the unique code to return the appropriate `Context` object.

Changes to the Use-Case Controller

The use-case controller, `UCMaintainRltnshp`, will require structural changes to accommodate the fact that it is now a session bean. However, the use-case pathway operations will remain intact with the exception of the following changes:

- Just as with the servlet, the entity beans used by the controller must return a home interface reference before we can work with them.
- The `TransactionContext` object and all the unit-of-work management code that wrapped the calls to the beans in the non-EJB solution must be removed. These are no longer necessary because the container will manage the transactions according to the assembly descriptor covered earlier in this chapter.

Let's start by looking at the differences in the structure of the revised `UCMaintainRltnshp` class:

```
package com.jacksonreed;

import java.util.Enumeration;
import java.util.Random;
import javax.ejb.SessionBean;
import javax.ejb.SessionContext;
import javax.ejb.CreateException;
import javax.ejb.DuplicateKeyException;
import javax.ejb.EJBException;

import javax.naming.InitialContext;

import javax.rmi.PortableRemoteObject;

import java.rmi.RemoteException;
import javax.naming.NamingException;

import javax.ejb.FinderException;
```

```
import javax.ejb.NoSuchEntityException;
import javax.ejb.ObjectNotFoundException;
import javax.ejb.RemoveException;

import javax.naming.NamingException;

public class UCMaintainRltnshpBean implements SessionBean {

  private static Random generator;
  private SessionContext sessionContext;

  public void ejbCreate() {
  }
  public void ejbPassivate() {
  }
  public void ejbRemove() {
  }
  public void ejbActivate() {
  }

  public void setSessionContext(SessionContext context) {
    sessionContext = context;
  }
```

The big visual difference between the controller implemented in Chapter 11 and this one is that we have quite a few more imports to support the EJB world, and we also have skeleton callback methods that we won't use. Notice that the controller implements `SessionBean`. Some practitioners lobby for creating adapter classes that the bean implements. Doing so allows you to hide all the empty callback operations you don't use and override the ones you need to use. I choose to leave them as they are, empty in the bean. It is clearer to see them there. You also avoid the problem of getting into a multiple inheritance quandary if your bean really does need to subclass another of your entity or session beans.

Next I will present two operations out of the new controller bean to show the differences from the solution laid out in Chapter 11. I think you will find that they are much cleaner because all the transaction logic is removed:

```
public CustomerValue rltnCustomerInquiry(String
customerNumber)
   throws NamingException, RemoteException, FinderException {
```

```
        CustomerHome customerHome;

        customerHome = lookupCustomerHome();

        Customer customer = customerHome.
                findByCustomerNumber(customerNumber);
        return customer.getCustomerValue();
    }
```

Gone is the reference to `TransactionContext` and the call to its `beginTran()` and `commitTran()` operations. We must still look up the `CustomerHome` interface as we did the `UCMaintainRltnshpHome` interface in the servlet. It is a local operation and is identical in intent. The exceptions coming back are defined in the `javax.ejb` package. They are all considered application-level exceptions. Let's now look at the `rltnAddCustomer()` operation:

```
    public void rltnAddCustomer(CustomerValue custVal)
        throws NamingException, RemoteException, FinderException {

        // Seed random generator
        seedRandomGenerator();

        CustomerHome customerHome;

        customerHome = lookupCustomerHome();

        // Generate a random integer as the key field
        custVal.setCustomerId(generateRandomKey());

       try {
           Customer myCustomer = customerHome.create(custVal);
       } catch (CreateException ce) {
           throw new EJBException (ce);
       }
    }
```

Gone are all the complicated `catch` blocks from the prior implementation, as well as the calls to the `beginTran()`, `commitTran()`, and `rollBackTran()` operations within `TransactionContext`. If the call to create the customer fails, `CreateException` (an application-level exception) is caught and `EJBException` (a system-level exception) is thrown. This action will immediately force a rollback by the container for the transaction. Remember that this method was set to `RequiresNew` by the assembly descriptor.

One more operation from the control class will be of interest because it really demonstrates the efficiency that EJB implementation brings to the architecture. It is the `rltnAddAddress()` operation:

```
public void rltnAddAddress(AddressValue addrVal, CustomerValue
custVal, RoleValue roleVal)
    throws NamingException, RemoteException, RemoveException {

    // Seed random generator
    seedRandomGenerator();

    RoleHome roleHome;
    roleHome = lookupRoleHome();
    AddressHome addressHome;
    addressHome = lookupAddressHome();
    CustomerHome customerHome;
    customerHome = lookupCustomerHome();

    // Generate a random integer as the primary-key field or
    // Role
    roleVal.setRoleId(generateRandomKey());

    // Generate a random integer as the primary-key field or
    // Address
    addrVal.setAddressId(generateRandomKey());

    try {
        Customer customer =customerHome.
                findByCustomerId(custVal.getCustomerId());

        Address myAddress = addressHome.create(addrVal);
        Address address = addressHome.
                findByAddressId(addrVal.getAddressId());

        Role myRole = roleHome.create(roleVal, address,
        customer);
   } catch (CreateException ce) {
        throw new EJBException (ce);
   } catch (FinderException fe) {
        throw new EJBException (fe);
   }
}
```

In this operation we are trying to create a new `RoleBean` object and a new `AddressBean` object, and then associate the `RoleBean` object with the `CustomerBean` object. This is a good example of several invocations to multiple beans; if something isn't found or created properly, we need to roll back. The `create()` operation for `RoleBean` takes in both the newly created `AddressBean` object and the `CustomerBean` object. When the `RoleBean` object sets these values in its `create()` method, CMP will ensure that the foreign keys are taken care of and the database is updated properly.

Creating a BMP Implementation

It may seem awkward that we started with what might seem like a very hands-on implementation in Chapter 11, followed by the very hands-off implementation that CMP provides, only to end with another relatively hands-on implementation with BMP. But there's a reason. I firmly believe that as the EJB vendor community embraces the EJB 2.0 specification, and in particular its support for a common CMP standard, fewer projects will choose BMP as a solution. It may be necessary sometimes, but lifting the burden of writing and managing SQL calls from the project team eliminates at least 20 to 25 percent of the effort. It also shortens the testing cycle; the ripple effect is exponential.

Let's examine what is necessary to make the *Maintain Relationships* use-case a BMP implementation. Much of the work is already done for us. Here are the relevant issues:

- The work that was done to `RemulakServlet`, the JSPs, and the `UCMaintainRltnshp` use-case controller to support the enhanced CMP implementation remains the same for BMP.
- The entity beans using CMP require substantial changes, but in structure only, to support BMP. Modified versions of the DAO classes introduced in Chapter 11 will be required to handle the SQL interaction with the database.

The changes boil down to adding calls to the DAO classes within the appropriate callback methods. Let's start by looking at `CustomerBean` as a BMP entity:

```
package com.jacksonreed;

import java.io.Serializable;
import java.util.Enumeration;
import java.util.Vector;
import java.util.Collection;

import javax.ejb.CreateException;
import javax.ejb.DuplicateKeyException;
import javax.ejb.EJBException;
import javax.ejb.EntityBean;
import javax.ejb.EntityContext;
import javax.ejb.FinderException;
import javax.ejb.NoSuchEntityException;
import javax.ejb.ObjectNotFoundException;
import javax.ejb.RemoveException;
import java.rmi.RemoteException;
import javax.naming.InitialContext;
import javax.naming.NamingException;
import javax.sql.DataSource;
import java.util.List;
import java.util.Iterator;
import java.util.ArrayList;

public class CustomerBean implements EntityBean {

   final static boolean VERBOSE = true;

   private EntityContext ctx;

   private Integer customerId;
   private String customerNumber;
   private String firstName;
   private String middleInitial;
   private String prefix;
   private String suffix;
   private String lastName;
   private String phone1;
   private String phone2;
   private String EMail;
   private ArrayList roleValue;
   private ArrayList orderValue;
```

The beginning of the bean looks very much like its `CustomerBean` counterpart in Chapter 11, with the exception that it implements

EntityBean. I won't show all the accessors for the attributes; they appear just as they do in the Chapter 11 version. The big difference with BMP is that the accessors aren't declared abstract public. Next we have the callback operations we are obligated to implement because we're dealing with an entity bean. We will focus on the ejbCreate() method:

```
public void ejbCreate(CustomerValue custVal) throws
  CreateException {
    customerInsert(custVal);
}
```

This method, which the UCMaintainRltnshp control class accesses via the matching create() stub in the CustomerBeanHome interface, invokes a local operation, customerInsert():

```
public void customerInsert(CustomerValue custVal)
        throws EJBExeption {

        try {
          setCustomerValue(custVal);
          DataAccess custDAO = new CustomerDAO();
          custDAO.insertObject(custVal);
          custDAO = null;
        } catch (DAODBUpdateException ae) {
            throw new EJBException (ae);
        } catch (DAOSysException se) {
            throw new EJBException (se);
        }
  }
```

The customerInsert() operation is the same one as in Chapter 11—just slimmed down a bit. There is no longer a TransactionContext object being passed in or one being sent out with the creation of the CustomerDAO object, but we are working through the DataAccess interface just as before.

Let's now visit the CustomerDAO class, which has a new constructor:

```
public CustomerDAO() throws DAOSysException  {
      InitialContext initCtx = null;

      try {
        initCtx = new InitialContext();
        DataSource ds = (javax.sql.DataSource)
```

```
          initCtx.lookup("java:comp/env/jdbc/remulak-bea");
        dbConnection = ds.getConnection();

      } catch(NamingException ne) {
        log("Failed to lookup JDBC Datasource. Please double
        check that");
        log("the JNDI name defined in the resource-description
        of the ");
        log("EJB's weblogic-ejb-jar.xml file is the same as the
        JNDI");
        log("name ");
        log("for the Datasource defined in your config.xml.");
        throw new DAOSysException(ne);

      } finally {
        try {
          if(initCtx != null) initCtx.close();
        } catch(NamingException ne) {
          log("Error closing context: " + ne);
          throw new DAOSysException(ne);
      }
    }
  }
```

In the constructor we attain a reference to our JDBC data source and establish a connection. The lookup is done through JNDI, and this part of the application will also vary depending on the container product. The difference will be more syntax versus functionality. The lookup must happen regardless of the vendor. What follows is the `insertObject()` operation that the `CustomerBean`'s `ejbCreate()` operation instigated:

```
public void insertObject(Object model) throws
                DAOSysException, DAODBUpdateException {

    CustomerValue custVal = (CustomerValue) model;

    PreparedStatement stmt = null;
    try {
        String queryStr = "INSERT INTO " + "T_Customer" + " (" +
          "customerId, " +
          "customerNumber, " +
          "firstName, " +
          "middleInitial, " +
          "prefix, " +
```

```
            "suffix, " +
            "lastName, " +
            "phone1, " +
            "phone2, " +
            "eMail) " +
            "VALUES " +
            "(?, ?, ?, ?, ?, ?, ?, ?, ?, ?)";

        stmt = dbConnection.prepareStatement(queryStr);

        int i = 1;
        stmt.setInt(i++, custVal.getCustomerId().intValue());
        stmt.setString(i++, custVal.getCustomerNumber());
        stmt.setString(i++, custVal.getFirstName());
        stmt.setString(i++, custVal.getMiddleInitial());
        stmt.setString(i++, custVal.getPrefix());
        stmt.setString(i++, custVal.getSuffix());
        stmt.setString(i++, custVal.getLastName());
        stmt.setString(i++, custVal.getPhone1());
        stmt.setString(i++, custVal.getPhone2());
        stmt.setString(i++, custVal.getEMail());

        int resultCount = stmt.executeUpdate();
        if ( resultCount != 1 )
            throw new DAODBUpdateException
                ("ERROR inserting Customer in" +
          " Customer_TABLE!! resultCount = " + resultCount);
    } catch(SQLException se) {
        throw new DAOSysException
          ("Unable to insert item " +
          custVal.getCustomerId() + " \n" + se);
    } finally {
        closeStatement(stmt);
        closeConnection();
    }
}
```

The logic is identical to the `CustomerDAO` version from Chapter 11. The only minor exception is that the reference to the `TransactionContext` object is gone and the connection itself is maintained locally in the `dbConnection` attribute, which was set in the constructor.

That completes our BMP preview. The complete source code is available (as described in preface of this book) to allow a full investigation of the differences. All the other operations in the bean follow the same pattern that we see with the insert.

A Road Most Traveled

The Technology Decision

Today, applications taking a server-centric approach to their design must consider their alternatives. If the transaction volume will be quite small and is not anticipated to grow over time, the solution presented in Chapter 11 is viable. The major downside of this approach is the extra coding necessary for managing your own transaction scope. If, however, the application volume will grow over time and the need for clustering services arises to provide very high throughput, then a commercial application server product is absolutely essential. This is where the need for an EJB solution becomes even more apparent.

Enterprise JavaBeans have really caught on in the marketplace. I feel we will also continue to see a shift away from bean-managed persistence and toward container-managed persistence. Prior to the EJB 2.0 specification, the message from Sun on CMP wasn't very clear, bordering on ambiguous; too much was left to vendors to implement how they saw fit. With EJB 2.0, very little is left to the imagination of EJB vendors, and that's a good thing. Now CMP entity beans will be truly transportable across EJB vendor products. But by far the biggest saving from CMP is the complete removal of SQL coding. On many projects I have seen an increase of up to 25 percent in the productivity of the team going the CMP route—nothing to scoff at.

In considering design strategies for a project, keep in mind some of the basic lessons put forward in this book:

- Employ the Model 2 strategy for your front components—that is, have a servlet that acts as a user interface controller that brokers the requests from the client. It may benefit the design to have a user interface controller for each use-case. It may be beneficial to use the command pattern in the servlet that allows the dynamic invocation of beans that implement each unique action the servlet must implement. Use JavaServer Pages to present the view to the client.
- Every use-case should have a use-case control class. Each use-case controller should have operations that map to the happy and alternate pathways through the use-cases. These pathway operations are completely documented in the form of the sequence or collaboration diagrams.

- Use value objects wherever possible. Network chatter must be kept to a minimum or performance will suffer. Value objects contain only attributes and accessors, no business logic.
- The use of data access objects can go a long way toward further separating the layers of the application. BMP solutions and non-EJB solutions can benefit from the same design strategy.

The Process of Getting There

I still contend that the technology is the easy part. Identifying all the requirements and having the backing of your user are key. Confirming for users that you understand what they want is the true challenge. Use-case analysis, coupled with two other key UML constructs—class and sequence/collaboration diagrams—comes closer to meeting that challenge than anything I have seen in the 25 years I have been in the software industry.

Too often we on the technology side lose sight of the fact that most of us are in this business to satisfy a paying client. If we can't find a way to communicate the needs of the client better and manage the ensuing project with some level of predictability that it will be a success, we are not doing our job.

So pick a process, any process, and stick to it. Make it a lean process, one that produces artifacts that are absolutely necessary and that have a traceable thread both forward and backward. The days are gone when we were judged by the thickness of the analysis and design deliverables we produced. Users pay for software, not paper documents. Give it a try; it really isn't as hard as it sounds.

I hope you have enjoyed this book as much as I enjoyed writing it. Again, remember to download the code from my Web site (*www.jacksonreed.com*), where the entire Remulak application is available for inspection. Happy learning!

Checkpoint

Where We've Been

- A visual modeling tool is necessary to expedite the development of program code. The primary sources for the code are the class and component diagrams.

- Just as forward engineering is beneficial, it is important to reverse-engineer the application code into the visual model. This iterative process—forward engineering, coding, and then reverse engineering—is ongoing throughout the project lifecycle.
- Not one line of SQL is necessary to implement the container-managed persistence (CMP) model as implemented in the Enterprise JavaBean 2.0 specification.

APPENDIX A The Unified Process Project Plans

IN THIS APPENDIX

In this book I have stressed the importance of a sound project plan. I even went so far as to say that without a sound lifecycle process and accompanying project plan, you will fail. *The Unified Process, according to Rational Software, is in implementation by more than 1,000 companies worldwide. In this appendix I want to show the project plan templates that come with the product. Although their true benefit comes from being used in conjunction with the product, they will help the project team become familiar with what a sound project plan should encompass. I want to thank Per Kroll of Rational Software for seeking the permissions necessary to present these plans, and Ensemble Systems* (http://www.ensemble-systems.com), *who originally created the plans*

Before diving into the plans, you will notice that the Unified Process covers quite a bit of ground. In particular, it identifies over 103 different artifacts that a project team might produce during the course of a project. From my experience with the Unified Process, I have identified what I call the ten essential artifacts *that most projects of any size would likely produce:*

1. *Vision (including the Supplementary Specification)*
2. *Requirements Management Plan*
3. *Software Requirements Specification*

4. *Software Architecture Document*
5. *Software Development Plan*
6. *Design Model*
7. *Test Model*
8. *Implementation Plan*
9. *Configuration Management Plan*
10. *Deployment Plan*

Some of these artifacts are composite in that they contain other artifacts. For instance, the Design Model contains things such as class diagrams and sequence diagrams. Again, this is my perspective on those artifacts that are absolutely essential. For different types of projects, my list would change. In the case of a Request for Proposal (RFP), I would produce only the Vision, Software Requirements Specification, and Software Architecture Document.

As mentioned in Chapter 1, the Unified Process, out of the box, should be tailored to fit the needs of a project. Some projects will demand more artifacts and more steps in the project plan than others. The higher the risk is, the more attention needs to be paid to ensuring that the risks are mitigated. This mitigation process may consist of more elaborate deliverables and/or more tasks to complete on a project plan.

In summary, don't unfairly judge the Unified Process because it covers so many areas and in such great depth about the software development process. The intent of the product is to provide the team with a complete collection of best practices, allowing the team to produce what it believes will best meet its needs.

The Plans

The plans I present here cover three categories. The first plan, which the project team must create from scratch, is called the **phase plan**. The Unified Process does not provide a template for this plan because it is unique to each project. This plan represents the milestones and iterations found for the lifecycle of the project. The target audience of this plan is senior management.

The second category of plan is the high-level **overview plan** for the phase. These are also called *workflow plans.* There will be one overview plan for each iteration within a phase. These plans are at a macro level in that they represent groups of project activities that must be accomplished by the team. Each task found on the overview plan will explode into detailed activities on the activity plan that follows. The target audience of this plan consists of the day-to-day project managers of the project.

The third category of plan is the lower-level **activity plan** for the phase. There will be one activity plan for each iteration within a phase. These plans are at a detailed level, the level at which actual time would be reported and tracked. Activities roll up to the overview plan, which then rolls up to the phase plan. The target audience of this plan consists of both the day-to-day project managers and the individual team members.

FIGURE A-1 *The Unified Process phase plan for Remulak Productions*

	ℹ	Task Name
1		⊟ **Inception**
2		Conceptual Prototype
3		LifeCycle Objective Milestone
4		⊟ **Elaboration**
5		Iteration 1 - Remulak Package 1 Use Cases
6		Architectural Prototype
7		Iteration 2 - Remulak Package 2 Use Cases
8		Architectural Baseline
9		Iteration 3 - Remulak Package 3 Use Cases
10		Lifecycle Architectural Milestone
11		⊟ **Construction**
12		Iteration 1 - Remulak Package 1 Use Cases
13		Iteration 2 - Remulak Package 2 Use Cases
14		Iteration 3 - Remulak Package 3 Use Cases
15		⊟ **Transition**
16		Production Handover Planning

FIGURE A-2 *Inception phase: Overview plan*

	Task Name
1	⊟ **Project Management**
2	Conceive New Project
3	Evaluate Project Scope and Risk
4	Develop Software Development Plan
5	Plan for Next Iteration
6	Manage Iteration
7	Monitor and Control Project
8	Reevaluate Project Scope and Risk
9	⊟ **Business Modeling**
10	Assess Business Status
11	Identify Business Processes
12	Refine Business Processes
13	Design Business Process Realizations
14	Refine Roles and Responsibilities
15	Explore Process Automation
16	⊟ **Requirements**
17	Analyze the Problem
18	Understand Stakeholder Needs
19	Define the System
20	Manage the Scope of the System
21	Refine the System Definition
22	Manage Changing Requirements
23	⊟ **Analysis and Design**
24	Perform Architectural Synthesis
25	⊟ **Test**
26	Plan Test
27	⊟ **Environment**
28	Prepare Environment for Project
29	Prepare Environment for an Iteration
30	Prepare Guidelines for an Iteration
31	Support Environment During an Iteration
32	⊟ **Configuration & Change Management**
33	Plan Project Configuration and Change Control
34	Create Project CM Environments
35	Change and Deliver Configuration Items
36	Manage Baselines and Releases
37	Manage Change Requests
38	Monitor and Report Configuration Status

FIGURE A-3 *Inception phase: Detailed plan*

	Task
1	**Project Management**
2	**Conceive New Project**
3	Identify and Assess Risks
4	Develop Business Case
5	Initiate Project
6	Project Approval Review
7	**Evaluate Project Scope and Risk**
8	Identify and Assess Risks
9	Develop Business Case
10	**Develop Software Development Plan**
11	Develop Measurement Plan
12	Develop Risk Management Plan
13	Develop Product Acceptance Plan
14	Develop Problem Resolution Plan
15	Define Project Organization and Staffing
16	Define Monitoring & Control Processes
17	Plan Phases and Iterations
18	Compile Software Development Plan
19	Project Planning Review
20	**Plan for Next Iteration**
21	Develop Iteration Plan
22	Develop Business Case
23	Iteration Plan Review
24	**Manage Iteration**
25	Acquire Staff
26	Initiate Iteration
27	Assess Iteration
28	Iteration Evaluation Criteria Review
29	Iteration Acceptance Review
30	**Monitor and Control Project**
31	Schedule and Assign Work
32	Monitor Project Status
33	Report Status
34	Handle Exceptions and Problems
35	Project Review Authority (PRA) Project Review
36	**Reevaluate Project Scope and Risk**
37	Identify and Assess Risks
38	Develop Business Case
39	**Requirements**
40	**Analyze the Problem**
41	Capture a Common Vocabulary
42	Find Actors and Use Cases
43	Develop Vision
44	Develop Requirements Management Plan
45	**Understand Stakeholder Needs**
46	Capture a Common Vocabulary

FIGURE A-3 *(continued)*

47	Elicit Stakeholder Requests
48	Develop Vision
49	Find Actors and Use Cases
50	Manage Dependencies
51	⊟ **Define the System**
52	Capture a Common Vocabulary
53	Find Actors and Use Cases
54	Manage Dependencies
55	⊟ **Manage the Scope of the System**
56	Develop Vision
57	Manage Dependencies
58	Prioritize Use Cases
59	⊟ **Refine the System Definition**
60	Detail a Use Case
61	Detail the Software Requirements
62	Model the User Interface
63	Prototype the User Interface
64	⊟ **Manage Changing Requirements**
65	Structure the Use-Case Model
66	Manage Dependencies
67	Review Requirements
68	⊟ **Analysis and Design**
69	⊟ **Perform Architectural Synthesis**
70	Architectural Analysis
71	Construct Architectural Proof-of-Concept
72	Assess Viability of Architectural Proof-of-Concept
73	⊟ **Test**
74	⊟ **Plan Test**
75	Plan Test
76	⊟ **Environment**
77	⊟ **Prepare Environment for Project**
78	Assess Current Organization
79	Develop Development Case
80	Develop Project-Specific Templates
81	Select & Acquire Tools
82	⊟ **Prepare Environment for an Iteration**
83	Develop Development Case
84	Develop Project-Specific Templates
85	Launch Development Case
86	Set Up Tools
87	Verify Tool Configuration & Installation
88	⊟ **Prepare Guidelines for an Iteration**
89	Develop Business-Modeling Guidelines
90	Develop Use-Case Modeling Guidelines
91	Develop User-Interface Guidelines
92	Develop Design Guidelines

FIGURE A-3 *(continued)*

ID	Task Name
93	Develop Programming Guidelines
94	Develop Manual Styleguide
95	Develop Test Guidelines
96	Develop Tool Guidelines
97	⊟ **Support Environment During an Iteration**
98	Support Development
99	⊟ **Configuration & Change Management**
100	⊟ **Plan Project Configuration and Change Control**
101	Establish CM Policies
102	Write CM Plan
103	Establish Change Control Process
104	⊟ **Create Project CM Environments**
105	Setup CM Environment
106	Create Integration Workspaces
107	⊟ **Change and Deliver Configuration Items**
108	Create Development Workspace
109	Make Changes
110	Deliver Changes
111	Update Workspace
112	Create Baselines
113	Promote Baselines
114	⊟ **Manage Baselines and Releases**
115	Create Deployment Unit
116	Create Baselines
117	Promote Baselines
118	⊟ **Manage Change Requests**
119	Submit Change Request
120	Update Change Request
121	Review Change Request
122	Confirm Duplicate or Rejected Change Request
123	Verify Changes in Build
124	⊟ **Monitor and Report Configuration Status**
125	Report on Configuration Status
126	Perform Configuration Audits

FIGURE A-4 *Elaboration phase: Overview plan*

	Task Name
1	⊟ **Project Management**
2	Manage Iteration
3	Monitor and Control Project
4	Reevaluate Project Scope and Risk
5	Plan for Next Iteration
6	Refine Software Development Plan
7	⊟ **Requirements**
8	Analyze the Problem
9	Understand Stakeholder Needs
10	Define the System
11	Manage the Scope of the System
12	Refine the System Definition
13	Manage Changing Requirements
14	⊟ **Analysis and Design**
15	Define a Candidate Architecture
16	Analyze Behavior
17	Design Components/Design Real-Time Components
18	Design the Database
19	Refine the Architecture
20	⊟ **Implementation**
21	Structure the Implementation Model
22	Plan the Integration
23	Implement Components
24	Integrate Each Subsystem
25	Integrate the System
26	⊟ **Test**
27	Plan Test
28	Design Test
29	Implement Test
30	Execute Tests in Integration Test Stage
31	Execute Tests in System Test Stage
32	Evaluate Test
33	⊟ **Environment**
34	Prepare Environment for an Iteration
35	Prepare Guidelines for an Iteration
36	Support Environment During an Iteration
37	⊟ **Configuration & Change Management**
38	Change and Deliver Configuration Items
39	Manage Baselines and Releases
40	Manage Change Requests
41	Monitor and Report Configuration Status

FIGURE A-5 *Elaboration phase: Detailed plan*

	Task Name
1	⊟ **Project Management**
2	⊟ **Plan for Next Iteration**
3	Develop Iteration Plan
4	Develop Business Case
5	⊟ **Develop Software Development Plan**
6	Develop Measurement Plan
7	Develop Risk Management Plan
8	Develop Product Acceptance Plan
9	Develop Problem Resolution Plan
10	Define Project Organization and Staffing
11	Define Monitoring & Control Processes
12	Plan Phases and Iterations
13	Compile Software Development Plan
14	Project Planning Review
15	Iteration Plan Review
16	⊟ **Manage Iteration**
17	Acquire Staff
18	Initiate Iteration
19	Assess Iteration
20	Iteration Evaluation Criteria Review
21	Iteration Acceptance Review
22	⊟ **Monitor and Control Project**
23	Schedule and Assign Work
24	Monitor Project Status
25	Report Status
26	Handle Exceptions and Problems
27	Project Review Authority (PRA) Project Review
28	⊟ **Reevaluate Project Scope and Risk**
29	Identify and Assess Risks
30	Develop Business Case
31	⊟ **Requirements**
32	⊟ **Analyze the Problem**
33	Capture a Common Vocabulary
34	Find Actors and Use Cases
35	Develop Vision
36	Develop Requirements Management Plan
37	⊟ **Understand Stakeholder Needs**
38	Capture a Common Vocabulary
39	Elicit Stakeholder Requests
40	Develop Vision
41	Find Actors and Use Cases
42	Manage Dependencies
43	⊟ **Define the System**
44	Capture a Common Vocabulary
45	Find Actors and Use Cases
46	Manage Dependencies

FIGURE A-5 *(continued)*

ID	Task Name
47	⊟ **Manage the Scope of the System**
48	Develop Vision
49	Manage Dependencies
50	Prioritize Use Cases
51	⊟ **Refine the System Definition**
52	Detail a Use Case
53	Detail the Software Requirements
54	Model the User Interface
55	Prototype the User Interface
56	⊟ **Manage Changing Requirements**
57	Structure the Use-Case Model
58	Manage Dependencies
59	Review Requirements
60	⊟ **Analysis and Design**
61	⊟ **Define a Candidate Architecture**
62	Architectural Analysis
63	Use-Case Analysis
64	⊟ **Analyze Behavior**
65	Identify Design Elements
66	Use-Case Analysis
67	Review the Design
68	⊟ **Design Components/Design for Real-Time**
69	Use-Case Design
70	Class Design
71	Subsystem Design
72	Review the Design
73	⊟ **Design the Database**
74	Class Design
75	Database Design
76	Review the Design
77	⊟ **Refine the Architecture**
78	Identify Design Mechanisms
79	Identify Design Elements
80	Incorporate Existing Design Elements
81	Describe the Run-time Architecture
82	Describe Distribution
83	Review the Architecture
84	⊟ **Implementation**
85	⊟ **Structure the Implementation Model**
86	Structure the Implementation Model
87	⊟ **Plan the Integration**
88	Plan System Integration
89	⊟ **Implement Components**
90	Plan Subsystem Integration
91	Implement Component
92	Fix a Defect
93	Perform Unit Tests

FIGURE A-5 *(continued)*

94	Review Code
95	⊟ **Integrate Each Subsystem**
96	Integrate Subsystem
97	⊟ **Integrate the System**
98	Integrate System
99	⊟ **Test**
100	⊟ **Plan Test**
101	Plan Test
102	⊟ **Design Test**
103	Design Test
104	⊟ **Implement Test**
105	Implement Test
106	Design Test Packages and Classes
107	Implement Test Components and Subsystems
108	⊟ **Execute Tests in Integration Test Stage**
109	Execute Test
110	⊟ **Execute Tests in System Test Stage**
111	Execute Test
112	⊟ **Evaluate Test**
113	Evaluate Test
114	⊟ **Environment**
115	⊟ **Prepare Environment for an Iteration**
116	Develop Development Case
117	Develop Project-Specific Templates
118	Launch Development Case
119	Set Up Tools
120	Verify Tool Configuration & Installation
121	⊟ **Prepare Guidelines for an Iteration**
122	Develop Use-Case Modeling Guidelines
123	Develop Business-Modeling Guidelines
124	Develop User-Interface Guidelines
125	Develop Design Guidelines
126	Develop Programming Guidelines
127	Develop Manual Styleguide
128	Develop Test Guidelines
129	Develop Tool Guidelines
130	⊟ **Support Environment During an Iteration**
131	Support Development
132	⊟ **Configuration & Change Management**
133	⊟ **Change and Deliver Configuration Items**
134	Create Baselines
135	Promote Baselines
136	Create Development Workspace
137	Make Changes
138	Deliver Changes
139	Update Workspace
140	⊟ **Manage Baselines and Releases**
141	Create Deployment Unit

FIGURE A-5 *(continued)*

142	Create Baselines
143	Promote Baselines
144	⊟ **Manage Change Requests**
145	Submit Change Request
146	Update Change Request
147	Review Change Request
148	Confirm Duplicate or Rejected Change Request
149	Verify Changes in Build
150	⊟ **Monitor and Report Configuration Status**
151	Report on Configuration Status
152	Perform Configuration Audits

FIGURE A-6 *Construction phase: Overview plan*

	Task Name
1	⊟ **Project Management**
2	Plan for Next Iteration
3	Manage Iteration
4	Monitor and Control Project
5	Reevaluate Project Scope and Risk
6	⊟ **Requirements**
7	Manage Changing Requirements
8	⊟ **Analysis and Design**
9	Design Components/Design for Real-Time
10	Design the Database
11	Refine the Architecture
12	⊟ **Implementation**
13	Plan the Integration
14	Implement Components
15	Integrate Each Subsystem
16	Integrate the System
17	⊟ **Test**
18	Plan Test
19	Design Test
20	Implement Test
21	Execute Tests in Integration Test Stage
22	Execute Tests in System Test Stage
23	Evaluate Test
24	⊟ **Environment**
25	Prepare Environment for an Iteration
26	Prepare Guidelines for an Iteration
27	Support Environment During an Iteration
28	⊟ **Configuration & Change Management**
29	Change and Deliver Configuration Items
30	Manage Baselines and Releases
31	Manage Change Requests
32	Monitor and Report Configuration Status

FIGURE A-7 *Construction phase: Detailed plan*

	Task Name
1	**Project Management**
2	**Plan for Next Iteration**
3	Develop Iteration Plan
4	Develop Business Case
5	**Develop Software Development Plan**
6	Develop Measurement Plan
7	Develop Risk Management Plan
8	Develop Product Acceptance Plan
9	Develop Problem Resolution Plan
10	Define Project Organization and Staffing
11	Define Monitoring & Control Processes
12	Plan Phases and Iterations
13	Compile Software Development Plan
14	Project Planning Review
15	Iteration Plan Review
16	**Manage Iteration**
17	Acquire Staff
18	Initiate Iteration
19	Assess Iteration
20	Iteration Evaluation Criteria Review
21	Iteration Acceptance Review
22	**Monitor and Control Project**
23	Schedule and Assign Work
24	Monitor Project Status
25	Report Status
26	Handle Exceptions and Problems
27	Project Review Authority (PRA) Project Review
28	**Reevaluate Project Scope and Risk**
29	Identify and Assess Risks
30	Develop Business Case
31	**Requirements**
32	**Manage Changing Requirements**
33	Structure the Use-Case Model
34	Manage Dependencies
35	Review Requirements
36	**Analysis and Design**
37	**Design Components/Design for Real-Time**
38	Use-Case Design
39	Class Design
40	Subsystem Design
41	Capsule Design
42	Review the Design
43	**Design the Database**
44	Class Design
45	Database Design
46	Review the Design

FIGURE A-7 *(continued)*

ID	Task Name
47	⊟ **Refine the Architecture**
48	Identify Design Mechanisms
49	Identify Design Elements
50	Incorporate Existing Design Elements
51	Describe the Run-time Architecture
52	Describe Distribution
53	Review the Architecture
54	⊟ **Implementation**
55	⊟ **Plan the Integration**
56	Plan System Integration
57	⊟ **Implement Components**
58	Plan Subsystem Integration
59	Implement Component
60	Fix a Defect
61	Perform Unit Tests
62	Review Code
63	⊟ **Integrate Each Subsystem**
64	Integrate Subsystem
65	⊟ **Integrate the System**
66	Integrate System
67	⊟ **Test**
68	⊟ **Plan Test**
69	Plan Test
70	⊟ **Design Test**
71	Design Test
72	⊟ **Implement Test**
73	Implement Test
74	Design Test Packages and Classes
75	Implement Test Components and Subsystems
76	⊟ **Execute Tests in Integration Test Stage**
77	Execute Test
78	⊟ **Execute Tests in System Test Stage**
79	Execute Test
80	⊟ **Evaluate Test**
81	Evaluate Test
82	⊟ **Environment**
83	⊟ **Prepare Environment for an Iteration**
84	Develop Development Case
85	Develop Project-Specific Templates
86	Launch Development Case
87	Set Up Tools
88	Verify Tool Configuration & Installation
89	⊟ **Prepare Guidelines for an Iteration**
90	Develop Use-Case Modeling Guidelines
91	Develop Business-Modeling Guidelines
92	Develop User-Interface Guidelines
93	Develop Design Guidelines

FIGURE A-7 *(continued)*

94	Develop Programming Guidelines
95	Develop Manual Styleguide
96	Develop Test Guidelines
97	Develop Tool Guidelines
98	⊟ **Support Environment During an Iteration**
99	Support Development
100	⊟ **Configuration & Change Management**
101	⊟ **Change and Deliver Configuration Items**
102	Create Baselines
103	Promote Baselines
104	Create Development Workspace
105	Make Changes
106	Deliver Changes
107	Update Workspace
108	⊟ **Manage Baselines and Releases**
109	Create Baselines
110	Promote Baselines
111	Create Deployment Unit
112	⊟ **Manage Change Requests**
113	Submit Change Request
114	Update Change Request
115	Review Change Request
116	Confirm Duplicate or Rejected Change Request
117	Verify Changes in Build
118	⊟ **Monitor and Report Configuration Status**
119	Report on Configuration Status
120	Perform Configuration Audits

FIGURE A-8 *Transition phase: Overview plan*

1	⊟ **Project Management**
2	Plan for Next Iteration
3	Manage Iteration
4	Monitor and Control Project
5	Close-Out Project
6	⊟ **Requirements**
7	Manage Changing Requirements
8	⊟ **Analysis and Design**
9	Refine the Architecture
10	⊟ **Implementation**
11	Plan the Integration
12	Implement Components
13	Integrate Each Subsystem
14	Integrate the System
15	⊟ **Test**
16	Plan Test
17	Design Test
18	Implement Test
19	Execute Tests in Integration Test Stage
20	Execute Tests in System Test Stage
21	Evaluate Test
22	⊟ **Deployment**
23	Plan Deployment
24	Develop Support Material
25	Manage Acceptance Test (At Development Site)
26	Produce Deployment Unit
27	Manage Acceptance Test (At Installation Site)
28	Package Product
29	Provide Access to Download Site
30	⊟ **Environment**
31	Prepare Environment for an Iteration
32	Prepare Guidelines for an Iteration
33	Support Environment During an Iteration
34	⊟ **Configuration & Change Management**
35	Change and Deliver Configuration Items
36	Manage Baselines and Releases
37	Manage Change Requests
38	Monitor and Report Configuration Status

FIGURE A-9 *Transition phase: Detailed plan*

ID	Task
1	**Project Management**
2	**Plan for Next Iteration**
3	Develop Iteration Plan
4	Develop Business Case
5	**Develop Software Development Plan**
6	Develop Measurement Plan
7	Develop Risk Management Plan
8	Develop Product Acceptance Plan
9	Develop Problem Resolution Plan
10	Define Project Organization and Staffing
11	Define Monitoring & Control Processes
12	Plan Phases and Iterations
13	Compile Software Development Plan
14	Project Planning Review
15	Iteration Plan Review
16	**Manage Iteration**
17	Acquire Staff
18	Initiate Iteration
19	Assess Iteration
20	Iteration Evaluation Criteria Review
21	Iteration Acceptance Review
22	**Monitor and Control Project**
23	Schedule and Assign Work
24	Monitor Project Status
25	Report Status
26	Handle Exceptions and Problems
27	Project Review Authority (PRA) Project Review
28	**Close-Out Project**
29	Project Acceptance Review
30	Prepare for Project Close-Out
31	**Requirements**
32	**Manage Changing Requirements**
33	Structure the Use-Case Model
34	Manage Dependencies
35	Review Requirements
36	**Analysis and Design**
37	**Refine the Architecture**
38	Identify Design Mechanisms
39	Identify Design Elements
40	Incorporate Existing Design Elements
41	Describe the Run-time Architecture
42	Describe Distribution
43	Review the Architecture
44	**Implementation**
45	**Plan the Integration**
46	Plan System Integration

FIGURE A-9 *(continued)*

ID	Task Name
47	⊟ **Implement Components**
48	Plan Subsystem Integration
49	Implement Component
50	Fix a Defect
51	Perform Unit Tests
52	Review Code
53	⊟ **Integrate Each Subsystem**
54	Integrate Subsystem
55	⊟ **Integrate the System**
56	Integrate System
57	⊟ **Test**
58	⊟ **Plan Test**
59	Plan Test
60	⊟ **Design Test**
61	Design Test
62	⊟ **Implement Test**
63	Implement Test
64	Design Test Packages and Classes
65	Implement Test Components and Subsystems
66	⊟ **Execute Tests in Integration Test Stage**
67	Execute Test
68	⊟ **Execute Tests in System Test Stage**
69	Execute Test
70	⊟ **Evaluate Test**
71	Evaluate Test
72	⊟ **Deployment**
73	⊟ **Plan Deployment**
74	Develop Deployment Plan
75	Define Bill of Materials
76	⊟ **Develop Support Material**
77	Develop Training Materials
78	Develop Support Materials
79	⊟ **Manage Acceptance Test (At Development Site)**
80	Manage Acceptance Test
81	⊟ **Produce Deployment Unit**
82	Write Release Notes
83	Develop Installation Artifacts
84	⊟ **Manage Acceptance Test (At Installation Site)**
85	Manage Acceptance Test
86	⊟ **Package Product**
87	Release to Manufacturing
88	Verify Manufactured Product
89	Create Product Artwork
90	⊟ **Provide Access to Download Site**
91	Provide Access to Download Site
92	⊟ **Environment**
93	⊟ **Prepare Environment for an Iteration**

FIGURE A-9 *(continued)*

ID	Task
94	Develop Development Case
95	Develop Project-Specific Templates
96	Launch Development Case
97	Set Up Tools
98	Verify Tool Configuration & Installation
99	**Prepare Guidelines for an Iteration**
100	Develop Use-Case Modeling Guidelines
101	Develop Business-Modeling Guidelines
102	Develop User-Interface Guidelines
103	Develop Design Guidelines
104	Develop Programming Guidelines
105	Develop Manual Styleguide
106	Develop Test Guidelines
107	Develop Tool Guidelines
108	**Support Environment During an Iteration**
109	Support Development
110	**Configuration & Change Management**
111	**Change and Deliver Configuration Items**
112	Create Baselines
113	Promote Baselines
114	Create Development Workspace
115	Make Changes
116	Deliver Changes
117	Update Workspace
118	**Manage Baselines and Releases**
119	Create Baselines
120	Promote Baselines
121	Create Deployment Unit
122	**Manage Change Requests**
123	Submit Change Request
124	Update Change Request
125	Review Change Request
126	Confirm Duplicate or Rejected Change Request
127	Verify Changes in Build
128	**Monitor and Report Configuration Status**
129	Report on Configuration Status
130	Perform Configuration Audits

APPENDIX B The Synergy Process Project Plan

IN THIS APPENDIX

The Synergy Process project plan presented here is for projects that don't plan on using the Unified Process and intend to build their own process. Developed through work on real projects, this plan has served me well over the years.

This appendix presents the plan that I have found invaluable. It initially started out as a plan for just client/server-based projects, regardless of methodology. It has been through the paces, and the good part is that it is meant as a baseline to build your own plan. I don't expect you to follow every task in the plan. The plan must be molded for your own project needs.

A few items are worth pointing out:

1. *Every high-level task, such as "Inception—Project Scope" (see Figure B-1), will always be composed of the same task sections:*
   - ***Management tasks:** These are usually administrative in nature, but they are also very focused and strategic.*
   - ***Execution tasks:** These are what I call "doer" tasks. They represent the prime work necessary to produce the bulk of the deliverables that will be delivered to the project sponsor.*
   - ***Education tasks:** These are the education steps necessary for certain team members to be successful on the project.*

2. *The timeline is moot because the unique characteristics, composition, and effort level required for completion of the work of each project will vary. For estimating projects, see Appendix C.*

3. *On my Web site,* www.jacksonreed.com, *where all the source code for this book is available, you will find a copy of this project plan. It is in Microsoft Project 2000 format. I have also included a copy of it in HTML format.*

The Plan

FIGURE B-1 *Synergy Process model: Elaboration phase*

1		⊟ **Inception - Project Scope**
2		⊟ **Management Tasks**
3	✓	Identify Business Unit Sponsor
4		Define Roles and Responsibilities
5		Establish Business Objectives
6		Assign Project Team
7		Assess Project Risks
8		Establish Risk Assessment/Mitigation Procedures
9		Establish Problem Resolution Procedures
10		Establish Change Control Procedures
11		Refine Business Objectives
12		Establish Preliminary Project Releases
13		Estimate Preliminary Project Releases
14		Prepare Project Charter
15		Kickoff Initial Increment
16		⊟ **Execution Tasks**
17		⊟ **Scoping - Iter#1**
18		Assess/select CASE Toolkit
19		Identify Project Features
20		Identify Actors
21		Identify Events
22		Create Event Table
23		⊟ **Scoping - Iteration#2**

FIGURE B-1 *(continued)*

ID		Task Name
24		Identify Use Cases from Events Table
25		Identify Happy Path (Basic Course of Events) - name only
26		Identify Alternate Course of Events - name only
27		Identify Exceptions - name only
28		Identify Shadow Use Cases- name only
29		Prioritize Basic and Alternate Course of Events
30		⊟ **Scoping - Iteration#3**
31		Create Happy Path Activity Detail
32		Assess Network Impact
33		Assess Operations Impact
34		Assess Preliminary Execution Architecture
35		⊟ **Education Tasks**
36		Prepare/Analyze Skills Assessment
37		Prepare Training Plan
38		Conduct Basic Object Training
39		⊟ **Elaboration - Requirements Gathering - Cycle1**
40		⊟ **Management Tasks**
41		Monitor Project Plan
42		Monitor Politics
43		Monitor Expectations
44		Assess Project Plan
45		Assess Project Risks
46		Re-affirm Release Cycles/Dates
47		Assess Change Control
48		⊟ **Execution Tasks**
49		Document Repository Standards
50		Identify Modeling Standards
51		Create Preliminary Test Cases from Course of Events
52		⊟ **Requirements Gathering - Iter#1**
53		Create Course of Event Detail for Alternate Paths
54		Create Course of Event Detail for Exception Paths
55		Identify/Categorize Business Rules
56		Brainstorm Classes (nouns)
57		Filter Classes
58		⊟ **Requirements Gathering - Iter#2**
59		Class Associations and Multiplicity
60		Create Initial Class Diagram
61		⊟ **Requirements Gathering - Iter#3**
62		Add any known attributes/operations
63		⊟ **Education Tasks**
64		Conduct UI Prototype Training
65		Conduct Database Training
66		Conduct Object Construction Training
67		⊟ **Elaboration - Requirements Gathering - Cycle2**
68		⊟ **Management Tasks**
69		Monitor Project Plan

FIGURE B-1 *(continued)*

ID	Task Name
70	Monitor Politics
71	Monitor Expectations
72	Assess Project Plan
73	Assess Project Risks
74	Assess Change Control
75	⊟ **Execution Tasks**
76	⊟ **User Interface Prototype - Iter#1**
77	Select UI Prototyping Tool
78	Build/Buy UI Standards Tool
79	Create UI Structure Charts from Use Case Paths
80	Identify UI objects from Use Cases
81	Validate UI Structure Chart
82	Build Prototype
83	Validate UI Prototype Functionality
84	Validate UI Prototype Usability
85	⊟ **Requirements Gathering - Iter#2**
86	Create Sequence Diagram-Happy Path
87	Create Sequence Diagram-Alternate Paths
88	Create Collaboration Diagrams (where appropriate)
89	Update Class Diagram-Attributes/Operations
90	⊟ **Requirements Gathering - Iter#3**
91	Identify Classes with Dynamic Behavior
92	Create State Diagrams for Classes
93	Update Class Diagram-Attributes/Operations
94	Create Activity Diagrams
95	⊟ **Requirements Gathering - Iter#4**
96	Object/Location Matrix
97	Object/Volume Matrix
98	Event/Frequency Matrix
99	Assess Network/Operations Impact
100	⊟ **Education Tasks**
101	Conduct UI Prototype Training
102	Conduct Database Training
103	Conduct Object Construction Training
104	⊟ **Elaboration - Execution Architecture - Cycle3**
105	⊟ **Management Tasks**
106	Monitor Project Plan
107	Monitor Politics
108	Monitor Expectations
109	Assess Project Plan for Design
110	Assess Project Risks
111	⊟ **Execution Tasks**
112	Assess Operations Impact
113	Assess Network Impact
114	Update Test Plans
115	⊟ **Technology Architecture**

FIGURE B-1 *(continued)*

116	Select Database Technology
117	Select Hardware Platform
118	Select Network Infrastructure
119	Select Construction Tools
120	Select Support and Implementation tools
121	⊟ **Application Architecture**
122	Determine Build/Buy Strategy
123	Establish security requirements
124	Select Internet Tools
125	Select Partitioning Models
126	Map Tools to Partitioning Models
127	Select Application Component Interfaces
128	⊟ **Data Access Architecture**
129	Establish Data Stewards
130	Select Data Access APIs
131	Assess Data Distribution Requirements
132	Assess Data Synchronization Requirements
133	Assess Replication Technology
134	⊟ **Education Tasks**
135	Architecture Awareness Training
136	Client/Server & Object Tools Awareness Training
137	Component Building and Language Training
138	⊟ **Construction-Database-Cycle 1**
139	⊟ **Management Tasks**
140	Monitor Project Plan
141	Monitor Politics
142	Monitor Expectations
143	Assess Project Plan for Construction
144	Assess Project Risks
145	⊟ **Execution Tasks**
146	Assess Operations Impact
147	Assess Network Impact
148	⊟ **Database Design - Iter#1**
149	Assess Object Impact on Relational Design
150	Verify Data Distribution Scenarios
151	Verify Usage Matrix Accuracy
152	Apply DBMS Transform Rules to ERD
153	Validate Physical Design
154	Denormalize Physical Design
155	⊟ **Build Database Environment - Iter#2**
156	Create Tables
157	Create Indexes
158	Create Views
159	Establish Locking Standards
160	Establish Recovery Standards
161	Establish Disk Storage Management Standards

FIGURE B-1 *(continued)*

ID	Task Name
162	Validate Server Selection
163	Formalize Database Stress Test Plans
164	⊟ **Education Tasks**
165	Configuration Management Training
166	Debugging Techniques Training
167	⊟ **Construction - Component - Cycle 2**
168	⊟ **Management Tasks**
169	Monitor Project Plan
170	Monitor Politics
171	Monitor Expectations
172	Assess Project Plan for Construction
173	Assess Project Risks
174	⊟ **Execution Tasks**
175	Assess Operations Impact
176	Assess Network Impact
177	⊟ **Component Design - Iter#1**
178	Assess Object Impact to Component Strategy
179	Verify Process Distribution Scenarios
180	Verify Usage Matrix Accuracy
181	Apply UML Artifacts to Partitioning Model
182	Allocate Client Tasks
183	Allocate Server Tasks
184	Design Process Components
185	Create Component/Deployment Diagrams
186	Finalize Design Model
187	⊟ **Component Build - Iter#2**
188	Code Process Components
189	Reassess UI Screen Dialogues
190	Code UI Screen Dialogs
191	Identify Batch Streams
192	Code Batch Streams
193	Formalize component Stress Test Plans
194	⊟ **Education Tasks**
195	Configuration Management Training
196	Debugging Techniques Training
197	⊟ **Construction - Network - Cycle 3**
198	⊟ **Management Tasks**
199	Monitor Project Plan
200	Monitor Politics
201	Monitor Expectations
202	Assess Project Plan for Construction
203	Assess Project Risks
204	⊟ **Execution Tasks**
205	Assess Operations Impact
206	Assess Network Impact
207	Establish Existing Network Baseline

FIGURE B-1 *(continued)*

ID	Task Name
208	Validate Unique Network Requirements
209	Update Physical CRUD with Network Parameters
210	Simulate Network Load
211	Validate Network Load Against Baseline
212	Formalize Network Stress Test Plans
213	⊟ **Education Tasks**
214	Configuration Management Training
215	Debugging Techniques Training
216	⊟ **Transition**
217	⊟ **Management Tasks**
218	Monitor Project Plan
219	Monitor Politics
220	Monitor Expectations
221	Assess Project Plan for Construction
222	Assess Project Risks
223	Allocate Resources for Beta and Maintenance Support
224	Formulate Production Handover Strategy
225	Establish Final Acceptance Criteria for Handoff
226	Conduct Beta Post-Mortem
227	Conduct Production Post-Mortem
228	Conduct Maintenance Handoff Post-Mortem
229	⊟ **Execution Tasks**
230	⊟ **Deployment Beta - Iter#1**
231	Select Software Distribution Tool
232	Create install sets and deployment plans
233	Create database creation and build scripts
234	Create Beta Test Directory Structures
235	Create Beta Environment
236	Execute Install Set
237	Assess Beta Results and Track Trouble Reports
238	Prioritize and Implement Changes
239	⊟ **Deployment Production - Iter#2**
240	Create install sets and deployment plans
241	Create database creation and build scripts
242	Create Production Directory Structures
243	Create Production Environment
244	Execute Install Set
245	⊟ **Deployment Maintenance - Iter#3**
246	Create post-delivery maintenance plans
247	Accept Production System
248	Establish Trouble Reporting and Help Desk Integration Strategy
249	Establish Service Pack Release Strategy
250	⊟ **Education Tasks**
251	Software Distribution Tool Training
252	Help Desk Support Training

APPENDIX C

Estimating Projects on the Basis of Use-Cases

IN THIS APPENDIX

Countless times I have heard presenters and consultants alike dodge the issue of estimating person-hours and completion dates for project deliverables. Unfortunately, estimating project deliverable timelines isn't an easy proposition. Most of us, including me, typically use our own personal rule-of-thumb approaches to come up with estimates. The more software development one does, the more accurate this approach is. But regardless of the level of skill, a better approach is necessary to account for personal biases, as well as for projects that don't have a staff with a wealth of experience.

Rational Software acquired Ivar Jacobson's Objectory AB in 1995. Along with that purchase came the excellent research conducted by Gustav Karner, then of Objectory AB, in estimating person-hours for software projects on the basis of use-cases. Although this work was based on earlier work by Allan Albrecht using function point analysis, it brought unique insight because it used artifacts that were derived directly from the use-case.

The Objectory Process is based on four separate inputs:

1. *Weighting of actors*
2. *Weighting of use-cases*
3. *Weighting of technical factors*
4. *Weighting of project participants*

Weighting Actors

Karner's approach begins by weighting actors. The rating is based on whether the actor is ranked as *simple, average,* or *complex.*

Simple actors fall into the category introduced in Chapter 1 of this text as *external systems.* In the case of Remulak Productions, good examples are the interfaces to the accounting system and the credit card system. These types of actors have a well-defined interface and are very predictable as to their reaction to the output the system in question provides or to the input it receives from the interface.

Average actors fall into the category introduced in Chapter 3 as *hardware devices* or *timers.* In the case of Remulak Productions, good examples are the timers necessary to kick off given reports and to create the interface to the accounting system. Although these actors are predictable, they require more effort to control and are usually more prone to errors than simple actors are.

Complex actors fall into the category introduced in Chapter 3 as *humans.* The majority of actors in Remulak Productions are good examples, including the customer service clerk, the supplier, and the billing clerk. These types of actors are the most difficult to control and are totally unpredictable. Although a graphical user interface or even a text-based interface can enforce edits and controls, more complexity is involved with unknown actors that maintain their free will, doing as they please.

For Remulak Productions, we rate the actors involved as follows:

- **Customer:** Complex
- **Order clerk:** Complex
- **Customer service clerk:** Complex
- **Manager:** Complex
- **Time:** Average
- **Billing clerk:** Complex
- **Accounting system:** Simple
- **Credit card system:** Simple
- **Shipping clerk:** Complex
- **Packaging clerk:** Complex
- **Supplier:** Complex

TABLE C-1 *Weighting Factors for Actors*

Type of Actor	Description	Factor
Simple	External systems	1
Average	Hardware or timers	2
Complex	Humans	3

Table C-1 is the table used to apply the actor weighting factor as input to the estimating process.

Using the factors outlined in Table C-1 to weight Remulak's actors, we can deduce the following about Remulak Productions:

- 2 Simple × 1 = 2
- 1 Average × 2 = 2
- 8 Complex × 3 = 24

The result is an actor weight of 28 (2 + 2 + 24).

Weighting Use-Cases

Now let's consider the use-cases. The primary feature of the use-cases that we judge is their pathways. The number of pathways determines the weighting factor. The pathways consist of both the happy path and the alternate pathways through the use-case. In addition, if there are many primary exception pathways, these should also be included. If the exceptions are incidental or simple error situations, don't consider them. Remember the story I told in Chapter 4: For some applications, errors are more important than the happy path.

One area where I modify the approach used by Karner is the inclusion of *includes, extends,* and *generalize* extensions on the use-case diagram. Karner elects not to include these, but this is a concern because many of these use-cases are very robust and are much more than an alternative path (as is outlined by *extends,* for instance). In the text of this book, I refer to many of the include and extend use-cases as shadow use-cases. My recommendation is to include all use-cases, regardless of their type.

Another consideration is that the granularity of a use-case can be a bit subjective. Some analysts tend to create use-cases that are more coarse-grained, while others make them more fine-grained. This leveling issue can also influence the resulting weighting.

Table C-2 is the table used to apply the use-case weighting factor as input to the estimating process.

For Remulak Productions, we rate the use-cases as follows:

- ***Maintain Orders*** (12 pathways): Complex
- ***Process Orders*** (7 pathways): Average
- ***Maintain Relationships*** (4 pathways): Average
- ***Decision Support*** (11 pathways): Complex
- ***Invoicing*** (3 pathways): Simple
- ***Shipping*** (6 pathways): Average
- ***Maintain Inventory*** (6 pathways): Average
- ***Security*** (5 pathways): Average
- ***Architecture Infrastructure*** (5 pathways): Average

These factors lead us to deduce the following about Remulak Productions:

1 Simple × 5 = 5

6 Average × 10 = 60

2 Complex × 15 = 30

The result is a use-case weight of 95 (5 + 60 + 30).

Now we need to add the actor total to the use-case total to get what is called the **unadjusted use-case points** (**UUCP**). Later this number will

TABLE C-2 *Weighting Factors for Use-Cases*

Type of Use-Case	Description	Factor
Simple	3 or fewer pathways	5
Average	4 to 7 pathways	10
Complex	More than 7 pathways	15

be further adjusted according to both the technical and project team characteristics. For Remulak Productions, we get the following UUCP:

UUCP = 28 actor weight points + 95 use-case weight points = **123**

Weighting Technical Factors

The next step in our estimating process is to consider the technical factors of the project. To do this, use Table C-3 to assign a rating between 0 (irrelevant) and 5 (essential) for each topic. After rating each topic, multiply the weight by the rating to get an extended weight. The total extended weight for all technical factors is called the *T factor.*

TABLE C-3 *Weighting Factors for Technical Factors*

Technical Factor	Weight	Rating	Extended Weight (weight × rating)	Reason
1. Distributed system	2	3	6	The system must be able to scale.
2. Response or throughput performance objectives	1	2	2	Although response times aren't "hard," they must be tolerable.
3. End-user efficiency (online)	1	3	3	The system must be easy to comprehend.
4. Complex internal processing	1	1	1	There is very little complex processing.
5. Reusability of code	1	3	3	The code must be extensible to add future functionality.
6. Ease of installation	0.5	2	1	Installation will be minimal to two different sites.
7. Ease of use	0.5	4	2	The system must be easy to use.
8. Portability	2	0	0	There are no portability requirements.
9. Ease of change	1	3	3	The system must be changeable as the needs of Remulak evolve.
10. Concurrency	1	1	1	At present, there are few concurrency issues.

(continued)

TABLE C-3 *(continued)*

Technical Factor	Weight	Rating	Extended Weight (weight × rating)	Reason
11. Special security features	1	2	2	There will be security requirements in future releases, but they are basic.
12. Direct access for third parties	1	2	2	There are Internet access requirements for order inquiry.
13. Requirement for special user training	1	0	0	There are no special training requirements.
T factor			**26**	

Now that we have the T factor, we plug the value into a formula to obtain the **technical complexity factor** (**TCF**): TCF = 0.6 + (0.01 × T factor). This formula gives us the following result for Remulak Productions:

$$\textbf{TCF} = 0.6 + (0.01 \times 26) = \textbf{0.86}$$

Weighting Project Participants

The last factor to consider deals with the experience level of the project team members. This is called the **environmental complexity factor** (**ECF**). Take each factor in Table C-4 and assign it a rating between 0 and 5. Consider the following contexts:

- For the first four factors, 0 means no experience in the subject, 3 means average, and 5 means expert.
- For the fifth factor, 0 means no motivation for the project, 3 means average, and 5 means high motivation.
- For the sixth factor, 0 means extremely unstable requirements, 3 means average, and 5 means unchanging requirements.
- For the seventh factor, 0 means no part-time technical staff, 3 means average, and 5 means all part-time technical staff.

TABLE C-4 *Weighting Factors for Project Participants*

Technical Factor	Weight	Rating	Extended Weight (weight × rating)	Reason
1. Use of a formal process	1.5	3	4.5	Project team has average experience with using the Synergy Process.
2. Application experience	0.5	5	2.5	Users are very knowledgeable about Remulak's needs.
3. Object-oriented experience	1	0	0	The development team and users have virtually no knowledge about object-oriented concepts.
4. Lead analyst capability	0.5	5	2.5	The lead analyst must be very competent.
5. Motivation	1	5	5	There must be high motivation to get the project up and running.
6. Stability of requirements	2	5	10	Requirements must be unchanging.
7. Number of part-time workers	–1	0	0	There must be no part-time staff.
8. Difficulty of programming language	–1	3	–3	Visual Basic is very easy to learn and apply, but the staff isn't very familiar with it.
E factor			**21.5**	

- For the eighth factor, 0 means easy-to-use programming language, 3 means average, and 5 means very difficult programming language.

The total extended weight for all environmental factors is called the *E factor.* Now that we have this value, we plug it into a formula to obtain the environmental complexity factor: ECF = 1.4 + (–0.03 × E factor). For Remulak Productions, we get the following:

$$\textbf{ECF} = 1.4 + (-0.03 \times 21.5) = \textbf{0.755}$$

Use-Case Points

Now that we have the three components we need—UUCP, TCF, and ECF—we are ready to calculate a bottom-line number, called **use-case points (UCP)**. The formula is UUCP × TCF × ECF. For Remulak Productions, then, we get the following value:

$$\textbf{UCP} = 123 \times 0.86 \times 0.755 = \textbf{79.86}$$

The Project Estimate

In his research, Karner applies 20 person-hours for each UCP. Doing the same, we would end up with a 1597.2 person-hours (20 × 79.86) for the Remulak project. For a 32-hour-per-week schedule with one person doing the work, this would amount to approximately 50 person-weeks.

Because 5 people are working on this project, we should allow about 10 weeks to finish the job. However, after considering time for unproductive meetings, communication issues, and show-and-tell sessions (you know, the ones that are never scheduled but you find yourself doing a lot of), we will add 4 additional weeks to the schedule. The total for the project, then, is 14 weeks.

Although Karner's approach isn't cast in stone, nor does it profess to provide the magic number, it is an excellent approximation. Others have suggested areas for improvement. In their excellent book *Applying Use Cases: A Practical Guide,* Geri Schneider and Jason Winters suggest that care should be given to the environmental complexity factor (ECF). She suggests counting the number of factors 1 through 6 that have a rating (not an extended weight) of less than 3 and the number of factors 7 and 8 that have a rating of greater than 3. If the total is 2 or less, use 20 person-hours per UCP. If the total is 3 or 4, use 28 person-hours per UCP. She goes on to indicate that if the total is 5 or more, some attention is needed because the risk for failure is very high. Using her criteria, we are still in good shape with 20 person-hours per UCP.

Use Karner's heuristics; they are the best I have seen up to now for estimating projects using the artifacts from UML (primarily the use-case). Tweak it where necessary, but remember that this approach is designed to prevent the sometimes dangerous rule-of-thumb estimates that we are so quick to provide but quite often overrun and regret.

APPENDIX D Sample Project Output

IN THIS APPENDIX

In the body of this book I used several examples to demonstrate the deliverables of the project as we moved through the phases of the Unified Process. At the introduction of those examples I referred to this appendix for more detail. That detail follows.

Use-Case Definitions

Recall that in Chapter 4 we defined many use-cases and then assigned them to one of three Remulak project increments. Providing for a more informed estimate while still at an early stage of the project requires an in-depth flyby of all the project's use-cases. At a minimum, before estimating a project, we must do the following:

1. Identify events.
2. Identify use-cases.
3. Assign events to use-cases.
4. Identify happy paths for all use-cases.
5. Identify alternate pathways for all use-cases.

6. Produce detailed task steps for all use-case happy paths.
7. Assign use-cases to project increments (both use-cases and pathways may need to be assigned because they may be split across increments).
8. Describe in detail all use-case pathways for the project's first increment.

Steps 1 through 5 were completed in the book, primarily in Chapter 4. The subsections that follow contain the completed use-case templates for all of Increment 1. A look at the happy paths for each use-case follows the templates.

The *Process Orders* Use-Case

Name: Process Orders.

Description:
This use-case starts when an order is either initiated or inquired about. It handles all aspects of the initial definition and authorization of an order, and it ends when the order clerk completes a session with a customer.

Author(s): Rene Becnel.

Actor(s): Order clerk.

Location(s): Newport Hills, Washington.

Status: Pathways defined.

Priority: 1.

Assumption(s):
Orders will be taken by the order clerk until the customer is comfortable with the specialized services being provided.

Precondition(s):
Order clerk has logged into the system.

Postcondition(s):

- Order is placed.
- Inventory is reduced.

Primary (Happy) Path:

- Customer calls and orders a guitar and supplies, and pays with a credit card.

Alternate Pathway(s):

- Customer calls and orders a guitar and supplies, and uses a purchase order.
- Customer calls and orders a guitar and supplies, and uses the Remulak easy finance plan to pay.
- Customer calls and orders an organ, and pays with a credit card.
- Customer calls and orders an organ, and uses a purchase order.

Exception Pathway(s):

- Customer calls to place an order using a credit card, and the card is invalid.
- Customer calls with a purchase order but has not been approved to use the purchase order method.
- Customer calls to place an order, and the desired items are not in stock.

The *Maintain Orders* Use-Case

Name: Maintain Orders.

Description:

This use-case starts when an order is modified in any way. It handles all aspects of the order modification, and it ends when the order clerk completes the order modification session.

Author(s): Rene Becnel.

Actor(s): Order clerk.

Location(s): Newport Hills, Washington.

Status: Pathways defined.

Priority: 1.

Assumption(s):

Orders will be modified by the order clerk.

Precondition(s):

Order clerk has logged into the system.

Postcondition(s):

- Order is modified.
- Inventory is reduced or increased.

Primary (Happy) Path:
Customer calls to inquire about an order's status.

Alternate Pathway(s):

- Customer calls to change a product quantity for one order item on an order.
- Customer calls to cancel an order.
- Customer calls to add a new item to an order.
- Customer calls to delete an item from an order.
- Customer calls to change the shipping terms of an order.
- Customer buys an extended warranty on an item.
- Customer calls to change the billing method on an order.

Exception Pathway(s):

- Customer calls to cancel an order that can't be found in the system.
- Customer calls to add a warranty to an item that is no longer valid for the time that the product has been owned.
- Customer calls to add to an order, and the product to be added can't be found in the system.

The *Maintain Inventory* Use-Case

Name: Maintain Inventory.

Description:
This use-case starts when a product is ordered and/or added to stock. It handles all aspects of inventory management, and it ends when either new stock is ordered or new stock has been accounted for in inventory.

Author(s): Rene Becnel.

Actor(s): Supplier.

Location(s): Newport Hills, Washington.

Status: Pathways defined.

Priority: 1.

Assumption(s):
Only products carried by Remulak are ordered or processed into inventory (i.e., unauthorized products are not sold).

Precondition(s):

Replenished products have product numbers assigned.

Postcondition(s):

- Product is ordered.
- Product is checked into inventory.

Primary (Happy) Path:

Product arrives at the warehouse with a copy of the purchase order attached.

Alternate Pathway(s):

- Product arrives at the warehouse with a purchase order that is attached but incomplete as to the products ordered.
- Product is ordered to replenish stock on hand.
- Product is ordered to fill a special order.
- Product is ordered to fill a back order.
- Products are accounted for through a physical inventory count.

Exception Pathway(s):

Product arrives with no attached purchase order or bill of lading.

The *Shipping* Use-Case

Name: Shipping.

Description:

This use-case starts when an order is either completely ready or partially ready for shipment. It handles all aspects of shipping, and it ends when the order is shipped and is either partially filled or completely filled.

Author(s): Rene Becnel.

Actor(s): Packaging clerk, shipping clerk.

Location(s): Newport Hills, Washington.

Status: Pathways defined.

Priority: 1.

Assumption(s):

For an order to be partially fulfilled, the customer must have authorized partial shipments.

Precondition(s):
Packaging clerk and shipping clerk have valid access to the system and are logged on.

Postcondition(s):
Order is shipped.

Primary (Happy) Path:
Entire order is shipped from stock on hand to a customer.

Alternate Pathway(s):
- Partial order is shipped from stock on hand to a customer.
- Entire order is shipped to a customer sourced directly from a third-party supplier.

Exception Pathway(s):
Order is ready to ship, and there is no shipping address.

The *Invoicing* Use-Case

Name: Invoicing.

Description:
This use-case starts when an order is invoiced to a customer. It handles all aspects of invoicing, and it ends when the order is invoiced and payment is received.

Author(s): Rene Becnel.

Actor(s): Accounting system, billing clerk.

Location(s): Newport Hills, Washington.

Status: Pathways defined.

Priority: 1.

Assumption(s):
- For an invoice to be produced, there must be a valid order.
- An order can have more than one invoice (to accommodate authorized partial shipments).
- Invoicing is interfaced to accounting nightly.

Precondition(s):
Billing clerk has valid access to the system and is logged on.

Postcondition(s):

- Order is invoiced, and/or funds are collected.
- The accounting system is updated as to the invoiced orders.

Primary (Happy) Path:

Order is invoiced and sent to the customer, indicating that payment was satisfied via credit card billing.

Alternate Pathway(s):

- Overdue notice is sent to a customer for a past-due account.
- Subledger transactions are interfaced to the accounting system.

Exception Pathway(s):

None

The *Maintain Relationships* Use-Case

Name: Maintain Relationships.

Description:

This use-case starts when a relationship with a customer or supplier requires attention. It handles all aspects of Remulak's relationships with customers and suppliers, and it ends when a relationship is either created or maintained for a customer or supplier.

Author(s): Rene Becnel.

Actor(s): Customer service clerk.

Location(s): Newport Hills, Washington.

Status: Pathways defined.

Priority: 1.

Assumption(s):

For a customer to order a product or a supplier to ship products, their relationships must be established.

Precondition(s):

Customer clerk has valid access to the system and is logged on.

Postcondition(s):

Relationship is either created or maintained.

Primary (Happy) Path:
Customer calls to change his/her mailing address.

Alternate Pathway(s):

- Customer calls to change his/her default payment terms and payment method.
- New customer is added to the system.
- Prospective customer is added to the system.
- New supplier is added to the system.
- Supplier calls to change its billing address.

Exception Pathway(s):
None.

The *Decision Support* Use-Case

Name: Decision Support.

Description:
This use-case starts when a predefined or undefined request for information is made. It handles all aspects of decision support effort, and it ends when a reply is formulated for the inquiry.

Author(s): Rene Becnel.

Actor(s): Manager.

Location(s): Newport Hills, Washington.

Status: Pathways defined.

Priority: 1.

Assumption(s):
None.

Precondition(s):
Manager has valid access to the system and is logged on.

Postcondition(s):
Reply is formulated for request.

Primary (Happy) Path:
Manager requests a back-order status report.

Alternate Pathway(s):
It is time to print the back-order report.

Exception Pathway(s):
None.

Happy Path Task Steps

This section contains the detailed task steps for all of the use-case happy paths.

The *Process Orders* Happy Path:

Customer calls and orders a guitar and supplies, and pays with a credit card

1. Customer supplies customer number.
2. Customer is acknowledged as current.
3. For each product that the customer desires:
   3.1 Product ID or description is requested.
   3.2 Description is resolved with its ID if necessary.
   3.3 Quantity is requested.
   3.4 Item price is calculated.
4. Extended order total is calculated.
5. Tax is applied.
6. Shipping charges are applied.
7. Extended price is quoted to the customer.
8. Customer supplies credit card number.
9. Customer's credit card is validated.
10. Inventory is reduced.
11. Sale is finalized.

The *Maintain Orders* Happy Path:

Customer calls to inquire about an order's status

1. Customer supplies order number.
2. Order number is acknowledged as correct.
3. Order header information is supplied, along with key customer information, for verification.

4. For each order line that the order contains, the following information is provided:
   4.1 Product description
   4.2 Quantity ordered
   4.3 Product price
   4.4 Extended product price
   4.5 Estimated shipping date
5. Extended order total is calculated.
6. Tax is applied.
7. Shipping charges are applied.
8. Extended order total is quoted to the customer.

The *Maintain Inventory* Happy Path:

Product arrives at the warehouse with a copy of the purchase order attached

1. Purchase order (PO) is verified for validity.
2. Accompanying PO is compared with the actual product shipment received.
3. Shipment items received are acknowledged as matching the PO.
4. Product's quantity on hand is updated to reflect new inventory amount.
5. For each order line that is back-ordered that matches the product received:
   5.1 Inventory is allocated.
   5.2 Inventory is assigned to the order line.

The *Shipping* Happy Path:

Entire order is shipped from stock on hand to a customer

1. Order is assigned to a shipping clerk.
2. Order is assigned to a packaging clerk.
3. Order is pulled from stock by a packaging clerk.
4. Order line items are packaged for shipment.
5. Shipping method and cost are verified by shipping clerk.
6. Order is shipped.

The *Invoicing* Happy Path:

Order is invoiced and sent to the customer, indicating that payment was satisfied via credit card billing

1. Existence of order number is validated.
2. For each order line with product in stock:
   2.1 The product quantity is drawn from inventory.
   2.2 An invoice line item is generated.

The *Maintain Relationships* Happy Path:

Customer calls to change his/her mailing address

1. Customer number is validated.
2. Customer's addresses are returned.
3. Changes to mailing address are accepted by customer service clerk.

The *Decision Support* Happy Path:

Manager requests a back-order status report

1. Each order with a line item that is presently back-ordered is printed.

Database Support

This section of deliverables deals with the Data Definition Language (DDL) statements necessary to support Microsoft or Sybase SQL Server, as well as Oracle. In most cases the differences between SQL Server and Oracle DDL, at least for the data types used in the Remulak project, are restricted to simple formatting issues and the use of `DateTime` in SQL Server versus `Date` in Oracle.

Note that the Java code written for the Remulak project and the accessing SQL statements found in the DAO modules will work on both platforms unmodified.

Microsoft SQL Server 7.0

```
CREATE TABLE T_Address (
       addressLine1 VARCHAR (30) NOT NULL,
       addressLine2 VARCHAR (30) NOT NULL,
       addressLine3 VARCHAR (30) NOT NULL,
       city VARCHAR (30) NOT NULL,
       state CHAR (2) NOT NULL,
       zip VARCHAR (15) NOT NULL,
       addressId int NOT NULL
)
GO

CREATE TABLE T_Customer (
       customerId int NOT NULL,
       customerNumber CHAR (14) NOT NULL,
       firstName CHAR (20) NOT NULL,
       lastName CHAR (20) NOT NULL,
       middleInitial CHAR (10) NOT NULL,
       prefix CHAR (4) NOT NULL,
       suffix CHAR (4) NOT NULL,
       phone1 CHAR (15) NOT NULL,
       phone2 CHAR (15) NOT NULL,
       eMail VARCHAR (30) NOT NULL
)
GO

CREATE TABLE T_Guitar (
       stringCount int NOT NULL,
       right CHAR (5) NOT NULL,
       fretLess CHAR (5) NOT NULL,
       make VARCHAR (20) NOT NULL,
       model VARCHAR (20) NOT NULL,
       age int NOT NULL,
       productId int NOT NULL,
       guitarId int NOT NULL
)
GO

CREATE TABLE T_Invoice (
       invoiceNumber int NOT NULL,
       invoiceId int NOT NULL,
       invoiceAmount DECIMAL(17,2) NOT NULL,
       invoiceDate DATETIME NOT NULL
)
```

```
GO

CREATE TABLE T_Role (
        role int NOT NULL,
        roleId int NOT NULL,
        addressId int NOT NULL,
        customerId int NOT NULL
)
GO

CREATE TABLE T_Order (
        orderId int NOT NULL,
        invoiceId int NULL,
        customerId int NOT NULL,
        orderNumber CHAR (10) NOT NULL
)
GO

CREATE TABLE T_OrderHeader (
        orderDateTime DATETIME NOT NULL,
        terms VARCHAR (30) NOT NULL,
        salesPerson VARCHAR (20) NOT NULL,
        orderHeaderId int NOT NULL,
        orderId int NOT NULL
)
GO

CREATE TABLE T_OrderLine (
        quantity int NOT NULL,
        iscount DECIMAL(17, 2) NOT NULL,
        dmextendedUnitPrice DECIMAL(17, 2) NOT NULL,
        orderLineId int NOT NULL,
        productId int NOT NULL,
        orderId int NOT NULL
) ON PRIMARY
GO

CREATE TABLE T_OrderSummary (
        orderSummaryId int NOT NULL,
        discount DECIMAL(17, 2) NOT NULL,
        courtesyMessage VARCHAR (50) NOT NULL,
        orderId int NOT NULL
)
GO
```

```
CREATE TABLE T_Payment (
       paymentId int NOT NULL,
       paymentAmount DECIMAL(17, 2) NOT NULL,
       paymentDate DATETIME NOT NULL
)
GO

CREATE TABLE T_Product (
       productId int NOT NULL,
       description VARCHAR (50) NOT NULL,
       price DECIMAL(17, 2) NOT NULL,
       discount DECIMAL(17, 2) NOT NULL,
       quantityOnHand int NOT NULL,
       eoq int NOT NULL,
       refproductId int NULL,
       productType int NULL
)
GO

CREATE TABLE T_SheetMusic (
       sheetId int NOT NULL,
       pages int NOT NULL,
       productId int NOT NULL
)
GO

CREATE TABLE T_Shipment (
       shipmentId int NOT NULL,
       shipmentDateTime DATETIME NOT NULL
)
GO

CREATE TABLE T_Supplies (
       supplyId int NOT NULL,
       independent CHAR (5) NOT NULL,
       productId int NOT NULL
)
GO

CREATE TABLE T_SysCode (
       sysCodeId int NOT NULL,
       name CHAR (12) NOT NULL,
       code CHAR (4) NOT NULL,
       description VARCHAR (20) NOT NULL
)
```

```
GO

CREATE VIEW Guitar_V(
    stringCount,
    right,
    fretLess,
    make,
    model,
    age,
    guitarId,
    productId,
    description,
    price,
    discount,
    quantityOnHand,
    eoq,
    productType)

    AS SELECT
    T_Guitar.stringCount,
    T_Guitar.right,
    T_Guitar.fretLess,
    T_Guitar.make,
    T_Guitar.model,
    T_Guitar.age,
    T_Guitar.guitarId,
    T_Product.productId,
    T_Product.description,
    T_Product.price,
    T_Product.discount,
    T_Product.quantityOnHand,
    T_Product.eoq,
    T_Product.productType

    FROM T_Guitar,T_Product
    WHERE T_Guitar.productId=T_Product.productId
GO

CREATE VIEW SheetMusic_V(
    pages,
    sheetId,
    productId,
    description,
    price,
    discount,
```

```
    quantityOnHand,
    eoq,
    productType)

    AS SELECT
    T_SheetMusic.pages,
    T_SheetMusic.sheetId,
    T_Product.productId,
    T_Product.description,
    T_Product.price,
    T_Product.discount,
    T_Product.quantityOnHand,
    T_Product.eoq,
    T_Product.productType

    FROM T_SheetMusic,T_Product
    WHERE T_SheetMusic.productId=T_Product.productId
GO

CREATE VIEW Supplies_V(
    independent,
    supplyId,
    productId,
    description,
    price,
    discount,
    quantityOnHand,
    eoq,
    productType)

    AS SELECT

    T_Supplies.independent,
    T_Supplies.supplyId,
    T_Product.productId,
    T_Product.description,
    T_Product.price,
    T_Product.discount,
    T_Product.quantityOnHand,
    T_Product.eoq,
    T_Product.productType

    FROM T_Supplies,T_Product
    WHERE T_Supplies.productId=T_Product.productId
GO
```

DDL for Oracle (Version 8.1.0)

```
CREATE TABLE T_Address (
      addressLine1 VARCHAR (30) NOT NULL,
      addressLine2 VARCHAR (30) NOT NULL,
      addressLine3 VARCHAR (30) NOT NULL,
      city VARCHAR (30) NOT NULL,
      state CHAR (2) NOT NULL,
      zip VARCHAR (15) NOT NULL,
      addressId int NOT NULL)

CREATE TABLE    T_Customer  (
       customerId   int  NOT NULL,
       customerNumber   CHAR  (14) NOT NULL,
       firstName   CHAR  (20) NOT NULL,
       lastName   CHAR  (20) NOT NULL,
       middleInitial   CHAR  (10) NOT NULL,
       prefix   CHAR  (4) NOT NULL,
       suffix   CHAR  (4) NOT NULL,
       phone1   CHAR  (15) NOT NULL,
       phone2   CHAR  (15) NOT NULL,
       eMail   VARCHAR  (30) NOT NULL)

CREATE TABLE    T_Guitar  (
       stringCount   int  NOT NULL,
       right   CHAR  (5) NOT NULL,
       fretLess   CHAR  (5) NOT NULL,
       make   VARCHAR  (20) NOT NULL,
       mmodel   VARCHAR  (20) NOT NULL,
       age   int  NOT NULL,
       productId   int  NOT NULL,
       guitarId   int  NOT NULL )

CREATE TABLE    T_Invoice   (
       invoiceNumber   int  NOT NULL,
       invoiceId   int  NOT NULL,
       invoiceAmount   DECIMAL (17, 2) NOT NULL,
       invoiceDate   date NOT NULL)

CREATE TABLE    T_Role   (
       role   int  NOT NULL,
       roleId   int  NOT NULL,
       addressId   int  NOT NULL,
       customerId   int  NOT NULL )
```

```
CREATE TABLE    T_Order  (
       orderId  int  NOT NULL,
       invoiceId  int  NULL,
       customerId  int  NOT NULL,
       orderNumber  CHAR  (10) NOT NULL )

CREATE TABLE    T_OrderHeader  (
       orderDateTime  date NOT NULL,
       terms  VARCHAR  (30) NOT NULL,
       salesPerson  VARCHAR  (20) NOT NULL,
       orderHeaderId  int  NOT NULL,
       orderId  int  NOT NULL )

CREATE TABLE    T_OrderLine  (
       quantity  int  NOT NULL,
       discount  DECIMAL (17, 2) NOT NULL,
       extendedUnitPrice  DECIMAL (17, 2) NOT NULL,
       orderLineId  int  NOT NULL,
       productId  int  NOT NULL,
       orderId  int  NOT NULL )

CREATE TABLE    T_OrderSummary  (
       orderSummaryId  int  NOT NULL,
       discount  DECIMAL (17, 2) NOT NULL,
       courtesyMessage  VARCHAR  (50) NOT NULL,
       orderId  int  NOT NULL )

CREATE TABLE    T_Payment  (
       paymentId  int  NOT NULL,
       paymentAmount  DECIMAL (17, 2) NOT NULL,
       paymentDate  date NOT NULL)

CREATE TABLE    T_Product  (
       productId  int  NOT NULL,
       description  VARCHAR  (50) NOT NULL,
       price  DECIMAL (17, 2) NOT NULL,
       discount  DECIMAL (17, 2) NOT NULL,
       quantityOnHand  int  NOT NULL,
       eoq  int  NOT NULL,
       refproductId  int  NULL,
       productType  int  NULL )

CREATE TABLE    T_SheetMusic  (
       sheetId  int  NOT NULL,
       pages  int  NOT NULL,
       productId  int  NOT NULL )
```

```
CREATE TABLE    T_Shipment  (
        shipmentId   int  NOT NULL,
        shipmentDateTime   date  NOT NULL )

CREATE TABLE    T_Supplies  (
        supplyId   int  NOT NULL,
        independent   CHAR  (5) NOT NULL,
        productId   int  NOT NULL )

CREATE TABLE    T_SysCode  (
        sysCodeId   int  NOT NULL,
        name   CHAR  (12) NOT NULL,
        code   CHAR  (4) NOT NULL,
        description   VARCHAR  (20) NOT NULL )

CREATE VIEW Guitar_V(
    stringCount,
    right,
    fretLess,
    make,
    model,
    age,
    guitarId,
    productId,
    description,
    price,
    discount,
    quantityOnHand,
    eoq,
    productType)

    AS SELECT
    T_Guitar.stringCount,
    T_Guitar.right,
    T_Guitar.fretLess,
    T_Guitar.make,
    T_Guitar.model,
    T_Guitar.age,
    T_Guitar.guitarId,
    T_Product.productId,
    T_Product.description,
    T_Product.price,
    T_Product.discount,
    T_Product.quantityOnHand,
    T_Product.eoq,
    T_Product.productType
```

```
    FROM T_Guitar,T_Product
    WHERE T_Guitar.productId=T_Product.productId

CREATE VIEW SheetMusic_V(
    pages,
    sheetId,
    productId,
    description,
    price,
    discount,
    quantityOnHand,
    eoq,
    productType)

    AS SELECT
    T_SheetMusic.pages,
    T_SheetMusic.sheetId,
    T_Product.productId,
    T_Product.description,
    T_Product.price,
    T_Product.discount,
    T_Product.quantityOnHand,
    T_Product.eoq,
    T_Product.productType

    FROM T_SheetMusic,T_Product
    WHERE T_SheetMusic.productId=T_Product.productId

CREATE VIEW Supplies_V(
    independent,
    supplyId,
    productId,
    description,
    price,
    discount,
    quantityOnHand,
    eoq,
    productType)

    AS SELECT

    T_Supplies.independent,
    T_Supplies.supplyId,
    T_Product.productId,
    T_Product.description,
    T_Product.price,
```

```
T_Product.discount,
T_Product.quantityOnHand,
T_Product.eoq,
T_Product.productType

FROM T_Supplies,T_Product
WHERE T_Supplies.productId=T_Product.productId
```

APPENDIX E

BEA WebLogic Application Server

IN THIS APPENDIX

The WebLogic application server from BEA Systems continues to lead the market in the commercial application server arena. Although WebLogic jockeys back and forth with IBM's WebSphere, it is a good example of an application server that supports the EJB 2.0 specification.

One element of the WebLogic environment that is crucial for using it successfully is the console (see Figure E-1). The tree view on the left-hand side of the screen shows the various areas that the developer can both monitor and adjust. Figures E-2 through E-4 explore a few.

Note: WebLogic is a world-class application server, but it has stiff competition from IBM's WebSphere. One area in which WebLogic excels is its support of the various WebLogic newsgroups on the Internet. Usually you have to wait no more than a day or so for excellent help. You can always call in for support, but the newsgroups are very useful.

FIGURE E-1 *WebLogic initial console screen*

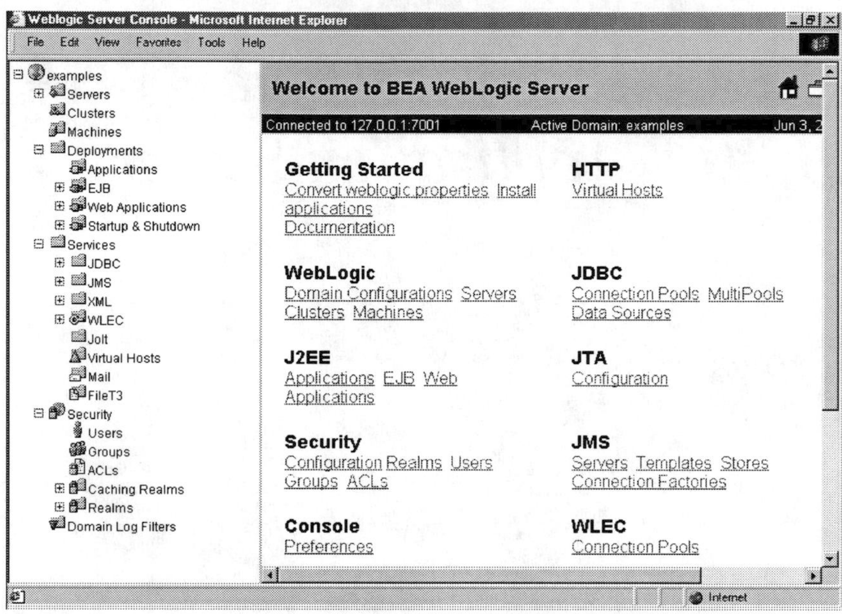

FIGURE E-2 *The* `ejb20_remulak` *EJB deployment*

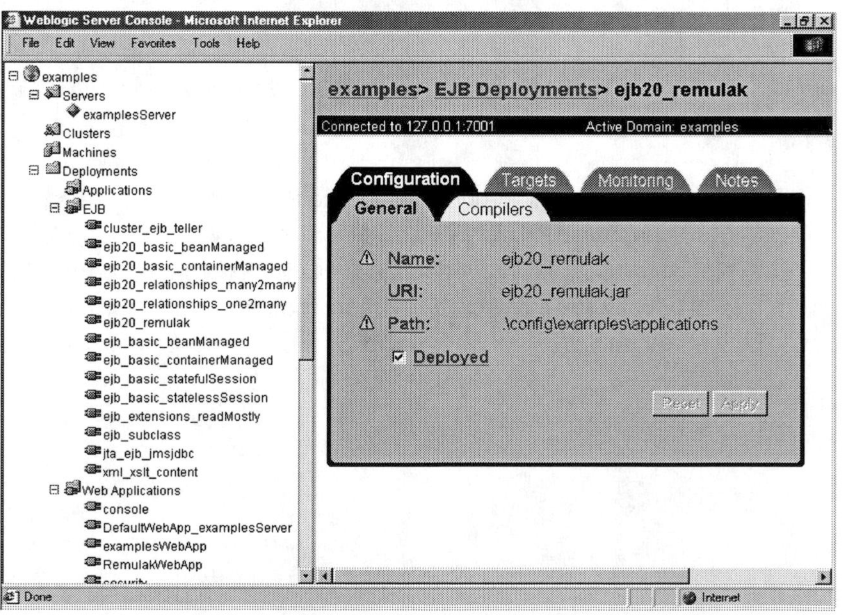

FIGURE E-3 *The RemulakWebApp Web application*

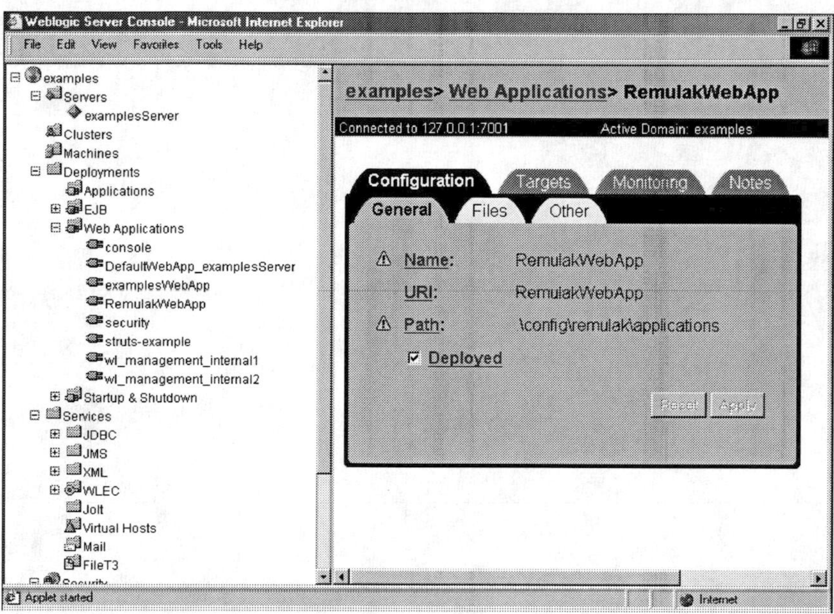

FIGURE E-4 *Remulak's JDBC pool*

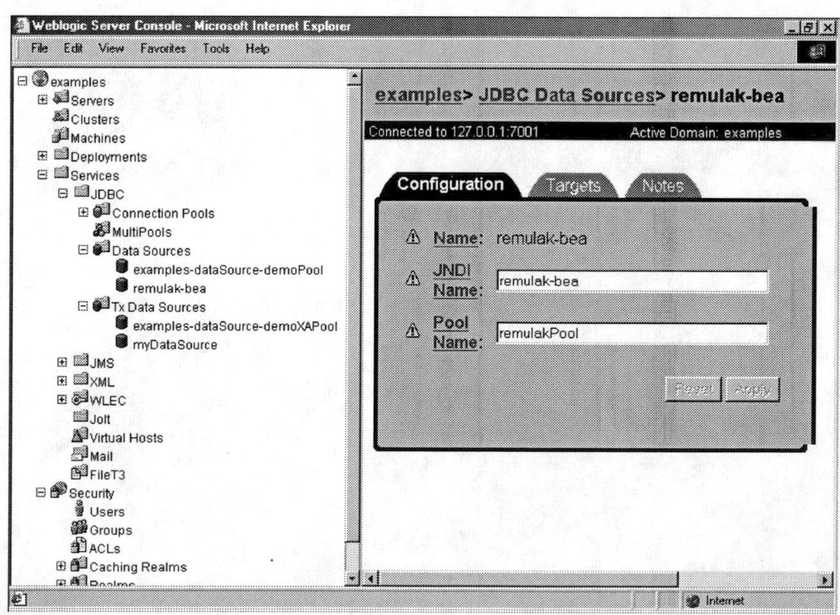

Bibliography

Many books have influenced my thought and approach on this project. Anyone who considers writing today must have fuel for the mind, and these sources provided me with quite a bit of power.

Chapter 1

Booch, Grady, James Rumbaugh, and Ivar Jacobson. *The Unified Modeling Language User Guide*. Addison-Wesley, Reading, MA, 1999.

Jacobson, Ivar, Grady Booch, and James Rumbaugh. *The Unified Software Development Process*. Addison-Wesley, Reading, MA, 1999.

Kruchten, Philippe. *The Rational Unified Process: An Introduction* (2nd ed.). Addison-Wesley, Boston, MA, 2000.

Reed, Paul R., Jr. *Object-Oriented Analysis and Design Using the UML* (Seminar material). Jackson-Reed, Colorado Springs, CO, 1992-2001.

Reed, Paul R., Jr. *The Rational Unified Process: An Introduction and Implementation Perspective* (Seminar material). Jackson-Reed, Colorado Springs, CO, 1992-2001.

Reed, Paul R., Jr. *Requirements Gathering Using Use Cases and the UML* (Seminar material). Jackson-Reed, Colorado Springs, CO, 1992-2001.

Rumbaugh, James. *OMT Insights: Perspectives on Modeling from the Journal of Object-Oriented Programming*. SIGS Books, New York, 1996.

Rumbaugh, James, Ivar Jacobson, and Grady Booch. *The Unified Modeling Language Reference Manual.* Addison-Wesley, Reading, MA, 1999.

Chapter 4

Cockburn, Alistair. *Writing Effective Use Cases.* Addison-Wesley, Boston, 2000.

Jacobson, Ivar, Magnus Christerson, Patrik Jonsson, and Gunnar Overgaard. *Object-Oriented Software Engineering: A Use Case Driven Approach.* Addison-Wesley, Reading, MA, 1992.

Reed, Paul R., Jr. *Requirements Gathering Using Use Cases and the UML* (Seminar material). Jackson-Reed, Colorado Springs, CO, 1992-2001.

"Using Legacy Models in CBD (Component Based Development)." *Component Strategies,* November 1998. Published electronically; no longer available.

Chapter 5

Jacobson, Ivar, Magnus Christerson, Patrik Jonsson, and Gunnar Overgaard. *Object-Oriented Software Engineering: A Use Case Driven Approach.* Addison-Wesley, Reading, MA, 1992.

Chapter 6

Gottesdiener, Ellen. *Object-Oriented Analysis and Design Using the UML* (Seminar material). EBG Consulting, Carmel, IN, 1995-2001.

Tasker, Dan. *The Problem Space: Practical Techniques for Gathering and Specifying Requirements Using Objects, Events, Rules, Participants, and Locations.* 1993. Published electronically; no longer available.

Chapter 8

Bergsten, Hans. *Java Server Pages.* O'Reilly, Beijing, 2001.

Kassem, Nicholas, and Enterprise Team. *Designing Enterprise Applications with the Java™ 2 Platform* (Enterprise ed.). Addison-Wesley, Boston, 2000.

Monson-Haefel, Richard. *Enterprise JavaBeans* (2nd ed.). O'Reilly, Cambridge, MA, 2000.

Reed, Paul R., Jr. *Object-Oriented Analysis and Design Using the UML* (Seminar material). Jackson-Reed, Colorado Springs, CO, 1992-2001.

Chapter 9

Bergsten, Hans. *Java Server Pages.* O'Reilly, Beijing, 2001.

Kassem, Nicholas, and Enterprise Team. *Designing Enterprise Applications with the Java™ 2 Platform* (Enterprise ed.). Addison-Wesley, Boston, 2000.

Marinescu, Floyd. *Details Object.* 2000. Available at *www.serverside.com, http://theserverside.com/patterns/thread.jsp?thread_id=79.*

Chapter 11

Bergsten, Hans. *Java Server Pages.* O'Reilly, Beijing, 2001.

Kassem, Nicholas, and Enterprise Team. *Designing Enterprise Applications with the Java™ 2 Platform* (Enterprise ed.). Addison-Wesley, Boston, 2000.

Chapter 12

Bergsten, Hans. *Java Server Pages.* O'Reilly, Beijing, 2001.

Kassem, Nicholas, and Enterprise Team. *Designing Enterprise Applications with the Java™ 2 Platform* (Enterprise ed.). Addison-Wesley, Boston, 2000.

Monson-Haefel, Richard. *Enterprise JavaBeans* (2nd ed.). O'Reilly, Cambridge, MA, 2000.

Index

C

F

G

H

I

T

All material previously distributed by CD-ROM is now available at http://www.awprofessional.com